Developing Professional Java™ Applets

K.C. Hopson
Stephen E. Ingram

201 West 103rd Street
Indianapolis, Indiana 46290

To my wife, Ann, whose love, patience, assistance, and encouragement made it possible for me to write this book.—K.C. Hopson

To my wife, Anne, and my son, Mitchell; their love and encouragement gave me the strength to write this book.—Stephen Ingram

Copyright © 1996 by Sams.net Publishing

FIRST EDITION

All rights reserved. No part of this book shall be reproduced, stored in a retrieval system, or transmitted by any means, electronic, mechanical, photocopying, recording, or otherwise, without written permission from the publisher. No patent liability is assumed with respect to the use of the information contained herein. Although every precaution has been taken in the preparation of this book, the publisher and author assume no responsibility for errors or omissions. Neither is any liability assumed for damages resulting from the use of the information contained herein. For information, address Sams.net Publishing, 201 W. 103rd St., Indianapolis, IN 46290.

International Standard Book Number: 1-57521-083-5

Library of Congress Catalog Card Number: 96-67126

98 97 96 95 4 3 2 1

Interpretation of the printing code: the rightmost double-digit number is the year of the book's printing; the rightmost single-digit, the number of the book's printing. For example, a printing code of 95-1 shows that the first printing of the book occurred in 1995.

Composed in AGaramond, Optima, and MCPdigital by Macmillan Computer Publishing

Printed in the United States of America

Trademarks

All terms mentioned in this book that are known to be trademarks or service marks have been appropriately capitalized. Sams.net Publishing cannot attest to the accuracy of this information. Use of a term in this book should not be regarded as affecting the validity of any trademark or service mark.

Java is a trademark of Sun Microsystems, Inc.

President, Sams Publishing *Richard K. Swadley*

Publishing Manager *Mark Taber*

Managing Editor *Cindy Morrow*

Marketing Manager *John Pierce*

Assistant Marketing Manager *Kristina Perry*

Acquisitions Editor
Mark Taber

Development Editor
Kelly Murdock

Software Development Specialist
Cari Skaggs

Production Editor
Lisa M. Lord

Copy Editors
Howard Jones
Anne Owen

Technical Reviewer
Greg Guntle

Editorial Coordinator
Bill Whitmer

Technical Edit Coordinator
Lynette Quinn

Formatter
Frank Sinclair

Editorial Assistant
Sharon Cox

Cover Designer
Tim Amrhein

Book Designer
Alyssa Yesh

Production Team Supervisor
Brad Chinn

Production
Mary Ann Abramson, Stephen Adams, Carol G. Bowers, Georgiana Briggs, Jeanne Clark, Jason Hand, Daniel Harris, Mike Henry, Clint Lahnen, Paula Lowell, Steph Mineart, Ryan Oldfather, Casey Price, Laura Robbins, Bobbi Satterfield, Ian Smith, SA Springer, Chris Wilcox

Overview

Contents

III Creating a Catalog Applet

VI Appendixes

Acknowledgments

We would like to thank our acquisitions editor, Mark Taber, our development editor, Kelly Murdock, and our production editor, Lisa Lord, for patiently guiding some lost sheep through their first book.

About the Authors

K.C. Hopson is president of Geist Software and Services, Inc., an independent consultant firm in the Baltimore/Washington D.C. metro area. However, K.C. thrives in cyberspace and enjoys using it anywhere in the world. He specializes in distributed computing solutions and has deep experience in GUI programming (especially Windows), relational databases, and client/server programming. K.C. was a lead architect of the software used in Bell Atlantic's Stargazer interactive television system and writes regularly about Java. K.C. has a B.S. in applied mathematics from the University of California-Irvine and a master's in computer science from the University of Maryland, Baltimore County. In his spare time, K.C. enjoys his family, worships music of all kinds, studies history, and loves literature.

K.C. can be reached at `chopson@universe.digex.net`, or visit his home page at `http://www.universe.digex.net/~chopson`.

Stephen E. Ingram is an computer consultant in the Washington D.C. metro area, specializing in embedded data communications and object-oriented design. He holds an electrical engineering degree from Virginia Tech and has been programming for 15 years. He was the architect behind the language of Bell Atlantic's Stargazer interactive television project; it was here that he first encountered Java. When he's not working, Steve likes to sail the Chesapeake Bay with his wife and son. Steve can be reached at `singram@qnet.com`.

Introduction

Java is frequently described as a programming language for the Internet. This reference mainly alludes to Java's ability to be executed as an *applet,* which is a program that runs inside a Java-enabled World Wide Web browser, such as Netscape Navigator 2.0 or HotJava. Applets naturally function as small programs that can enhance your Web page. This stems from Java's structure as a distributed language and its corresponding ability to load small pieces of code as needed. In the short run, programmers will use Java to add small snippets of code, such as animations, to enhance a Web page experience.

Java applets, however, are much more than small programs that supplement Web pages. Java is a sophisticated and extendable environment, providing the foundation for building industrial-strength applications. This power stems from Java's many facets—from its object-oriented nature to its simplicity to its ability to function in distributed environments. Consequently, to view Java as a "neat" tool for sprucing up your Web pages is a serious understatement of its capabilities. Java applets will appear in more guises than just the Internet, and Java's role inside internal networks—the so-called "Intranet"—is already being given serious consideration.

Developing Professional Java Applets aims to help bring Java applets out of the world of lightweight programs—like simple animations—into the world of practical programming. This book attempts to fill a gap that has been seriously lacking in currently existing Java literature: a book full of serious, practical, and professional Java projects and examples. The projects in this book illustrate how to create Java applets that solve real-life problems, and they do so in such a way that you will learn all the general features, as well as subtleties, of Java while you're working through practical applications of serious projects. In doing so, you will not only become a more capable Java programmer, but you might also develop insights on how to use Java to create a great new application.

Who Should Read This Book

Developing Professional Java Applets is intended for people who do not want to spend 200 pages learning basic Java (such as `for` loops), but want to quickly step into serious Java programming. To do this, however, requires you to have some background. In general, a basic background in programming and a rudimentary understanding of the principles of object-oriented programming should be enough. If you have any of the following credentials, then you are set:

- Have read and understood another book or literature on the basics of Java.
- Have some experience in C or C++.

If you are lacking these credentials, don't worry. Just take more time going through the first part of the book (an introduction to Java). If you have the background just described, however, this book will lead you deep into Java programming before you know it!

How This Book Is Organized

This book is based on the Java Development Kit (JDK), version 1.0. Most of the chapters of *Developing Professional Java Applets* have a tutorial section that covers some JDK topics, followed by a serious chapter project. The chapter project is accompanied by a discussion of the project's general architecture, as well as any Java subtleties it might uncover. By the time you are done with any given chapter, you will have been exposed to at least one serious Java programming concept.

Part I of the book is a quick overview of the fundamentals of Java programming. If you have no experience with Java, this part should be enough to get you ready for the heart of the book. It includes plenty of examples to illustrate key ideas. However, the book's focus is on practical Java programming, so some of the discussions of Java basics are terse. However, almost all the topics broached in Part I will reappear frequently throughout the rest of the book.

Parts II through IV are the heart of the book. Each of these parts walks through a serious project over the course of three chapters. By the end of each part, you will not only have seen the development of a major project, but will have attained some deep understanding of one or more crucial topics in Java programming.

In Part II, you'll see the development of a spreadsheet applet. This applet will guide you through the basics of Java's graphical toolkit, **AWT**. You will not only learn the general workings of AWT, but will also be exposed to some of its hidden gems, such as its Toolkit class. Since (at least for a while) most Java applets will use AWT as the basis for their user interfaces, a solid understanding of the package is indispensable. Part II also includes in-depth discussions of **I/O streams** in Java, as well as an exploration of Java's powerful approach to **exception handling**.

Part III uses a catalog-style applet to introduce you to the more advanced concepts of **URL streams**, **threads**, and **image processing**. This catalog applet shows how to tie information on one catalog page to that on another. The applet features a media loader that uses threads and advanced imaging concepts to bring in images that may be needed in the future; this is a "preloader" that can be used to reduce the latencies often associated with images. By the end of this part, you will have been through some of Java's most complex features.

Part IV takes you into the world of Java **client/server programming**. It introduces you to Java **network programming** through the creation of an **HTTP** server. This server will actually download Java applets to a client! You will also be shown how to use Java **native methods**—code written in C—by tying in databases (through the **ODBC** mechanism) to your server. Finally, you will see an applet that gets data from the server as it changes in real-time—what the book calls "**live data.**" After this part of the book, you will have seen serious treatments of most of the major concepts in Java programming.

Part V lets you have a little break—but just a little one. Rather than one large project, each chapter has a smaller project. The focus is on more advanced uses of images and threads, but there is also a discussion of HotJava and its content-handling features. The goal of Part V is to further refine the knowledge you have gained in the first four parts of the book. By the time the book ends, you should feel that you have a solid understanding of everything needed to build high-quality, professional Java applets.

Thoughts Before Starting

There are a variety of Web sites cropping up that help you with various aspects of Java. The main launching pad for Java is `http://www.javasoft.com/`, which is where you can download the latest Java release and all kinds of first-rate documentation. The newsgroup `comp.lang.java` has excellent discussions of all aspects of Java programming, from novice to advanced. A couple of other Web sites, such as `http://www.digitalfocus.com/` and `http://www.gamelan.com/`, offer good starting places for exploring Java in cyberspace.

Finally, it should be pointed out that the JDK 1.0 is not without bugs. An unfortunate side-effect of this is that some features that work on one platform might not work on another. If you are having isolated, inexplicable problems running any of the applets in this book, consider downloading the latest version of the JDK for your platform.

I

Java Applet Development

1

The Java Development Environment

Java is a programming language that provides a foundation for developing Internet applications. Java does this through *applets*, which are programs executed as part of a Web page and displayed with a Java-enabled browser, such as HotJava or Netscape Navigator 2.0. However, Java's features need to be understood in a context much broader than just running Internet applications. Java is a language designed to solve a variety of problems that have plagued the computing community for years; running well on the Internet is almost a by-product of solving these problems.

What are these problems? And how does Java solve them? This chapter will attempt to answer those questions. Through the course of this chapter, you will be given the background needed for understanding why Java, applets, and the Internet are such a natural match. This background will not only help you better understand the techniques used to program the Java applets developed throughout this book, but the extra knowledge of the "big picture" may also help you come up with novel ways to apply this new technology. Java and the Internet are very much like the old Western frontier—pathfinders who break new ground may find the gold that lies underneath.

Tough Problems in Search of One Solution

A key word often used when discussing the "information superhighway" is *convergence*. People talk about the convergence of telecommunications and computing, television and computers, consumer appliances and telecommunications, and so forth. Each of these converging factors comes from areas of technology that, until recently, have not had much in common. For example, the technology of fiber optics does not have much to do directly with the problems of computing. At the same time that these *disparate* technologies have converged, there have also been pressures from *within* computing to bring together disciplines historically considered unrelated. This convergence within computing has been brought about by various pressures that have arisen:

- An overwhelming need to deal with the *software crisis* has developed. This term has been coined to describe problems that have plagued the software community. Software development has been marred by high cost, low quality, and ever-increasing demand; these problems have been both caused and exacerbated by increasing software complexity. Because of these trends, there is tremendous interest in any technique that can increase the productivity of software developers, improve reliability, and make it easier to design software that tackles complex problems. Over the last decade the technology that has been viewed as having the best chance of successfully dealing with these problems is *object-oriented programming*. Object-oriented features of abstraction, encapsulation, and modularity are particularly well suited for making complex real-world problems easier to model and, hence, design. A true object-oriented language's support for inheritance and dynamic binding improves software reuse and also, as a consequence, programmer productivity. The garbage collection facility in some object-oriented languages improves *reliability* by freeing the programmer from the intricate concerns of memory management.

- The predominance of a variety of operating systems and platforms has created a heavy demand for *portable* software. Programs need to be written that will not only run on several different platforms, but do so in a way that fits into the native "look and feel" of the environment. Furthermore, portable software needs to have the *high performance* that is typical of the software written for the target platform. Interest in software that is portable but slow is waning rapidly.
- The rapid growth of computer networks has been matched by a corresponding rise of interest in *distributed computing*. This discipline is concerned with the problems of software distributed across multiple computers. Distributed computing issues include interprocess communication, concurrent processing, data sharing and replication, and security. Although the Internet is the most well-known distributed environment, it is in just the early stages of using the full potential of distributed computing. Until recently, for example, there has been no solution to the problem of dynamically downloading an application both efficiently and securely. *Efficiency* is important since you want to download only the code you need when you need it; you don't want to wait thirty minutes to download a 3MB application. Even more important, you need to be concerned with the *security* of the code. You won't run applications from the Internet if it means giving the green light to hackers around the world to attack your hard disk. You also do not want a poorly written Internet application to crash your system—the software has to be *reliable*.

Each of these problems has been seriously addressed from many fronts, but no approach has simultaneously addressed all these problems. For example, there might be a programming language that's good for rapid development but isn't portable, or a development environment might be portable, but could not work in a distributed environment without opening you up to serious breaches of security. A single solution to all these problems has been lacking...until Java!

Why Java Is a Comprehensive Solution

The designers of Java created a programming environment to attack each and every one of these problems. As a comprehensive solution to these pressing issues, Java needs to be understood as not just a programming language, but as a general-purpose environment. Its unique combination of a programming language, compiler, and runtime environment provides a general architecture well suited for addressing many of the concerns that have been plaguing the computing community for years. This general development environment is often referred to with the solitary term *Java*.

In part, Java's evolution into a comprehensive solution stems from its twisted history of being a language for general consumer electronics to being one for PDAs and set-top boxes for interactive television. Features common to each of these potential platforms include severe memory constraints and the need to support multiple operating systems. These problems forced the language to address the problems of distributed computing, efficiency, security, portability, and reliability. For Java to be a successful language, furthermore, it would also have to address the problems associated with the software crisis—it would need to be object-oriented.

Being object-oriented carried another bonus for Java. The object-oriented message-passing model of invoking class methods makes it a natural for network-based application development. Consequently, being object-oriented is one of the cornerstones of Java, so it's a good place to begin a tour of its general architectural features.

Why Object-Oriented Is Important

Why is it important for Java to be an object-oriented language? As stated before, modern programming languages need to address the problems of the software crisis. Perhaps the most serious difficulty a software engineer encounters is the inherent complexity involved in modeling a real-world problem. Through the past decades of computing, analysis techniques have come in and out of fashion that aim to make modeling the world a more comprehensible and stable practice. When you were taking your first classes in programming, you might have seen flowcharts used as a modeling tool. The Structured Analysis school of thought uses data flow diagrams to model the world. These approaches have some contributions to make, but they have one serious problem: they are heavily oriented toward the *procedural* side of the activities being modeled. The problem with a procedural approach is that it does not translate well to software that is compact, easy to maintain, and reusable. In its worst implementations, a system based on the procedural model has a different function for every different type of procedure that could occur. You have probably seen such systems—they are so incomprehensible and hard to follow that the only goal of the poor soul who has to maintain the system is to "just make it work."

Object-oriented analysis, design, and programming is a radical departure from the procedural model. Its focus is not on the procedures of the modeled world, but on the *objects* appearing in it. Objects are a natural thing to model because that's what the world is made of. Planes, dogs, and computers are all objects. Even abstract concepts, such as a priority queue, can be thought of as an object. What all objects have in common is that they have *state* and *behavior*. For example, the state of a plane can be partially indicated by its speed and location, but its behavior might be represented by its ability to change altitude.

Another feature of objects is that they are self-contained; in other words, they are *modular*. When modeling a car engine, for example, you can focus on the characteristics of each object in the engine as opposed to the flow of gas and energy through it. The object model breaks the engine down into a series of components that can be described on their own terms, as opposed to what they are in a complex global view of things. Instead of writing a single huge procedure describing what's going on in the car, you can focus on how each of the individual elements behaves.

Finally, objects have the quality of being hierarchical. A large complex object, a house, for example, consists of other objects, such as its physical structure, the electrical system, the plumbing, and so forth. These are in turn made up of yet other objects, such as a chimney, the light switches, and a sink. These can be broken down into yet smaller components such as wood, wires, and pipes. By modeling a system based on *hierarchy*, you can use the model of smaller, more easily understood objects, such as a wire, to construct more complex objects, such as a light switch. Since the switch is now seen as an object that consists of yet simpler objects, its complexity is easier to understand and manage.

In object-oriented systems, objects communicate through a *message-passing* mechanism. When an object receives a message, it may change its state and behavior as part of the response. For example, sending a message of "play" to a CD player object might result in the CD playing a music track. This message-passing aspect of objects translates very nicely into the needs of network programming, where transactions are carried out by the mechanism of messages. It is particularly well suited to distributed systems because objects communicate by a standard message-passing mechanism, in which the actual location of the objects becomes less important. If your object needs to talk to an object, it isn't particularly important if it is on your computer or a remote host. All that really counts is that the object gets your message.

Java as an Object-Oriented Language

Java is unusual for an object-oriented programming language in that it is "objects all the way down." Unlike C++, which is a confusing combination of objects and functions, everything in Java is an object. Strings are objects, numbers are objects, threads are objects, even applets are objects. Because of this, Java has all the helpful features of object-oriented systems just described. Its core constructs of classes, objects, methods, and instance variables are, by their very nature, managed in a modular fashion. Java's support for inheritance allows you to build new classes from other classes. Each class you construct becomes a tool that can be used to create yet more complex classes.

Java's particular object-oriented implementation allows it to have yet even more desirable features than those already discussed. It has a runtime *garbage collector* that removes objects from memory that you no longer need. No longer will your program run out of memory because you forgot to explicitly delete an object. The garbage collector, which your program doesn't even have to be aware of, does this for you. Furthermore, Java's total orientation toward objects removes another construct that has been a blight of programmers—the pointer. Java hides almost all aspects of memory management from the programmer. C or C++ programmers who have had to deal with complex bugs caused by the misuse of pointers or bad pointer arithmetic will no longer have to deal with this entire class of problems. In Java, you will never deal with pointers, only objects. Because of this combination of garbage collection and removal of the pointer construct, Java has generally taken the problem of memory management away from you. Consequently, programs written in Java are more *reliable.*

Java's unique object-oriented implementation gives it another set of desirable characteristics—*simplicity* and *familiarity*. In many ways, its syntax is similar to C and C++, thus making it familiar. On the other hand, it strips out all the programming constructs of this language that are historical artifacts contributing little to writing object-oriented programs. For example, the structure construct is removed because everything in Java is an object. Unions are removed because they make you think too much about how memory is laid out, a low-level memory consideration that Java's garbage collection and removal of pointers tries to abolish. Other procedural features of C and C++ that are removed include functions, which are replaced by class methods; preprocessor constructs, such as `typedef` and `ifdef`; the hated `goto` statement; and, of course, pointers. Java also replaces the complex and troublesome multiple inheritance of C++ by a simpler combination of single inheritance and interfaces. With all these features in mind, Java becomes a simpler and easier language to use.

Java has all the object-oriented features discussed in the previous section. It uses message passing to let objects communicate, and it supports *dynamic binding*, allowing a message to be sent to an object even though its specific type may not be known until runtime. Abstract classes and interfaces enable you to specify a design without having to worry about a specific implementation. With Java's access control constructs, you can define different levels of access to your class's methods and variables that are available to external classes.

Java as a Portable Environment

Portability is critical to success in the emerging world of networked applications and commerce. On the Internet, you cannot make assumptions about what kind of platform your applet will run on. Not only do you have to write software that will run on the client's underlying architecture—such as 80x86, PowerPC, or 68000 series—but you must also ensure it will have the correct look and feel of the native interface. To make things even tougher, this software needs to be fast and compact.

Java takes a multipronged approach to this challenge. At the heart of this approach is the fact that the Java compiler generates *bytecodes* that are *interpreted* at runtime. The fact that bytecodes are generated is important because it avoids the problem of basing the binary code on a basic set of primitive types—such as integers and floating point—that would be tied to a specific platform. For example, even something as simple as an integer data type is implemented in a different manner on different platforms (16-bit on some, 32-bit on others). Java defines its own set of primitive data types and reconstructs large 16-bit or 32-bit values at runtime by composing them out of individual bytecodes. Java consistently uses the big-endian format to do this, thus avoiding another portability conflict about how platforms store primitive data types. You can also quickly and efficiently convert the bytecodes at runtime to the underlying native formats if necessary. In short, Java's underlying encoding scheme is *architecture-neutral.*

The bytecode-based system is important to writing a portable interpreter. The bytecodes generated by the compiler are based on the specification of a *Java Virtual Machine,* which, as its name suggests, is not a specific hardware platform but a machine implemented in software. The virtual machine is very similar to a real CPU with its own instruction set, storage formats, and registers. Since it is written in software, however, it is portable. All that's needed to take Java code compiled on one platform and run it on another is to provide a Java interpreter and runtime environment. The runtime system is written in an easily portable fashion. Once you have this system, everything becomes easy. You don't even have to port the Java compiler—it is written in Java!

Another advantage of the Java interpreter is that it improves software development by eliminating the link phase of the development process. You can go straight from compiling your code to executing it. Linking actually occurs at runtime through mechanisms discussed in the section "Java as a Secure Environment."

A couple of higher-level features also improve Java's portability. The Abstract Window Toolkit (or AWT) is constructed to be a visual interface that is portable across platforms. This way your applets will look good regardless of the underlying interface. They will have the proper "look and feel" on Microsoft Windows, the Macintosh, or X-Windows. Although not a portability issue in the strict sense, Java stores characters by using the 16-bit Unicode format as opposed to the 8-bit ASCII standard. Unicode is used if you need to support international character sets. Since the Internet is an international network, this consideration is important.

Java as High Performance

One of the reasons why Java's portable solution is such a coup is that interpreted platforms have generally been very slow. Often their performance is so poor that systems based on these interpreters have been unusable. Java's bytecode system, however, provides a "lean and mean" interpreted solution. It isn't based on multimegabyte executable "image" files. Rather, the runtime system works with small binary *class files* compiled to Java virtual machine code. These files typically have a size of only a few kilobytes.

However, Java offers more than just the byte-code system to get high performance. Since the byte-code system is at a low level, it can be easily converted at runtime to the native platform. Just-in-time Java compilers will be out in the near future to allow this. Another performance enhancement is a by-product of another Java feature. When a class is brought into memory at runtime, it runs through a verification process as part of the Java security mechanism (discussed in the section "Java as a Secure Environment"). This process not only guarantees that the code you are loading is secure, but the end result is code that requires less runtime checks. These checks, which otherwise would hurt performance, now don't need to be executed. For example, the runtime system does not have to check for stack overflows on verified code.

One of the key features that Java offers to improve performance is *multithreading.* Most interactive applications are characterized by large periods of time during which the user pauses between actions to decide what to do next. In traditional single-threaded environments, the application may sit idle during such periods. In multithreaded environments, however, the application can perform other tasks during these types of delays or at any other time. This is critical for network applications, which can take long periods of time to load files. Wouldn't it be more efficient if you could read the current page of text while the next page is being downloaded? Multithreading also greatly improves the usability of multimedia applications. For example, you need to be able to interact with your system while a sound or a movie is playing. Multithreading is useful for even more down-to-earth things, such as running a background thread that spell checks your document as you are typing in words.

You can use Java's easy-to-use multithreading environment to perform all kinds of optimizations to your program. In fact, the designers of Java have taken great pains to make sure it's easy to write multithreaded programs. Historically, writing multithreaded applications has been quite difficult—a key reason they have appeared infrequently. Furthermore, Java uses threads to improve its own performance. The garbage collector that takes care of your memory management concerns runs in the background as a low-priority thread. So even when your program is doing nothing, the garbage collector could be busy optimizing memory!

There are some other interesting things Java does to guarantee good performance. As stated earlier, Java is "objects all the way down." In some object-oriented systems, primitives such as integers and floating point numbers are implemented only as objects. So to perform an operation such as adding two numbers, you actually have to call an object method. If you are doing some serious number crunching, this will absolutely kill your performance. Java has an intermediate solution to resolve the dilemma between having good performance and being a pure object-oriented system. It implements "type wrappers" to take primitives, such as numbers, and make them appear as objects. This way, methods—such as converting numbers to strings—can be performed by using the object-oriented method style. However, if you need to work with raw data types, you can use the primitive formats to produce such things as CPU-intensive images like fractals. Java can even be used to create the computation-hungry Mandelbrot set. It's rather remarkable that Java can do this; if you don't believe it can, then see Chapter 14, "Advanced Image Processing."

If you really need that final push to your performance, Java can link to executable code written in a low-level native language such as C. Java code that does this is said to use *native methods*. This technique can also be used to implement platform-specific features. However, using native methods is not without its drawbacks; it will probably compromise the portability of your code. Fortunately, Java performance is generally good enough that you don't need to bring in native methods very often.

Finally, it is important to remember that the Java community is constantly working on techniques to improve performance but not compromise all the other features of Java, such as portability. The just-in-time compilers that will be out later this year are among the most impressive of such optimizations.

Java in the World of Distributed Computing

Much of what has been discussed so far makes Java well suited for network computing. In particular, the lightweight nature of the binary class files makes it possible to download Java code without serious performance hits. Multithreading is also critical for latency-laden network operations; your applet can download code and resources in the background while the end user is deciding the next action to take. Portability frees you from knowing how your applet will run and what it will look like on your potential client's unknown platform.

Another feature of Java that makes it excellent for distributed computing is that it's *dynamic.* Since there is no linking phase after compilation, the resolution of references is put off until runtime. Java also does not calculate the layout of objects in memory until they are used at runtime. Consequently, if you add a new method to one class, you don't have to recompile another class that uses the class but not the method. In C++, you are constantly having to recompile multiple classes because one is "dependent" on the other—this is known as the "fragile superclass problem." In its typical efficient manner, Java solves the superclass problem while taking care of other issues. Since the Java dynamic system removes difficulties caused by unnecessary dependencies, it's easy to download a special subclass to handle a specific situation without worrying about "linking" problems.

The Java development package also gives you a variety of good communication constructs. The message-passing mechanism of its objects can be used to let two different applets communicate; this is known as "inter-applet communication." Sockets, pipes, and thread synchronization constructs also provide other easy-to-use communication mechanisms. In short, Java provides all the basics for creating distributed systems.

Java as a Secure Environment

Although distributed systems are extremely powerful, they open the door to a range of security problems, which are particularly serious on a vast open network like the Internet. For normal data transmission, you have to be concerned with someone eavesdropping on your information as it passes through the network. If you have a server on the Internet, you have to worry about someone breaking in and wreaking havoc on your internal network. And if you're downloading applications from the net, you have to worry about it causing damage to your host system.

The kind of damage a poorly written application could inflict on your host spans a range of extremes. On one hand, a poorly written application can misuse the resources of your system, taking resources you might need elsewhere. For example, a C program that mismanages memory can simply take memory that another one of your applications needs. If the program is really bad, it can cause your system to lock up. Fortunately, it's usually easy to recover from such problems. However, the other end of the extreme is not quite so innocent. A malicious program can attack some of the most critical resources of your computer, such as your hard disk, causing damage less easily fixed. If the program is a virus, it can be even more pernicious. It can lie in wait for weeks or even months, then one day pounce on your computer and connecting network, causing hours or even days of lost work time. If this attack came from an application that you ran from the World Wide Web, you would probably be reluctant to use the Web again. Consequently, bad Web programs not only threaten your system, but the viability of the Web as a whole.

The designers of Java know just how important security is. For this reason, they built a multi-layered security system whose presence is felt throughout Java. This security model consists of four main layers:

- The **language** itself is designed to be safe. A strict **compiler** prevents generating bytecodes that don't completely follow extensive safety rules.
- A runtime **bytecode verifier** that inspects class bytecodes as they are loaded into the system. Since code loaded at runtime has already passed through the compilation stage, Java cannot know that it hasn't been produced by a malicious or weak compiler that does not follow all the language's safety rules.
- Once code has been verified, it needs to be loaded into a runtime namespace. This is performed by a module called the **Class Loader**, represented by a like-named class. Java has a different namespace depending on whether the loaded class came from a local file system or across a network. These separate namespaces prevent a class from passing itself off as a new low-level class. Therefore, it can't do such things as replacing the existing Security Manager (discussed briefly in the next bulleted item).
- The final layer performs checks on the code as it's being executed. This layer makes sure the code does not violate any security restrictions defined for the current environment; it's generally represented by a module called the **Security Manager**, which corresponds to a Java class of a similar name. An applet that can delete a file on your computer is an example of something that falls under the auspices of the Security Manager. The workings of Security Managers can vary on different environments. Extremely conservative Java-enabled browsers, such as Netscape Navigator, actually prevent applets from reading or writing to your local file system altogether. The HotJava browser, on the other hand, can be configured to authorize file operations more flexibly.

Figure 1.1 gives an overview of the lifetime of Java code as it travels through the layers of security. Those modules related to security are set off in boldface.

Since security is such a critical part of Java, it is worth taking a moment to look at it in greater detail. In doing so, you will get some greater insight into the inner workings of Java.

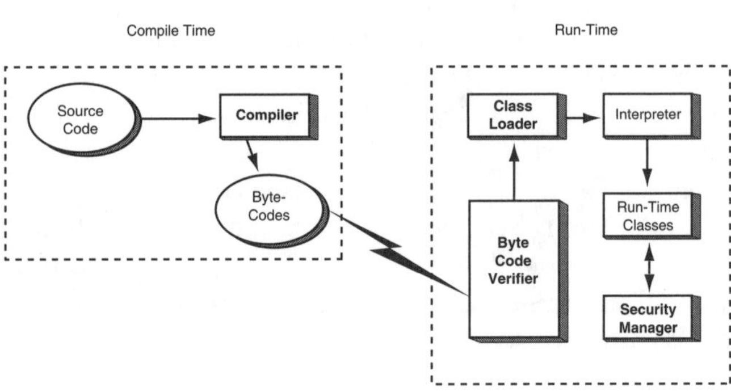

FIGURE 1.1.
The Java life-cycle in relationship to its security layers.

First Security Layer: The Language and Compiler

You have already seen a couple of reasons why Java is a secure language. A key ingredient here is removing pointers from Java. Without pointers, a bad or malicious program cannot invade the memory space of other applications. This removes a major source of attack for viruses. For example, a threatening program cannot use Java as a launching pad to directly attack your operating system kernel. Furthermore, the absence of pointers makes the Java applet itself more secure and reliable. An applet won't crash because of a "dangling pointer," as is often the case in C and C++.

Another security feature of the language is its class access mechanism. Classes can control the kinds of access other classes have to their methods and variables. There are four access modifiers, ranging from `public`, which indicates availability to all classes, to `private`, which makes a method or variable accessible only from within the class where it's defined. These modifiers can make your class more secure by denying other classes access to critical behavior. For example, if you have a class that manages critical data in a private method, another class cannot invoke that method to change the data. Access modifiers will be discussed in more detail in the next section.

The compiler uses very strict checking to ensure adherence to these and other Java language constructs. Java is a strongly typed language, so runtime bugs aren't introduced because of freely casting one type of object to another. A language like C is notorious for its loose casting mechanism. A pointer to a structure can be fairly easily cast into a long integer, and vice versa. When such casting is done incorrectly, pernicious and difficult-to-find bugs can be introduced, but this kind of casting is eliminated in Java. All casts must be explicit, and those that don't follow the semantics of the language are disallowed. Because the compiler is so strict, many errors that would otherwise appear at runtime are caught at compilation. Since runtime bugs are potentially dangerous and can be time-consuming and difficult to track down, it's good to catch as many mistakes as possible during compilation. Java's strict compiler is one reason the environment is said to be *robust*.

Second Security Layer: The ByteCode Verifier

The bytecode verifier is the most critical line of defense in the Java security system. If a rogue class can get through this layer, you could be in real trouble! However, this is unlikely. The verifier uses various techniques, including a theorem prover, to ensure that the bytecodes of the class being loaded do not violate any of the structural constraints Java places on incoming code. The verifier is, therefore, positioned to catch any potential malicious actions caused by bytecodes produced by a hostile compiler or subject to post-compilation tampering.

Verification goes through a couple of steps. The first step is to verify the format of the incoming file to make sure it is indeed a Java class and has been properly constructed. The next step is much more complex. The verifier basically sets out to prove that the code has a variety of properties. If the bytecodes make it through this phase of the verifier, then you'll know the following things:

- The code does not cause stack overflows or underflows.
- The operand types of the bytecode opcodes are proper. For example, an opcode that works with an integer operand cannot have an operand that is an object reference.
- No illegal casting is attempted.
- Object access rules are followed.

As a result of these properties being proved, the runtime system will know a couple of other important things, the most important being no forged pointers in the code.

A beneficial side effect of the verification process is that the interpreter is free from performing many of these checks as the code is being executed. For example, it does not need to conduct expensive checks to see if a stack overflow is about to occur. Because such checks are not necessary, the interpreter will run much faster.

Another security-related step occurs when the interpreter loads the verified bytecodes. When the interpreter brings in a class, it defines the *memory layout* of the class. Recall that this is a feature of Java's dynamic linking used to solve the "fragile superclass" problem. Dynamic linking also has a security advantage. In traditional languages, memory is laid out at compile time. A malicious programmer, knowing the layout of memory in the executable code, could then tamper with the pointers to get around security problems. Since Java performs memory layout at runtime, however, this potential security bypass is thwarted.

Third Security Layer: The Class Loader

After a class is verified, it's ready for runtime use. The Class Loader brings each class into a unique *namespace* that corresponds to its origin. The default namespace is for classes that come from the local file system. Such classes are called *built-ins*; they can never be replaced by a class that comes from an external source because there is a separate namespace for each network source of classes. When a class is referenced, Java looks first for a built-in class. If it isn't found, then Java inspects the namespace of the referencing class. This approach prevents network classes from replacing a built-in, or a class from one network source overriding one from another source. The security implications of this approach are subtle but important. Java tries to implement as much as possible through Java classes; for example, the Security Manager module is represented by a SecurityManager class, you get access to system resources through the System class, and, as will be seen shortly, class loader policies are implemented by ClassLoader classes. By preventing built-ins from being overridden, Java protects critical modules, such as the SecurityManager or System. It's easy to imagine what could happen if a network class was allowed to replace the SecurityManager class.

Subclasses of the ClassLoader class are used to enforce namespace policies. The Class Loader system can consist of multiple instances of ClassLoader subclasses. For example, one Class Loader can be used for classes brought from inside a firewall, but another Class Loader class can be used for those brought in from the Internet. The local file system, by default, does not use a ClassLoader class. Instead, it searches for classes in directories listed in the `CLASSPATH` environment variable; you can modify this path to include the directories that have your classes. Keep in mind that there's a subtle difference between the Class Loader mechanism, which applies to the entire Java runtime environment, and instances of the ClassLoader class, which implement specific policies.

Fourth Security Layer: The Security Manager

Even after a chunk of bytecode has gotten past the verifier and the class loader, it is still technically in a position to cause some damage. Suppose that a class downloaded from the Internet has some code to delete files from your hard disk. This can be done legitimately by calling the `delete()` method of the File class and so will pass the verifier and class loader. Fortunately, the final security layer, represented by the SecurityManager class (also known as the Security Manager), will prevent this from occurring. The Security Manager is responsible for enforcing a set of policies for protecting the runtime environment from unauthorized transactions. Whenever a potentially "dangerous" action is about to happen, the Security Manager is asked for authorization to perform the action. Based on how the manager is implemented, the action may be denied or granted.

Different browsers and applet viewers can use the Security Manager in an appropriate way. Once installed into the runtime system, the Security Manager cannot be replaced. These browsers may grant levels of authorization for different actions. For example, the Netscape Navigator has a very conservative Security Manager. The most dangerous class of actions, those of reading and writing from the hard disk, are prohibited altogether. On the other hand, the HotJava browser has a more flexible configuration. It can be set up to grant full disk access from applets loaded locally, some access to applets loaded from within the firewall, and no access for those brought in over the Internet.

A wide variety of actions are subject to authorization by the Security Manager. When a class is asked to perform a potentially dangerous action, such as a file delete, it will ask the SecurityManager class for authorization. If it isn't permitted, a security exception will occur. Besides all file-related activities, the actions of the most importance to security are network accesses. Once more, restrictions are usually based on how the SecurityManager is set up, but there are a few generalities. An applet loaded over the Internet can connect only to the host from which it originated; it will not be allowed to connect to anywhere from inside the client's firewall, nor will it be permitted to use the client to act as a launching pad into some other Internet site. An applet is also prevented from running as a network server (this has some implications that are explored later). Restrictions enforced by the SecurityManager will be discussed throughout the book as the appropriate topics dictate.

General Features of the Java Programming Language

You will now be guided through a very quick tour of the basics of the Java language. If you have experience with C or C++, then much will be familiar—you might want to skip over parts of this section. If you don't know these languages, don't worry. The basic mechanics of the language are easy, and you will see many examples throughout the book. Discussion of classes, methods, and objects will be postponed until the next chapter.

Data Types

As stated earlier, everything in Java is an object. The *partial* exception to this is the primitive data types. These data types have a standard size across all platforms; this standardization is a key aspect of Java's portability. Table 1.1 lists the primitive data types.

Table 1.1. Primitive Java data types.

Data Type	*Size*
`byte`	8-bit
`short`	16-bit
`int`	32-bit
`long`	64-bit
`float`	32-bit floating point
`double`	64-bit floating point
`char`	16-bit Unicode

If you are a C or C++ programmer, you might have noticed a couple of things. First of all, there is no `unsigned` type specifier. The `char` data type has been replaced by the `byte` primitive. The `char` type is now 16 bits, instead of the old 8 bits, because Java bases character data on the Unicode character set. Unicode is a standard that supports international characters, thus broadening the potential base in which your application can run. Although Unicode is a much broader standard than ASCII, you will probably have many opportunities to program in the 8-bit standard. Some default class behavior and localization methods will be available for doing this. This book will focus on ASCII output.

The only primitive data type not in Table 1.1 is `boolean`. A `boolean` variable cannot be converted to a number and has only two values: `true` or `false`.

You might have noticed that these primitive data types present a *partial* exception to Java's pure object-oriented nature. It is "partial" because Java has a suite of classes used to encapsulate these data types as objects. These classes are called *type wrappers* and are discussed in Chapter 2, "Object-Oriented Development in Java."

Literals

Literals are used to represent the primitive types. Integers are defined in a manner similar to C. They can be literally set to a decimal value, such as 10. A hexadecimal value is indicated with a leading 0x; 15 is represented by 0xF. Octal values (base 8) are prefaced by 0.

Floating point numbers are represented by the standard decimal point notation, such as 3.1415. These can be stored as a 32-bit `float` or a 64-bit `double`; the latter is the default. The notation style of 6.1D or 6.1F can also be used to designate the number as a `double` or `float`, respectively.

Characters can be represented by a single character in quotes such as `'a'`. Escape sequences are used to represent special characters and are preceded by a backslash (`\`). For example, tab is `\t`, newline is `\n`, and so forth. See your Java references for a listing of all the escape characters.

The last literal is not based on a primitive data type. Strings are represented by zero or more characters in double quotes. An example is `"This is a Java book!"`. The literal string can also use escape characters. For example, to add a new line to the previous example you would write: `"This is a Java book!\n"`.

String literals are implemented as objects of the String class. Operations on strings do not occur on character arrays (as in C), but through class methods; these operations are discussed in more detail in the next chapter.

Variables

Java has three types of variables: *instance*, *class*, and *local*. The first two types are talked about in the next chapter in the context of the discussion on classes. Local variables can be declared inside methods or blocks. *Blocks* are statements appearing in braces { }. Any local variable declared inside a left brace is valid until the right brace, at which point the variable goes out of scope.

Individual variables are declared in the general format:

```
<type> <variable name>
```

For example, to declare a `double` called pi:

```
double pi;
```

You can also asign a value to it:

```
double pi = 3.1415;
```

Variable names are prefaced by letters, an underscore, or a dollar sign. They can use most characters, including numbers. However some symbols, such as those used in operators, should not be used. For example, you should not call a variable `pi+3`.

Comments

Java has three comment styles. Two are similar to those used in C and C++. A double slash (//) means that everything to the end of the line should be ignored:

```
// Ignore this
```

Everything between the characters /* and */ is also ignored. This can be spread over several lines. If the first part of the comment starts with /**, then a special documenting feature is indicated. How this works is discussed in Chapter 14.

Operators

Table 1.2 lists a quick summary of operators in Java, which are fairly simple to use. The following code declares two integers, assigns values to them, and adds them to a third variable:

```
int x,y;
x = 3;
y = 4;
int z = x + y;
```

The final value is 7.

The following code applies the bitwise AND operator to the end of the previous example to get the value 4.

```
int q = z & 4;
```

You'll see examples of other categories of operators in the upcoming sections.

Table 1.2. Classification of operators.

Classification	*Operators*
Arithmetic	+ - * / %
Relational Operators	< > >= <= == != && || !
Bitwise Operators	& | ^ << >> >>> ~ &= |= ^=
Assignments	= += -= /= %=
Bitwise Assignments	&= |= <<= >>= >>>= ^=
Ternary Operator (if...else shorthand)	?:
Increment	++
Decrement	--

Expressions that have multiple operators are resolved according to where they are in a hierarchy of precedences, shown in Table 1.3. Operators higher up in the precedence table are evaluated first. If multiple operators on the same line have the same precedence, then they are resolved by left-right order. If you are confused or cannot remember precedence, then a nice rule is "When in doubt, use parentheses."

Table 1.3. Operator precedence.

. [] ()

++ — ! ~

* / %

+ -

<< >> >>>

< > <= >=

== !=

&

^

|

&&

||

?:

= and other assignments

Bitwise Assignments

Keywords and Conditionals

Table 1.4 lists Java keywords; they are reserved for Java statements, so you can't use them for things like variable names. They are identifiers for such things as data types, conditionals, control flow constructs, class definitions, and object implementations. Most of these keywords will be described in this and the next chapter. Those that are reserved but currently not implemented are italicized.

Table 1.4. Java keywords.

abstract	boolean
break	byte
byvalue	case
catch	char
class	*const*

continues

Table 1.4. continued

continue	default
do	double
else	extends
false	final
finally	float
for	*goto*
if	implements
import	instanceof
int	interface
long	native
new	null
package	private
protected	public
return	short
static	super
switch	synchronized
this	threadsafe
throw	transient
true	try
void	while

An `if...else` conditional is used to execute code based on whether a `boolean` test is `true`. Single statements can follow, or multiple statements can be declared in braces:

```
if (test == true)
  // ... A single statement to execute if test if true
else {
  // ... multiple statements to execute if test if false
}
```

The test must return a `boolean` value. This means an expression such as

```
if (1)
```

is not valid because it returns a `numeric`, but not a `boolean`. It's acceptable to nest `if...else` statements or call them in a nested series, such as `if...else...if...else...if...else`.

The latter can also be simulated with the `switch` conditional. Not being restricted to just boolean comparisons, the `switch` conditional uses a comparison with a general primitive to conduct its test. The following code uses an integer to perform its test:

```
switch ( Count ) {
        case 1:
            // ... test 1
            break;
        case 4: {
            // ... do some operation...
            return 0;
        }
        case 24: break;
        default:
            return -1;
        }
```

The `case` statements can appear in braces.

Loops

Java has three looping operations. The `for` construct loop is structured as follows:

```
for (init; test; post-test)
```

The first part of the expression is any initialization at the start of the loop. The test is a simple or complex expression. The last part is an expression such as an increment or decrement of a variable. The `for` loop is followed by a single statement or a block of code. For example,

```
 for (k = 0; k < 10; ++k) {
   // ... do something
}
```

loops ten times.

A `while` loop is just the test portion of the `for` loop:

```
while (test)
```

The `do...while` construct performs the test and the end of the loop:

```
do {
   // ... do something
} while (test);
```

The `break` construct is used to exit from a loop, and the `continue` statement skips to the next iteration of the loop. Labeled loops can also be used to control where to go in complex loops. If a label follows a `break` statement, then the code breaks out of the nearest loop that has the matching label. The following example effectively quits both loops when the variable `j` is greater than 100:

```
int i,j;
  quit: for (i = j = 0; i < 100; ++i) {
          for (int k = 0; k < 10; ++k) {
            // ... Do something
            if (j > 100)
               break quit;
         }
     }
```

If the `break` statement in this example was replaced by the following,

```
if (j > 100)
    continue quit;
```

then the code would jump to the next iteration of the outer `for` loop.

Arrays

Arrays are first-class objects in Java; they are not just a pointer to memory as in C. Consequently, Java arrays are a lot safer. You cannot indiscriminately assign an element to just any index in an array. Java makes sure the index is valid—this prevents the difficult-to-track memory access violations that occur so easily in C. If you try to access a bad array index in Java, an exception will be thrown and no action will be taken.

Because Java arrays are objects, their semantics are a little different from their counterparts in C or C++. The thing that confuses most new Java programmers is how to allocate a new array. First, you cannot declare an array with a prefixed size; it must be declared as an uninitialized variable:

```
int numbers[];    // For integer arrays
String myStrings[];  // For arrays of String objects
```

Another way to declare array variables is to put the braces after the type. Some programmers consider this method more readable.

```
String[] myStrings;
```

As you might have noticed from these examples, arrays can be used for both primitive data types and classes.

The next step is to create the array by using the `new` operator to construct an object instance; this will be discussed in more detail in the next chapter.

```
int numbers[] = new int[5];    // For integer arrays of length 5
String myStrings[] = new String[20];  // For arrays of length 20 of String objects
```

These examples create an `integer` array of 5 elements and a String array of 20 elements. However, the arrays still don't actually contain anything. Each slot is initialized to a default value. Integers are all set to `0`, and String elements are all set to `null` (indicating no object).

It's easy to add elements to the array after it's created, much as you do in C++. It is a zero-based system with integer indexes. Therefore, to assign the first element you would call the following:

```
myStrings[0] = "My First String"
numbers[0] = 10;
```

If you try to make an invalid assignment to an invalid index, an ArrayIndexOutOfBoundsException will be thrown:

```
numbers[10] = 10;
```

Chapter 2 covers how exceptions are handled; for now, you just need to know that such exceptions occur at runtime. The preceding error will not be caught by the compiler.

A `public` instance variable called *length* is used to get the size of an array:

```
int q = numbers.length;  // This is 5
```

Array sizes are final; any attempts to change the length variable will lead to problems.

Java doesn't support multidimensional arrays. However, they can be effectively simulated by using arrays of arrays, which can be initialized in several different ways. The simplest way is to define the array with preset sizes:

```
int k[][] = new int[5][4];
k[1][3] = 999;  // Assign a value to it
```

This example creates a 5 × 4 array of arrays assigned to the variable `k`. The second line shows that assigning an element to the array is straightforward, much like C or C++.

Another way to create a multidimensional array is to declare and then later assign its sizes:

```
int z[][];
int outerSize = 5;
int innerSize = 4;
z = new int[outerSize][innerSize];
```

Not all the dimensions need to be known at the time of allocation—only one dimension is required:

```
int j[][] = new int[5][];
j[0] = new int[4];
j[1] = new int[4];
```

In this example, the outer array is set to size 5, then two of its elements are set to arrays of size 4. It is interesting to note that the statement

```
j.length
```

will return size 5, but

```
j[0].length
```

will return size 4.

Applets and Standalone Applications

Java can work with two kinds of applications: *Applets*, as stated at the beginning of this chapter, are programs executed as part of a Web page and displayed with a Java-enabled browser; *standalone applications*, on the other hand, are general-purpose Java applications that don't need a browser to run. Although applets and standalone applications are compiled in a similar fashion, they are created differently.

Creating an Applet

Listing 1.1 shows the code of a minimum applet, which is stored in a file called FirstApplet.java on this book's CD-ROM. It is compiled with the following command line call to the Java compiler:

```
javac FirstApplet.java
```

The output from the compiler consists of Java bytecodes in a file called FirstApplet.class. This class code is ready to be directly run from the interpreter—no further steps are necessary.

The code consists of one class called FirstApplet, a subclass of the Applet class. The Applet class is used to tie the applet into the browser environment; it will be described in more detail in Chapter 6, "Building a Catalog Applet."

Listing 1.1. An applet that compiles but does nothing.

```
import java.applet.Applet;

public class FirstApplet extends Applet  {
}
```

To run the applet in the browser, you need to create an HTML file. Listing 1.2 shows the HTML text needed to run the applet. Note the second line of the listing: The <APPLET> tag is a special HTML extension used to launch Java applets; notice especially the `CODE` attribute. The value assigned to it indicates the class that will be run. In this case, it is the FirstApplet class that was just compiled. The <WIDTH> and <HEIGHT> tags are used to specify the bounding area of the applet, so you can control what the applet looks like on your Web page. How Applet tags are used in HTML files is discussed in more detail later in Chapter 6.

Listing 1.2. The HTML text to run the applet.

```
<TITLE>First Applet</TITLE>
<APPLET CODE="FirstApplet" WIDTH=300 HEIGHT=200>
</APPLET>
```

The program called appletviewer is used to run a Java applet from outside a browser. It's limited in capability—it lacks all the features that a browser has—but it's good for rapid development. You can launch an applet from appletviewer by passing it the name of the HTML file that starts the applet on the command line:

```
appletviewer FirstApplet.html
```

NOTE

Most of the projects and examples in the book can be run by loading the HTML in the example directory of the CD-ROM into the appletviewer program or a browser such as Netscape. When there are additional steps required, such as in the Part IV server programs, you should look at the README file in the working directory of the CD-ROM.

Creating a Standalone Application

Listing 1.3 shows the code of a simple standalone application, which is stored in a file called Standalone.java on this book's CD-ROM. Like the preceding sample applet, and class files in general, it's compiled with the program javac.

The code in a standalone application differs from an applet's code in two ways: first, standalone applications do not need an instance of the Applet class; second,they are started by a call to the `main()` method, as in C programs. The `main()` method is the first routine executed in the program, which you start by invoking the Java interpreter:

```
java Standalone
```

The .class extension should not be specified as part of the main parameter. Additional parameters can be specified after this; they are passed to the `main()` method as an array of String objects, as the example shows.

The example just prints text to the standard output console by using a call to the `println()` method of the System class: `System.out.println`. You will see this method invoked regularly throughout the book—it provides the same role for Java programmers as `printf()` does for C programmers. It will be used for both debugging and conveying program information.

Listing 1.3. A simple standalone application.

```
import java.lang.System;

public class Standalone {
  public static void main(String args[]) {
    System.out.println("Running standalone applet!");
  }
}
```

Applets Versus Standalone Applications

Most classes and methods can be used in both applets (which are tied to browsers) and standalone applications (which are not). Using a browser gives your applet access to a range of services, such as linking your applet to another Web page or using browser resources like the status bar. On the other hand, much of what you can do in an applet is restricted by a browser's security constraints. You don't have as much freedom to perform file and network operations as you do in a standalone application.

Sometimes the security restrictions of a browser force you to write a standalone application, as illustrated in the chapter on network servers in Part IV of this book. Such servers generally need to be written as standalone applications. Of course, security is both a blessing and a curse. It's a curse because it limits what you can do, but of course, if someone used that lax security to break into your system, you could end up with quite another view.

Consequently, there may come a time when people begin to write their own Security Managers into standalone programs to fit special needs. For example, a corporate "intranet" is a possibility.

This book, as its title indicates, will focus on applets. However, some features, such as network servers, are best created as standalone applications, so these will be used when appropriate.

Summary

Java is more than just an Internet programming language. It is a full-featured, object-oriented language in its own right. As the language matures, Java may be considered the language of choice for *all* object-oriented programming. In this way, Java might compete with major object-oriented languages, such as C++ or Smalltalk. It is entirely possible that corporations and other institutions will use Java for in-house applications, such as timesheets and client/server projects. Java will probably prove to be especially popular on intranets. So despite its billing as primarily an Internet language, Java's wide variety of features could establish it as the next major language in general, for uses ranging from in-house projects to commercial uses to the Internet and intranets to being the first language taught in universities. For this reason, Java is worth knowing, regardless of how you use the Internet.

Chapter 2 moves from this overview of Java's foundations to a deeper exploration of its object-oriented features. You will also be introduced to the Java Development Kit (JDK), which offers a large suite of classes for creating your applets. Techniques for writing more readable, efficient, and extendible code will also be discussed.

2

Object-Oriented Development in Java

Now that you're familiar with the general architecture of Java and its basic programming constructs, you're ready to look at Java's tools for object-oriented development. This chapter first looks at the simple, yet powerful, object-oriented features of the Java programming language. You then see how you can organize Java classes into libraries by using the *package mechanism*. Finally, you're introduced to the suite of class libraries provided with Java, known as the *Java Developer's Kit (JDK)* or the *Java API*.

Introduction to Java Classes and Objects

The starting place of object-oriented programming in Java is *classes*, which provide templates for specifying the state and behavior of an object at runtime. An *object* is said to be an *instance* of a class. For a given class and runtime session, there can be multiple object instances.

Basic Structure of a Class

A class generally consists of *variables* and *methods*. The following is a rudimentary example of a class called FirstClass:

```
class FirstClass {
   int firstVariable = 0; // Initially set to 0
   // Set the value of the variable...
   public void setValue(int newValue) {
      firstVariable = newValue;
   }
   // Get the variable value...
   public int getValue() {
      return firstVariable;
   }
}
```

This class consists of a single variable, called `firstVariable`, which is initially set to `0`. The class has two methods. The `setValue()` method is used to set `firstVariable` to the specified value. The `getValue()` method returns the current value of `firstVariable`.

The variable `firstVariable` is called an *instance variable*. This type of variable is defined for an instance of an object. It differs from a *local variable*, which is defined inside a block of code or a method. Suppose that a new method is defined to get half the value of `firstVariable`:

```
public int getHalf() {
      int half;  // A local variable
      half = firstVariable / 2;
      return half;
}
```

The variable `half` is a local variable; it will not exist after the `getHalf()` method is finished. However, the `firstVariable` instance variable hangs around until the object instance is destroyed.

Note that the `getHalf()` local variable isn't really needed. This method could have gotten the same results in a single `return` statement:

```
public int getHalf() {
     return firstVariable / 2;
}
```

Creating an Object Instance

After defining a class, you can use it as a runtime object. Use the `new` operator to create an instance of a class. You can use the following code to create an object instance of the FirstClass class:

```
FirstClass firstObject = new FirstClass();
```

The `new` operator does a couple of things. First, it allocates memory for the object. Recall that Java has automatic memory management; consequently, you don't have to explicitly allocate memory. The `new` operator also initializes instance variables. In this sample class, `firstVariable` is set to an initial value of zero. However, the explicit initialization to zero is not necessary; Java automatically sets instance variables to initial values such as zero or null.

The `new` operator also calls a *constructor.* A constructor is a method called when an object is instantiated. You can use a constructor to provide additional initialization. Constructors are discussed in greater detail in the "Constructors" section of this chapter.

Using Methods

A *method* has two parts: a *definition* and a *body.* The definition must have at least three components: a *return value*, a *name*, and a *parameter list.* These three components define the *signature* of a method. As you will see in the next section, signatures are important because you can use a method name multiple times in a class.

The return value of a method can be a primitive data type (such as `int`), a class name (such as String), or `void` if there is no return value. A method has zero or more parameters. If there are no parameters, the method consists of empty parentheses; otherwise, the parameters can be primitive data types or classes, separated by commas.

It's easy to call object methods. The following code instantiates a FirstClass object and manipulates its internal variable values:

```
FirstClass firstObject;  // Object not instantiated yet
firstObject = new FirstClass(); // Object instantiated!
// See what the default value of the object is...
int val = firstObject.getValue();
System.out.println("Value of firstObject = " + val);
// Set it to a new value...
firstObject.setValue(1000);
```

```
    System.out.println("Value of firstObject = " +
         firstObject.getValue());
      System.out.println("Half Value of firstObject = " +
         firstObject.getHalf());
```

Recall that `System.out.println` prints a string to standard output. In this example, the first `Print` statement outputs a value of `0`, which was the initialized value of `firstVariable`. The code then sets that variable to a value of `1000` by using the `setValue()` method. When its value prints again, a value of `1000` is output. Finally, the code calls the `getHalf()` method to print half the instance variable's value, namely `500`.

Overloading Methods

As mentioned earlier, a method has a signature. This is important because Java provides a mechanism for repeatedly using the same method name; this mechanism is called *overloading*. An overloaded method has the same name but different parameters. To illustrate overloading, a class is created that defines two instance variables. This class, called SecondClass, illustrates overloading by providing two methods of the same name to set the instance variables:

```
class SecondClass {
   int var1 = 1;
   int var2 = 2;
   // Set only the first variable
   public void setVar(int newVal1) {
      var1 = newVal1;
   }
   // Overloaded! Set both variables...
   public void setVar(int newVal1,int newVal2) {
      var1 = newVal1;
      var2 = newVal2;
   }
   // Get variable values...
   public int getVar1() {
      return var1;
   }
   public int getVar2() {
      return var2;
   }
}
```

The version of `setVar()` with one parameter sets the value of variable `1`; the `setVar()` version with two parameters sets both variable values. The following code shows how you can use this class:

```
SecondClass secondObject = new SecondClass();
      System.out.println("Var1=" + secondObject.getVar1()
         + " Var2= " + secondObject.getVar2());
      secondObject.setVar(1000);
      System.out.println("Var1=" + secondObject.getVar1()
         + " Var2= " + secondObject.getVar2());
      secondObject.setVar(secondObject.getVar1()/2,
         secondObject.getVar1());
      System.out.println("Var1=" + secondObject.getVar1()
         + " Var2= " + secondObject.getVar2());
```

After you call the first print method, the output is 1 and 2, the initialized values of the two variables. The code then uses the first version of setVar() to set the first variable to a value of 1000. The second print call prints the values 1000 and 2. Finally, the other setVar() method is called to set both variables. The first variable is set to half its existing value, and the second variable is set to half the existing value. Parameters resolve fully before passing to the called method. This means that half of the existing first variable value of 500 passes to the first parameter, but the full value of 1000 passes to the second parameter. The consequent printing displays 500 and 1000 for SecondClass object variables var1 and var2, respectively.

Periodically, you might hear method invocation called "message passing" or "sending a message." This is object-oriented "lingo" for talking about how two objects communicate. The reason that message passing is more than a buzzword is because of what goes on behind the scenes when a method is invoked. Because a method can be overloaded (and overridden, as you'll see in the section on "Method Overriding"), an invocation of an object actually results in the receiving object performing a lookup to see which method should be called. Consequently, it is more correct to call the procedure a "message passing" because the method invocation is not a direct call (such as calling a function in C) but a request for action.

Constructors

As stated earlier, *constructors* are a special type of method called when an object is initialized; their syntax is similar to that of methods, except they don't return values. The name of a constructor is the same as its class. A constructor is automatically called when an object is instantiated.

Now, rework the SecondClass class to illustrate constructors. First, add a default constructor:

```
class SecondClass {
   int var1;
   int var2;
   // Main constructor...
   public SecondClass() {
      var1 = 1;
      var2 = 2;
   }
   // ... OTHER METHODS GO HERE...
}
```

Rather than setting the values of the instance variables in their declaration, set them in the constructor. This constructor is called if you create an instance of SecondClass, as follows:

```
SecondClass secondObject = new SecondClass();
```

As with methods, you can overload constructors. Here is a constructor that defines the variable var1 at creation:

```
// Another constructor...
   public SecondClass(int var1) {
      this.var1 = var1;
      var2 = 2;
   }
```

To instantiate an object with this constructor, use the following:

```
SecondClass secondObject = new SecondClass(100);
```

This call creates an object with `var1` set to `100`; `var2` is set to `2`.

You may have noticed the curious way `var1` is set in the new constructor.

```
this.var1 = var1;
```

In this code, `this` refers to the current instance of the object, so use `this` to differentiate the `var1` of the object from that of the parameter. Because local variables and parameter variables are first in scope, they will be used unless the `this` keyword is used. Effectively, `this` appears in front of every call to an object's variable, so this is the `var2` initialization of the constructor:

```
this.var2 = 2;
```

To round out this example, you can use a third constructor to set both the variable's initial values:

```
// Define both values at initialization
   public SecondClass(int var1,int var2) {
      this.var1 = var1;
      this.var2 = var2;
   }
```

You can call this constructor with the following:

```
SecondClass secondObject = new SecondClass(100,200);
```

This call creates an object with `var1` set to `100`; `var2` is set to `200`.

What happens if there is no constructor, as in the earlier examples? In this case, the constructor of the class's *superclass* is called. This brings up the subject of *inheritance* in Java.

Inheritance in Java

One of the distinguishing features of object-oriented languages is *inheritance,* a mechanism you can use to create a new class by extending the definition of another class. It gives you a powerful way to increase the reusability of your code. You can take an old class and use it to create a new class by defining the differences between your new class and the old one. The old extended class is the *superclass*; the new extended class is the *subclass*. In Java, the process of extending one class to create a new class is called *subclassing*.

Subclassing

Java uses the `extends` keyword to indicate the creation of a new class as a subclass of an existing class. To illustrate subclassing, the following code creates a simple class that keeps a record of people's first and last names. It has a default constructor that simply initializes the two names, a constructor for storing String parameters, and a `list()` method that dumps the current values to standard output.

```
class SimpleRecord {
   String firstName;
   String lastName;
   // Default constructor
   public SimpleRecord() {
      firstName = "";
      lastName = "";
   }   // Constructor...
   public SimpleRecord(String firstName, String lastName) {
      this.firstName = firstName;
      this.lastName = lastName;
   }
   // List the elements of the record...
   public void list() {
      System.out.println("First Name: " + firstName);
      System.out.println("Last Name: " + lastName);
   }
}
```

To instantiate the class with a name and dump its contents, use the following:

```
SimpleRecord simple = new SimpleRecord("Thomas","Jefferson");
simple.list();
```

You can use the `extends` operator to *derive* from the SimpleRecord class a new class with additional address information:

```
class AddressRecord extends SimpleRecord {
   String address;
   // Default constructor
   public AddressRecord() {
      firstName = "";
      lastName = "";
      address = "";
   }
   // Constructor...
   public AddressRecord(String firstName, String lastName,
    String address) {
      this.firstName = firstName;
      this.lastName = lastName;
      this.address = address;
   }
}
```

Notice how this new AddressRecord class inherits the `firstName` and `lastName` variables from the SimpleRecord class. It also inherits the `list()` method. Therefore, if you call

```
record = new AddressRecord("Thomas","Jefferson",
         "Monticello");
record.list();
```

you create a fully initialized AddressRecord object. However, the `list()` method prints only the name variables because this call ultimately results in calling the SimpleRecord `list()` method. The reason for this is because you haven't explicitly defined a `list()` method in the AddressRecord. However, you can address this limitation through method overriding.

Method Overriding

Use *method overriding* when you need a subclass to replace a method of its superclass. Recall that each method has a signature. When you override a method, you are defining a new method that replaces the method in the superclass that has the same signature. Whenever you call a method, Java looks for a method of that signature in the class definition of the object. If Java doesn't find the method, it looks for a matching signature in the definition of the superclass. Java continues to look for the matching method until it reaches the topmost superclass.

To add a `list()` method to the AddressRecord class that displays the address, all you need to do is add this code to the class definition:

```
// List the elements of the record...
   public void list() {
      System.out.println("First Name: " + firstName);
      System.out.println("Last Name: " + lastName);
      System.out.println("Address: " + address);
   }
```

The `list()` method call from the previous example will now print the following results:

```
First Name: Thomas
Last Name: Jefferson
Address: Monticello
```

Calling Superclass Methods

You may have noticed that the AddressRecord `list()` method duplicates some code of the SimpleRecord `list()` method. Namely, it duplicates the following:

```
System.out.println("Last Name: " + lastName);
System.out.println("Address: " + address);
```

You can eliminate this redundancy. Recall that one of the points of inheritance is that a subclass takes an existing class and extends its definition. Because the `list()` method of SimpleRecord already has some of the behavior of the AddressRecord class, you should be able to use the SimpleRecord `list()` method as part of the base behavior of the AddressRecord class.

Use the `super` keyword to refer to a superclass. The `super` keyword is appropriate for the current problem being discussed because calling the superclass of AddressRecord has some of the behavior the `list()` method needs. Consequently, the `list()` method of AddressRecord is modified to call the SimpleRecord `list()` method before specifying additional behavior:

```
public void list() {
      super.list();
      System.out.println("Address: " + address);
   }
```

This code now prints the full name and address, as mentioned in the preceding section's definition of `list()`.

Calling Superclass Constructors

You can use the `super` keyword to call the constructor of the superclass. The only difference from the previous use of `super` is that you call it without any method definition. For example, the two constructors of AddressRecord are modified to call the SimpleRecord constructor before performing its own initialization:

```
// Default constructor
   public AddressRecord() {
      super();
      address = "";
   }
   // Constructor...
   public AddressRecord(String firstName, String lastName,
    String address) {
      super(firstName,lastName);
      this.address = address;
   }
```

You can call the default constructor (no parameters) or another constructor with `super` as long as the constructor with the matching signature exists.

You can use the `this` keyword in a similar manner to call methods within your class. For example, suppose that you need a constructor that just adds an address to the AddressRecord class, with the other fields set to empty strings. You can do this by using the following code:

```
public AddressRecord(String address) {
      this();
      this.address = address;
   }
```

This code calls the default constructor of the AddressRecord class, which in turn calls the SimpleRecord default constructor. At this point, all the fields are set to empty strings. The code then assigns the specified String to the address field, and you're ready to go.

You might wonder what the superclass of SimpleRecord is; the answer is in the next section.

Important Core Classes

Now that you have seen the fundamentals of classes in Java, it's time to see how some of the basic classes in Java work. Because these classes are used throughout Java, you should be familiar with them.

The Object Base Class

The Object class is *the* base class of all classes in Java—the ultimate superclass of all classes. Because of its primary nature, the methods of the Object class are present in all other classes, although custom methods often override them.

The Object class has a variety of interesting methods. Each Object has its own String representation. This may be a system-generated name or something generated by the class. For example, a String object's representation is the string itself. You get an Object's String representation in two ways:

```
Object o = new Object();
System.out.println("Object = " + o);
System.out.println("Object = " + o.toString());
```

In the second line of the preceding example, the Object itself is provided as part of the printout. The Object's `toString()` method is actually called when an Object is provided as part of the `print` statement. Consequently, the second and third lines are functionally equivalent. The `toString()` method should be overridden if you want a custom String representation; it is overriden throughout the Java class libraries.

The `finalize()` method is the closest thing Java objects have to a destroy method. Recall that Java has automatic memory management so you don't have to explicitly delete objects. The *garbage collector* removes unreferenced objects from memory. When an object is about to get "garbage collected," its `finalize()` method is called. This can be overridden if you need to do some custom cleanup, such as closing a file or terminating a connection. However, because garbage collection doesn't happen at predictable times, you need to use the `finalize()` method carefully. You can also call the method manually, as in right before removing a reference.

Each class in Java has a class *descriptor*. The Class class represents this descriptor, which you access by using the `getClass()` method of the Object class. You cannot modify the returned class descriptor. However, you can use it to get all kinds of useful information. For example, the `getSuperclass()` method returns the class descriptor of a class's superclass. For example, to get the superclass of a String, you can call the following:

```
String s = "A string";
System.out.println("String superclass = " +
        s.getClass().getSuperclass());
```

The `getName()` method of Class returns the name of the class.

You may notice the `wait()` and `notify()` methods of the Object class. These are complex methods related to threaded processing, which is discussed in detail in Chapter 8, "Adding Threads to Applets."

String Classes

As stated in Chapter 1, *string literals* are implemented as objects of the String class. You can create strings in a variety of ways. First, you can assign a String to a literal, as has been shown. You can also use String arithmetic to concatenate one String to another. For example, the second string in

```
String s1 = "A string";
String s2 = s1 + " with some additional text";
```

is set to `"A string with some additional text"`. You can also use other operators, such as `+=`, in String arithmetic. String concatenation also works with primitive data types. For example, this is a valid operation:

```
String s = "This is number " + 6;
```

Although you cannot change String objects after creating them, you can apply methods to them to yield new String objects. For example, you can use the `substring()` method to return a String starting at a specific index. You can also apply other operations. The `length()` method returns the length of the String. For example, the following methods applied on the above String objects print `with some additional text`:

```
System.out.println(s2.substring(s1.length()));
```

A series of overloaded `valueOf()` methods is particularly useful. These methods take a primitive data type and return a String representation. The following code sets the String variable `s` to `100`.

```
int i = 100;
String s = String.valueOf(i);
```

Notice that the preceding example didn't use any instance of the String class to invoke the `valueOf()` method. This is because `valueOf()` is a *class method*, which means that the method is global to the class, not to a specific instance of the class. Class methods (sometimes called *static methods*) are discussed in the section "Class Methods and Class Variables" later, but keep this syntax in mind when you see it.

The `equals()` method returns a boolean indicating whether two String objects have identical internal strings. The call

```
s2.equals(s);
```

using the String variables from the previous example returns `false`. The String class has many methods; you'll see many of these used in the examples and chapter projects of this book.

Another type of string class is StringBuffer. Unlike the String class, you can modify a StringBuffer object after you've created it. You typically construct a StringBuffer object with a String as the lone parameter, although other variations are possible. After construction, you can use operations like `append()` to modify its state. Using the two String variables again in an example, the following code creates the same String value as variable `s2`, except with a period concatenated to the end:

```
StringBuffer sb = new StringBuffer(s2);
sb.append('.');
System.out.println(sb);
```

The StringBuffer class has some of the same methods as String, and you usually use it in close conjunction with String objects.

Type Wrappers

As pointed out in Chapter 1, "The Java Development Environment," Java had some important design decisions to make regarding primitive data types like integers and floating point numbers. On one hand, designers of Java wanted it to be "objects all the way down," while on the other hand, it needed good performance. In other object-oriented languages, such as Smalltalk, everything is an object, including a number. To perform a mathematical operation would then actually be an application of a method. However, this purity comes at the expense of performance; methods calls are relatively expensive compared to, say, an addition of two integers.

Java uses a middle-ground approach. You can work with the primitive data types directly so that

```
int x = 2 + x2;
```

does not result in an object method call. However, if you want to use numbers or other data types of objects, you can use instances of a special set of classes called *type wrappers*. Each of the primitive data types has a type wrapper class, as shown in Table 2.1.

Table 2.1. Type wrapper classes.

Class	*Description*
`Boolean`	Object wrapper for the `boolean` data type
`Character`	Object wrapper for the `char` data type
`Double`	Object wrapper for `double` data type
`Float`	Wrapper for `float` data type
`Integer`	Wraps `integer` data type
`Long`	Type wrapper for `long` data type
`Number`	A superclass that defines methods of numeric type wrappers

You can create wrappers in a variety of ways depending on the data type. You can create instances of the Integer class in two ways:

```
Integer I1 = new Integer(6);
Integer I2 = new Integer("6");
```

Once created, you can apply a suite of methods. You can use some of these to convert the internal value to a new data type. For example, the preceding code returns a double value for the integer `6`:

```
double dbl = I1.doubleValue();
```

As with the String class, you can employ class methods to perform operations on primitive data types without creating an instance of a class. For example, the following code converts a string to an integer:

```
int i = Integer.parseInt("6");
```

If the String cannot be converted to a number, a NumberFormatException object is thrown. Exceptions are discussed later in the section "Introduction to Exception Handling."

Finally, the type wrappers provide public variables that give information about such things as the upper and lower bounds of a data type. To get the maximum value a `double` primitive type can have, you may call the following:

```
System.out.println("Max double value: " + Double.MAX_VALUE);
```

The `MAX_VALUE` public variable is a class variable of the Double class and is declared as static as in class methods. You learn more about these types of variables in the section "Class Methods and Class Variables."

NOTE

Now that you have seen some of Java's core classes, you can gain some further insight into Java arrays; as stated earlier, arrays are first-class objects. Because Object is the base class, this implies that arrays are subclasses of the Object class. Actually there is a class called Array, which is a direct subclass of Object. For each primitive type and class, there is a subclass of Array. Thus, there is a String[] and int[] class. Inheritance relationships are also maintained in this Array hierarchy. Turning back to the first inheritance example, the AddressRecord[] class is a subclass of SimpleRecord[].

Because arrays are subclasses of Object, this means that you can apply Object methods to it. For example, this is legal:

```
String s[] = new String[4];
System.out.println("S Superclass: " + s.getClass().getSuperclass());
```

Therefore, you can assign arrays to Objects. These are all valid calls:

```
String s[] = new String[4];
Object oArray[] = s;
int numbers[] = new int[4];
System.out.println(numbers);
Object o = numbers;
```

However, you cannot explicitly subclass an array.

More about Classes

It is time to go back to the mechanics of using Java classes. However, with the basics and a description of some core classes behind you, you're ready for some more advanced class constructs.

Access Modifiers

Java uses access control modifiers to specify the level of visibility a method or variable has to other classes. Java has four levels of access: `public`, `private`, `protected`, and `package`. The first three are straightforward and may be familiar; the `package` access level is a little more involved.

The `public` modifier indicates that you can access a variable by any class or method. Constructors are usually `public`, as in the AddressRecord example from earlier:

```
class AddressRecord extends SimpleRecord {
   // Default constructor
   public AddressRecord() {
     //...
   }
}
```

You can also declare a variable as `public`. For example, you can extend the AddressRecord class to have two `public` variables to indicate whether the address is for the Internet or is physical:

```
class AddressRecord extends SimpleRecord {
   public int INTERNET_ADDRESS = 0;
   public int PHYSICAL_ADDRESS = 1;
   // ... Constructors and methods...
   }
}
```

You can use the following code to print its values:

```
AddressRecord a = new AddressRecord();
      System.out.println("Physical Address = " +
         a.PHYSICAL_ADDRESS);  // which is 1
```

You use the `protected` accessor to restrict access only to subclasses of the protected class. This accessor allows you to design classes so that you can specify methods only of use to subclasses. For example, you can make the name variables of SimpleRecord `protected`. This restricts their use to a subclass, such as AddressRecord. This is how the variable portion of SimpleRecord is defined:

```
class SimpleRecord {
   protected String firstName;
   protected String lastName;
   // ... Constructors and methods...
}
```

The AddressRecord class can continue to use these variables, but outside classes cannot access them.

The `private` accessor indicates that a variable or method is not available to any other class except the one in which it appears. For example, recall that the `list()` method of SimpleRecord is called by the AddressRecord subclass. This can happen because access to the method is allowed. However, if the method is declared as `private`,

```
private void list()
```

then AddressRecord will not be able to access the method. A compilation error will therefore arise when you try to compile the AddressRecord class.

The last and default form of access, `package`, does not directly correspond to an accessor keyword. *Packages*, as discussed in the section of the same name, are a way of creating libraries of classes. If you do not specify an access control modifier, a method or variable is accessible to all classes in the `package`. The `package` level of access is a way of saying that the method or variable is accessible to all classes that are "friends" with, or the same `package` as, the class they're contained in.

Class Methods and Class Variables

Sometimes you may need to have information that is global to a class and shared by every instance of that class. One reason you might want to do this is for values that do not change, as in defining mathematical constants, like pi. Or you may want to define a version number for a class. Finally, if your class is providing a service that is used throughout an applet, you may want to make its data global to the class so that objects can share the information.

Class methods and *class variables* are employed to define data that is local to a class and not an object. For this reason, class variables are different from instance variables. Class methods and class variables are declared by using the `static` keyword, which sometimes results in them being referred to as *static methods* and *static variables*.

From the ever present AddressRecord example, you can make the two public address flags into class variables by adding the `static` keyword:

```
class AddressRecord extends SimpleRecord {
   public static int INTERNET_ADDRESS = 0;
   public static int PHYSICAL_ADDRESS = 1;
   // ... Constructors and methods...
   }
}
```

This is more efficient than the previous use that just declared the addresses as `public`. By adding the `static` keyword, you have indicated that these flags are global to the class and not the particular instance.

Class methods are even more interesting. In Part III of this book, you will create a class that keeps track of images that have been loaded in memory. This class information is kept across invocations of applets, so some of this class information doesn't need to be tied to a particular instance. In fact, there is only one instance of the class, and it is invoked by the class itself! The class does this through a private constructor. Here are some of the code highlights:

```
public class MediaLoader {
   // Cache is hashtable...
   static Hashtable cache = new Hashtable(cacheSize);

   // The loader is static and so can be created only once
   private static MediaLoader loader = new MediaLoader();

   // Private internal constructor
   private MediaLoader() {
      // ... various initilization goes on here...
   }

   // Return reference to this MediaLoader object
   public static MediaLoader getMediaLoader() {
      return loader;
   }
   // ... internal methods..
}
```

A lot of interesting things are going on here. A `cache`, which is used to store images, is declared as a class variable. One of the neat things about Java is the flexibility with which you can structure your code. Note how this initialization is not within a method but is part of the class definition; remember that because the `cache` variable is `static`, it is a class variable and thus is not tied to an object instance.

The next step is even more unusual. The loader class initializes itself! The constructor is `private` and not `public`, so no other object can create an instance of the loader. Instead, the class calls the `private` constructor and stores the instantiated loader object into a *private class variable*. In effect, the class is saying, "Make only one instance of this class, and only I know it!"

How do other objects use this MediaLoader object? They do so by calling the last method listed, `getMediaLoader()`. It is a class method and so is not tied to any instance. The job of the method is to return a *reference* to the `private` instance of the object. The other objects can then use this reference to call the `public` methods of the loader class. These methods will not be declared as `static`.

To keep things simple, suppose that the loader has a `public` method called `getImage()`, with no parameters. Another object calls the method as follows:

```
MediaLoader ref = MediaLoader.getMediaLoader(); // Get the reference!
ref.getImage(); // Call the method!
```

Note how you call the class method `getMediaLoader()` by prefacing it with the name of the class. Because class methods are global to the class, you do not need an instance of the class.

The preceding call also could have been accomplished in one line of code:

```
MediaLoader.getMediaLoader().getImage();
```

This method-chaining technique prevents you from creating short-lived variables; you can use the object returned from one method call as the object to be used in the next method call.

While class methods are extremely powerful, they have some restrictions. In particular, they can work only on class variables. If you think about it, the reason for this is obvious: They cannot work on instance variables because there may not be an instance for them to work with!

The various techniques you have seen in the MediaLoader class are used throughout the Java Developer's Kit (JDK). You sometimes see classes that you cannot figure out how to use. In this situation, look for methods named something like `getReference` or `getDefault`; these may return a reference to an object instance of that class. You would then employ them in a fashion similar to the MediaLoader class.

The `final` Modifier

You use the `final` modifier to indicate that something cannot be changed or overridden. If the `final` modifier is applied to a variable, it is effectively made into a *constant*. In the AddressRecord example, the address flags are set to their best form by adding the `final` modifier:

```
class AddressRecord extends SimpleRecord {
   public static final int INTERNET_ADDRESS = 0;
   public static final int PHYSICAL_ADDRESS = 1;
   // ... Constructors and methods...
   }
}
```

Without the `final` modifier, other classes could change the value of the variable by calling something like

```
AddressRecord.INTERNET_ADDRESS = 6;
```

With the `final` modifier attached to `INTERNET_ADDRESS`, however, this line of code would generate a compiler error. This is because `final` variables cannot be modified.

If a method is declared as `final`, it cannot be subclassed. Because `private` methods cannot be subclassed, they are effectively `final`. Note, however, that the converse does not hold. It is useful to declare methods as `final` whenever it is appropriate. This allows the Java compiler to make some optimizations, thus improving the performance of your code. If the compiler knows that a method cannot be subclassed, it can do such things as "in-lining" the method wherever it is called. Because a `final` method cannot be subclassed, runtime lookups for matching method signatures as part of the subclassing mechanism are not necessary.

To declare a method as `final`, place the modifier as follows:

```
public final void list()
```

You can also declare classes as `final`. This means that the class cannot be subclassed. The main reason you may want to declare a class as `final` is related to security. In the JDK, many classes are `final`. The reason for this is clear if you think about it. For example, suppose that you could subclass the System class! It would then be relatively easy to subvert the security of a client. Final classes may also be subject to some compiler optimizations, thus providing an additional reason for declaring a class as `final`.

NOTE

The term *accessor methods* refers to methods used to set and retrieve a variable. This is the preferred way of constructing a class rather than declaring everything as `public`. In the SimpleRecord class, the preferred way to set or retrieve the `firstName` variable of an object is to create methods like

```
public void setFirstName(String firstName) {
      this.firstName = firstName;
   }
   public String getFirstName() {
      return firstName;
   }
```

where the variable `firstName` is not declared as `public`. While writing a `set` or `get` method for every accessible variable may seem tedious, it is better than declaring everything `public`. If you make instance variables `public`, you're compromising the principle of encapsulation. By exposing `public` instance variables to objects that use your class, you're making the outside world aware of how your class works. You may then lose the freedom to modify the inner workings of your class. For example, if you want to rename or delete a `public` instance variable, you may not be able to do so because all kinds of classes are using this variable! This very bad practice departs from all the good principles of object-oriented programming. So while it may seem painful now to write large numbers of `set` or `get` methods, you're saving yourself time down the road. If you have a good editor, it won't take that much time anyway.

The term *accessor class* is sometimes used to refer to classes that do nothing more than hold data reachable through accessor methods; the classes have no behavior per se. For C programmers, you will often want to write an accessor class where you would normally create a structure.

The `null` Keyword and More About Garbage Collection

The `null` keyword indicates that something has no instance. By default, an uninitialized class variable is set to `null`. Sometimes you might want to do this explicitly—simply for code readability—if your variable will not be initialized for a while.

The biggest use of `null` occurs when you no longer need an object. For example, suppose that you create a local variable in a long and involved method that refers to an instance of the Integer class. You use the Integer object for a while, and then you want to indicate that it is no longer needed. You can do this with the `null` keyword:

```
Integer I = new Integer(6);
// ... do something with the object...
I = null;
```

You can achieve the same result in other ways. You can enclose the variable in a block statement; when the variable goes out of scope, the object will no longer be referenced. If you reuse the variable for another object reference, the old object will no longer be referenced:

```
Integer I = new Integer(6);
// ... do something with the object...
I = new Integer(9);  // Old Integer reference is gone...
```

Why would you want to set something to `null`? Recall that Java's memory management is through a garbage collector. This garbage collector removes objects from memory that are no longer referenced. If your variable was the only reference to the object, then after the reference is removed, the object is a candidate for garbage collection. Remember that the garbage collector is a low-priority thread, so the object may not be cleaned up immediately. If you are really tight on memory, you can call the garbage collector explicitly via the System class:

```
System.gc();
```

Like all methods in the System class, `gc()` is a class method, so you don't have to create any instance to use it. The kind of situations in which you might want to call the garbage collector explicitly is after involved operations that consume a large number of objects and system resources. Do not call the collector in a loop, however. The `gc()` operation runs the full collector, so the collector's execution will take a moment or so.

Scoping Rules

When a variable is referenced inside a method, Java first looks in an enclosing block for a declaration. If a declaration is not found, Java travels up the nested blocks until it reaches the method definition. If the variable is found anywhere inside a method, the variable has priority over a similarly named instance or class variable. This is why you often see code like the following:

```
public SimpleRecord(String firstName, String lastName) {
      this.firstName = firstName;
      this.lastName = lastName;
}
```

The `this` keyword is used here to differentiate the instance variable from the local variable.

If the referenced variable is not found inside the method, Java searches the class. If the reference variable still is not found, Java travels up the class hierarchy (until the Object class is reached), inspecting the superclasses for the variable. You have seen how this works in the "Inheritance in Java" section.

Casting Rules

Use *casting* when you need to convert an object or primitive of one type to another type. For example, you may want to convert a `double` to an `int`, or a subclass to its superclass. Casting allows you to do this, although the rules of casting can be complicated. The key thing to remember about casting is that it does *not* affect the object or value being cast. However, the receiver of the cast constitutes a new object or a new type.

Casting primitive data types occurs quite often, such as when you are reading in a stream of data. How the cast occurs depends on the precision of the types involved in the cast. Precision relates to how much information the type can contain; for example, a floating point type such as `double` or `float` has more precision than a simple number like `int`. Likewise, `double` has more precision than `float` because it is 64-bit as opposed to 32-bit. Whenever you transfer data from a less precise type to a more precise type, explicit casting is *not* required:

```
int i = 3;
double pi = i + .14159;
```

On the other hand, transferring data from a more precise type to a less precise type requires casting. This is because data may be lost in the casting. Java forces you to explicitly cast because it wants you to be aware of the possible danger of such a conversion:

```
double pi = 3.14159;
int i = (int)pi;  // This is set to 3 (you lost the .14159!)
```

Casting between objects is a little more complicated. To illustrate casting, look at the Hashtable class of the JDK. This class takes instances of the Object class and places them into a hash table via a method called `put()`, where a String is used as a key. To retrieve them from the table, you invoke `get()`, which takes a String key and returns the corresponding Object.

Recall that Object is a superclass of all classes; every class is a subclass of Object. Suppose that you have a class called MyClass and a String that will be used as a key, placed in a variable `key`. You can place it in a Hashtable object, indicated by the variable `hash`, as follows:

```
MyClass MyObject;
hash.put(key,MyObject);
```

Because you want to keep your object, MyObject, as an instance of MyClass, don't cast it when you call `put()`. This is acceptable because MyClass is a subclass of Object.

Suppose that you want to actually store MyObject as a proper Object. In other words, you want to cast a subclass to a superclass. You would then cast it as follows:

```
hash.put(key,(Object)MyObject);
```

By doing this, however, you lose the functionality of MyObject.

Suppose that you store the MyObject in the original example, without casting. When you retrieve the object, it is returned as an Object. You can convert the Object returned by `get()` to the original MyObject by casting:

```
MyClass MyObject;
hash.put(key,MyObject);
// ... do something...
MyClass MyObject2 = (MyClass)hash.get(key);   // Get back original MyObject
```

In this case, you're using casting to convert a superclass to a subclass. You can then use the variable `MyObject2` as an instance of MyClass. It will be identical to the original `MyObject` variable.

If you structure the code in the following way, you will have problems:

```
MyClass MyObject;
hash.put(key,(Object)MyObject);
// ... do something...
MyClass myObject2 = (MyClass)hash.get(key);   // Don't do this!
```

Problems will occur because MyObject was stored in this case as an Object. When you retrieve it, even after casting, it is not really an instance of MyObject any more because that data was lost. If you try to use a `MyObject` method or variable after this, you get a runtime exception.

You cannot cast indiscriminately. If you try to convert two sibling classes (they are not derived from each other), you get a compilation error:

```
AddressRecord a = new AddressRecord("Thomas","Jefferson","Monticello");
String s = (String)a;   // THIS WILL NOT COMPILE!
```

You cannot cast primitive data types to objects or vice versa. However, you can effectively perform these conversions by using the type wrapper classes discussed earlier in this chapter.

Other Keywords

You use the `instanceof` operator to test if a class is an instance of another. A subclass will be an instance of its superclass, but not vice versa. For example, the first three of the following print statements will display `true`. (Recall that AddressRecord is a subclass of SimpleRecord.) Only the last test will be `false`.

```
AddressRecord a = new AddressRecord();
System.out.println((a instanceof SimpleRecord));  // true
System.out.println((a instanceof AddressRecord));  // true
SimpleRecord b = new SimpleRecord();
System.out.println((b instanceof SimpleRecord));  // true
System.out.println((b instanceof AddressRecord));  // false
```

Another important modifier is `synchronized`. You will see this modifier in code throughout this book and in the JDK. The `synchronized` modifier is related to coordinating thread processing; it is discussed in depth in Part III of the book.

Introduction to Exception Handling

One of the great challenges for programmers is how to handle runtime errors in a graceful and efficient manner. In traditional programming, developers manage problems by passing success or failure codes in `return` statements. The calling functions then check the return code in an `if...else` statement. If the function succeeds, one chain of action is called; otherwise, another course of action is taken.

There are a couple of problems with this approach. First, this approach results in bloated code. To have to put an `if...else` check around every function call increases the size of your code by several factors. Even worse, this traditional approach does not enforce strong error checking. Because of sloppiness or overconfidence, programmers often ignore return codes. If there is a problem in an unchecked function call, however, the program may end up reaching a dangerous state that eventually culminates in an abnormal termination. The ensuing search for the cause of the error would probably prove to be quite painful because the source of the problem is not readily apparent.

Fortunately, Java's strongly enforced implementation of exception handling makes it easier to track down errors. In fact, many errors are caught by the compiler instead of at runtime. If the problem does happen at runtime, however, a stack trace makes the difficulty easy to spot. Furthermore, Java's error-handling mechanism does not result in the kind of code bloat typical of traditional programming. Java's way of handling errors is through a programming construct called an *exception handler*.

Structure of an Exception Handler

An *exception handler* is often called a *try-catch block* because of its structure. It is typified by a block of code called a *try block*, which is where you attempt to execute your normal course of action. The code marches right through the block if there is no problem. If there is an error, however, Java or the called method may generate an object that may indicate the problem. This object is called an *exception object* and is passed off to the runtime system in search of a way to handle the error. The act of passing an exception object to the runtime system is called *throwing an exception*.

The job of the catch block of an exception handler is to catch any exception objects thrown from within the try block. It can then perform any cleanup or message notification as a consequence of the error.

A simple example can illustrate the basics of writing an exception handler. Suppose that you need to divide two numbers. Division, of course, can be the cause of a frequent problem: divide-by-zero errors. However, the following code handles this problem in a graceful manner:

```
int z = 0;
try {
    z = x/y;
    System.out.println("Z = " + z);
}
catch (Exception e) {
    System.out.println("Divide by zero error.");
}
```

If the variable y in this example is not 0, the division goes fine, and the result is printed. However, if the variable is 0, an exception is thrown. The Java runtime system will then try to find an exception handler to manage the error. Fortunately, Java will not have to look very far. The catch clause in the exception handler catches the thrown exception. This handler prints the fact that there is a divide-by-zero error to standard output.

An exception handler has an optional block placed at the end of the code called the *finally block*, which provides code to be executed regardless of whether an exception occurs.

```
int z = 0;
try {
    z = x/y;
    System.out.println("Z = " + z);
}
catch (Exception e) {
    System.out.println("Divide by zero error.");
}
finally {
    System.out.println("Finally: Z = " + z);
}
```

Regardless of what happens in the division operation, the last print statement is invoked.

When to Catch Exceptions

When should you catch an exception? Sometimes exceptions are generated as a result of a normal runtime violation, such as a division error or an array out of bounds. However, methods can also explicitly throw exceptions. A method can declare that it can throw an exception via the `throws` clause.

For example, it was stated earlier that the Integer class has a method, called `parseInt()`, that takes a String and converts it to an `int` data type. When the String cannot be converted to a number, however, the `parseInt()` method throws a NumberFormatException object.

The following code tries to convert some Strings to integers and prints their values:

```
String s = "100";
String s2 = "Not a number";
try {
      System.out.println("The first number is: " +
         Integer.parseInt(s));
      System.out.println("The second number is: " +
         Integer.parseInt(s2));
}
catch (NumberFormatException e) {
      System.out.println("Cannot convert String to number!");
}
```

The first conversion succeeds, but the second fails. The NumberFormatException generated is caught by the exception handler, and an error message is printed. The calling code knows that `parseInt()` throws this kind of exception because of how the method is declared:

```
public static int parseInt(String s) throws NumberFormatException
```

The `throws` section of the declaration indicates that the method may throw a certain type of exception if an operation cannot be performed. Whenever you use a method that has a `throws` clause, you should probably catch the type of exception the method throws. Depending on the type of exception thrown, an exception handler may or may not be required for a successful compile. Categories of exceptions are discussed in more detail in the next chapter.

To throw an exception, you use the `throw` keyword. The `throw` statement passes a throwable object that follows it to the runtime environment, which then begins trying to find an exception handler to catch the object. The method that throws the exception is no longer executed after the `throw` statement is invoked.

Exceptions, like everything else in Java, are objects. Consequently, you can generate an exception object by instantiating it with the `new` operator. You would then use the `throw` keyword to throw the object. Because the `parseInt()` method throws a NumberFormatException, it's likely that there is a line of code in the method similar to the following:

```
throw new NumberFormatException();
```

Exception Handlers and Exception Classes

As indicated in the previous section, exceptions have different types, or more specifically, classes. For example, NumberFormatException refers to a specific class. When an exception is generated, the Java runtime system looks for an *appropriate* handler to catch the exception. The details of this process are explained in the next chapter, but remember that whether or not a handler is appropriate has to do with the class of the exception.

To clarify this, consider a couple of exception classes. The ArithmeticException class represents errors caused by illegal arithmetic operations, usually divided by zero. Objects of class ArrayIndexOutOfBoundsException are thrown when an invalid array index is accessed. The Exception class is used to represent the general class of exceptions; the other exception classes that have been discussed are actually subclasses of Exception.

The following example shows how these exceptions are used:

```
try {
      int x = Integer.parseInt(s);
      int y =Integer.parseInt(s2);
      int index =Integer.parseInt(s3);
      int a[] = new int[5];
      a[index] = x/y;
      System.out.println("Everything worked!");
}
catch (ArithmeticException e) {
      System.out.println("Arithmetic exception");
}
catch (ArrayIndexOutOfBoundsException e) {
      System.out.println("Array index out of bounds exception");
}
catch (NumberFormatException e) {
```

```
    System.out.println("Cannot convert String to number!");
}
catch (Exception e) {
      System.out.println("Generic exception");
}
```

The first part of the code takes three input Strings and tries to convert them into integers; if the conversion fails, a NumberFormatException object is thrown. However, the third `catch` clause will catch the thrown object. If the clause were not there, the last `catch` clause would catch the problem because NumberFormatException is a subclass of Exception. The general rule is this: Java searches the `catch` clauses in the order they are declared, looking for a handler that either matches the class of the exception thrown or is a superclass of it. The runtime system will use the first handler that matches. If no appropriate handler is found, Java will go up the runtime stack and look at the next method. Java looks for an appropriate handler in the same way. This process repeats until the top of the stack is reached or until an appropriate handler is found. If there is no appropriate handler, Java dumps the stack trace to standard output. Depending on the nature of the class being thrown, the program may terminate abnormally.

After the Strings are converted to numbers, the program tries to divide the numbers. If the program divides by zero, an ArithmeticException object is thrown. The object is caught by the ArithmeticException `catch` clause, although the `Exception` clause also would have handled it.

Finally, the code assigns the divided number to an array index. If the index is illegal, an ArrayIndexOutOfBoundsException is thrown. However, there is also an appropriate handler for it, so the code finishes gracefully.

Nested Exceptions

You can also nest exceptions. To illustrate this, look at the following rework of the preceding example:

```
int y = 0;
int z = 0;
int z = 0;
int index = 0;
int a[] = new int[5];
try {
      x = Integer.parseInt(s);
      y =Integer.parseInt(s2);
      index =Integer.parseInt(s3);
      a[index] = x/y;
      System.out.println("Everything worked!");
}
    catch (ArithmeticException e) {
      System.out.println("Arithmetic exception. Try to assign Zero");
      try {
         a[index] = x/z;  // Try another division to the index
      }
      catch (ArithmeticException e2) {
         System.out.println("Another Arithmetic exception");
      }
```

```
}
catch (ArrayIndexOutOfBoundsException e) {
      System.out.println("Array index out of bounds exception");
}
catch (NumberFormatException e) {
      System.out.println("Cannot convert String to number!");
}
catch (Exception e) {
      System.out.println("Generic exception");
}
```

If the `int` variable `y` evaluates to `0`, an ArithmeticException is thrown. When it is caught, the code attempts to perform yet another division. Unfortunately, this is also a divide-by-zero error. Fortunately, this is caught in a nested ArithmeticException catch block. If there were no divide-by-zero problem but the index were illegal, the outer ArrayIndexOutOfBoundsException `catch` clause would catch the exception.

You learn more about exception handling in the next chapter. You see how Java organizes its exception classes, what methods to use, and how to use them. The following chapter also discusses how to write your own exception classes within the framework established by Java.

Organizing Projects in Java

You've seen a wide variety of constructs that Java uses to help you develop classes. These are useful for quickly getting an applet up and running. But what happens if you are working on a large-scale project that requires a carefully designed and organized class hierarchy? How will Java help you manage all of the classes required in such an environment?

Fortunately, Java provides a variety of constructs that help you develop large-scale software as well as small applets. These constructs range from those that help you lay out your design to those that help you pull the pieces together. With these techniques in hand, you can use Java to design applets that can meet your current requirements and can be used as a foundation for future development.

Abstract Methods

Suppose that you're defining a class that manages files on your hard disk. You can define most of the high-level methods, such as how to list files and their attributes; however, you can't define low-level behavior, such as how you actually get the file attributes. Because this is platform dependent, you want to leave this behavior as undefined so it can be implemented for practical purposes.

In Java, you use *abstract methods* and *abstract classes* to define a template for a class that is well defined except for a few methods. A class is abstract if one or more methods are defined by the `abstract` keyword. The following case shows how you might structure the discussed file manager as an abstract class:

```
abstract class FileManager {
   // Abstract class that enumerates files...
   public abstract String enumerateFiles(String file);
   // Practical implementation. List all files
   // using abstract enumerateFiles...
   public void dir() {
     // ... call enumerateFiles...
   }
   // ... other methods
}
```

In this example, the only abstract method is `enumerateFiles()`, which provides the low-level implementation of getting a file attribute. However, this is enough to make the class abstract. All the other methods are well defined, so if you create a class that provides a practical implementation of `enumerateFiles()`, the class will be ready to use. As long as a class is abstract, though, it cannot be instantiated.

You need to subclass the FileManager class to create a class that can be implemented. Here is one way to do it:

```
class MyFileManager extends FileManager {
   // Enumerate all files...
   public String enumerateFiles(String file) {
      // ... do the platform specific operation...
   }
}
```

This class uses all the methods of FileManager and is ready to be instantiated.

There are a couple of restrictions in creating abstract methods. Constructors and `private` or `static` methods cannot be declared as abstract. (If you think about the semantics of these, it should be clear why they cannot be abstract.) You also cannot replace a `superclass` method with an `abstract` method.

Interfaces

If you have a class that is nothing but abstract methods, it's better not to use the `abstract` keyword. Java provides a technique called *interfaces*, which you can use to define a template of behavior. Like abstract methods, interfaces cannot be instantiated. Interfaces differ from abstract methods, however, in that no interface methods can have a body. Interfaces are strictly templates.

By their nature, interfaces are a way of defining a *design*. It specifies the kinds of behaviors that something needs to have. Classes that *implement* the interface are said to provide the *implementation* of the design.

Interfaces are also Java's way of dealing with the limitations of single inheritance. Unlike C++, Java avoids multiple inheritance because of all the problems related to it, such as name ambiguity. Interfaces are a way of adding behavior to a class without compromising its fundamental behavior. However, a class can implement multiple interfaces and so simulate multiple inheritance.

The following example shows how interfaces are used. Suppose that you're working for a printer company. You have a well-defined and tested Printer class and a Document class that represents what is to be printed. However, your company wants to move into the fax and copier markets, so a multifunction printer will be developed.

You define two interfaces for copiers and fax machines as follows:

```
interface Copier {
  public void copyDocument(Document d);
}

interface Fax {
  public void transmitDocument(Document d);
}
```

These interfaces define the behavior that a copier and fax machine should have, respectively. You can also add this behavior to the Printer class to get the desired multifunction printer. You can implement these interfaces in a class that is a subclass of Printer:

```
class MultiFunctionPrinter extends Printer
 implements Copier, Fax {
  public void copyDocument(Document d) {
   // Practical implementation of Copier...
  }
  public void transmitDocument(Document d) {
   // Practical implementation of Fax...
  }
}
```

You now have a multifunction Printer class!

It should be noted that interfaces can have variables but cannot have modifiers.

Packages

Packages are a mechanism for grouping classes and interfaces. Every class or interface has a package. You can explicitly name the package in which it appears by using the `package` statement:

```
package myPackage;
```

If no package is specified, a default package is used (usually represented by the current directory).

Java has a hierarchical naming convention for naming packages, known as a *dot notation*. The top level of the notation represents the producer of the source file, such as "java." After that, you would name subhierarchies. For example, the JDK has a package called "lang" that is used to house classes related to the basic mechanics of programming in Java. The String class is in the "lang" package. You can therefore refer to the class from anywhere in your source code as `java.lang.String`. This dot structure is reflected in the directory organization of the source code files that make up the package. Thus, the String.java file will be located off a java/lang subdirectory.

Given this, the `package` declaration for the String class would be

```
package java.lang;
```

The `package` declaration must be the first non-comment, non-white space line in the file.

The `import` statement allows you to use a class defined in another package or source file. You can use the `import` statement in several ways. You can define the full reference to the class, as in the following:

```
import java.lang.String;
```

You can also bring in all classes in a package by specifying a wildcard:

```
import java.lang.*;
```

Anything imported is thereafter treated as part of the current package for the purposes of compilation.

You can also reference a class in the code by using the full package reference:

```
java.lang.String s = "A string";
```

NOTE

The Java runtime system looks for classes by the path specified by the `CLASSPATH` environment variable. You can specify multiple directories in the path. For example:

```
CLASSPATH=\java\classes;.
```

This path looks first in a Java directory for the class files and then in the current directory.

If the runtime system cannot find the class requested, it may look in the current directory, even if it was not specified in `CLASSPATH`.

A final note about *compilation units*: A compilation unit is a source code file that has *at most* one public class or interface. The file must be the same name as the `public` declaration, followed by the .java suffix. So if your source code declares a public class SimpleRecord, the file it appears in must be named SimpleRecord.java. While this convention may seem annoying at first, it will prove to be helpful because your files will give a quick listing of your public classes. The convention also helps you write more modular and easier-to-maintain code.

The Java Developer's Kit

You have now seen all of the fundamentals of Java programming. However, one last thing needs to be discussed. The *Java Developer's Kit (JDK)* is a series of class libraries organized as packages that give you a set of tools for creating software based on Java. The JDK consists of over

150 classes that provide functionality ranging from manipulating Strings to working with network sockets. A large number of these classes are used and explained throughout this book. Many of them are subject to extended tutorials, while others are explained in the course of describing a chapter project. A quick overview of the JDK will get you ready for the in-depth coverage that follows.

Eight packages make up the JDK. These packages are represented by the "java." notation mentioned earlier:

- **java.lang:** This package contains classes related to the basic workings of the Java environment. Such activities include wrappers for basic data types and strings, classes for managing threads, a class for mathematical operations, a wide variety of classes for describing exceptions, the System class, and the Object base class. The classes in this package appear throughout this book.
- **java.io:** Classes for controlling file and stream operations. The fundamentals of using this package are introduced in Chapter 4, "Enhancing the Spreadsheet Applet." The java.io classes for stream operations are employed in many of the chapter projects.
- **java.util:** This package provides a series of utility classes: a class for manipulating dates; basic data structure classes, such as hash tables and stacks; a class and interface for writing classes that use the model-view paradigm; and a tool for parsing Strings. Classes in the java.util package are used throughout this book.
- **java.applet:** This package contains the Applet class that ties your applet to its working environment, such as a browser. It also has a class that allows you to more directly exploit the native browser's capabilities. Classes of the java.applet package are explored in detail in Chapter 6, "Building a Catalog Applet," and are employed throughout this book.
- **java.awt:** The *AWT (Abstract Window Toolkit)* package provides simple and advanced tools used to direct the visual interface of a Java applet. The most important of the AWT tools is a set of standard controls that allow you to interact with the applet, such as buttons and text fields. Because AWT is one of the cornerstones of Java applet programming, Part II of this book is dedicated to exploring the package. Furthermore, various techniques for using AWT classes appear throughout the remainder of this book.
- **java.awt.image:** This "sub-package" of AWT provides the underpinnings for using images in Java. Although it's a complex package, it is also very powerful. This package is explored in depth in Part III of this book and in Chapter 14, "Advanced Image Processing."
- **java.awt.peer:** This package is used to tie AWT widgets to the underlying platform. Because you will be more concerned with the AWT classes than with the inner workings of these peers, this package is not discussed in the following chapters.

- **java.awt.net:** The classes in this package are used to write Java network programs. This package includes sockets classes for both the client and the server and classes for referencing URLs. Part IV of this book explores this package in depth and uses its classes to build a Java-based HTTP server.

Summary

This first part of this book has introduced you to the fundamentals of Java. You're now ready to dive head first into the world of Java programming. Wear your safety belt! Each chapter that follows will have an involved project that explores a feature of Java in depth. Some of these projects are quite involved and touch on many of the classes in the JDK. By the end of Chapter 4, you will have been presented with almost every major aspect of writing an applet in Java (and more!). You're encouraged to explore these projects on your computer. Modify the code to give extra functionality or to add print statements to help you understand what is going on. The emphasis of this book is learning by example, so there will be no shortage of code to look at!

II

Developing a Spreadsheet Applet with the AWT Package

3

Building a Spreadsheet Applet

This chapter starts with an overview of AWT (the Abstract Window Toolkit) and its general features and then details the basic structure of AWT and its most important classes. A discussion of more advanced aspects of exception handling follows. AWT and exception handling will be important in developing the first version of the spreadsheet applet, discussed in detail in the last section of this chapter. The visual and user-interface features of the applet will rely on AWT. The underlying spreadsheet engine will make active use of exception handling, particularly when validating and calculating formulas.

Overview of AWT: Part 1

AWT forms the basis for graphical user-interface programming in Java. The AWT package offers a large variety of tools for creating graphic widgets such as buttons, list boxes, and scrollbars. A graphics class can be used for two-dimensional drawing operations, such as displaying polygons, painting text, and setting fonts and colors, and graphical operations, such as clipping and scaling. Beyond all this, AWT provides an underlying foundation for interfacing with the user. A series of methods handle events produced by the user and the system, such as mouse clicks and keystrokes. In short, AWT gives you a set of tools for writing simple applets and a basis for developing classes that can be used to create more sophisticated programs. Chapters 4, "Enhancing the Spreadsheet Applet,"and 5, "Adding Graphs and Scrollbars to the Spreadsheet," will have the other parts of the AWT tutorial.

AWT Classes

Figure 3.1 illustrates the hierarchy of the most important classes in the AWT package; they are used for a variety of services:

- **Component** is the foundation of controls such as buttons and labels. It is also the superclass of more sophisticated controls, such as dialog boxes, and even the Applet class.
- **Container** is a class that contains Components or other Containers.
- **Panel** is a visual Container that can be used to hold other components, such as buttons, list boxes, and other Containers.
- **Applet** is the base class for creating an applet. It starts the program and ties it to the native browser.
- **Window** is used for popup-style components, such as dialog boxes.
- **Font** can be used to create fonts customized by such features as point size and style.
- **Event** encapsulates user- and system-initiated events, such as mouse clicks, keyboard strokes, and the shutdown of an applet.
- **Graphics** is mainly used when a Component needs painting. This class encapsulates a wide range of functions, including drawing polygons, text, and images, plus setting the Fonts and Colors to create what is drawn.

- **MenuComponent** provides the foundation for creating drop-down, checkbox, and other menus.

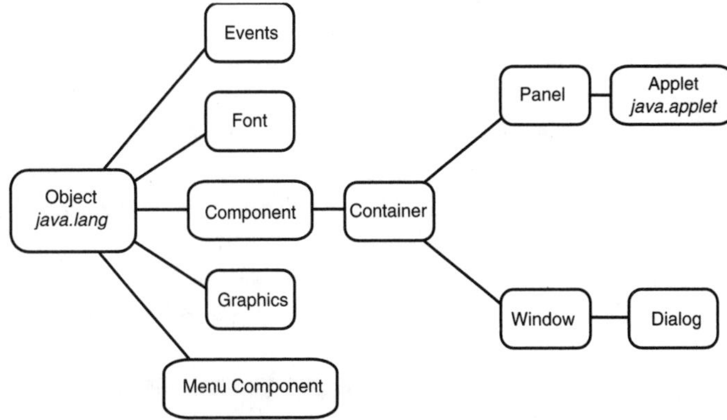

FIGURE 3.1.
Hierarchy of significant AWT classes.

Most of these classes are discussed and illustrated in more detail throughout this and subsequent chapters.

Components and Containers

Component classes are used for coordinating all aspects of a visual control. A variety of Component methods can be used to process events, enable or disable a control, set fonts and colors, and manage the control's visual display. The most widely used Components will be those simple ones that are part and parcel of creating a user interface. These include labels, buttons, list boxes, and choice menus. However, more sophisticated Component subclasses can be used to manage these primitive controls. The following list shows the primitive Component classes; these simpler classes are derived directly from Component.

Primitive Component Classes
Button
Canvas
Checkbox
CheckboxGroup
Choice
Label
List
Scrollbar
TextComponent
TextArea (extends TextComponent)
TextField (extends TextComponent)

The Component hierarchy complements these primitive controls with classes based on the Container class. Containers are used to hold Component classes and other Containers. Panels, Windows, Dialogs, and Applets are all notable Container subclasses. The Container classes are presented in more detail shortly.

You can use the primitive controls in Table 3.1 to quickly produce a functional applet. Figure 3.2 shows such an applet; with five components, it enables the user to choose what to display and when to display it. A choice between painting nothing, a rectangle, or text is offered. The class that does the drawing is a custom subclass of the Canvas Component called DrawCanvas, located in the middle of the applet. At the bottom of the screen is a Panel with Button and Choice objects. The Choice menu object lets the user decide what is to be painted when the Button object is clicked (or when the applet repaints). A TextField object at the top of the screen is used to specify which text will be displayed, if text is used.

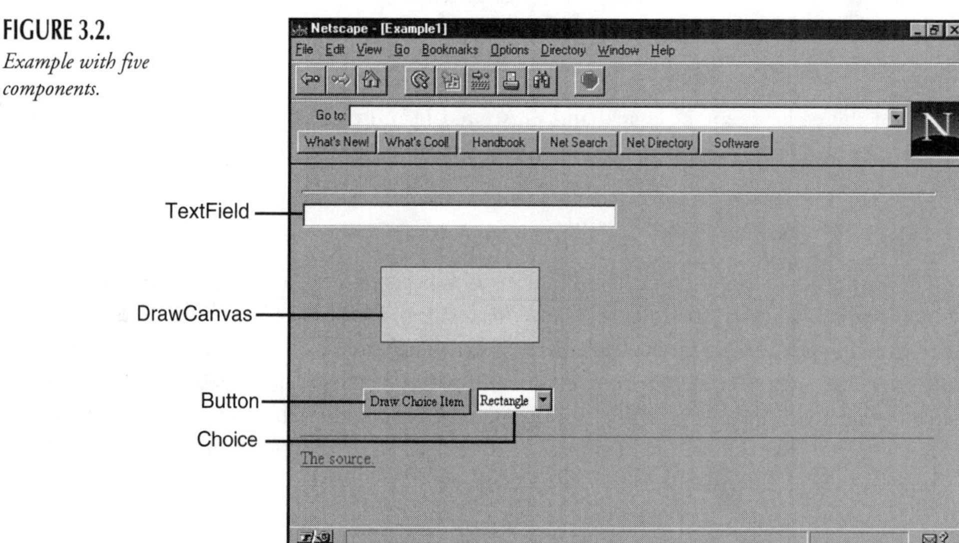

FIGURE 3.2.
Example with five components.

Listing 3.1 provides the code for this example. Although the applet is simple, it illustrates a lot of features. The `init()` portion of the applet class (called `Example1`) shows how easy it is to create and add classes to the applet display. The `handleEvent()` method overrides the default event handler and is used to trap button clicks. The code checks to see whether the action came from its button. If so, it forces the DrawCanvas object to repaint. The user's selection in the Choice box will then be reflected.

The DrawCanvas class inherits the features of Canvas and adds its own custom functions to it. When it is drawn with the `paint()` method, the class queries the applet about the user's selections and paints accordingly. This `paint()` method can be issued either when the user clicks the button or when a certain region of the canvas needs to be redrawn. The `paint()` method is part of all Component classes. It must be overridden, as in the DrawCanvas class, if any custom drawing needs to be done.

The `paint()` method takes as its sole parameter an instance of the Graphics class. This class offers different methods that can be used to set the features of the area being drawn. For example, the DrawCanvas class uses the `drawString()` method to put some text up on the drawing area. The `drawRect()` and `fillRect()` methods paint a rectangle that draws a border rectangle and its interior, respectively. These rectangles are painted a color established by the `setColor()` method. Since the `paint()` method and the Graphics class are at the basis of drawing AWT images, you will see more examples of these throughout the rest of the book.

Listing 3.1. An applet with five components.

```
import java.awt.*;
import java.lang.*;
import java.io.*;
import java.applet.*;

// This program illustrates a simple applet with a TextField,
// Panel, Button, Choice menu, and Canvas.
public class Example1 extends Applet  {
TextField tf;
DrawCanvas c;
Button drawBtn;
Choice ch;
// Add the Components to the screen...
public void init() {

 // Set up display area...
 resize(300,200);
 setLayout(new BorderLayout());

 // Add the components...
 // Add the text at the top.
 tf = new TextField();
 add("North",tf);

 // Add the custom Canvas to the center
 c = new DrawCanvas(this);
 add("Center",c);

 // Create the panel with button and choices at the bottom...
 Panel p = new Panel();
 drawBtn = new Button("Draw Choice Item");
 p.add(drawBtn);
 // Create the choice box and add the options...
 ch = new Choice();
 ch.addItem("Rectangle");
 ch.addItem("Empty");
 ch.addItem("Text");
 p.add(ch);
```

continues

Listing 3.1. continued

```
 add("South",p);
}

// Handle events that have occurred
public boolean handleEvent(Event evt) {
switch(evt.id) {
 // This can be handled
 case Event.ACTION_EVENT: {
  if(evt.target instanceof Button)    {
   // Repaint canvas to use new choices...
   c.repaint();
   }  // end if
   return false;
 }
 default:
  return false;
 }
}

// Return the current choice to display...
public String getChoice() {
 return ch.getSelectedItem();
}

// Return the text in the list box...
public String getTextString() {
 return tf.getText();
}
}

// This is a custom canvas that is used for drawing
// text, a rectangle, or nothing...
class DrawCanvas extends Canvas {
Example1 e1app;
 // Constructor - store the applet to get drawing info...
 public DrawCanvas(Example1 a) {
  e1app = a;
 }
 // Draw the image per the choices in the applet...
 public synchronized void paint (Graphics g) {
  // Get the current size of the display area...
  Dimension dm = size();
  // Draw based on choice...
  String s = e1app.getChoice();
  // Calculate center coordinates...
  int x,y,width,height;
  x = dm.width/4;
  y = dm.height / 4;
  width = dm.width / 2;
  height = dm.height / 2;
  // Paint a rectangle in the center...
  if (s.compareTo("Rectangle") == 0) {
   // Draw the rectangle in the center with colors!
   g.setColor(Color.blue);
   g.drawRect(x,y,width,height);
   g.setColor(Color.yellow);
```

```
    g.fillRect(x + 1,y + 1,width - 2,height - 2);
   } // end if
   // Get the text in the applet and display in the middle...
   if (s.compareTo("Text") == 0) {
    String displayText = e1app.getTextString();
    g.setColor(Color.red);
    g.drawString(displayText,x,y + (height/2));
   }
  }
}
```

The other Component in this example is a Panel, which is a subclass of Container. In the example, the Panel contains the Button and Choice objects. Containers are good for managing a group of Components and have a special meaning in AWT regarding how an object is displayed. Containers function as a broker for how a component within it is presented. If a component's display coordinates are outside the region of a container, it is clipped. More importantly, Containers provide a mechanism for *how* an object is presented, especially its size and position. This is closely tied to how Layouts work, discussed briefly in the following section.

One interesting aspect of AWT is that the Applet class is derived from Panel. This may seem unusual at first; however, an Applet really functions as a Container. Objects that do not fit within its area are clipped in display, and if the Applet is destroyed, so are the objects within it. Given this, the Applet class can be easily understood as simply a Panel with additional functions that tie it to the workings of the native browser.

The Window, Frame, and Dialog classes are also Containers that figure prominently. These are used to create objects that "pop up" outside the space of the applet, giving a multidimensional feel to an otherwise "flat" Web page. These classes will be discussed in more detail in the next chapter.

Layouts

For someone who has not seen Java applet code before, one question that might immediately come to mind from the previous example is: How does the program know where to position the Component objects on the screen? After all, there is no coordinate information in the code. And what do code expressions like `add("North", tf)` mean?

The key to understanding the previous code and how AWT displays components in general is a knowledge of layouts. Containers rely on layouts to give you a way to determine the size and position of the components within it. Every container is tied to a single instance of a layout. The layout that a container uses is either set by default or through programming. In Listing 3.1, the layout of the Applet object, Example1, is set to an instance of the BorderLayout class by the line:

```
setLayout(new BorderLayout());
```

Since the Panel class is also a container, it too has a layout. The default class, FlowLayout, is used in the example.

Layouts are an important part of AWT because they take care of a major issue in Java: portability. Although the language portion of Java takes care of software portability concerns, it cannot, by nature, take care of visual portability issues. Namely, how can Java guarantee that an applet developed on a specific GUI (such as Windows 95) and on a specific monitor resolution (such as VGA) have a proper look and feel on other platforms? The AWT package was designed to solve this problem. By providing a level of abstraction above the native GUI, it can hide the specifics of the underlying environment from the developer. Layouts are key elements of the visual part of the abstraction mechanism. By taking control of the sizing and positioning of components, layouts free the developer from having to worry about how to write an applet that looks good on the variety of monitor resolutions in the field. Layouts dynamically calculate how to present a component by looking at the native display-coordinate system at runtime; the sizing and positioning of the components is based on this runtime information.

All layouts are derived from the LayoutManager interface, which specifies how a layout needs to function. AWT provides five classes (described in the following sections) that set up the LayoutManager interface. This range of layouts allows the developer to choose the appropriate layout manager for the requirements at hand; if these choices aren't enough, a new class can be written. In fact, Java developers have already created several custom layout classes. Various incarnations of a RelativeLayout class have been created that lets you state where components go in relation to each other. By navigating the Java home pages on the Internet, you might find a layout class that better fits your development needs. Some of the entry points to Java on the Internet are mentioned in this book's Introduction.

Border Layout

In Listing 3.1, the applet specifies adding new components through an unusual scheme that uses such terms as "North" and "South". This scheme reflects how the BorderLayout class works. In the example, BorderLayout is tied to the Example1 applet class when the `setLayout()` method is invoked. This method indicates that the Example1 object, which is an instance of Container, is tied to the BorderLayout object. When a Container uses BorderLayout, a Component is added through a command of this form:

```
add(String direction, Component);
```

Direction is one of the following Strings: `"North"`, `"South"`, `"East"`, `"West"`, and `"Center"`. In short, the BorderLayout class uses a directional scheme to position a component based on one of the five direction strings. A component set to the `"North"` direction is set to the top of the container, one that is set to `"South"` is positioned at the bottom, and so forth. The size of the components is determined by other runtime information, such as the size of the container (usually set by the `resize()` method) and the attributes of the displayed component. The default behavior of BorderLayout gives the component set to the `"Center"` direction any space not used by the other components. In Listing 3.1, the Example1 applet dimensions are set to 300×200 pixels. The TextField and Panel objects are relatively small and so are set comfortably at the top and bottom of the applet. The remaining display is then used for the `"Center"` component, the DrawCanvas object. This object takes up the bulk of the applet display area.

That the BorderLayout class can display up to only five components (corresponding to the five directions) might concern users; however, this is not really a problem. Recall that since containers can hold other containers, this limitation does not really exist. Consequently, an applet can contain Panel objects, which in turn can contain other containers, and so forth.

In the example, the Panel class is used to align the button and choice box on the same row. The Panel class can be used as a kind of "toolbar," displaying components along the top or bottom of the screen. It exemplifies this behavior because its default layout is the FlowLayout class (see the following section).

Flow Layout

The FlowLayout class is good for displaying components horizontally across the container. It is the default layout for Panels, which can be set to function like a toolbar or to contain related Components, such as OK and Cancel buttons. In most cases, the FlowLayout class will present components across a single row. However, if the components do not fit on one row, a new row is started.

Figure 3.3 illustrates a modification of Listing 3.1, which adds another Choice menu to the left of the button (whose text has been modified). The canvas uses this new Choice object to pick the color used to paint the object chosen in the other Choice menu. Since the order of when a component is added to a container is important in determining the layout display, the color Choice object is added before the button.

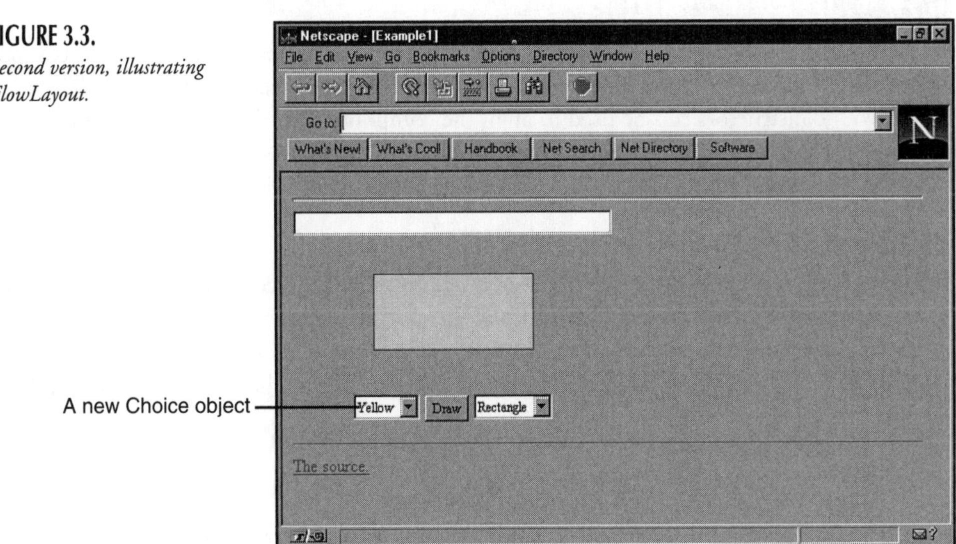

FIGURE 3.3.
Second version, illustrating FlowLayout.

The following code modifies the `init()` method in Listing 3.1 to build the Panel object shown in Figure 3.4. It is inserted in the source code after the DrawCanvas object is created, but before the Button is made.

```
// Create the panel with button and choices at bottom...
Panel p = new Panel();
// Explicitly set to flow layout...
p.setLayout(new FlowLayout());
// Add color choice to left of button...
colorChoice = new Choice();
colorChoice.addItem("Yellow");
colorChoice.addItem("Red");
colorChoice.addItem("Blue");
p.add(colorChoice);
// Add button...
```

The code explicitly creates a new FlowLayout object for the Panel to use. This is unnecessary, but it illustrates how a FlowLayout object could be set up for Container objects in general.

To use the color Choice menu in the DrawCanvas code, add a method to the Example1 class to return the color selection:

```
// Get the color to be displayed....
// Convert the String to a Color object
Color getColor() {
 String s = colorChoice.getSelectedItem();
 if (s.compareTo("Yellow") == 0)
  return Color.yellow;
 if (s.compareTo("Red") == 0)
  return Color.red;
 return Color.blue;
}
```

The DrawCanvas class modifies its color code to get the color choice from the applet class:

```
g.setColor(e1app.getColor());
```

You can specify other features of FlowLayout to customize its appearance. By default, components within a container using FlowLayout are aligned along the center. However, alternative FlowLayout constructors can be used to align the components to the left or the right. Figure 3.4 shows how the Panel in the example would look if it were right-aligned. The following code line is all you need to add to modify how the layout is established:

```
p.setLayout(new FlowLayout(FlowLayout.RIGHT));
```

You can specify the number of pixels between the components in a container using FlowLayout in an alternative constructor. This difference in the spacing between the components is known as the *gap value*. Both the horizontal and vertical gap values can be set in FlowLayout. Most of the LayoutManager classes support setting gaps. The discussion of the next layout, GridLayout, will illustrate how to use gap values.

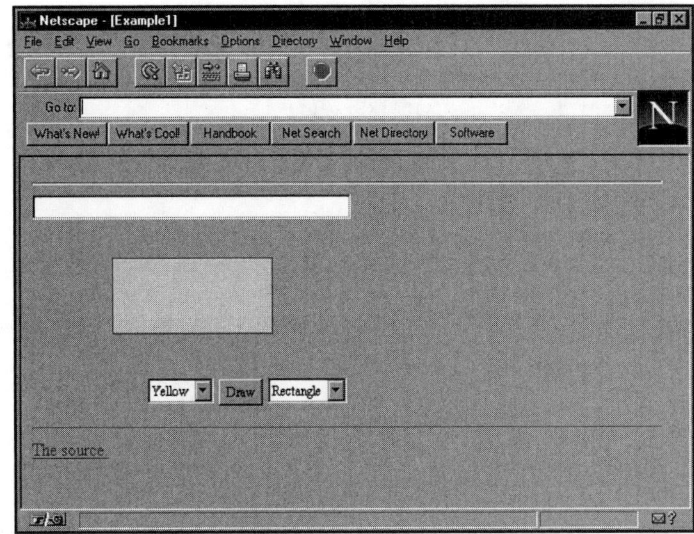

FIGURE 3.4.
The FlowLayout panel is right-justified.

GridLayout

The GridLayout class is used to set a matrix of components along a number of rows and columns. Since the size of each row and column is the same, each component in the grid has the same size. Each new component added to the container using GridLayout is positioned to the next index in the grid. If the row is not full, it is added to the next column; if it is, a new row is started and the component is added to the new column.

Figure 3.5 illustrates an applet set to use GridLayout. It is a 5×5 matrix of Buttons. Listing 3.2 shows the code used to create this applet and illustrates the use of gap values. In this case, a horizontal gap of 10 and a vertical gap of 20 is specified in the constructor.

Listing 3.2. Creating an example using GridLayout.

```
import java.awt.*;
import java.lang.*;
import java.applet.*;

// Class used for illustrating Grid Layouts...
public class GridLayoutExample extends Applet  {
 // Set up a matrix of numbers to be displayed in a grid...
 public void init() {
  // Set up display area...
  resize(300,200);
  // Set the layout to a 5 by 5 grid with
  // a horizontal gap of 10 and a vertical gap of 20
  int rowsAcross = 5;
  int rowsDown = 5;
  setLayout(new GridLayout(rowsAcross,rowsDown,10,20));
```

continues

Listing 3.2. continued

```
  // Fill the grid with buttons filled with numbers...
  int matrixSize = rowsAcross *rowsDown;
  for (int i = 0; i < matrixSize; ++i) {
   // Make a label set to the current number...
   // Add it to the grid...
   add(new Button(Integer.toString(i)) );
  }
 }
}
```

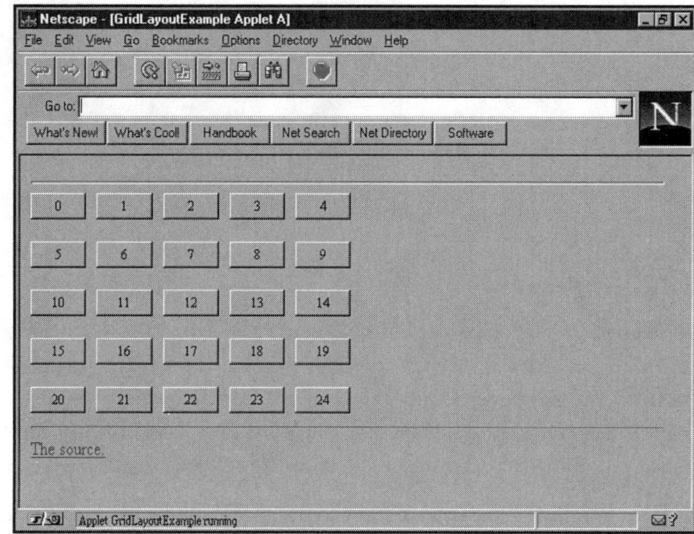

FIGURE 3.5.
An example using GridLayout.

The code ends with a `for` loop that adds Buttons to the grid. As the number increases, each Button is added across and down the applet display area. The code that creates the numeric name of the Button is interesting because it illustrates a static method of the type wrapper class, Integer, that can be used to convert an integer to a String without creating a new object.

An alternative constructor enables you to create a GridLayout without horizontal and vertical gaps.

GridBagLayout

The most complex layout class provided with the Java API is GridBagLayout. While it is superficially similar to the GridLayout class, it differs significantly by not requiring the components in the grid to be the same size. GridBagLayout uses a helper class called GridBagConstraints to specify how the component is displayed in relation to the container's other components. GridBagLayout can guarantee a logical display of components because it replaces the use of hard-code coordinates with a relative structure of how the components should visually interrelate.

Figure 3.6 and Listing 3.3 show an example of using GridBagLayout. As the code illustrates, this class is much more complex than the other layouts. The key to using GridBagLayout is understanding its interaction with the GridBagConstraints helper. To describe it in high-level terms, GridBagLayout and GridBagConstraints use a system of weighting and relative flags to determine how things will be positioned and sized. To see how this works, look at some of the GridBagConstraints variables summarized in Table 3.1. The variables starting with "grid" specify positioning in relation to the other components in the row or column. The GridBagConstraints constant `REMAINDER` means that the object should be the last item in the row or column. A value of `1`, on the other hand, indicates that it should be positioned normally. The `weightx` and `weighty` variables determine space distribution of the components in relation to each other. A weight of `1` indicates that the item should be positioned evenly with other items of weight `1`. On the other hand, a weight of `0` will give a component a lower priority in sizing. If the weight variables are not set to a nonzero value, the default distribution will be moved toward the center of the container.

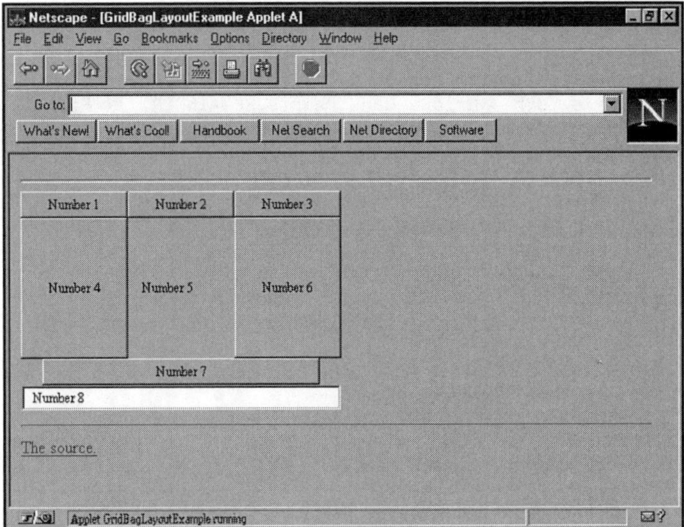

FIGURE 3.6.
An example using GridBagLayout.

Listing 3.3. Creating an example using GridBagLayout.

```
import java.awt.*;
import java.lang.*;
import java.applet.*;

// Class used for illustrating GridBagLayouts...
public class GridBagLayoutExample extends Applet  {
 // A complex set of buttons
 public void init() {
  // Just reuse these over & over...
  Button b;
```

continues

Listing 3.3. continued

```
Label l;
// Set up display area...
resize(300,200);
// Create the GridBagLayout and its helper...
GridBagLayout g = new GridBagLayout();
setLayout(g);
GridBagConstraints gbc = new GridBagConstraints();
// *************************************
// Put up a row of three equal size buttons...
// *************************************
// This tells the layout to use the full horizontal
// and vertical height if the display area is not filled...
gbc.fill = GridBagConstraints.BOTH;
// Distribute horizontal space evenly between buttons
gbc.weightx = 1.0;
// Create and add the three buttons...
b = new Button("Number 1");
g.setConstraints(b,gbc);
add(b);
b = new Button("Number 2");
g.setConstraints(b,gbc);
add(b);
b = new Button("Number 3");
gbc.gridwidth = GridBagConstraints.REMAINDER; // Fill up the row...
g.setConstraints(b,gbc);
add(b);
// *************************************
// Put up a button, a label, and a button
// that uses the remaining height area...
// *************************************
b = new Button("Number 4");
gbc.gridwidth = 1;  // Reset to normal...
gbc.weighty = 1.0;  // Force it to use remaining height...
g.setConstraints(b,gbc);
add(b);
l = new Label("Number 5");
g.setConstraints(l,gbc);
add(l);
b = new Button("Number 6");
gbc.gridwidth = GridBagConstraints.REMAINDER; // Fill up the row...
g.setConstraints(b,gbc);
add(b);
// *************************************
// Make a normal height button with insets...
// *************************************
gbc.weighty = 0.0; // Normal height;
gbc.gridheight = 1;
gbc.weightx = 0.0;  // Use up the row...
gbc.insets.left = 20;
gbc.insets.right = 20;
b = new Button("Number 7");
g.setConstraints(b,gbc);
add(b);
// *************************************
// Finally add a text field across the bottom...
// *************************************
```

```
   gbc.insets.left = 0;    // Reset these...
   gbc.insets.right = 0;
   TextField t = new TextField("Number 8");
   g.setConstraints(t,gbc);
   add(t);
  }
}
```

Table 3.1. The GridBagConstraints variables.

Variables	*Description*
`gridx, gridy`	Specifies the upper-left display of the grid cell. A value of `GridBagConstraints.RELATIVE` indicates that the component is to be placed just right of or below the component just added before.
`gridwidth, gridheight`	Indicates the number of grid cells in its display area. The `GridBagConstraints.REMAINDER` value specifies that it is the last cell in the row or column. `GridBagConstraints.RELATIVE` indicates that it is the next to last cell in the row or column.
`fill`	Indicates what to do if the display area is not filled. If this value is set to `GridBagConstraints.BOTH`, then it will fill up the display area.
`ipadx, ipady`	Used to specify internal padding to add to the component's minimum size.
`insets`	Sets the external padding around the component's display area.
`anchor`	A directional scheme to indicate where a component should go if it does not fill up the display area. The `GridBagConstraints.CENTER` variable is the default value.
`weightx, weighty`	Determines space distribution. The default value of zero results in the components clumping together in the middle of the display. Otherwise, the value indicates a weighting in relation to the other row and column components.

Look at the Java API documentation for more information about these variables.

The spreadsheet project throughout this part of the book uses GridBagLayout. In particular, the frame initialization uses this class to set how the text field, spreadsheet canvas, and scrollbars are positioned in relation to each other. Look at these examples to get more ideas about how GridBagLayout works.

CardLayout

The CardLayout class allows the developer to flip through a series of displays. The flipping action of CardLayout is similar to HyperCard or other card-based programs. This card style of presentation differentiates CardLayout from the other layouts in that only one card of information is displayed at a time.

The typical way to use CardLayout is to tie it to a container, like a Panel. A series of cards can then be added to the container. Every time a component is added to a container that uses CardLayout, a new "card" is added. A variety of methods can be used to flip through the cards. For example, the `first()` method goes to the first card in the deck, `next()` goes to the next card, `show()` goes to a card with a certain name, and so on.

Listing 3.4 provides the source code for a program that can be used to flip through a deck displaying different graphical images. It is similar to the first example in this chapter.

Listing 3.4. Creating an example using CardLayout.

```
import java.awt.*;
import java.lang.*;
import java.applet.*;

// This class illustrates card layouts by drawing a different
// shape for a variety of cards...
public class CardLayoutExample extends java.applet.Applet  {
 // Each card consists of a canvas that draws the name
 // of the card...
 Panel p;
 CardLayout panelLayout;
 int index = 0;
 int lastIndex;
 public void init() {
  String name;
  // Set up display area...
  resize(300,200);
  setLayout(new BorderLayout());

  // Create the panel that uses CardLayout
  p = new Panel();
  panelLayout = new CardLayout();
  p.setLayout(panelLayout);
  add("Center",p);

  // Add a canvas to each card
  // The name variable is the shape to display...
CardLayoutDrawCanvas c; // Reuse these...
  // Add the rectangle...
  name = "Rectangle";
  c = new CardLayoutDrawCanvas(name);
  p.add(name,c);

  // Add the oval display...
  name = "Oval";
```

```
  c = new CardLayoutDrawCanvas(name);
  p.add(name,c);

  // Add the round rectangle display...
  name = "RoundRect";
  c = new CardLayoutDrawCanvas(name);
  p.add(name,c);

  // Show the first card...
  index = 0;
  lastIndex = 2;
  panelLayout.first(p);
 }

 // A mouse click takes you to the next card...
 public boolean mouseDown(Event ev, int x, int y) {
  // Go to the next card or to beginning
  if (index != lastIndex) {
   panelLayout.next(p);
   ++index;
  }
  else {  // Go to first card...
   panelLayout.first(p);
   index = 0;
  }
  return true;
 }

}

// This is a custom canvas that is used for drawing
// text, a rectangle, or nothing...
class CardLayoutDrawCanvas extends Canvas {
 String name;
 // Constructor - store the applet to get drawing info...
 public CardLayoutDrawCanvas(String s) {
  name = s;
 }
 // Draw the image per the choices in the applet...
 public synchronized void paint (Graphics g) {
  // Get the current size of the display area...
  Dimension dm = size();
  // Draw based on choice...
  // Calculate center coordinates....
  int x,y,width,height;
  x = dm.width/4;
  y = dm.height / 4;
  width = dm.width / 2;
  height = dm.height / 2;
  // Paint a rectangle in the center...
  if (name.compareTo("Rectangle") == 0) {
   // Draw the rectangle in the center with colors!
   g.setColor(Color.blue);
   g.drawRect(x,y,width,height);
   g.setColor(Color.yellow);
   g.fillRect(x + 1,y + 1,width - 2,height - 2);
  } // end if
```

continues

Listing 3.4. continued

```
  // Paint an oval in the center...
  if (name.compareTo("Oval") == 0) {
   // Draw the rectangle in the center with colors!
   g.setColor(Color.blue);
   g.drawOval(x,y,width,height);
   g.setColor(Color.yellow);
   g.fillOval(x + 1,y + 1,width - 2,height - 2);
  } // end if
  if (name.compareTo("RoundRect") == 0) {
   // Draw the rectangle in the center with colors!
   int rounding = dm.width / 8;
   g.setColor(Color.blue);
   g.drawRoundRect(x,y,width,height,rounding,rounding);
   g.setColor(Color.yellow);
   g.fillRoundRect(x + 1,y + 1,width - 2,height - 2,
     rounding,rounding);
  } // end if
 }
}
```

Event Handling

Programs written for most GUI environments take actions based on events initiated by the user or the system. If the user clicks the mouse, a "mouse click" event is issued. If the program wants to handle the mouse click, it needs to insert some code to trap for any mouse click event. The program may pass the event on to a default handler if it doesn't want to handle the event. The default handler encapsulates an object's standard behavior. For example, when you click a button, it should reflect the action by showing a pressing motion. This default behavior should occur regardless of whether the program processes the mouse click event.

As stated earlier, the visual controls the user interacts with in the AWT environment are derived from the Component class. A critical method of this class is `handleEvent()`, which is used to process incoming events and relay them to the appropriate handler methods. Any component that needs to manage specific events will need to override this method with its own handler.

In this chapter's initial example, the canvas object that draws shapes and text was repainted every time the user clicked the Draw button. (See Figure 3.3 and Listing 3.1.) The program made this happen by adding the following code to the applet class, Example1:

```
// Handle events that have occurred
public boolean handleEvent(Event evt) {
switch(evt.id) {
 // This can be handled
 case Event.ACTION_EVENT: {
  if(evt.target instanceof Button)    {
   // Repaint canvas to use new choices...
```

```
      c.repaint();
      }  // end if
      return false;
   }
   default:
    return false;
   }
}
```

This code overrides the default handler of the Applet class (which is a subclass of Component). The sample applet would do very little if this code had not been added. Even though the default handler was overridden, the code can still allow default behavior to occur. The return code from the method tells the parent of the component what should happen next. If the method returns true, then the event has been completely handled and should not be passed to the parent. On the other hand, a false return value allows the event to be passed on. The event handler of the component's superclass can also be called through this expression:

```
return super.handleEvent(evt);
```

The `handleEvent()` method takes as its sole parameter an instance of the Event class. This class encapsulates information about the event that occurred. The `id` integer variable of the class represents the type of event that occurred. The most widely captured event is the one with the `id` `ACTION_EVENT`. Each class of component has a specific action tied to it. For example, the action for a Button object is its selection, such as a mouse click. For TextField objects, the action is the entry of the Return key in the text field.

Other types of frequently caught events are those prefixed by `KEY_` and `MOUSE_`, which represent keyboard and mouse events, respectively. Other events include scrollbar actions and window events, such as Minimize or Destroy.

In the preceding code, the `handleEvent()` method traps for button selections. When the button is selected, an event with an `ACTION_EVENT` ID is generated. Recall, however, that this example also had a TextField. To differentiate the button selection from a text field Return keystroke, the code needs to tell what class of object issued the event. It does this by looking at the Event target variable. In the example's code, the program checks to see whether the target is a button by using the `instanceOf` operator.

Other information can be found in Event variables. An optional argument, the `arg` variable, provides information specific to the Event, such as the Object of an action. For mouse events, the `x` and `y` variables can be used to get the mouse position. The key variable is used to determine which keystroke corresponds to a `KEY_` event.

The Component class also has helper methods that can be used if the user wants to manage events in a simpler manner than `handleEvent()` provides. These helper methods are actually called by `handleEvent()`. However, the overriding of `handleEvent()` is not required to use the helper methods.

In the CardLayout example, cards were flipped by overriding the `mouseDown()` method, which was declared as follows.

```
public boolean mouseDown(Event ev, int x, int y)
```

This is used to trap mouse clicks, passing the current location of the mouse in the x and y parameters. This call actually begins in the `handleEvent()` method, which traps for events of ID `MOUSE_DOWN`. When such events are issued, `handleEvent()` reacts by calling `mouseDown()`. If this is overridden by the object in question, its version of the method will be called. Like `handleEvent()`, the return value of the helper methods indicate whether the event has been completely handled.

Table 3.2 lists the available Event helper methods, which are all part of the definition of the Component class.

Table 3.2. Event helper methods.

Method	*Description*
`mouseEnter`	Mouse enters the Component's area
`mouseExit`	Mouse leaves the Component's area
`mouseMove`	Mouse has moved
`mouseDown`	Mouse has been pressed down
`mouseDrag`	Mouse has moved while it is pressed down
`mouseUp`	Mouse click has been released
`keyDown`	Keyboard character has been pressed
`keyUp`	Keyboard character has been released
`action`	An action has occurred to the Component
`gotFocus`	The input focus has been placed on the Component
`lostFocus`	The Component has lost input focus

Exception Classes

Although the basics of exception handling were discussed in the first part of the book, there is a lot more to managing exceptions in Java than just the "try-catch" clause. The class of exceptions that is thrown and what information can be gleaned from the thrown object are also important topics. This part of exception handling is related to Java's exception class hierarchy, the subject of this section.

The Throwable Class

All throwable objects in Java are an instance of, or are subclassed from, the Throwable class, which encapsulates the behaviors found in all the throwable classes that are part of the Java API. One widely used method of Throwable is `getMethod()`. This prints out a detail message attached to the thrown object. The detail message will give extra information regarding the nature of the error. If the default constructor of the thrown object is used, a system-generated detail message will be provided. If you want a custom message, on the other hand, an alternative constructor can be used.

A couple of examples will illustrate using detail messages. Suppose an operation is performed that results in an error. The following code will catch the thrown object and print out the detail message:

```
try {
  // ... do something that causes an exception, such as divide by zero
}
catch (Throwable t) {
  // Print out the detail message of the error...
  System.out.println(t.getMessage());
}
```

In another case, suppose that the same code wants to rethrow the message with its own custom detail message if there is an error. The other constructor for Throwable can be used in this situation to construct the custom message:

```
try {
  // ... do something that causes an exception, such as divide by zero
}
catch (Throwable t) {
  // Throw a new Throwable object with
  // Custom detail message...
  throw new Throwable("This method threw an exception");
}
```

When the new Throwable is caught and `getMessage()` is invoked, the program will get the String `"This method threw an exception"` instead of a system-generated message.

Other methods in Throwable can be used for getting the state of the runtime stack when the error occurred. The `printStackTrace()` method, for example, prints to standard error the kind of stack output that you often see when a Java program terminates abnormally.

Exception Class Hierarchy

All the other exception classes in the Java API behave similarly to the Throwable class. They differ only in how they are located in the hierarchy of class exceptions. Java divides errors into two general groupings, indicated by two parent classes derived from Throwable. The Exception class represents the kind of errors that occur in a normal programming environment, such as file not found, array index out of bounds, null pointers, divide by zero, and so forth. These are "soft" errors, the type of difficulty that a program should be able to easily recover from. In general, Exception classes represent errors that are meant to be caught by the calling method whenever they occur. Classes derived from the Error class, on the other hand, represent more serious errors that can occur at unpredictable times and are often fatal in nature. An extreme case of such an Error is a failure within the Java virtual machine. If this occurs, often the best you can hope for is an orderly shutdown of the program. Because of their unpredictable and catastrophic nature, Error objects do not have to be caught in exception handlers. In general, programs will be written to catch only classes derived from the Exception class.

NOTE

From a terminological standpoint, "exception" (lowercase) is used to refer to all classes of thrown objects. The term "error" (lowercase also) refers to the circumstances that cause the object to be thrown.

As mentioned in the first part of this book, a method establishes that it throws an Exception that has to be caught in its declaration. For example, this is the constructor for the class that opens a file for output:

```
public FileOutputStream(String name) throws IOException
```

This declaration means that an instance of IOException is thrown whenever the file specified in the String cannot be opened. The IOException class is derived from Exception, so any code that uses this FileOutputStream constructor must catch this exception. This means that code using this constructor must be generally structured as follows:

```
try {
 FileOutputStream fo = new FileOutputStream("MyFile");
 // … write the file…
{
catch (IOException e) {
  // …Handle the file open problem…
}
```

With one notable exception, all methods that throw objects of type Exception must be called in an exception handler that catches the Exception. However, Java provides a branch of Exceptions of thrown objects that do not have to be caught. These are derived from the RuntimeException class. Subclasses of the RuntimeException class are those problems that would be too cumbersome to trap every time they may occur. For example, all accesses to arrays could result in an exception because the index into the array could be bad. However, it would be unwieldy to put an exception handler around all array calls. There would also be a performance hit. Even worse are instances of the NullPointerException class being thrown, which theoretically could occur anywhere in the program.

Just because an exception is a subclass of RuntimeException, however, doesn't mean that a good program should not trap for the thrown object. For example, the ArithmeticException usually indicates a divide by zero error. It is good programming to trap for this error whenever it occurs. In most cases, division doesn't often occur in a program. Consequently, a clause like the following is appropriate for many division operations:

```
try {
 result = divider / divisor;
}
catch (ArithmeticException e) {
 System.out.println("Divide by zero error!");
 result = 0;
}
```

On the other hand, it is acceptable to have a divide operation that is not part of an exception handler, since ArithmeticException is a subclass of RuntimeException. Here is a list of the subclasses of RuntimeException:

The Subclasses of RuntimeException
ArithmeticException
ArrayIndexOutOfBoundsException
ArrayStoreException
ClassCastException
IllegalArgumentException
IllegalMonitorStateException
IllegalThreadStateException
IndexOutOfBoundsException
NegativeArraySizeException

Exception Handlers and Throwable Classes

The Exception class hierarchy serves a more fundamental purpose in Java programming than just providing a way to order exception classes; it plays an important role in determining how an exception is handled. When an exception is thrown, Java looks for an exception handler to catch the thrown object. It first looks in the method where the error occurred, checking to see whether it has an appropriate exception handler—one that is the class or a superclass of the exception thrown. Recall that an exception handler can have multiple catch statements. The catch statements should be ordered in such a way that a subclass is listed before any of its superclasses. Here is a possible exception handler for managing a variety of problems:

```
try {
 // ... some bad arithmetic operation
 // ... or maybe a bad array access
 // ... or a null errror
}
catch (ArithmeticException e) {
 // Handle the exception...

}
```

```
catch (RuntimeException e) {
 // Handle the runtime exception…
}
catch (Exception e) {
 // Handle the Exception…
}
catch (Throwable e) {
 // Handle the thrown object…
}
```

Recall that ArithmeticException is a subclass of RuntimeException. The latter is derived from Exception, which in turn is a subclass of Throwable. In this example, a divide by zero error throws an ArithmeticException, which is handled in the first catch statement. On the other hand, a NullPointerException or a bad array access will result in a RuntimeException object being thrown, which is handled in the second catch statement. A serious problem of class Error will not be handled until it reaches the last catch statement, which will catch the thrown object since Error is a subclass of Throwable. This example illustrates that the exception class hierarchy is a critical part of Java's strategy for resolving exceptions.

If the method that caused an object to be thrown does not have an appropriate exception handler, the object percolates up the call stack, and this process of finding an appropriate handler is repeated. If it reaches the top of the stack and no appropriate handler is found, the program will terminate abnormally.

Writing Custom Exception Handlers

It's easy to write your own exception handler. A class is simply created that extends the class that should function as the superclass. If a new IOException handler is needed, for example, it could be written as the following:

```
public class CustomIOException extends IOException { }
```

The hard part, however, is deciding what the superclass of the handler should be. In general, it should not be a subclass of Error since these are reserved for "hard" system problems. Using RuntimeException should also be discouraged because of an interesting controversy over whether there should even be such a thing as a RuntimeException class. This is because, in some ways, the use of RuntimeException classes defeats some of the goals of exception handling. By definition, a RuntimeException object does not have to be caught, but this would then increase the likelihood of an exception not being caught at all, forcing the program to terminate abnormally. This defeats a key goal of exception handling, which is to have a graceful resolution of problems. Thus, the use of RuntimeException is reserved for classes of errors that would occur too frequently to have an exception handler every time the pertinent methods are called.

This leaves the subclasses of Exception as the best candidate for being the superclass of new exception classes. Some good examples can be found in the organization of the exceptions in the Java IO package. One of the constructors for the FileInputStream class tries to open up the input file specified in its String parameter. If the file cannot be opened, a FileNotFoundException is thrown. This class is derived from the IOException class, which is based on Exception. Other file error classes are also derived from IOException. Therefore, the IOException class marks a hierarchy for problems related to input/output operations.

Suppose a new set of classes is being created for database operations. It might be helpful to create a new hierarchy of exceptions that correspond to database problems. The class at the top of this hierarchy might be called DatabaseException, which could be derived from Exception since it marks a new branch of the Exception hierarchy. For errors related to problems with the database key, you could create a KeyException class derived from DatabaseException. If the key could not be found, then you could add a KeyNotFoundException, whose superclass is KeyException. These new Exceptions could be declared as follows:

```
public class DatabaseException extends Exception { }

public class KeyException extends DatabaseException { }

public class KeyNotFoundException extends KeyException { }
```

In the following example, a method that tries to find a record could then be declared as throwing a KeyNotFoundException if the record is not found:

```
public findRecord(Key index) throws KeyNotFoundException
```

The code that invokes this method then can be structured as follows:

```
try {
  db.findRecord(myKey);
}
catch (KeyNotFoundException e) {
 // Handle the key not found exception...
}
catch (KeyException e) {
 // Handle the exception due to a bad key
}
catch (DatabaseException e) {
 // Handle any database exception...
}
catch (Exception e) {
 // Handle the Exception...
}
```

Chapter Project: Spreadsheet Applet, Version 1

The project in this chapter is a spreadsheet applet that supports rudimentary formula operations and other basic behavior. This version of the project has the following behaviors:

- The program produces a spreadsheet of the size specified in the HTML parameter list. The rows are indicated by alpha characters ranging from *A* to *Z*. The columns are numbered from 0 to the number of columns minus one. The individual cells in the spreadsheet are labeled accordingly. Therefore, the upper-left cell is A0. The spreadsheet cells support only numeric values of precision double.

- The user can change the value of a cell by clicking on a valid cell. A numeric value, a formula, or an empty string can then be entered into the text field at the top of the screen. When the user hits return, the new value is validated and entered into the cell, and the spreadsheet cell values are recalculated.
- The program supports several formulas. Arithmetic formulas of MULT, ADD, SUB, and DIV operate on two cells and return the double value resulting from it. For example, MULT(C3,B3) returns the value in cell C3 times the value in cell B3. The SUM(cell1,cell2) operation returns the values of all the sums between cell1 and cell2 when these cells share a common row or column. The spreadsheet supports cell recursion on formulas, so a cell with a formula can be included in the formula operation of another cell.
- The applet has a basic menu with Quit and New spreadsheet commands.

Figure 3.7 shows how the spreadsheet applet appears in a browser. More advanced features, such as scrollbars, dialog boxes, and graphs, will be explored in the upcoming chapters. The version of the spreadsheet currently presented aims to illustrate many of the features of AWT and exception handling discussed in the first section of this chapter.

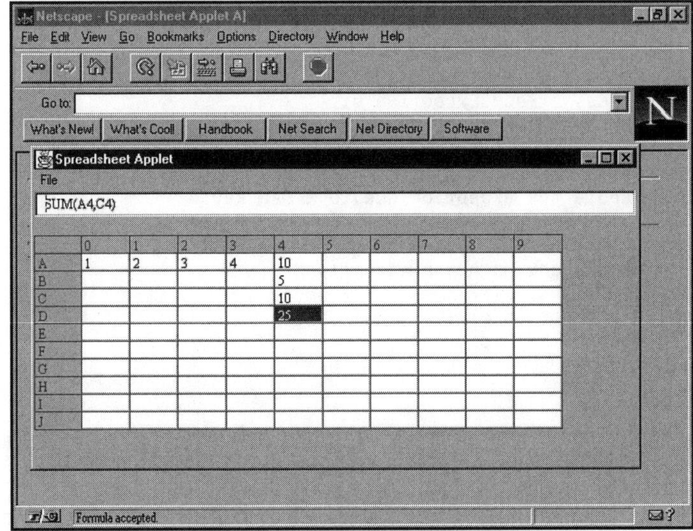

FIGURE 3.7.
The first version of the spreadsheet applet.

Class Organization

Table 3.3 explains the classes used in this chapter's version of the spreadsheet applet.

Table 3.3. Spreadsheet classes.

Class	*Description*
Cell	Contains a String and evaluated value corresponding to a single cell.
CellContainer	Contains a matrix of Cells. The String in each Cell is evaluated according to whether it is a formula, a literal numeric value, or an empty cell.
FormulaParser	Used to parse out the individual string fragments that make up a single formula. Converts literal strings to their numeric values.
FormulaParserException	An Exception that is thrown if a formula is ill constructed.
ArgValue	A FormulaParser helper class used to store information about an argument in a formula.
SpreadsheetCell	Provides for the visual presentation of a single Cell.
SpreadsheetContainer	Manages the visual presentation of a matrix of SpreadsheetCells. Provides an interface for changing the value of a cell. Supports the display of a currently highlighted cell.
SpreadsheetFrame	Provides the main presentation of the spreadsheet by displaying the SpreadsheetContainer, managing mouse selections on that spreadsheet, reading a text field for changing cell values, and handling a simple menu.
SpreadsheetApplet	Responsible for creating, showing, and hiding the SpreadsheetFrame that provides the visual display of this applet.

The Cell Class

This class stores a String and its evaluated value for a single cell. It performs no validation in terms of the validity of any formulas or nonnumeric values contained in the String. A variable is used to mark whether the cell has been evaluated, although the setting of this variable is of interest only to the classes that use Cell.

Listing 3.5. The Cell class.

```
// A cell contains the formula  for an individual cell
// However, it does not know what to do with it and simply
```

continues

Listing 3.5. continued

```
// returns its contents...
public class Cell {
 String s;
 double evaluatedValue;
 boolean evaluated;  // True if the cell has been evaluated
 // Constructor creates empty StringBuffer as reference...
 public Cell() {
  s = "";
  evaluatedValue = 0.0;
  evaluated = true;
 }
 // Takes a StringBuffer and makes it the cell's data...
 public void setCellString(StringBuffer s) {
  this.s = new String(s);
  evaluated = false;
 }
 // Takes a StringBuffer and makes it the cell's data...
 public void setCellString(String s) {
  this.s = s;
  evaluated = false;
 }
 // Return the current contents of the Cell
 public String getCellString() {
  return s;
 }
 // Set the evaluated value of a cell...
 public void setEvalValue(double val) {
  evaluated = true;
  evaluatedValue = val;
 }
 // Set the evaluated value of a cell...
 public void setEvalValue(int val) {
  setEvalValue((double)val);
 }
 // See if a cell has been evaluated...
 public boolean getEvaluated() {
  return evaluated;
 }
 // Get the evaluated value of a cell...
 public double getEvalValue() {
  return evaluatedValue;
 }
 // Set a cell to unevaluated...
 public void setEvaluated(boolean eval) {
  evaluated = eval;
 }
}
```

The Cell Container Class

This class consists of a matrix of Cells. Its main constructor creates the matrix based on the number of rows and columns provided in its constructor. Public methods allow setting or retrieving values of individual cells based on a row and column index. If this index is bad, an

IllegalArgumentException is thrown. The most interesting feature of this class is its ability to evaluate formulas. The `recalculateAll()` method forces a reevaluation of all the Cell values in the matrix. It works with the FormulaParser class to see how a formula will be calculated. If the formula relies on a Cell that contains yet another formula, the program recurses into finding out the evaluated formula value of that cell. The recursion occurs in the `calculateCell()` and `parseFormula()` methods, which determine the numeric value of a specific Cell. The recursion stops when a Cell with a literal (that is, a number) value is found. When a Cell's formula or literal value has been fully evaluated, the Cell is updated accordingly. The calculation process provides a good illustration of exception handling because they are widely used to handle formula parsing errors and illegal formula operations.

Listing 3.6. The CellContainer class.

```
// The CellContainer class contains a matrix of Cell data.
// The class is responsible for making sure
// that the formulas in the cells are evaluated properly...
public class CellContainer {
 int numRows;
 int numColumns;
 Cell matrix[];
 // Constructs an empty container...
 public CellContainer() {
  numRows = 0;
  numColumns = 0;
  matrix = null;
 }
 // Constructs a matrix of cells [rows X columns]
 public CellContainer(int rows,int columns) throws IllegalArgumentException {
  numRows = rows;
  numColumns = columns;
  // Throw an exception if the row/col values are no good...
  if ((numRows <= 0) || (numColumns <=0)) {
   numRows = 0;
   numColumns = 0;
   matrix = null;
   throw new IllegalArgumentException();
  }

  // Create the Cell matrix...
  int numCells = numRows * numColumns;
  matrix = new Cell[numCells];
  for (int i = 0; i < numCells; ++i)
   matrix[i] = new Cell();
 }

 // Sets the new value of a cell...
 public void setCellFormula(StringBuffer s,int row,int col) {
  setCellFormula(s.toString(),row,col);
 }

 // Sets the new value of a cell...
 public void setCellFormula(String s,int row,int col) {
```

continues

Listing 3.6. continued

```
  // Get the index into the matrix...
  int index;
  try {
   index = getMatrixIndex(row,col);
  }
  catch (IllegalArgumentException e) {
   System.out.println("Invalid CellContainer index.");
   return;
  }
  // Set the value of the cell...
  matrix[index].setCellString(s);
 }

 // Get the string contents of a cell...
 public String getCellFormula(int row,int col)  throws IllegalArgumentException {
  // Get the index into the matrix...
  int index;
  try {
   index = getMatrixIndex(row,col);
  }
  catch (IllegalArgumentException e) {
   throw e;
  }
  // Good index. Return string...
  return matrix[index].getCellString();
 }

 // Get the cell at certain index...
 public Cell getCell(int row,int col)  throws IllegalArgumentException {
  // Get the index into the matrix...
  int index;
  try {
   index = getMatrixIndex(row,col);
  }
  catch (IllegalArgumentException e) {
   throw e;
  }
  // Good index. Return Cell...
   return matrix[index];
 }

 // Calculate the matrix index given a row and column...
 // Throw an exception if it is bad...
 int getMatrixIndex(int row,int col) throws IllegalArgumentException {
  // Kick out if there are negative indexes...
  if ((row < 0) || (col <0))
   throw new IllegalArgumentException();
  // Also reject too large indexes...
  if ((row >= numRows) || (col >= numColumns))
   throw new IllegalArgumentException();
  // Everything is OK. Calculate index...
  return ((numColumns * row) + col);
 }

 // Validate a formula by seeing whether it matches the basic syntax...
 public String validateFormula(Cell c,String newFormula) throws
```

```
➥FormulaParserException {
// Convert all alphas to Upper Case
  String convertedFormula = newFormula.toUpperCase();
  // Get old formula of cell and temporarily set cell value there...
  String oldFormula = c.getCellString();
  // Set up the parser to validate the cell...
  FormulaParser f = new FormulaParser(convertedFormula);
  // Validate the cell...
  try {  // Set up the formula parser...
   // Get the type of formula it is...
   int typeFormula = f.getType();
   // If it's empty, return Success...
   if (typeFormula == f.EMPTY)
    return convertedFormula;
   // Check to see whether literal is valid...
   if (typeFormula == f.LITERAL) {
    f.getLiteral();  // Ignore the return value...
    return convertedFormula;
   } // end if
   // If it's a formula, you need to parse it...
   parseFormula(c,f);
  }
  catch (Exception e) {
   throw new FormulaParserException();
  }
  // Return the converted string...
  return convertedFormula;
 }

 // Recalculate the values in all the cells...
 public void recalculateAll() {
  if (matrix == null)
   return;
  // Invalidate the formulas...
  invalidateFormulas();
  // Go through each cell and calculate its value...
  // Go row-wise across, as this is how things are probably set up
  int i,j;
  for (i = 0; i < numRows; ++i) {
   for (j = 0; j < numColumns; ++j) {
    if (matrix[(i * numColumns) + j].getEvaluated() == false) {
     calculateCell(i,j);
    }
   } // end column for
  } // end row for
}

 // Recalculate an individual cell...
 // Update its evaluation when complete...
 double calculateCell(int row,int col) {
  // Get the index of the calculation...
  int index;
  try {
   index = getMatrixIndex(row,col);
  }
  catch (IllegalArgumentException e) {
```

continues

Listing 3.6. continued

```
   return 0.0;  // Bad index...
  }

  // Set up the parser to recalculate the cell...
  FormulaParser f = new FormulaParser(matrix[index].getCellString());
   // First get the type...
   int typeFormula = f.getType();
   // If it's empty, you're done...
   if (typeFormula == f.EMPTY) {
    matrix[index].setEvalValue(0.0);
    return 0.0;
   }
   // If it's a literal, you can also finish quickly...
   if (typeFormula == f.LITERAL) {
    // It better be some kind of number...
    try {
     double dbl = f.getLiteral(); // Get the double value...
     matrix[index].setEvalValue(dbl);
     return dbl;
    }
    // Some kind of invalid string...
    catch(FormulaParserException e) {
     System.out.println("Invalid literal at [" + row + "," + col + "]");
     matrix[index].setEvalValue(0.0);
     return 0.0;
    }
   }
   // Formulas got to be parsed and maybe recurse, however...
   double dbl;
   try {
    dbl = parseFormula(matrix[index],f);
   }
   catch (Exception e) {
    System.out.println("Invalid formula at [ " + row + "," + col + "]");
    dbl = 0.0;
   }
   matrix[index].setEvalValue(dbl);
   return dbl;
  }

  // Parse out a formula...
  // Assumes formula parser is set to a certain formula...
  double parseFormula(Cell c, FormulaParser f) throws FormulaParserException {
   // Figure out what type of formula it is...
   try {
    int op = f.getOperation();
    // Get the arguments...
    ArgValue arg1 = new ArgValue();
    ArgValue arg2 = new ArgValue();
    f.getOpArgs(arg1,arg2);
    // Sum operation is different from rest...
    if (op != f.SUM) { // SUM is even worse...
     double val1,val2;
     // Get the values...
     // See if you have to recurse...
     if (arg1.getType() == arg1.CELL)
```

```
    val1 = calculateCell(arg1.getRow(),arg1.getColumn());
   else
    val1 = arg1.getLiteral();
   if (arg2.getType() == arg1.CELL)
    val2 = calculateCell(arg2.getRow(),arg2.getColumn());
   else
    val2 = arg2.getLiteral();
   // Perform the operation...
   switch (op) {
    case f.ADD:
     return (val1 + val2);
    case f.MULT:
     return (val1 * val2);
    case f.DIV:
     try {   // Handle divide by zero errors...
      double ret = val1 / val2;
      return ret;
     }
     catch (ArithmeticException e) {
      // Divide by zero!
      return 0.0;
     }
    case f.SUB:
     return (val1 - val2);
    default:
     break;
   }  // end switch...
  } // end if
  else {  // Sum...
   double dbl = 0.0;
   int index;
   // Validate row-wise or column operation...
   if ((arg1.getType() != arg1.CELL) || (arg2.getType() != arg2.CELL))
    throw new FormulaParserException();
   // Row-wise or column-wise...
   if (arg1.getRow() == arg2.getRow()) {
    if (arg2.getColumn() < arg1.getColumn())
     throw new FormulaParserException();
    for (int i = arg1.getColumn(); i <= arg2.getColumn(); ++i) {
     // Skip cases where the cells are the same...
     index = getMatrixIndex(arg2.getRow(),i);
     if (matrix[index] == c)
      continue;
     // If OK, then recurse...
      dbl += calculateCell(arg2.getRow(),i);
    } // end for
    return dbl;
   }
   else if (arg1.getColumn() == arg2.getColumn()) {
    if (arg2.getRow() < arg1.getRow())
      throw new FormulaParserException();
    for (int i = arg1.getRow(); i <= arg2.getRow(); ++i) {
      // Skip cases where the cells are the same...
      index = getMatrixIndex(i,arg2.getColumn;
      if (matrix[index] == c)
       continue;
```

continues

Listing 3.6. continued

```
        // If OK, then recurse...
        dbl += calculateCell(i,arg2.getColumn());
       } // end for
       return dbl;
    }
    throw new FormulaParserException();
   }
   return 0.0;
  }
  catch (FormulaParserException e) {
   throw e;
  }
 }

// Invalidate all cells that are formulas to force recalculation...
 void invalidateFormulas() {
  // Set up the parser to get the cell type...
  FormulaParser f = new FormulaParser();
  int numCells = numRows * numColumns;
  for (int i = 0; i < numCells; ++i) {
   f.setFormula(matrix[i].getCellString());
   if (f.getType() == f.FORMULA)
    matrix[i].setEvaluated(false);
  } // end for
 }

 // Get the number of rows in the container
 int getNumRows() {
  return numRows;
 }

 // Get the number of columns in the container
 int getNumColumns() {
  return numColumns;
 }
}
```

The FormulaParserClass

This class is used to parse the elements of a single formula. Its public integer variables are used to indicate what kind of operation (such as SUM) is being performed or whether the formula is a literal or empty value. It uses internal hints to keep track of the current parsing operation. It not only returns the type of operation the formula performs, but also the contents of its arguments. For example, the formula SUM(A0,A3) results in the first argument being parsed into row 0 and column 0 (corresponding to A0) and row 0 and column 3 (cell A3). These are stored in the helper ArgValue class. A FormulaParserException object is thrown if there is anything wrong with the formula or literal.

For the sake of saving space, you are referred to the accompanying CD-ROM for the source code of this class.

The FormulaParserException Class

This exception is thrown when a String does not contain a proper formula, for any of a variety of reasons. It is a subclass of IllegalArgumentException.

Listing 3.7. The FormulaParserException class.

```
// This class is an Exception thrown when a
// formula is an invalid format...
public class FormulaParserException extends IllegalArgumentException { }
```

The ArgValue Class

This class does little more than hold information about an argument. Public integer variables are used to indicate whether the argument is a literal or cell value. If it is the former, the class stores the converted double value. If it is a cell in a spreadsheet, then its converted row and column values are stored.

In the interest of saving space, see the accompanying CD-ROM for the source code of this class.

The SpreadsheetCell Class

This class is used to draw the contents of an individual Cell. It is an extension of the Canvas class and has a custom `paint()` method that is used to draw the Cell at specific coordinates. It gets the evaluated value of the Cell to determine what to display. The text and background color of the Cell can be set through public methods. It is also possible to indicate that the literal Cell value should be painted and the evaluated value should be ignored.

Listing 3.8. The SpreadsheetCell class.

```
import java.awt.*;
import java.lang.*;

// This class ties the contents of an individual
// SpreadsheetCell to a single data Cell.
// The evaluated contents of
// that cell are returned to the SpreadsheetContainer...
public class SpreadsheetCell extends Canvas {
 Cell c;  // The cell this is tied to...
 boolean literal;  // If set to true, automatically paint what's in
                   // cell string...
 Color fillColor;
 Color textColor;
 public SpreadsheetCell(Cell c,boolean literal) {
```

continues

Listing 3.8. continued

```
  super();
  this.c = c;
  this.literal = literal;
  // Set the color defaults...
  fillColor = Color.white;
  textColor = Color.black;
 }

 // Set the fill color
 public void setFillColor(Color clr) {
  fillColor = clr;
 }

 // Set the text color
 public void setTextColor(Color clr) {
  textColor = clr;
 }

 // Return the reference to the cell...
 public Cell getCell() {
  return c;
 }

 // Set the cell string...
 public void setString(String s) {
  c.setCellString(s);
 }

 // Get the current string value in the cell...
 public String getString() {
  return c.getCellString();
 }

 // This will return the text to the current evaluated contents
 // of the cell...
 public synchronized void paint(Graphics g,int x,int y,int width,int height) {
  String s = c.getCellString();
  String textPaint;
  // If this is a literal value, then print what it has...
  if (literal == true)
   textPaint = s;
  else {
   // Otherwise, display formula only if cell is not empty...
   if (s.compareTo("") == 0)
    textPaint = s;
   else  // Otherwise, show evaluate value...
    textPaint = String.valueOf(c.getEvalValue()) ;
  } // end else
  // Set up drawing rectangle...
  g.setColor(Color.blue);
  g.drawRect(x,y,width,height);
  g.setColor(fillColor);
  g.fillRect(x + 1,y + 1,width - 2,height - 2);
  // Clip the text if necessary...
  int textWidth;
  int len = textPaint.length();
  int effWidth = width - 4;
```

```
  // Loop until text is small enough to fit...
  while (len > 0) {
   textWidth = g.getFontMetrics().stringWidth(textPaint);
   if (textWidth < effWidth)
    break;
   —len;
   textPaint = textPaint.substring(0,len);
  } // end while
  // Draw the string
  g.setColor(textColor);
  g.drawString(textPaint,x + 4,y + (height - 2));
 }

 // Return the literal value...
 public boolean getLiteral() {
  return literal;
 }

}
```

The SpreadsheetContainer Class

This class constructs the spreadsheet to be displayed. It takes as input an instance of CellContainer that contains the matrix being operated on. It constructs a matrix of Spreadsheet cells, each of which is tied to an individual Cell in the CellContainer, except for the headers. These are represented by SpreadsheetCells (set to a literal value) created on the boundaries of the spreadsheet to display the row and column headers.

The SpreadsheetContainer class is derived from the Canvas class. It overrides the `paint()` method to draw the SpreadsheetCells. It goes across and down the spreadsheet matrix repeatedly calling the SpreadsheetCell's `paint()` method, providing the coordinates of where it should be drawn. Note the `update()` method that is called before `paint()`; this was added to prevent flicker. The default behavior of `update()` is to blank out the painting area with a white color; this causes a "flicker" until the `paint()` method is next called. By overriding `update()` with a direct call to `paint()`, however, you can avoid the flicker. Try removing the `update()` method from the SpreadsheetContainer class, and you can see the flicker that results.

The SpreadsheetContainer class also controls the currently highlighted cell by setting the background and text color of the highlighted SpreadsheetCell. It also overrides the `handleEvent()` method so it can trap mouse clicks. It checks to see whether the mouse is over a valid cell; if so, it is given the highlight.

Listing 3.9. The SpreadsheetContainer class.

```
import java.awt.*;
import java.lang.*;
```

continues

Listing 3.9. continued

```
// This class contains the cells that make up a spreadsheet...
public class SpreadsheetContainer extends Canvas {
 CellContainer c;  // The actual spreadsheet data...
 int numRows;
 int numColumns;
 SpreadsheetCell matrix[];
 int cellWidth; // These are set in the paint routine...
 int cellHeight;
 SpreadsheetCell newHighlight;
 SpreadsheetCell oldHighlight;

 // Construct container.  Create internal paint matrix tied to
 // the data container...
 public SpreadsheetContainer(CellContainer ctnr) {
  super();
  // Load the container and set up the display...
  loadContainer(ctnr);
 }

 // Take a cell container and load set the spreadsheet
 // to use it. Put the highlight in the first cell...
 void loadContainer(CellContainer ctnr) {
  c = ctnr; // Store the CellContainer...

  // Get size of spreadsheet...
  numRows = c.getNumRows() + 1;
  numColumns = c.getNumColumns() + 1;

  // Create the SpreadsheetCell matrix...
  matrix = new SpreadsheetCell[numRows * numColumns];

  // Add the cells to the grid...
  int i,j,index;
  char ch;

  // Add the column labels across the top...
  for (j = 0; j < numColumns; ++j) {
   // Create a literal cell for each column...
   matrix[j] = new SpreadsheetCell(new Cell(),true);
   // Set the cell contents and color...
   if (j > 0)
    matrix[j].setString(String.valueOf((j - 1)) );
   matrix[j].setFillColor(Color.lightGray);
   matrix[j].setTextColor(Color.blue);
  } // end for

  // Create the individual rows...
  for (i = 1; i < numRows; ++i) {
   // Set up the row header...
   index = (i * (numColumns));
   matrix[index] = new SpreadsheetCell(new Cell(),true);
   ch = (char)('A' + (i - 1));
   matrix[index].setString(String.valueOf(ch) );
   matrix[index].setFillColor(Color.lightGray);
   matrix[index].setTextColor(Color.blue);
   // Now set the container cells...
```

```
   for (j = 1; j < numColumns; ++j) {
    index = (i * (numColumns)) + j;
    matrix[index] = new SpreadsheetCell(c.getCell(i - 1,j - 1),false);
    // Set the colors...
    matrix[index].setFillColor(Color.white);
    matrix[index].setTextColor(Color.black);
   }  // end inner for...
  } // end outer for

  // Highlight the upper-left cell...
  index = getIndex(1,1);
  newHighlight = matrix[index];
  oldHighlight = newHighlight;
  setCellHighlight(newHighlight,true);
 }

 // Attach a new container to the spreadsheet...
 public void newCellContainer(CellContainer ctnr) {
  // Load the container and set up the display...
  loadContainer(ctnr);
  repaint();
 }

 // Return the currently highlighted row...
 public SpreadsheetCell getHighlight() {
  return newHighlight;
 }

 // Get the index into the matrix for a row or column...
 int getIndex(int row, int col) {
  return ((row * numColumns) + col);
 }

 // Handle mouse clicks...
 void setMouseHighlight(int x, int y) {
  // First figure out what cell is at those coordinates...
  newHighlight = calculatePaint(null,false,x,y);
  // Make it the new highlight if it is not a border element...
  if ((newHighlight != null) && (newHighlight.getLiteral() == false) ) {
   // Turn off old highlight...
   if ((oldHighlight != null) && (oldHighlight != newHighlight))
    setCellHighlight(oldHighlight,false);
   // Set new highlight...
   setCellHighlight(newHighlight,true);
   oldHighlight = newHighlight;
   // Notify parent of change...
   notifyParentOfHighlight(newHighlight);
  }
 }

// Highlight a cell
 // If boolean is on then highlight; else set to normal...
 void setCellHighlight(SpreadsheetCell sc,boolean on) {
  if (on == true) {   // Highlight it!
   sc.setFillColor(Color.red);
   sc.setTextColor(Color.white);
```

continues

Listing 3.9. continued

```
 } // end if
 else {   // Set to normal...
  sc.setFillColor(Color.white);
  sc.setTextColor(Color.black);
 } // end else...
 // Force the cell to repaint...
 repaint();
}

// Update message sent when repainting is needed...
// Prevent paint from getting cleared out...
public void update(Graphics g) {
 paint(g);
}

// Draw the displayable spreadsheet contents...
public synchronized void paint (Graphics g) {
 // Go through the calculations of the paint while painting...
 calculatePaint(g,true,0,0);
}

// This goes through the motions of calculating what is on the
// screen and either calculates coordinates or paints...
// If it is not paint, returns cell that fits in hit region...
SpreadsheetCell calculatePaint(Graphics g,boolean bPaint,int xHit,int yHit) {
 // Get the current size of the display area...
 Dimension dm = size();
 // Calculate the cell width and height
 // Cell should be wide enough to show 8 digits...
 if (bPaint == true) {
  cellWidth = g.getFontMetrics().stringWidth("12345.67");
  cellHeight = g.getFontMetrics().getHeight();
 } // end if

 // Figure out how many rows and cols can be displayed
 int nCol = Math.min(numColumns,dm.width / cellWidth);
 int nRow = Math.min((numRows + 1),dm.height / cellHeight);

 // Draw the cells...
 int index,i,x,j,y;
 —nRow;
 // Go across the rows...
 for (i = 0; i < nRow; ++i) {
  y = cellHeight + (i * cellHeight);
  // Go across the colomns...
  for (j = 0; j < nCol; ++j) {
   index = (i * numColumns) + j;
   // Paint if told to...
   if (bPaint == true) {
    matrix[index].paint(g, (j * cellWidth),y,
     cellWidth,cellHeight);
   } // end if
   else { // Otherwise see whether cell fits...
    x = (j * cellWidth);
    // See whether it fits in the column...
```

```
      if ((xHit >= x) && (xHit < (x + cellWidth))) {
       // See whether it fits in the row...
       if ((yHit >= y) && (yHit < (y + cellHeight))) {
        return matrix[index];
       } // end if
      } // end if
     }
    }  // end column for
   } // end row for
   return null;  // Only used if paint is false...
  }

  // Notify parent that there is a new Highlight...
  void notifyParentOfHighlight(SpreadsheetCell sc) {
   // Create new event with highlight cell as arg
   Event ev = new Event(this,Event.ACTION_EVENT,sc);
   // Send it to the parent...
   getParent().deliverEvent(ev);
  }

  // Handle mouse clicks to spreadsheet...
  public boolean handleEvent(Event evt) {
   switch(evt.id) {
    // Mouse clicks. See whether you should highlight
    // cell on spreadsheet...
    case Event.MOUSE_DOWN: {
     if (evt.target instanceof SpreadsheetContainer)
      setMouseHighlight(evt.x,evt.y);
     return false;
    }
    default:
     return false;
   }
  }

  // Handle to change to a formula...
  // Throws an exception if the formula is invalid...
  public void replaceFormula(SpreadsheetCell sc,String newFormula) throws
➥IllegalArgumentException {
 String convertedFormula;
   // First validate the formula...
   try {
    convertedFormula = c.validateFormula(sc.getCell(),newFormula);
   }
   // If formula is invalid, rethrow an exception...
   catch (FormulaParserException e) {
    throw new IllegalArgumentException();
   }
   // Add converted formula to cell...
   sc.setString(convertedFormula);
   // Recalc...
   c.recalculateAll();
   // Repaint...
   repaint();
  }
 }
```

The SpreadsheetFrame Class

The SpreadsheetFrame class is responsible for presenting the spreadsheet applet to the user. Its most important component is the SpreadsheetContainer class, displayed in the middle of the applet. It creates the CellContainer class that is passed to the SpreadsheetContainer. It also has a TextField object used to edit the individual Cell values. The components of SpreadsheetFrame are displayed using the GridBagLayout manager.

When the user clicks on a cell in the SpreadsheetContainer, the SpreadsheetFrame class gets a notification of the current cell highlighted and sticks the text of the cell into the TextField. When the user enters the text, the new formula is validated, and the spreadsheet is redisplayed with the recalculated values.

The SpreadsheetFrame also has a menu attached to it. Currently, the only menu options are Quit and New for a new spreadsheet. Frames and menus will be discussed in more detail in the next chapter.

Listing 3.10. The SpreadsheetFrame Class.

```
// THIS CLASS IS NOT PUBLIC! Compile in same file as SpreadsheetApplet class.
// This is the frame that controls that user interaction
// with the applet.  It creates the initial spreadsheet data
// and visual container, along with the input field for
// changing values of a cell, the scrollbars, and the menus
class SpreadsheetFrame extends Frame {
 CellContainer c;    // The actual spreadsheet data...
 SpreadsheetContainer s;  // The spreadsheet view
 Scrollbar hScroll;  // The scrollbars...
 Scrollbar vScroll;
 GridBagLayout g;    // Layout for Frame
 MenuBar mbar;  // The frames menu...
 TextField t;  // The text field for the spreadsheet...
 SpreadsheetCell currHighlight;  // The currently highlighted cell...
 Applet appl; // The applet...
 int numRows;  // Keep the initial parameters...
 int numCols;

 // The constructor for the spreadsheet frame takes the
 // values of the size of the Spreadsheet...
 public SpreadsheetFrame(Applet a,int rows, int cols) {
  super("Spreadsheet Applet");

  // Set the initial size and layouts...
  resize(300,200);
  g = new GridBagLayout();
  setLayout(g);
  appl = a;  // Store the applet...
  numRows = rows;
  numCols = cols;

  // Create the new container based on the applet parameters...
  try {
   c = new CellContainer(rows,cols);
```

```
  }
  catch (IllegalArgumentException e) {
   System.out.println("Invalid Spreadsheet parameters");
   dispose();
  }

  // Add some fake data to see how it works...
  addTestData();

  // Create display components...
  addDisplayComponents();

  // Add the menu choices to the frames
  addMenuItems();

  // Pack before display...
  pack();
  resize(300,200);  // Then reset to default value...
  show();
 }

 // Handle system and user events...
 public boolean handleEvent(Event evt) {
  switch(evt.id) {
   case Event.WINDOW_DESTROY: {
    dispose();   // Kill the frame...
    return true;
   }
   // This can be handled
   case Event.ACTION_EVENT: {
    String menu_name = evt.arg.toString();
    if (evt.target instanceof MenuItem)    {
     // Exit...
     if(menu_name.equals("Quit"))
    dispose();  // Kill the frame...
     // New Spreadsheet...
     if(menu_name.equals("New"))
      newSpreadsheet();
    }  // end if
    if (evt.target instanceof TextField)    {
     validateNewFormula();
     return true;
    }  // end if
    if (evt.target instanceof SpreadsheetContainer) {
     changeInputFormula((SpreadsheetCell)evt.arg);
     return true;
    }
    return false;
   }
   default:
    return false;
  }
 }

// Add the menu choices to the frames
 void addMenuItems() {
```

continues

Listing 3.10. continued

```
  mbar = new MenuBar();
  Menu m = new Menu("File");
  m.add(new MenuItem("New"));
  m.addSeparator();
  m.add(new MenuItem("Quit"));
  mbar.add(m);
  setMenuBar(mbar);
 }

 // Add the spreadsheet and input field
 // to display...
 void addDisplayComponents() {
  GridBagConstraints gbc = new GridBagConstraints();
  // Create an input field across the top...
  gbc.fill = GridBagConstraints.BOTH;
  gbc.weightx = 1.0;
  gbc.gridwidth = GridBagConstraints.REMAINDER;
  t = new TextField();
  g.setConstraints(t,gbc);
  add(t);

  // Create the spreadsheet display...
  gbc.fill = GridBagConstraints.BOTH;
  gbc.weightx = 1.0;
  gbc.weighty = 1.0;
  gbc.gridwidth = GridBagConstraints.RELATIVE;
  gbc.gridheight = 10;
  s = new SpreadsheetContainer(c);
  g.setConstraints(s,gbc);
  add(s);

  // Set initial formula for text field...
  changeInputFormula(s.getHighlight());
 }

 // Change the formula of the input field to that of
 // the Object argument, which is a spreadsheet cell...
 void changeInputFormula(SpreadsheetCell sc) {
  // Set the text box with the formula...
  if (sc != null)
   t.setText(sc.getString());
  else
   t.setText("");
  // Store the currently highlighted cell...
  currHighlight = sc;
 }

 // A text field formula has been entered...
 // Validate it and update spreadsheet...
 // Update text field where necessary...
 void validateNewFormula() {
  // Put up wait icon for calculations...
  int oldCursor = getCursorType();
  setCursor(WAIT_CURSOR);
  try {
```

```
    // Replace the formula.  If no problem, then
    // spreadsheet will be recalculated...
    s.replaceFormula(currHighlight, t.getText());
    appl.getAppletContext().showStatus("Formula accepted.");
   }
   catch (Exception e) {  // Handle illegal exception...
    // Let browser status bar know about error...
    // Get the status bar from the AppletContext...
    appl.getAppletContext().showStatus("Illegal Formula syntax:
➥Use SUM,ADD,SUB,MULT,DIV");
}
   // Always place the converted formula in the text field...
   changeInputFormula(s.getHighlight());
   setCursor(oldCursor);
  }

  // Reload spreadsheet with blank data...
  void newSpreadsheet() {
   // Create the new container based on the applet parameters...
   try {
    c = new CellContainer(numRows,numCols);
    s.newCellContainer(c);
    // Set initial formula for text field...
    changeInputFormula(s.getHighlight());
   }
   catch (IllegalArgumentException e) {
    System.out.println("Invalid Spreadsheet parameters");
    dispose();
   }
  }

  // Just some test data...
  void addTestData() {
   c.setCellFormula("1",0,0);
   c.setCellFormula("2",0,1);
   c.setCellFormula("3",0,2);
   c.setCellFormula("4",0,3);
   c.setCellFormula("SUM(A0,A3)",0,4); // Should be 10
   // c.setCellFormula("ADD(A0,A3)",0,4);  // Should be 5
   // c.setCellFormula("ADD(A0,4)",0,4);  // Should be 5
   // c.setCellFormula("ADD(1,4)",0,4);  // Should be 5
   c.recalculateAll();
  }
}
```

The SpreadsheetApplet class

This class takes the applet parameters and determines the size of the spreadsheet to be constructed. If the parameters are bad, default values are used. When row and column sizes of the spreadsheet are determined, an instance of the SpreadsheetFrame class is created and the visual portion of the program begins. When the user moves away from the current Web page, the spreadsheet is hidden; it is redisplayed if the user returns.

Listing 3.11. The SpreadsheetApplet class.

```
// This file describes the applet class that manages the
// spreadsheet program.

import java.awt.*;
import java.lang.*;
import java.applet.*;

//  This applet kicks off the SpreadsheetFrame
//  that manages the spreadsheet program.
public class SpreadsheetApplet extends Applet  {
 SpreadsheetFrame fr;
 public void init() {
  int rows = 10;  // Default if params are no good...
  int cols = 10;
  // Get the HTML parameters
  // and try to convert to a good value...
  // Get the row...
  try {
   String param = getParameter("rows");
   int temp = Integer.parseInt(param);
   if ((temp > 1) && (temp < 26))
    rows = temp;
   else
    throw new IllegalArgumentException();
  }
  catch (Exception e) {   // Display error to browser...
   getAppletContext().showStatus("Invalid row parameter. Using default...");
  }
  // Get the column...
  try {
   String param = getParameter("columns");
   int temp = Integer.parseInt(param);
   if ((temp > 1) && (temp < 40))
    cols = temp;
   else
    throw new IllegalArgumentException();
  }
  catch (Exception e) {
   getAppletContext().showStatus("Invalid column parameter. Using default...");
  }

  // Create the spreadsheet frame
  fr = new SpreadsheetFrame(this,rows,cols);
 }

 // If returning to screen, show frame...
 public void start() {
  // Redisplay the applet...
  try {
   fr.show();
  }
  // Handle any problem...
  catch(Exception e) {       }
 }
```

```
 // Hide the frame upon leaving...
 public void stop() {
  // Handle where it may have been disposed...
  try {
   fr.hide();
  }
  // Handle any problem...
  catch(Exception e) {        }
 }

}
```

Summary

In this chapter, you have read about many of the basics of AWT and seen it applied to the creation of a non-trivial spreadsheet. In Chapter 4, "Enhancing the Spreadsheet Applet," you will see how dialog boxes, streams, colors, and fonts can be applied to improve the spreadsheet applet. More of the fundamentals of AWT will be discussed in the context of these enhancements. You will also see a practical example of streams as the ability to save and open a spreadsheet is added to the applet.

4

Enhancing the Spreadsheet Applet

The previous chapter laid the foundations for the spreadsheet applet to be developed throughout this part of the book. In creating this first version of the spreadsheet, Chapter 3, "Building a Spreadsheet Applet," introduces many of the fundamental concepts of AWT programming. It also discusses exception handling and practical ways to handle errors in a Java application. However, this first version of the spreadsheet applet also includes elements such as menus and frames that were not discussed at the time they were presented. These concepts are expanded on in this chapter.

While exploring these aspects of Java programming, this chapter will illustrate more features of the AWT package, and discussing the Dialog classes will lead to the practical addition of dialog boxes to the spreadsheet applet. Custom dialog boxes will be created for the purposes of selecting the color and font of a spreadsheet cell; they will be accessed through an expanded menu and their selections will be made through upgraded classes. This chapter also includes an introduction to streams programming, which is used to add the capability of saving and reading a spreadsheet file. Security issues related to file storage in Java will be an important part of this discussion.

Overview of AWT: Part 2

The previous chapter's version of the spreadsheet applet did not cover how to use the Frame and Menu classes. These features of AWT are actually closely related. The Frame class also has a common relationship with the Dialog class because they both are from the same superclass, Window; therefore, dialog boxes will also be covered in this section.

AWT applications can also be enhanced through the support of multiple colors and fonts. Using them can not only make an applet more visually pleasing, but can also give the user more freedom in customizing the spreadsheet's display. The Color, Font, and FontMetrics classes that make this possible are, therefore, also an appropriate topic of discussion here.

Windows and Frames

The Window class is used in AWT to create "popup" windows that appear outside the constraints of the normal browser area allocated to an applet. The Window class is derived from the Container class and so can contain other components. Unlike applet components tied directly to a browser page, Window classes are not restricted to a prespecified area of the screen. Window objects can be resized as their immediate requirements dictate. AWT can perform this automatically through the Window class's `pack()` method; it works with the Window layout (by default, BorderLayout) to arrive at the optimal presentation of the window, given its contained components and screen resolution. Typically, `pack()` is called before a window is displayed. Windows are not made visible until the `show()` method is called. They are removed from the screen, and their resources freed, when the `dispose()` method is invoked.

The Frame class extends Window by adding a title bar, a border for resizing, support for menus, and the ability to modify the system cursor to various states such as waiting or moving. For most GUI platforms, the Frame's title bar will be tied to system control boxes, such as minimize, maximize, or destroy. Consequently, the Frame class has all the elements necessary to make an applet look like a "real" application, complete with menus and system controls.

Figure 4.1 and Listing 4.1 present a simple Frame applet that changes the cursor to a state based on the button selected. The applet class, FrameCursorApplet, does little more than launch the main frame, FrameCursor. The constructor for this frame begins by calling the frame super constructor. The sole parameter in this case is the caption displayed on the title bar. The layout for the Frame is then set. The default is BorderLayout, but in this case, you want a three by two grid matrix, hence the use of GridLayout. The buttons are added to the frame next, with names representing the cursor state to be selected. After all the components have been added, the `pack()` method is invoked so that the button placement can be optimized. Since this optimized placement will result in a small frame (six buttons sized tightly around the label text doesn't take much space), the `resize()` method is called to make the frame a larger size. Finally, the frame is displayed with the `show()` method.

When a button is selected, the custom method `SetCursor()` is invoked. This method takes the button label and figures out which cursor should be displayed. The Frame `setCursor()` method is used to set the cursor state; its parameter is a static integer defined as part of the Frame class.

NOTE

You might see the message `Untrusted Java Applet Window` in your Netscape browser when applet frames are displayed. However, this is not cause for alarm—it is just a security message.

Listing 4.1. Code for Frame applet that changes the cursor state.

```
import java.awt.*;
import java.lang.*;
import java.applet.*;

// This applet simply starts up the frame used to
// show different frame cursors...
public class FrameCursorApplet extends Applet  {
    public void init() {
      // Create the frame with a title...
      new FrameCursor("Frame Cursors");
   }
}

// The frame for letting the user pick different
// cursors to display...
```

continues

Listing 4.1. continued

```
class FrameCursor extends Frame {
   // Create the frame with a title...
   public FrameCursor(String title) {
      // Call the superclass constructor...
      super(title);
      // Create a grid layout to place the buttons...
      setLayout(new GridLayout(3,2));
      // Add the buttons for choosing the cursor...
      add(new Button("Default"));
      add(new Button("Wait"));
      add(new Button("Hand"));
      add(new Button("Move"));
      add(new Button("Text"));
      add(new Button("SE Resize"));
      // Pack and display...
      pack();
      resize(300,200); // Make it a reasonable size...
      show();
   }

   // Handle events...
   public boolean handleEvent(Event e) {
      switch(e.id) {
         case e.WINDOW_DESTROY:
            dispose();  // Erase frame
            return true;
            case Event.ACTION_EVENT:
            if (e.target instanceof Button)
               SetCursor((Button)e.target);
            return true;
         default:
            return false;
      }
   }

   // Set the cursor based on the button chosen...
   void SetCursor(Button btn) {
      // Get the label of the button...
      String selection = btn.getLabel();
      //Set the cursor based on that label...
      if (selection.equals("Wait"))
            setCursor(Frame.WAIT_CURSOR);
      else if (selection.equals("Hand"))
            setCursor(Frame.HAND_CURSOR);
      else if (selection.equals("Move"))
            setCursor(Frame.MOVE_CURSOR);
      else if (selection.equals("Text"))
            setCursor(Frame.TEXT_CURSOR);
      else if (selection.equals("SE Resize"))
            setCursor(Frame.SE_RESIZE_CURSOR);
      else // Just use the default...
            setCursor(Frame.DEFAULT_CURSOR);
   }
}
```

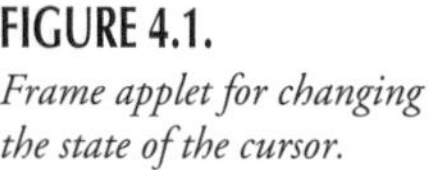

FIGURE 4.1.
Frame applet for changing the state of the cursor.

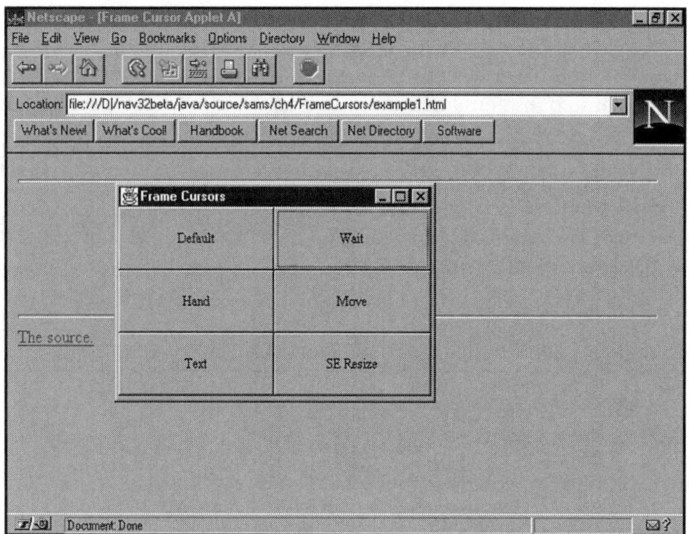

The current state of the cursor can be retrieved with the `getCursorType()` method, and the `getTitle()` and `setTitle()` Frame methods can be used for getting and setting the title bar caption, respectively. Similarly, the `getIconImage()` and `setIconImage()` methods can be used to set the image display of an iconized frame.

Menus

Frames and menus are closely related since the Frame class is the only AWT class with built-in support for menus. Frames implement the MenuContainer interface, which is used to contain menu components. These components are defined by the MenuComponent class, the superclass of all menu components. It defines a set of methods pertinent to individual menu items. For example, the `getFont()` and `setFont()` MenuComponent methods are used to control the font selection of the menu object.

Menus can be illustrated by modifying the previous example to use menus, instead of buttons, to change the state of a cursor. Listing 4.2 shows the code that performs this. The constructor of the Frame class, called FrameMenuCursor, shows how to add menus to a frame. The first step is creating a MenuBar object. The menu bar is tied to the frame with the `setMenuBar()` method of the Frame class. This makes the MenuBar object the default menu for the frame.

The next step is to add the individual menus to the menubar. The Menu class is used as a container of individual menu items or other menus. In this applet, the two menus are File and Cursor. The Menu constructor takes these strings as its sole parameter, thus defining the text to be associated with the menu. The menus are then added to the menu bar through the MenuBar `add()` method. The `remove()` method can be used to delete a Menu from a MenuBar.

The final step in menu creation is to add the individual menu items, defined by the MenuItem class. This class is a subclass of MenuComponent and provides additional operations to be performed on a menu item. MenuItem methods can be used to set the menu label and to disable or enable an item. The constructor for the MenuItem has as its sole parameter the item label that will be initially displayed. The `add()` method is used to add an instance of MenuItem to a Menu.

Listing 4.2. Code for applet that uses menus to change cursor state.

```
import java.awt.*;
import java.lang.*;
import java.applet.*;

// This applet simply starts up the frame
// which provides a menu for setting cursors...
public class FrameMenuCursorApplet extends Applet {
   public void init() {
      // Create the frame with a title...
      new FrameMenuCursor("Menu Based Cursors");
   }
}

// The frame for letting the user pick different
// cursors to display...
class FrameMenuCursor extends Frame {
   // Create the frame with a title...
   public FrameMenuCursor(String title) {
      // Call the superclass constructor...
      super(title);

      // Add the menus...
      // First create the menu bar
      MenuBar mbar = new MenuBar();
      setMenuBar(mbar); // Attach to the frame...

      // Add the File submenu...
      Menu m = new Menu("File");
      mbar.add(m);  // Add to menu bar
      // Add Quit to the submenu...
      m.add(new MenuItem("Quit"));

      // Add the Cursor submenu...
      m = new Menu("Cursor");
      mbar.add(m);  // Add to menu bar

      // Add the cursor selections to the submenu...
      m.add(new MenuItem("Default"));
      m.add(new MenuItem("Wait"));
      m.add(new MenuItem("Hand"));
      m.add(new MenuItem("Move"));
      m.add(new MenuItem("Text"));
```

```
      m.add(new MenuItem("SE Resize"));

      // Pack and display...
      pack();
      resize(300,200); // Make it a reasonable size...
      show();
   }

   // Handle events...
   public boolean handleEvent(Event e) {
      switch(e.id) {
         case e.WINDOW_DESTROY:
            dispose();  // Erase frame
            return true;
         case e.ACTION_EVENT:
            // Process menu selection...
            if (e.target instanceof MenuItem) {
               // Get the name of the menu selection..
               String menuName = e.arg.toString();
               // Dispose of frame if quit is chosen...
               if (menuName.equals("Quit"))
                     dispose();
               // Otherwise, set the cursor...
               if (menuName.equals("Default"))
                     setCursor(Frame.DEFAULT_CURSOR);
               if (menuName.equals("Wait"))
                     setCursor(Frame.WAIT_CURSOR);
               if (menuName.equals("Hand"))
                     setCursor(Frame.HAND_CURSOR);
               if (menuName.equals("Move"))
                     setCursor(Frame.MOVE_CURSOR);
               if (menuName.equals("Text"))
                     setCursor(Frame.TEXT_CURSOR);
               if (menuName.equals("SE Resize"))
                     setCursor(Frame.SE_RESIZE_CURSOR);
               return true;
            } // end if
            return true;
         default:
            return false;
      }
   }
}
```

A MenuItem can be removed from a Menu with the `remove()` method, much as it is in the MenuBar class. A separator, dividing menu items, can be added with the `addSeparator()` method of the Menu class. This is useful for menus that have different categories of options.

The current example also illustrates how to process menu selections. When a menu item is selected, an `ACTION_EVENT` is issued. The `instanceof` operator can be used in the handler to verify that the target of the action is a menu. By taking the Event argument (the `arg` variable) and converting it to a string, the program can get the name of the menu item. Through the name, the appropriate course of action can then be taken. In this example, the Quit menu item forces the frame to shut down by using the `dispose()` method. The other menu choices result in a new state for the cursor.

It should be mentioned that the CheckboxMenuItem class can be implemented for menus that need to use checkmarks to indicate whether the item has been selected. This is handy for menu items that toggle.

Dialogs

Like the Frame class, the Dialog class is a subclass of Window. Dialogs differ from Frames in a couple of subtle ways, however. The most important of these differences is that Dialogs can be *modal*. When a modal Dialog is displayed, input to other windows in the Applet is blocked until the Dialog is disposed. This feature points to the general purpose of Dialogs, which is to give the user a warning or a decision to be made before the program can continue. Although non-modal, or *modeless*, Dialogs are supported, most Dialogs are modal.

There are two constructors for the Dialog class. Both take a Frame object as a parameter; they also take a boolean flag, which indicates whether the dialog should be modal. If the flag is set to true, the dialog is modal. The constructors differ only in a parameter that specifies whether the dialog should have a title caption. It is this constructor that is used in the example that follows.

Figure 4.2 shows a variation of the previous applet, except that a Dialog is used to change the cursor state. Listing 4.3 shows the code for the Dialog class, called ChangeCursorDialog. The Frame class (still called FrameMenuCursor from the previous example) declares the dialog and instantiates it as follows:

```
ChangeCursorDialog dlg;
dlg = new ChangeCursorDialog(this,true,"Change the cursor");
```

The menu for this application is different from the previous example. The frame constructs the menu as follows:

```
// First create the menu bar
MenuBar mbar = new MenuBar();
setMenuBar(mbar); // Attach to the frame...

// Add the File submenu...
Menu m = new Menu("File");
mbar.add(m);  // Add to menu bar
// Add Dialog to the submenu...
m.add(new MenuItem("Cursor Dialog"));
// Add a separator
m.addSeparator();
// Add Quit to the submenu...
m.add(new MenuItem("Quit"));
```

Note that a separator is added to divide the two menu items.

When the Cursor Dialog menu item is chosen, the dialog box is presented with the following code:

```
if (menuName.equals("Cursor Dialog"))
    dlg.show(); // Make the dialog visible...
```

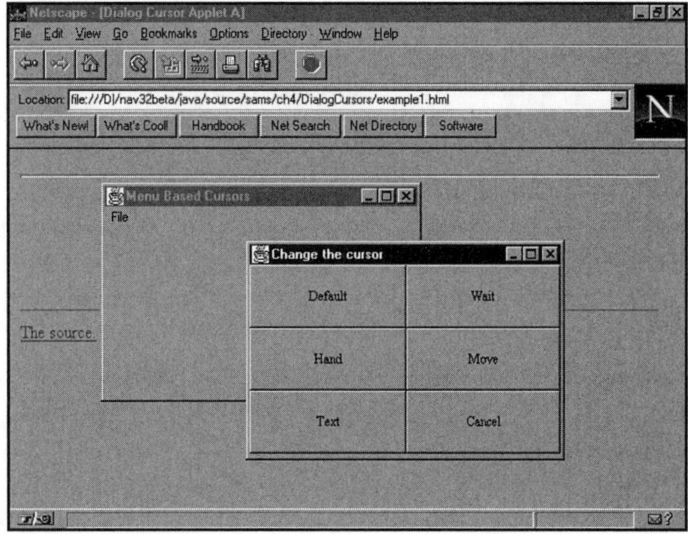

FIGURE 4.2.

Using Dialog to change the state of the cursor.

Listing 4.3. Code for a Dialog to change the cursor state.

```
import java.awt.*;
import java.lang.*;
import java.applet.*;

// Dialog that presents a grid of buttons
// for choosing the Frame cursor. A Cancel
// button exits the dialog...
class ChangeCursorDialog extends Dialog {
FrameMenuCursor fr;
// Create the dialog and store the title string...
public ChangeCursorDialog(Frame parent,boolean modal,String title) {
 // Create dialog with title
 super(parent,title,modal);
 fr = (FrameMenuCursor)parent;
 // The layout is Grid layout...
 setLayout(new GridLayout(3,2));
 // Add the button options
 add(new Button("Default"));
 add(new Button("Wait"));
 add(new Button("Hand"));
 add(new Button("Move"));
 add(new Button("Text"));
```

continues

Listing 4.3. continued

```
 add(new Button("Cancel"));
 // Pack and size for display...
 pack();
 resize(300,200);
}
// Look for button selections to
// change the cursor...
public boolean action(Event e,Object arg) {
     // If button was selected then exit dialog..
if (e.target instanceof Button) {
         // And possibly change the cursor...
         if (arg.equals("Default"))
            fr.setCursor(Frame.DEFAULT_CURSOR);
         if (arg.equals("Wait"))
            fr.setCursor(Frame.WAIT_CURSOR);
         if (arg.equals("Hand"))
            fr.setCursor(Frame.HAND_CURSOR);
         if (arg.equals("Move"))
            fr.setCursor(Frame.MOVE_CURSOR);
         if (arg.equals("Text"))
            fr.setCursor(Frame.TEXT_CURSOR);
         dispose();
    }
    return false;
}
}
```

Another AWT class called FileDialog is a subclass of Dialog. It is used for creating stock Load and Save dialog boxes. The upcoming tutorial has examples of the FileDialog class.

Colors

The Color class is used to set an object's colors. This class represents a color as a combination of RGB values. RGB is a 24-bit representation of a color composed of red, green, and blue byte values. This 24-bit representation is virtual since many platforms do not support 24-bit color. In these situations, Java maps the color to the appropriate value; this will usually be an index into a palette.

The Color class defines a set of stock color values, implemented as static variables. For example, Color.red is available with an RGB value of 255,0,0. Other colors supported are white, black, gray, green, blue, yellow, magenta, and cyan. Various Color constructors can also be used to define other colors. For example, the statement

```
Color col = new Color(0,0,120);
```

produces a dark blue color. Other methods, such as `darker()` and `brighter()`, can also be used to create a new Color object from an existing one.

There are generally two approaches to tying a color to an object. The first approach is to use methods provided by the Component class. The `setBackground()` and `setForeground()` methods are used to set the colors of an object in the two respective positions. For example, the following code creates a Panel object and sets its background to white:

```
Panel p = new Panel();
p.setBackground(Color.white);
```

You can use the respective methods prefixed by "get" to return the background and foreground colors of a component.

The other approach to setting a color occurs in the `paint()` method. Recall that a Graphics object is passed to this method. The `setColor()` method can then be used to set the color of the next items to be painted. For example, the following code paints a blue framed rectangle:

```
public synchronized void paint (Graphics g)
g.setColor(Color.blue);
g.drawRect(0,0,100,40);
```

The tutorial in this section gives more examples of using color. A dialog box presents a choice of colors through the use of colored components. The spreadsheet is modified to use these chosen colors when it is painted.

Fonts

Fonts are a critical aspect of graphics-based programming. Not only are they important for making an application attractive, they are a seminal part of programming a visual interface. Often how a component is sized or placed turns on what font is being used. The spreadsheet tutorial in this chapter, for example, uses the current dimensions of the font to determine how the spreadsheet cell should be sized and located. Therefore, there are two aspects of font programming: tying fonts to display components and getting font information to program how graphical objects are positioned. The former aspect generally falls in the domain of the Font class; the latter is tied to the FontMetrics class, although Font is involved here also.

To construct a Font object, you need a font name, style, and size. The font name represents a family of fonts, such as Courier. The font families available to an applet depend on where the program is running, and so decisions about what font is to be used should be made dynamically. The java.awt.Toolkit has a method called `getFontList()` that returns a string array of font names on the host system. An example of how this method is used is found in the next section and in the font dialog in the tutorial. The family of a Font can be retrieved through the `getFamily()` method.

The size of a font is its point size, such as 8 for a small font and 72 for a large one. There are three styles defined as constants in the Font class: `PLAIN`, `BOLD`, or `ITALIC`. The latter two can be combined to produce a font with both features. For example, you could create a Helvetica font that has a 36-point size and is both bold and italicized as follows:

```
Font f = new Font("Helvetica", Font.BOLD + Font.ITALIC,36);
```

Fonts can be tied to a component through the `setFont()` method. To create the previous font and tie it to a label, the following code could be invoked:

```
Label l = new Label("My Label");
l.setFont(new Font("Helvetica", Font.BOLD + Font.ITALIC,36));
```

A reference to a component's Font can be retrieved through `getFont()`.

Another way to use fonts is in the `paint()` method. The Graphics class used in `paint()` can have the current font set through the `setFont()` method. For example, Listing 4.4 provides the code for an applet that paints a series of Strings containing a row number. Figure 4.3 shows the output. When the `paint()` method begins, a new font is created and set to the graphics object; this font is now the current font used for the following graphics calls. The `drawString()` method is then called repeatedly with the y coordinate being dynamically calculated.

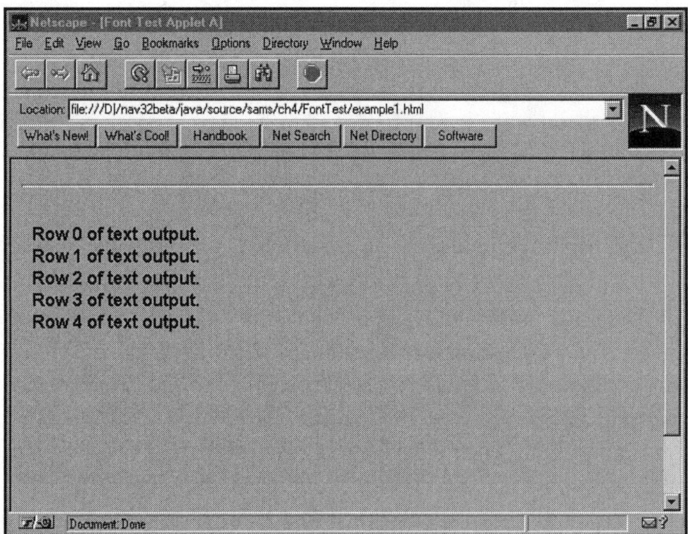

FIGURE 4.3.
A Font applet using hard-coded coordinates.

Listing 4.4. Code for Font applet using hard-coded coordinates.

```
import java.awt.*;
import java.lang.*;
import java.applet.*;

// This aspect throws a string into the applet
// display separated by a height difference of the
// current font
public class FontTest extends Applet  {
    public void paint(Graphics g) {
      int y;
      Font f = new Font("Helvetica",Font.BOLD + Font.PLAIN,16);
      g.setFont(f);
```

```
      for (int i = 0; i < 5; ++i) {
         y = 40 + (i * 20);
         g.drawString("Row " + i + " of text output.",10,y);
      } // end for
   }
}
```

There are a couple of things about this applet that are not quite optimal. First of all, it isn't good to create a new Font in the paint routine. Painting occurs frequently and font creation is an expensive operation. It is faster and more efficient to create the font only once, as in the `init()` method.

The other thing that might be avoided is using hard-coded values, which is notorious for displays that do not appear uniformly across different platforms. (After all, that is why AWT has layouts!) Although this applet might look decent across platforms, it gives an excuse for showing a better way of using coordinates. This is where the FontMetrics class comes in.

FontMetrics is used to get a variety of information about a Font object. Such information includes the font's dimensions, how big a String or character using that font would be, and so forth. Table 4.1 lists some of the methods of the FontMetrics class.

Table 4.1. FontMetrics methods.

Method	*Description*
`charWidth`	Returns width of character using this font.
`getAscent`	Returns the ascent of the font (distance between the baseline and top of the character).
`getDescent`	Returns descent of font (distance from the baseline of the font and its bottom).
`getHeight`	Returns total height of font (ascent + descent + leading).
`getLeading`	Returns the line spacing of the font.
`stringWidth`	Returns the number of pixels a String using this font will take.

You can retrieve a FontMetrics object for a specific font in a couple of ways. First of all, the FontMetrics object can be created from scratch by using its constructor; it takes the Font in question as its only parameter. The reference to the FontMetrics can also be taken directly from the Graphics class by using the `getFontMetrics()` method. The first technique is used when the program is not painting, but that is when the latter technique is applied. Finally, it could retrieve from the default toolkit with a method also named `getFontMetrics()`.The next section explains how the Toolkit class works.

Figure 4.4 shows an improved version of the Font applet through the use of FontMetrics; Listing 4.5 gives the new code. In this version of the applet, each of the String displays are equally incremented by the height of the font. The code calculates the height increment from the `getHeight()` method of the FontMetrics reference of the Graphics object. The new code is also more efficient than the previous example since it creates the font only once, at initialization.

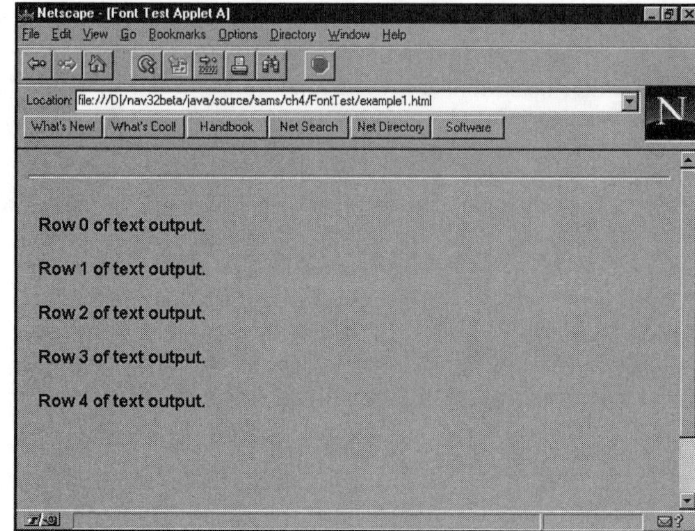

FIGURE 4.4.
A Font applet using FontMetrics.

Listing 4.5. Code for a Font applet that uses FontMetrics.

```
import java.awt.*;
import java.lang.*;
import java.applet.*;

// This aspect throws a string into the applet
// display separated by a height difference of the
// current font
public class FontTest extends Applet {
   Font f;
   // Create the font...
   public void init() {
     f  = new Font("Helvetica",Font.BOLD + Font.PLAIN,16);
   }
   // Paint using TextMetrics to set the height in even
   // increments...
   public void paint(Graphics g) {
      // Set the font
      g.setFont(f);
      // Always increment by twice the height of the font...
      int heightIncrement =  2 * g.getFontMetrics().getHeight();
      int y = 0;
      for (int i = 0; i < 5; ++i) {
         y += heightIncrement;
         g.drawString("Row " + i + " of text output.",10,y);
```

```
      } // end for
   }
}
```

The tutorial that follows will have even more examples of fonts, including a dialog box that can be used to select a font family, size, and style.

The Toolkit Class

The AWT Toolkit class provides the link between the AWT system-independent interface and the underlying platform-based toolkit (such as Windows). The class is abstract, so the `getDefaultToolkit()` method must be called to get a reference to the actual Toolkit object. Once this is done, all kinds of information about the underlying environment can be revealed. By working with the Toolkit, this underlying information can be used in a way that does not compromise portability.

For example, the following code gets a list of all the fonts available on the native platform and prints them out:

```
String fontList[] = Toolkit.getDefaultToolkit().getFontList();
    for (int i = 0; i < fontList.length; ++i)
       System.out.println(fontList[i]);
```

If the fonts used in an applet are derived from this list, versus using hard-coded font names, the portability of an applet will be improved. The `getFontMetrics()` method returns the screen metrics of a font.

Another useful Toolkit method is `getScreenSize()`. This returns the full-screen dimensions of the native platform. If you want to create a window that fills up the screen, these dimensions will be useful. The `getScreenResolution()` method returns the dots-per-inch resolution of the screen.

The Toolkit class also provides a variety of methods for using images, including a method for synchronizing the screen's graphics state. This `sync()` method can be used in animation to avoid flicker.

I/O and Streams

Streams are a traditional way of representing a connection between two objects. The types of streams that programmers are most familiar with are ones between I/O devices (such as files) and processes or streams between two memory structures. Each endpoint of a stream connection can have one or two channels: an input channel and an output channel. When a process is reading from a file, it reads from a stream that receives data from the file device's output channel. From the point of view of the process, it is managing an *input stream*. From the viewpoint of the file device, it is sending an *output stream*. Figure 4.5 illustrates the relationship.

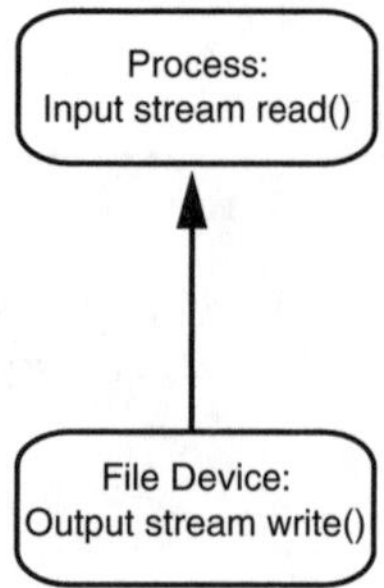

FIGURE 4.5.
Stream relationships when a process reads from a file.

The JDK package for managing input and output interactions, called java.io, has the stream concept at its foundation. It is structured on the notion of input and output streams just discussed. These stream classes permeate the Java programming environment. Their use ranges from file I/O to network programming to the widely used `System.out.println()` method. There are few things that will increase the capabilities of a Java programmer more than a full understanding of Java streams.

Structure of the java.io Package

As just stated, the java.io package is based heavily on the notion of input and output streams. This is made clear by the diagram of significant java.io classes, shown in Figure 4.6. The most important of these are, not surprisingly, the InputStream and OutputStream classes, which are generally used to read and write from a stream, respectively. They form the basis of an elaborate network of stream classes that make it easy to build high-level streams, such as those that work on newline delimited ASCII data, to low-level streams, such as one that manages data on a byte-by-byte level. How this works will be explored in the upcoming discussion of the two foundation classes and their subclasses.

Before engaging in a discussion of the input and output stream classes, it's useful to look at some of the other aspects of Java I/O programming. The File class can be used to get information about a file or directory on the host file system. For example, the following code checks to see whether a file exists in the current directory and lists what is in the grandparent directory.

```
myFile = new File("File.txt");
      System.out.println("The file " + myFile.getName()
            + " existence is " + myFile.exists());
      File myDirectory = new File("..\\..");
      String s[] = myDirectory.list();
      System.out.println("Directory contents: ");
      for (int i = 0; i < s.length; ++i)
         System.out.println(s[i]);
```

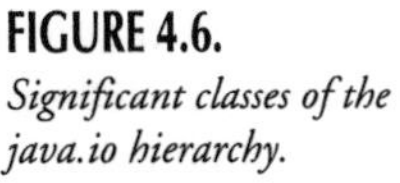

FIGURE 4.6.
Significant classes of the java.io hierarchy.

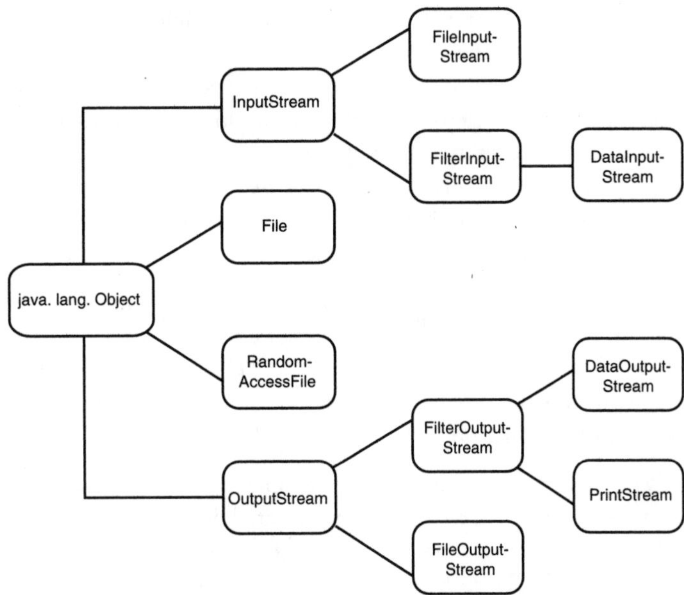

As you might have observed in the constructor for the directory object, the naming conventions are based on the host file system. Consequently, hard coding such conventions can result in nonportable code. Fortunately, the class provides some constants that can hide the platform-specific conventions. For example, the following code makes the directory constructor portable:

```
File myDirectory = new File(".." + File.separator + "..");
```

The File class also offers a variety of other file operations. This includes the ability to delete or rename a file, create a new directory, and inspect a file's attributes. Note, however, that these operations are subject to the native environment's security constraints, discussed in the following section.

I/O and Security

The Java language and its native environment (such as a browser) give you a sophisticated system of security layers. At the top of this security hierarchy is protection for the local file system. After all, the most prevalent methods for a virus to inflict pain on its victim is to destroy his or her file system. Consequently, protection of the file system where the applet is running is paramount.

A Java environment enforces a security policy through its security manager. This is implemented as an object through the SecurityManager class and is created once and only once by a browser at startup. Once established, a SecurityManager cannot be changed or replaced. The reasons for this are obvious. If a rogue applet can modify the SecurityManager object, then it can simply remove all access restrictions and wield unlimited power over your hard disk. However, it is possible to get a reference to the SecurityManager through the System object's `getSecurityManager()` method. Once obtained, methods can be applied on the object to see what security constraints are currently being applied.

The strictness of a security policy depends on the runtime Java environment. Netscape Navigator, for example, cannot perform any file operations. The simple File class example in the previous section causes a security violation. This occurs when the File `exists()` method is invoked, which is the first file operation in the code (the File constructor simply associates the String name with the object).

Sun's HotJava browser allows some file operations on the client running an applet. Note that where the applet is loaded from is important. The client is the site running the applet; the server is where the applet was loaded from. The security that concerns Java the most is that of the client site. In Hot Java, the operations allowed on the client are based on the concept of *access control lists*. By default, any file not covered in the list cannot be accessed in any fashion, including the simple File `exists()` operation. The access control list can be found in the properties file of the .hotjava directory located under the parent.

File security is even weaker for the appletviewer program that programmers can use to test an applet. In this environment, most file operations are allowed for applets loaded from the client. Some file operations performed by applets loaded from a server over the network are also permitted. Standalone Java applications have no file security. If a sophisticated Java application is being developed, such as over an internal corporate network, it probably would be best to create a subclass of SecurityManager to set up a security policy appropriate for that environment.

When a file operation violates a security policy, a SecurityException object is thrown. This can be caught by the program to prevent abnormal termination.

I/O Exceptions

Besides thrown SecurityException objects, Java I/O programs need to be concerned with handling other exceptions. In particular, they need to catch IOException objects that are thrown. The IOException class embraces the category of errors related to input/output operations. Many of the methods in the java.io package throw IOException objects that must be caught. The typical structure of code that performs I/O operations is, therefore, as follows:

```
try {
 // IO operations
}
```

```
catch (IOException e) {
  // Handle the error
}
```

Two subclasses of IOException are noteworthy. A FileNotFoundException object is thrown when there is an attempt to open a file that doesn't exist. For example, the constructor for the FileInputStream class tries to open the file specified in its parameter. If it cannot do so, an object of class FileNotFoundException is thrown.

Another notable subclass of IOException is EOFException, which typically occurs in read operations when an end of file has been reached. This indicates that there are no more bytes to be read.

InputStream Classes

Figure 4.7 illustrates the class hierarchy that descends from the InputStream class. InputStream is an abstract class that defines the basic operations that must be implemented by its subclasses. The most noteworthy of these is the `read()` method. This is used to read in bytes one at a time or into a byte array. The System.in variable, which represents that standard input stream, is based on the InputStream class and is now used to illustrate the `read()` method:

```
try {
         int b;
         b = System.in.read();
}
catch (IOException e) {
  // Handle any exception…
}
```

This example reads in a byte that is, confusingly, converted to an integer by the `read()` method. The method returns `-1` if there is no input to be read. For many subclasses of InputStream, an EOFException object is thrown in these circumstances.

Table 4.2 lists other notable methods of the abstract InputStream class.

Table 4.2. Notable InputStream methods.

Method	*Description*
`available`	A non-blocking way to find out number of bytes available to read.
`close`	Closes the input stream.
`mark`	Marks the current stream position.
`read`	Reads a byte or array of bytes.
`reset`	Resets stream to last marked position.
`skip`	Skips over specified number of input bytes.

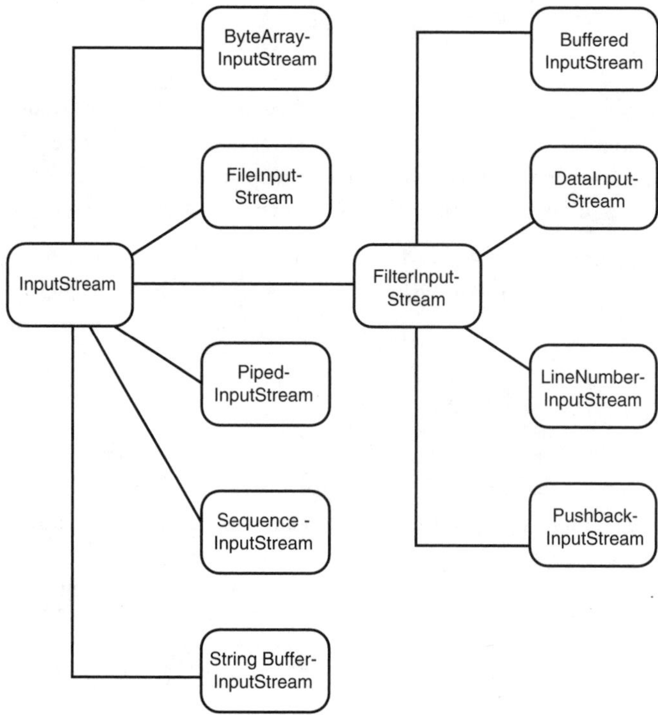

FIGURE 4.7.
InputStream classes.

FilterInputStream classes

The FilterInputStream class is at the top of a branch of the InputStream hierarchy that can be used to implement some very powerful operations. In particular, this class is used to chain a series of FilterInputStream classes so that one stream can process data before passing it "up" to the next stream. This chaining technique is excellent to use when encapsulating classes that interact with streams at a lower level (such as bytes) into streams that read in data at a higher level, such as Strings. The following example illustrates how this works.

As seen in the previous overview of the InputStream class, the System.in object reads data in a byte at a time. This will prove to be cumbersome for many standard input operations that typically want to work on String objects. Fortunately, FilterInputStream classes make it easy to abstract this byte-level functionality into a higher and more usable interface. The code in Listing 4.6 takes the System.in object and creates a DataInputStream object that can be used to read in a String of text delimited by a newline or EOF. This is then sent to the System.out object, which prints the string to the standard output stream.

Listing 4.6. Chaining Input Stream classes.

```
try {
        // Create the data input stream...
        DataInputStream dis =
           new DataInputStream(
              new BufferedInputStream(System.in));
        // Read in a line of text...
        String s = dis.readLine();
        // Send it to standard output...
        System.out.println(s);
     }
     // Handle any exceptions caused by the process...
     catch (IOException e) {
        // Just print out the error...
        System.out.println(e.getMessage());
     }
```

The first line inside the `try` clause is full of material; the innermost part of the clause introduces the BufferedInputStream class:

```
new BufferedInputStream(System.in)
```

This subclass of FilterInputStream simply allows the reading in of data more efficiently. Reading a file so that every byte request requires a new input read is very slow. The BufferedInputStream class reads data into a buffer in a series of large chunks. This prevents each request for a byte of data resulting in a read from the underlying input stream, such as a file or network read. If the BufferedInputStream already has the data in the buffer, it can return the data directly from its memory cache. This is also useful for operations that require movement back and forth in a stream, such as a "push back" of an unneeded byte. Since this class will improve the efficiency of input stream operations, it should be used liberally.

Once the BufferedInputStream object is created, it is used as the constructor for a DataInputStream object:

```
DataInputStream dis =
             new DataInputStream(
               new BufferedInputStream(System.in));
```

This code means that the DataInputStream object's request for input is actually made to a BufferedInputStream object. This object in turn makes its requests for input to the System.in object (which is based on InputStream) when it needs more data.

The code can now use DataInputStream methods, such as `readLine()`, to hide the underlying request of data at a byte-by-byte level. The DataInputStream methods return the data formatted in a data type that the user needs. In this case, `readLine()` reads in a String of text delimited by a new Line (a carriage return/line feed, or EOF). The delimiter is not included in the stream.

The DataInputStream class supports over a dozen data type operations, as listed in Table 4.3. These include most of the basic data types supported from Java, ranging from a single byte to an integer to a floating point number to a full-text String in Unicode format. The DataInputStream class is an implementation of the DataInput stream interface, which defines the data type methods that need to be supported.

Table 4.3. Data-type reads supported by DataInputStream.

Method	*Description*
`read`	Reads data into byte array.
`readBoolean`	Reads a boolean.
`readByte`	Reads an 8-bit byte.
`readChar`	Reads a 16-bit char.
`readDouble`	Reads a 64-bit double number.
`readFloat`	Reads a 32-bit floating point number.
`readInt`	Reads a 32-bit integer.
`readLine`	Reads String terminated by newline or EOF.
`readLong`	Reads a 64-bit long.
`readShort`	Reads a 16-bit short.
`readUTF`	Reads a Unicode formatted String.
`readUnsignedByte`	Reads an unsigned byte.
`readUnsignedShort`	Reads an unsigned 16-bit short.

From the powerful chaining operation supported by FilterInputStream, it's easy to imagine interesting new possible classes. For example, a WordProcessStream could be written to read paragraphs and images into a word processing application.

Two other FilterInputStream classes are worth mentioning. The LineNumberInputStream class associates the data streams with line numbers. This means that the class supports such operations as `setLineNumber()` and `getLineNumber()`. The PushBackInputStream class is used for the kind of operations that parsers typically perform. Parsers need methods such as `unread()`, which pushes a character back into a stream. This kind of operation is needed when a token has been identified by the parser.

Other InputStream classes

Although the FilterInputStream classes are the most powerful part of the InputStream hierarchy, other classes are also useful. If applets read from a file, an instance of the FileInputStream class will probably be used. It includes the same operations as its superclass, InputStream.

Therefore, it can be used to pass data to FilterInputStream classes, as in the previous section's example. Listing 4.7 shows how to use chaining to read an ASCII file and send its contents to standard output. Instead of creating the FilterInputStream classes from the System.in InputStream object, it is built from a FileInputStream object tied to the filename provided in the method parameter; if the file cannot be opened because it does not, an IOException object will be thrown.

Listing 4.7. Reading a file to standard output.

```
void readFileToStandardOut(String filename) {
      System.out.println("***** BEGIN " + filename + " *****");
      try {
         // Open the file...
         DataInputStream dis = new DataInputStream(
          new BufferedInputStream(
             new FileInputStream(filename)) );
         // Read lines until EOF is reached...
         String s;
         while((s = dis.readLine()) != null)
            System.out.println(s);
         // Close the file when done...
         dis.close();
      }
      // Handle any exceptions caused by the process...
      catch (IOException e) {
         // Just print out the error...
         System.out.println(e.getMessage());
      }
      System.out.println("***** END " + filename + " *****");
   }
```

As this example further illustrates, the powerful technique of stream chaining makes it easy to abstract away from the low-level implementation of reading from a file. In fact, except for the innermost part of the constructor, with this code it really doesn't matter if you're working on a file, the standard input stream, or even from a network!

However, if it's necessary to work with streams at the level of bytes, the ByteArrayInputStream class could be used. This takes a large array of bytes and uses it as the basis for input stream requests. Therefore, this is the constructor for the class:

```
ByteArrayInputStream bis = new ByteArrayInputStream(byteArray)
```

The `reset()` method sets the current position back to the beginning of the stream buffer. The StringBufferInputStream class functions in a manner similar to ByteArrayInputStream, except it works on a StringBuffer. Like ByteArrayInputStream, however, the `read()` methods return a single byte or an array of bytes.

The PipedInputStream class works with the PipedOutputStream class to send a stream of data from one channel to another. This is well suited for thread processing, in which one thread is producing data (the output) to another thread that's consuming it (the input). Piped streams is a classic technique of interprocess communication. Chapter 8, "Adding Threads to Applets," will provide a concrete example of piped streams.

Finally, the SequenceInputStream class can be used to take a series of InputStreams and treat them as if they were one stream. This could be useful for operations such as concatenating files.

OutputStream Classes

The OutputStream class is an abstract class that marks the top of the hierarchy of classes used for streamed output. Its major operations are represented by `write()` methods, which can be used to write an integer, a byte, or an array of bytes to a stream. The other methods of OutputStream are the `close()` method, which is used to close a stream, and the `flush()` method, which writes the contents of a buffered cache to the stream—this applies only to derivatives of OutputStream that implement buffering.

Figure 4.8 lists the output classes that descend from OutputStream. In many cases, the classes mirror the input classes shown in Figure 4.7. The most noteworthy of these, not surprisingly, is the FilterOutputStream class, which, like its FilterInputStream counterpart, is used to chain streams together. This class will be used as the starting point for a tour through the OutputStream classes.

FIGURE 4.8.
OutputStream classes.

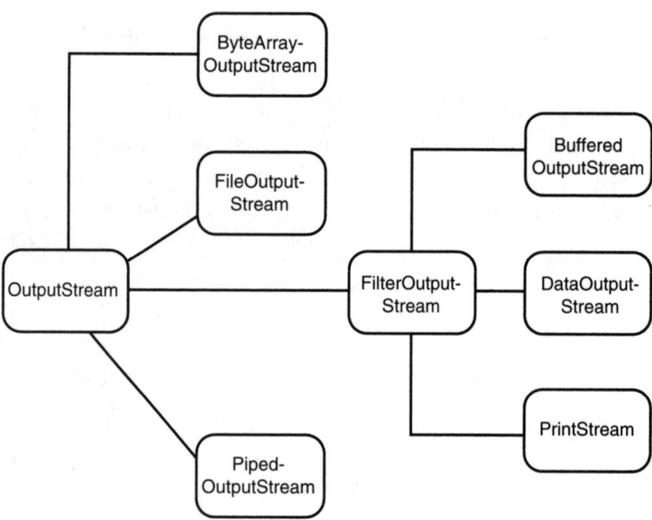

FilterOutputStream Classes and FileOutputStream

The FilterOutputStream class is used to chain streams together so that one stream can process data before passing it to the next stream in the chain. This is useful for cases in which the lowest level stream reads in data at a primitive level (such as bytes) and passes up to the interface layer, which manages streams in terms of Strings and other data types. This is well suited for operations such as writing to a file, as the following example illustrates.

Listing 4.8 shows a method that takes a string array and writes it to a file, which is formatted for ASCII text. As in the InputStream example of Listing 4.7, the key part of this method is the constructor. Its innermost statement consists of a constructor for a stream that writes to a file:

```
new FileOutputStream(filename)
```

Listing 4.8. Writing a string array to an ASCII file.

```
void writeStringsToFile(String s[],String filename) {
      try {
         // Create the output stream to a file...
         DataOutputStream out = new DataOutputStream(
          new BufferedOutputStream(
            new FileOutputStream(filename)) );
         // Write the strings out...
         for (int i = 0; i < s.length; ++i)
            out.writeBytes(s[i]);
         // Flush and close...
         out.flush();
         out.close();
      }
      // Handle any exceptions caused by the process...
      catch (IOException e) {
         // Just print out the error...
         System.out.println(e.getMessage());
      }
    }
```

The FileOutputStream opens a file with the designated filename. If the file previously exists, its contents will be lost. The FileOutputStream class has an alternate constructor that takes a File object. The File class was described in the section "Structure of the java.io Package." The created file can then be written to with the `write()` methods, which can take a single integer or a byte array.

In the example, the FileOutputStream is fed as input into the BufferedOutputStream. The use of this class is very useful for file write operations since it prevents disk writes from occurring every time the buffer is given some data. It only writes when the buffer's cache is full or when the `flush()` method is called.

Finally, the newly created BufferedOutputStream object becomes the source for the DataOutputStream object. Like the DataInputStream counterpart, the DataOutputStream works with general Java data types, such as bytes, integers, doubles, and Strings. Table 4.4 summarizes the write operations supported by DataOutputStream. These are fairly straightforward, except for the three methods used for writing out Strings. Recall that Java treats characters not as 8-bit ASCII bytes, but as 16-bit Unicode characters. This is important for creating international software. However, programmers often need to read and write data in its native form. The `writeBytes()` method takes a String and writes out each character in the 8-bit ASCII format. This is the method used in the example. The `writeChars()` method, on the other hand, writes data out in 16-bit Unicode characters. A file created this way will not look or behave like an ASCII file, so this method wasn't used in the example. The `writeUTF()` method writes a String out in a special Unicode format.

Table 4.4. Data-type writes supported by DataOutputStream.

Method	*Description*
`write(byte)`	Writes a byte.
`write(byte [],int, int)`	Writes a subarray of bytes.
`writeBoolean(boolean)`	Writes a boolean.
`writeByte(int)`	Writes an 8-bit byte.
`writeBytes(String)`	Writes a String out as 8-bit bytes. Use for writing out ASCII text.
`writeChar(int)`	Writes a 16-bit char.
`writeChars(String)`	Writes a String out as 16-bit Unicode characters.
`writeDouble(double)`	Writes a 64-bit double number.
`writeFloat(float)`	Writes a 32-bit floating point number.
`writeInt(int)`	Writes a 32-bit integer.
`writeLong(long)`	Writes a 64-bit long.
`writeShort(int)`	Writes a 16-bit short.
`writeUTF(String)`	Reads a Unicode formatted String.

The DataOutputStream class implements the DataOutput class. This defines the data-type write methods that need to be supported by the classes that implement data output streams.

At the end of the example, there are calls to `flush()` and `close()`. The `flush()` method forces the BufferedOutputStream object to send its cached contents to the FileOutputStream. This could also be called inside the `write` loop at appropriate intervals (such as when a prespecified number of bytes or Strings have been written). The `close()` method call closes in the FileOutputStream stream, and the file is now complete.

The other FilterOutputStream class is PrintStream. This is the class used to implement the standard output and error objects, System.out and System.err. Of course, its most noteworthy method is `println()`. This is actually an overloaded method that takes any of a variety of data types and writes it to the PrintStream (usually standard output) followed by a new line. The `println()` method is most widely used with String objects. This method is also noteworthy in that the stream is flushed every time it is called. The `print()` method functions similarly but with no newline appended. A `println()` or `flush()` method will cause output from `print()` to be written to the stream. Finally, a byte-based `write()` is also supported by PrintStream.

Other Output Classes

The PipedOutputStream class works with the PipedInputStream class to send a stream of data from one channel to another. Pipes are a classic technique of interprocess communication. You will find a concrete example of piped streams in Chapter 8.

The ByteArrayOutputStream is used for working with arrays of bytes. Its most interesting feature is that its internal array will grow as it receives data.

Other I/O Classes

Two other I/O classes need to be mentioned. The RandomAccessFile class implements both the DataInput and DataOutput interfaces. Consequently, it is the only stream class that supports both the read and write operations. This is good for more traditional programming in which files are read and updated interactively. The RandomAccessFile also supports file-positioning operations, such as `seek()`.

The StreamTokenizer stream can be used for tokenizing a stream. This is useful for the lexical analysis operations of a parser.

Tutorial

The spreadsheet applet from the previous chapter is enhanced in this tutorial to support dialog boxes and to introduce file storage to the spreadsheet data. Some new classes were written to create the dialog boxes, and classes from the previous section were modified to support new functioning.

For ease of reading, Figure 4.9 shows the spreadsheet applet again as it appears in a browser.

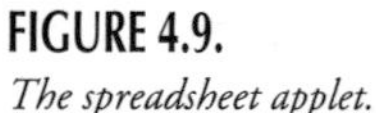

FIGURE 4.9.
The spreadsheet applet.

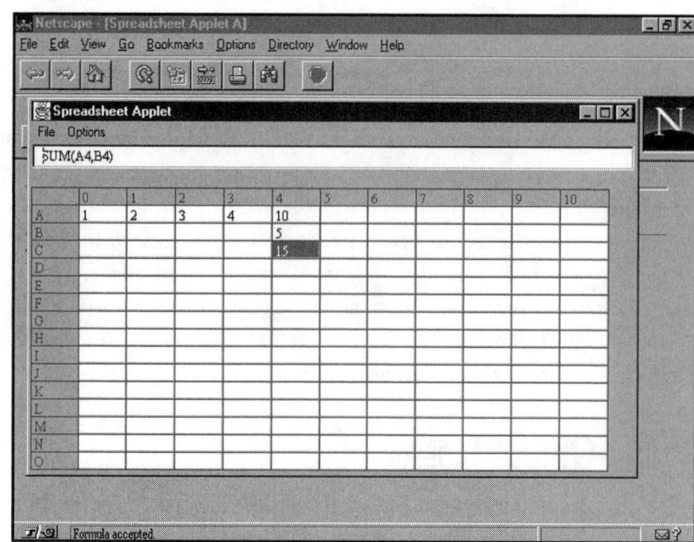

Class Organization

Table 4.5 enumerates the classes used in this chapter's version of the spreadsheet applet. Since many of these classes were created in the previous section, the new classes are delimited by having their name in bold. The classes that were modified have their names italicized.

Table 4.5. Spreadsheet classes.

Class	*Description*
Cell	Contains a String and evaluated value corresponding to a single cell.
CellContainer	Contains a matrix of Cells. The String in each Cell is evaluated according to whether it is a formula, a literal numeric value, or an empty cell. Can write or read its contents from a file.
FormulaParser	Used to parse out the individual string fragments that make up a single formula. Converts literal strings to their numeric values.
FormulaParserException	An Exception that is thrown if a formula is poorly constructed.
ArgValue	A FormulaParser helper class used to store information about an argument in a formula.
ChooseColorDialog	Dialog for choosing the color of a spreadsheet element.

Class	*Description*
colorDisplay	A canvas class that ChooseColorDialog uses to display how a spreadsheet cell would appear if certain colors were picked.
ColoredCheckbox	Draws a checkbox with its color set to a different color.
ColoredCheckboxGroup	Creates a group of colored checkboxes.
ChooseFontDialog	Dialog for choosing a font for the spreadsheet.
fontDisplay	A canvas class that ChooseFontDialog uses to display how a font looks.
SpreadsheetCell	Provides for the visual presentation of a single Cell.
SpreadsheetContainer	Manages the visual presentation of a matrix of SpreadsheetCells. Provides an interface for changing the value of a cell. Supports the display of a currently highlighted cell. Sets fonts and colors of SpreadsheetCells.
SpreadsheetFrame	Provides the main presentation of the spreadsheet by displaying the SpreadsheetContainer, managing mouse selections on that spreadsheet, reading a text field for changing cell values, and handling a menu for actions such as invoking dialog boxes.
SpreadsheetApplet	Responsible for creating, showing and hiding the SpreadsheetFrame that provides the visual display of this applet.

Adding the Color Dialog

The color dialog box lets you associate a color with various elements of a spreadsheet cell. You can set the foreground and background color of a cell in its normal state and also change the colors of the cell when it is highlighted. Figure 4.10 shows how the dialog appears in a browser.

How the Dialog Box Is Used

When the dialog box appears, the current settings of the spreadsheet cell colors are displayed. A list control in the top left shows which elements of the spreadsheet cell can be modified. These colors are normal foreground, normal background, highlighted foreground, and highlighted background. When you select a list item, the radio button for the corresponding color is highlighted. A text display underneath the list shows what the spreadsheet cell would look like with the given colors. The text display shows either the normal state (with both foreground and background colors) or the background state. If you select a new color with the radio button, the canvas object is updated to show what the new foreground and background combination would look like. The spreadsheet is updated with the color settings for the current list item when you select the Update button.

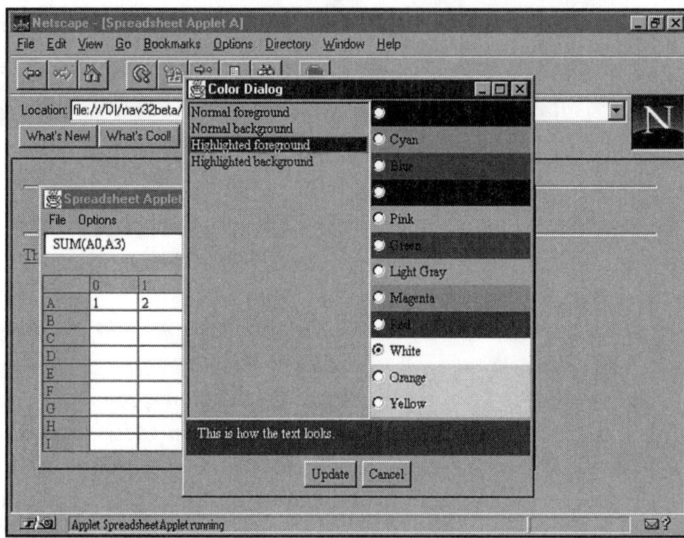

FIGURE 4.10.
The color dialog box.

The Construction of the Color Dialog Box

Four classes are used to construct the color dialog box. The ChooseColorDialog class is a subclass of Dialog and controls the main display and control of the dialog box. The colorDisplay class is a Canvas class derivative that draws text with colors corresponding to the selected foreground and background display. The ColoredCheckbox class draws a checkbox associated with a certain Color object; the background of the box is drawn according to that color. The ColoredCheckboxGroup class groups ColoredCheckbox items together so that they can function as part of a radio button group.

The discussion of the color dialog box begins with its underlying components. Listing 4.9 shows the code for the ColoredCheckbox class. Its most interesting feature is that it associates itself with a given Color object. It paints its background according to the Color and, through the `setIfColorMatches()` method, turns its checkbox on if the Color sent to it matches its internal color. The checkbox in this case is a radio button because the class is associated with a CheckboxGroup. Checkbox objects have radio buttons only if they are associated with a CheckboxGroup object; only one radio button in a checkbox group can be on at one time. If no checkbox group is specified for a checkbox object, then there are no restrictions on which boxes can be selected.

Listing 4.9. The ColoredCheckbox class.

```
// Class for creating a checkbox associated
// with a given color...
class ColoredCheckbox extends Checkbox {
   Color color;  // The color of this checkbox...
   // Constructor creates checkbox with specified color...
   public ColoredCheckbox(Color color, String label,
         CheckboxGroup grp, boolean set) {
         // Call the default constructor...
         super(label,grp,set);
         this.color = color;
         setBackground(color);
   }
   // Sets itself to true if it matches the color
   public void setIfColorMatches(Color match) {
      if (color == match)
         setState(true);
      else
         setState(false);
   }
   // Return the color matching this box...
   public Color getColor() {
      return color;
   }
}
```

The ColoredCheckboxGroup is used to contain ColoredCheckbox objects. Its constructor creates a preselected number of colored checkboxes to be associated with a Panel object. Here are the first few lines of the ColoredCheckboxGroup class declaration:

```
class ColoredCheckboxGroup extends CheckboxGroup {
   // Array to hold checkboxes...
   ColoredCheckbox c[] = new ColoredCheckbox[12];
   // Constructor. Create the checkboxes with
   // no default color chosen...
   public ColoredCheckboxGroup(Panel p) {
      // Call the default constructor...
      super();
      // Create the checkboxes and store in panel and reference array...
      c[0] = new ColoredCheckbox(Color.black,"Black",this,false);
      p.add(c[0]);
      c[1] = new ColoredCheckbox(Color.cyan,"Cyan",this,false);
      p.add(c[1]);
```

Strangely enough, ColoredCheckboxGroup is not a Container object. Consequently, the checkboxes need to be associated with a Panel to meet the needs at hand. Note the use of the Color constants in constructing the ColoredCheckbox objects. The reference array (variable c) is used in the other method of the class, `setMatchingColor()`, which is used to set the radio button of the ColoredCheckbox that matches a certain color:

```
public void setMatchingColor(Color match) {
      for (int i = 0; i < c.length; ++i)
         c[i].setIfColorMatches(match);
   }
```

Since ColoredCheckbox objects are self-identifying by color, this technique prevents a long and cumbersome walk through hard-coded color names to see which radio button should be turned on.

The colorDisplay class is a Canvas derivative that draws text (specified in the `displayText` String variable) with a specified foreground and background color. Listing 4.10 highlights some of the more interesting features of the class. The `paint()` method draws the canvas if a background and foreground color have been selected. It first starts getting the size of its drawing area through the `size()` method; this method is a standard part of subclasses of Component. It fills in the background color through the `setColor()` and `fillRect()` methods of the Graphics class. It then sets the color of the text to be displayed (the foreground). By getting the current FontMetrics, the canvas can figure out a good location for the text string; the `getHeight()` method returns the total height of the font. The `drawString()` method then draws the text at the specified location.

Listing 4.10. Portions of the colorDisplay class.

```
// The layout will call this to get the minimum size
   // of the object.  In this case, you want it to be at
   // least big enough to fit the display test...
   public Dimension minimumSize() {
      // Get the metrics of the current font...
      FontMetrics fm = getFontMetrics(getFont());
      return new Dimension(fm.stringWidth(displayText),
         2 * fm.getHeight());
   }

   // Paint the colors and text...
   public synchronized void paint(Graphics g) {
      if ((foreground == null) || (background == null))
         return;
      // Set background...
      Dimension dm = size();
      g.setColor(background);
      g.fillRect(0,0,dm.width,dm.height);
      // Draw the string
      g.setColor(foreground);
      // Set dimensions. Move just from left...
      FontMetrics fm = getFontMetrics(getFont());
      int x = fm.charWidth('W');
      // And center in height...
      int y = fm.getHeight();
      g.drawString(displayText,x,y);
   }
```

The `minimumSize()` method is used with layouts, which were discussed in the last chapter. When AWT is constructing the display of a group of components, it works with the layouts to decide what position and size a component should have. Sometimes, you might want a component to exercise some input into what its size will be. Two methods of the Component class can be invoked to do this. The `preferredSize()` method returns the Dimensions of the preferred size of the component. The `minimumSize()` method returns the smallest size in which the component should be made. In the case of the `colorDisplay()` class, it returns that the component should be wide enough to display the text String and twice as high as its current font. It does this by getting the FontMetrics of the current font and calling the `stringWidth()` and `getHeight()` methods respectively.

Finally, the dialog box is ready to be constructed. Figure 4.11 highlights the declarations and methods used to construct the color dialog box. The `createComponents()` method adds the components to the dialog box by using the complex `GridBagLayout()` class. The main thing that needs to be done here is to have most of the space taken up by the list control set to half the dialog box and the color checkboxes on the other half, as shown in Figure 4.10. The key reason for doing this is to set the GridBagConstraints `weighty` and `gridheight` variables to the appropriate values. By setting the former to `1.0`, this tells the layout that the associated components should be given preeminence in terms of the layout's height. When `weighty` is set to `0.0`, then the height of the corresponding components is given lower priority.

The `preferredSize()` method in Listing 4.11 returns the desired dimensions of the dialog box. It needs to be three times as wide as the longest string in the list component, and 24 times as high as the current font. This way everything should fit comfortably in the dialog box.

Listing 4.11. The construction of ChooseColorDialog.

```
// Dialog box for choosing display colors...
public class ChooseColorDialog extends Dialog {
   SpreadsheetFrame fr;    // What to update...
   ColoredCheckboxGroup colorGrp;  // To hold radio buttons of colors...
   SpreadsheetContainer s;
   List choiceList;  // List of color choices...
   colorDisplay d; // This is the text display...
   // Defines for listbox values...
   static int NORMAL_FORE = 0;
   static int NORMAL_BACK = 1;
   static int HILITE_FORE = 2;
   static int HILITE_BACK = 3;
   // Construct dialog to allow color to be chosen...
   public ChooseColorDialog(Frame parent,boolean modal) {
      // Create dialog with title
      super(parent,"Color Dialog",modal);
      fr = (SpreadsheetFrame)parent;
      // Create the dialog components...
      createComponents();
      pack();  // Compact...
      // Resize to fit everything...
      resize(preferredSize());
   }
```

continues

Listing 4.11. continued

```
// The layout will call this to get the preferred size
   // of the dialog.  Make it big enough for the listbox text
   // the checkboxes, canvas, and buttons...
   public Dimension preferredSize() {
      // Get the metrics of the current font...
      FontMetrics fm = getFontMetrics(getFont());
      int width = 3 * fm.stringWidth("Highlighted foreground");
      int height = 24 * fm.getHeight();
      return new Dimension(width,height);
   }

   // Create the main display panel...
   void createComponents() {
    // Use gridbag constraints...
    GridBagLayout g = new GridBagLayout();
    setLayout(g);
    GridBagConstraints gbc = new GridBagConstraints();
    // Set the constraints for the top objects...
    gbc.fill = GridBagConstraints.BOTH;
    gbc.weightx = 1.0;
    gbc.weighty = 1.0;
    gbc.gridheight = 10;

    // Add the listbox of choices...
    choiceList = new List();
    choiceList.addItem("Normal foreground");
    choiceList.addItem("Normal background");
    choiceList.addItem("Highlighted foreground");
    choiceList.addItem("Highlighted background");
    g.setConstraints(choiceList,gbc);
    add(choiceList);

    // Create the checkbox panel
    Panel checkboxPanel = new Panel();
    checkboxPanel.setLayout(new GridLayout(12,1));
    // Create the checkbox group and add radio buttons...
    colorGrp = new ColoredCheckboxGroup(checkboxPanel);
    colorGrp.setMatchingColor(Color.magenta);

    // Create checkbox panel to right...
gbc.gridwidth = GridBagConstraints.REMAINDER;
    g.setConstraints(checkboxPanel,gbc);
    add(checkboxPanel);

    // Display the color chosen...
    d = new colorDisplay("This is how the text looks.");

    // Add to grid bag...
    gbc.weighty = 0.0;
    gbc.weightx = 1.0;
    gbc.gridwidth = GridBagConstraints.REMAINDER;
    gbc.gridheight = 1;
    g.setConstraints(d,gbc);
    add(d);

    // Two buttons: "Update" and "Cancel"
```

```
    Panel p = new Panel();
    p.add(new Button("Update"));
    p.add(new Button("Cancel"));

    // Add to grid bag...
    gbc.gridwidth = GridBagConstraints.REMAINDER;
    g.setConstraints(p,gbc);
    add(p);
  }
```

Using the Dialog Box

Once the dialog box is displayed, its event loop is entered. Listing 4.12 details the `handleEvent()` method of the dialog box. This code has several subtleties worth noting. Most of the work is performed when an action occurs, as indicated by the `ACTION_EVENT` method. When a button is selected, the argument of the Event object is set to the name of the button. The `handleEvent()` method looks at this name to decide what to do. If the name is "Cancel," then the dialog box is removed from the screen with the `dispose()` method, and control returns to the calling frame. The Update button sets the spreadsheet colors according to what is currently highlighted. How this works will be discussed shortly.

Listing 4.12. The `handleEvent()` method of ChooseColorDialog.

```
// Wait for Cancel or OK buttons to be chosen...
public boolean handleEvent(Event e) {
    switch(e.id) {
       case Event.ACTION_EVENT:
         // Kill the dialog...
         if (e.arg.equals("Cancel")) {
            dispose();  // Remove Dialog...
            return true;
         }  // end if
         // Update colors on the spreadsheet...
         if (e.arg.equals("Update")) {
            setSpreadsheetColors();
            return true;
         }  // end if
         if (e.target instanceof Checkbox) {
            selectedRadioItem();
            return false;
         }
         return false;
       // User selected a listbox item...
       case Event.LIST_SELECT:
         // Set up caption colors and color choice highlight...
         if (e.target instanceof List) {
            selectedChoiceListItem();
            return false;
         }  // end list if
         return false;
```

continues

Listing 4.12. continued

```
        default:
          return false;
    } // end switch
}
```

If the target of the `ACTION_EVENT` is a Checkbox, then it means a radio button is selected, which calls the `selectedRadioItems()` method. This method sets the colorDisplay object's foreground or background color according to the radio button chosen and the current selection in the list.

If you click on a list item, a `LIST_SELECT` event is issued. In this case, this invokes the `selectedChoiceListItems()` method. It sets the colorDisplay object's settings according to the current list selection; this process needs to take into account both the foreground and background colors. The ColoredCheckboxGroup's `setMatchingColor()` method is called to set the radio button of the ColoredCheckbox object corresponding to the current list color.

See this book's accompanying CD-ROM for the full source code of the `selectedRadioItems()` and `selectedChoiceListItems()` methods.

Calling the Dialog Box

The SpreadsheetFrame object is responsible for bringing up the color dialog box. It declares a variable of the color dialog class as follows:

```
ChooseColorDialog colorDialog;  // Color Dialog...
```

In its constructor, the frame instantiates the color dialog box with the following:

```
colorDialog = new ChooseColorDialog(this, true);
```

This states that the frame is the parent of the dialog box and its appearance is modal. Recall that a modal dialog box does not allow input to other windows while it is being displayed.

A dialog box does not automatically appear when it is constructed; you do this with the `show()` method. The SpreadsheetFrame object is modified in this chapter's tutorial to add menu options for the new dialog boxes. Here is some of the code from the frame's `handleEvent()` method that results in the ChooseColorDialog object being displayed:

```
public boolean handleEvent(Event evt) {
 switch(evt.id) {
  case Event.ACTION_EVENT: {
   String menu_name = evt.arg.toString();
   if (evt.target instanceof MenuItem) {
    // Set colors...
    if(menu_name.equals("Colors..."))
      colorDialog.show();
    // … other menu choices…
```

The color dialog box overrides the `show()` method so it can do some setup before the dialog box appears:

```
public synchronized void show() {
      super.show(); // Call the default show method...
      // Get the spreadsheet container...
      s = fr.getSpreadsheetContainer();
      // Set the listbox default...
      choiceList.select(0);
      // Set up caption colors and color choice highlight...
      selectedChoiceListItem();
}
```

After calling the superclass show method, the dialog box gets a reference to the frame's SpreadsheetContainer object. It will need this to get and set the spreadsheet's colors. It then sets the list box selection to the first item. The last method called, `selectedChoiceListItem()`, sets the radio buttons and display canvas to values corresponding to the current list selection.

Setting the Spreadsheet Colors

The SpreadsheetContainer class needs to be modified slightly to support dynamically selecting colors. Fortunately, these changes are small since the SpreadsheetCell class, which represents the individual cells in the spreadsheet, was written to support colors in its first version presented in Chapter 3, "Building a Spreadsheet Applet."

Four `Color` variables are introduced to the SpreadsheetContainer class so that colors can be set dynamically:

```
Color normalForeColor = Color.black;
Color normalBackColor = Color.white;
Color highlightedForeColor = Color.white;
Color highlightedBackColor = Color.red;
```

Associated with the variable declarations are the default colors. These SpreadsheetCell colors have the background and foreground colors set, respectively, in code such as the following:

```
matrix[index].setFillColor(normalBackColor);
matrix[index].setTextColor(normalForeColor);
```

This code is from the SpreadsheetContainer constructor. The two `setFillColor()` and `setTextColor()` methods are also called when a cell is given the current highlight focus. In this case, the cell is given the highlight colors. Some code is repeated here from the SpreadsheetCell object's `paint()` method to illustrate how these colors are applied to the cell:

```
// Set up drawing rectangle...
g.setColor(Color.blue);
g.drawRect(x,y,width,height);
g.setColor(fillColor);
g.fillRect(x + 1,y + 1,width - 2,height - 2);
// Draw the string
g.setColor(textColor);
g.drawString(textPaint,x + 4,y + (height - 2));
```

The `fillColor` and `textColor` variables are set by the `setFillColor()` and `setTextColor()` methods, respectively.

Four accessor methods are added to the SpreadsheetContainer class for getting the normal and highlight Color variables. These are called by the `selectedChoiceListItem()` method of the ChooseColorDialog class to retrieve the colors to be displayed in the colorDisplay object.

When you click the Update button, the color dialog box's `setSpreadsheetColors()` is invoked to update the spreadsheet colors. This in turn calls the SpreadsheetContainer's `setNewColors()` method, which applies the four normal and highlight colors to each of the SpreadsheetCell objects that are not row or column headers. The container is then repainted, displaying the cells in their new colors.

Font Dialog Box

The discussion of the spreadsheet applet's font dialog box will not be as lengthy as the preceeding overview of the color dialog. In many ways, it is very similar, so a detailed explanation doesn't need to be repeated; refer to this book's CD-ROM for any details not covered in this overview.

Figure 4.11 shows the font dialog box. It is based on the ChooseFontDialog class, which displays its components in a two-column style similar to the color dialog box. The current font family, style, and size is shown in a Canvas display object of the fontDisplay class. This class is very similar to the colorDisplay class.

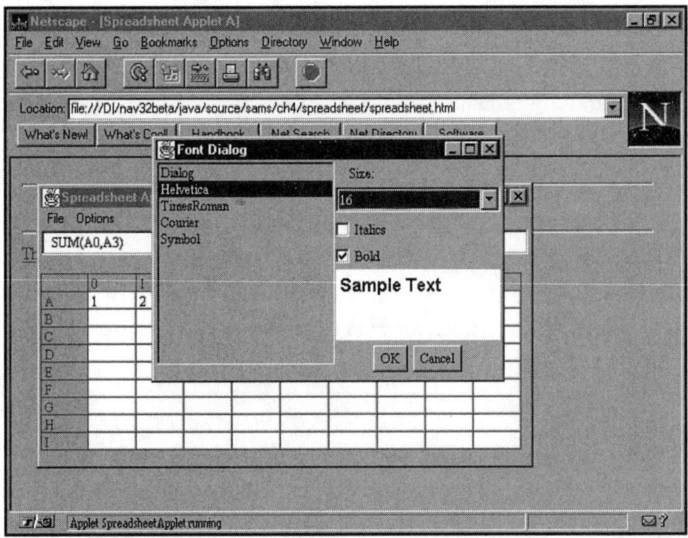

FIGURE 4.11.
The font dialog box.

The list component on the left side of the dialog box shows the fonts available on the current platform. It uses the AWT Toolkit class to get this information. Here is the code that creates the control and adds the font families:

```
// Add the listbox of choices...
   // Get the selection from the toolkit...
    choiceList = new List();
    String fontList[] = Toolkit.getDefaultToolkit().getFontList();
    for (int i = 0; i < fontList.length; ++i)
       choiceList.addItem(fontList[i]);
```

A choice box is added to the dialog box to enumerate font sizes that can be used. Two checkboxes are used to set the bold and italicized styles. If none of these are set, the font's style is set to plain.

Every time one of these controls is changed, the font display is updated with a new font. This happens in the `paintSample()` method, whose text is found in Listing 4.13. The variable `d` in the code represents the fontDisplay object.

Listing 4.13. The `paintSample()` method for displaying a font with selected attributes.

```
// Set the display canvas to show itself with
   // the currently selected font
   private synchronized void paintSample() {
      // Get the family to display
String fontName = choiceList.getSelectedItem();
      // Get its point size
      String fontSize = choiceSize.getSelectedItem();
      // Set its style
      int fontStyle = Font.PLAIN;
      if (checkItalics.getState())
            fontStyle += Font.ITALIC;
      if (checkBold.getState())
            fontStyle += Font.BOLD;
      // Create a font with the proper attributes...
      currentFont = new Font(fontName,fontStyle,
            Integer.parseInt(fontSize));
      // Set the new font on the canvas...
      d.setFont(currentFont);
      // Repaint it so the new font is displayed..
      d.repaint();
   }
```

When you select OK, the `setFont()` method of the SpreadsheetContainer class is called; the font created in the previous `paintSample()` code is passed as the parameter. This `setFont()` method overrides the default `setFont()` method, as seen in Listing 4.14. The method goes through every font in the container and sets it to the new font. The container is then repainted to show the new font. Figure 4.12 shows what the spreadsheet looks like when it is set with a Helvetica Bold 16-point font.

Listing 4.14. The SpreadsheetContainer `setFont()` method.

```
// Set the font for all the individual
  // spreadsheet cells...
   public synchronized void setFont(Font f) {
     super.setFont(f);
     int index;
     // Reload the font for each cell...
     for (int i = 0; i < numRows; ++i) {
      for (int j = 0; j < numColumns; ++j) {
       index = (i * (numColumns)) + j;
       // Set the colors...
       matrix[index].setFont(f);
      }  // end inner for...
     } // end outer for
     // Repaint to show new font...
     repaint();
   }
```

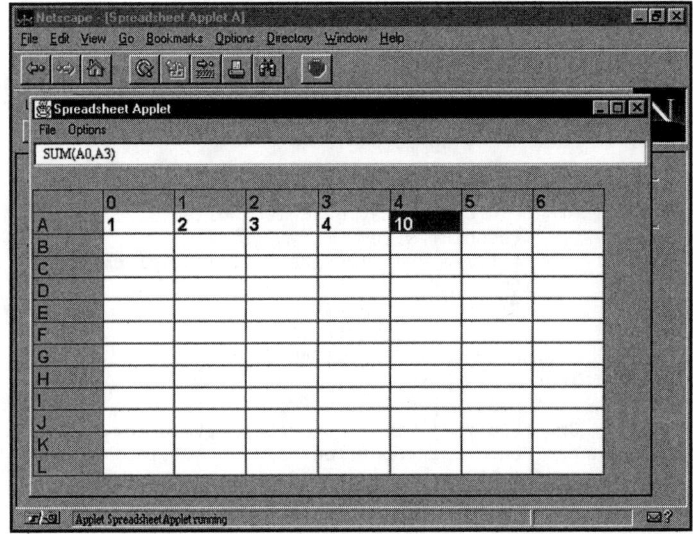

FIGURE 4.12.
The spreadsheet applet set to Helvetica Bold 16-point font.

The FileDialog Class

The FileDialog class is a subclass of Dialog used to provide a platform-independent approach to letting the user select what files are to be loaded or saved. Instances of the FileDialog class will usually mirror the underlying GUI conventions. For example, a FontDialog object for loading a file on the Windows 95 environment is shown in Figure 4.13. As you can see from the example, the dialog box follows the Windows 95 Open dialog box conventions.

FIGURE 4.13.
The load file FontDialog.

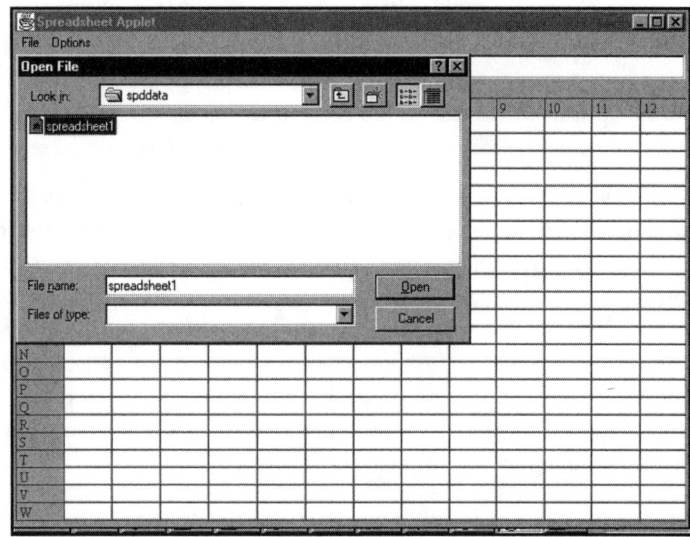

The FileDialog can be constructed to be in a mode to load a file or save a file. These dialog boxes look similar but perform slightly differently. For example, the Save version of the dialog box will notify the user that a file exists if a filename is given for a preexisting file. The SpreadsheetFrame class constructs a dialog box for both the load and save cases:

```
FileDialog openFileDialog;  // File Open Dialog...
FileDialog saveFileDialog;  // File Save Dialog...
openFileDialog = new FileDialog(this,"Open File",
               FileDialog.LOAD);
saveFileDialog = new FileDialog(this,"Save File",
               FileDialog.SAVE);
```

The integer flag in the last parameter of the constructors indicates the mode in which the dialog box should function.

When the dialog box is displayed with the `show()` method, it acts in a modal fashion so that input to the frame is blocked while it is up. After a choice has been made, the chosen file and directory can be retrieved with the `getFile()` and `getDirectory()` methods. The former will return a null value if the user had canceled out of the dialog box. If the names are valid, the SpreadsheetFrame class either saves or opens the specified spreadsheet file.

It is interesting to note that the FileDialog objects constructed here do not appear when the applet is run in Netscape Navigator. Recall that Netscape does not allow any file-based methods to be invoked from an applet. Consequently, there is no reason to even display FileDialog objects.

Saving a Spreadsheet File

The process of saving a spreadsheet file is surprisingly simple. What is saved is not the contents of the SpreadsheetContainer object, but the CellContainer object. This is because the former has some useless information like row/column headers, but the real data is in the CellContainer.

Listing 4.15 shows the CellContainer method for saving a file. This code was easy to generate because of the FilterOutputStream classes discussed in the overview of streams. The DataOutputStream variable `fs` is used to hide the complexities of the underlying BufferedOutputStream and FileOutputStream objects. The former is used as a cache so that every stream write does not result in a disk write. In short, BufferedOutputStream is used to improve performance. The inner part of the constructor, FileOutputStream, actually opens the file for writing. If there is a problem opening or writing the file at any point in the process, an IOException will be thrown. The `saveFile()` method simply rethrows the exception, forcing the calling method to catch the problem.

Listing 4.15. The CellContainer method for saving a file.

```
// Save the cell container to a file...
   public void saveFile(String filename) throws IOException {
      // Perform these file operations.  If anything goes wrong
      // an exception will be thrown.  This must be caught
      // by the calling method...
      // Open the file...
      DataOutputStream fs = new DataOutputStream(
            new BufferedOutputStream(
               new FileOutputStream(filename)));
      // Write out magic number
      fs.writeInt(magicNumber);
      // Write out row and column sizes
      fs.writeInt(numRows);
      fs.writeInt(numColumns);

      // Now go through each row and column and save...
      // Write out literal value followed by delimited...
      int numCells = numRows * numColumns;
      for (int i = 0; i < numCells; ++i) {
         fs.writeBytes(matrix[i].getCellString());
         fs.writeByte(delimiter);
      } // end for

      // Close the file. You're done!
      fs.close();
   }
```

The first thing written to the file is a magic integer number. This is used to indicate that the file is a spreadsheet file. The method for opening a spreadsheet file (discussed in the next section) will check for the existence of the magic number at the beginning of the file. If it isn't there, an exception will be thrown.

The `saveFile()` method writes out the magic number and the number of rows and columns out as integers, using the DataOutputStream `writeInt()` method. The method then loops through each element in the CellContainer matrix, writing out each cell's String contents followed by a delimiter (in this case, a tab). Recall that the CellContainer needs only the Cell's String value; the evaluated value can be generated on the fly by calling the CellContainer `reevaluate()` method.

The Cell string is written out through the `writeBytes()` method. Why not use a `writeString()` method? This does not exist because Java is a Unicode-based system. This means that 8-bit ASCII character strings need to be treated differently than 16-bit Unicode values. The `writeBytes()` method is used here so that ASCII data can be written out.

Opening a Spreadsheet File

Once a spreadsheet's contents have been saved to a file, it can be reopened through the CellContainer's `readFile()` method. This is detailed in Listing 4.16. Although it's similar to the `saveFile()` method in the previous section, it differs in some important ways. A major difference is that the `readFile()` method generates the Cell matrix of the CellContainer because `readFile()` is called from a new CellContainer constructor, which takes a filename as its parameter. This constructor does little more than call `readFile()`, which becomes responsible for setting up the Cell matrix.

Listing 4.16. The CellContainer method for reading in a file.

```
// Read in a file and create a new matrix to
   // accommodate the data...
   public void readFile(String filename) throws IOException {
      // Set everything to empty...
      numRows = 0;
      numColumns = 0;
      int magic;
      byte b;
      DataInputStream fs;
      try {
         // Open the file...
         fs = new DataInputStream(new BufferedInputStream(
            new FileInputStream(filename)) );
      }
      // Can't open file, quit out...
      catch (IOException e) {
         throw e;
      }
      // Now try to load the data...
      try {
           // Check the magic number
           magic  = fs.readInt();
           if (magic != magicNumber)
               throw (new IOException("Invalid magic number"));
           // Get the rows and columns...
```

continues

Listing 4.16. continued

```
            numRows = fs.readInt();
            numColumns = fs.readInt();
            if ((numRows <= 0) || (numColumns <=0) ||
             (numRows > maxRows) || (numColumns > maxColumns) )
                throw (new IOException("Invalid row/col settings"));
            int numCells = numRows * numColumns;
            // Allocate matrix...
            matrix = new Cell[numCells];
            // Now load the individual cells...
            for (int i = 0; i < numCells; ++i) {
                // Load the string up until delimited...
                StringBuffer s = new StringBuffer();
                while ((b = fs.readByte()) != delimiter)
                      s.append((char)b);
                // Add it to new Cell...
                matrix[i] = new Cell();
                matrix[i].setCellString(s);
            } // end for
            // Success! Close the file and leave...
            fs.close();
        }
        // If exception, then close file
        // and reset everything...
        catch (IOException e) {
           numRows = 0;
           numColumns = 0;
           fs.close();
           throw e;
        }
    }
```

Of course, the other difference between `saveFile()` and `readFile()` is that the latter works with an InputStream. The DataInputStream object `fs` builds on BufferedInputStream and FileInputStream objects, the latter of which actually opens the file for reading. The code uses `readInt()` to check the first few bytes of the file to make sure the magic number is present. If it isn't, an exception is thrown. The `readFile()` method throws an IOException if the magic number fails, the file is not found, or there is a problem with the read. The constructor does not catch thrown IOException objects, so it's up to the calling object to catch IOException objects.

The individual Cell Strings are created through multiple calls to `readByte()`. This is used with the String `append()` method to add byte characters to a new String until the delimiter is found. When this happens, a new Cell is created with the String and is assigned to the CellContainer matrix.

The SpreadsheetFrame object calls the CellContainer constructor that loads a file when the load FileDialog object is used. It takes the newly created CellContainer and sets it to the SpreadsheetContainer with the `newCellContainer()` method discussed in the previous chapter. This method uses the loaded CellContainer object to generate new SpreadsheetCell objects. It then repaints itself, displaying the new spreadsheet contents.

Summary

This chapter's tutorial provides several examples of how to use Dialogs. In doing so, it also illustrates more principles for using the Graphics object to paint colors and fonts, working with layouts to create more complex displays, and learning the subtleties of event handling. It also gives you an overview of Java streams with examples of how to read and write to files. This latter capability will be restricted depending on the browser environment (or lack thereof) in which a Java applet is being executed.

5

Adding Graphs and Scrollbars to the Spreadsheet

In the previous two chapters, you have developed a spreadsheet applet that supports general spreadsheet functionality, dialog boxes for setting fonts and colors, and saving and opening files. Along the way, many aspects of the AWT package have been discussed, from basic components to layouts to methods of the Graphics class to the AWT Toolkit.

With all these tools at hand, a few last touches can now be added to the applet. Scrollbars are added to the spreadsheet, as is support for marking cells. The latter will be used to generate the final feature of the spreadsheet applet, the runtime generation of graphs.

Since this chapter builds on the AWT tools explored in the earlier chapters, it will go straight into the tutorial. Any new AWT features that aren't covered in this exposition will be explained as part of the tutorial.

Tutorial

In this tutorial, you'll enhance the spreadsheet applet from the previous chapter to support scrollbars, cell marking, and dynamic graphs. Some new classes have been written to create the graphs and the supporting dialogs, and some classes from the previous section have been modified to support new functions.

Class Organization

Table 5.1 lists the classes used in this chapter's version of the spreadsheet applet. Since many of these classes were created in the previous chapter, the new classes have their names in boldface type; the classes that were modified have their names italicized.

Table 5.1. Spreadsheet classes.

Class	*Description*
Cell	Contains a String and evaluated value corresponding to a single cell.
CellContainer	Contains a matrix of Cells. The String in each Cell is evaluated according to whether it is a formula, a literal numeric value, or an empty cell. Can write or read its contents from a file.
FormulaParser	Used to parse out the individual string fragments that make up a single formula. Converts literal strings to their numeric values.
FormulaParserException	An Exception that is thrown if a formula is poorly constructed.
ArgValue	A FormulaParser helper class used to store information about an argument in a formula.

Class	*Description*
ChooseColorDialog	Dialog box for selecting the color of a spreadsheet element.
colorDisplay	A canvas class that ChooseColorDialog uses to display what a spreadsheet cell would look like if certain colors were picked.
ColoredCheckbox	Draws a checkbox with its colors set to a different color.
ColoredCheckboxGroup	Creates a group of colored checkboxes.
ChooseFontDialog	Dialog box for selecting a font for the spreadsheet.
fontDisplay	A canvas class that ChooseFontDialog uses to display what a font looks like.
GraphCanvas	A canvas class that actually paints a graph.
GraphData	An accessor class for holding data needed for drawing graphs.
GraphDialog	Dialog box that brings up the GraphCanvas that displays the requested graph.
SpreadsheetCell	Provides for the visual presentation of a single Cell.
SpreadsheetContainer	Manages the visual presentation of a matrix of SpreadsheetCells. Provides an interface for changing the value of a cell. Supports the display of a currently highlighted cell. Sets fonts and colors of SpreadsheetCells.
SpreadsheetFrame	Provides the main presentation of the spreadsheet by displaying the SpreadsheetContainer, managing mouse selections on that spreadsheet, reading a text field for changing cell values, and handling a menu for actions such as invoking dialog boxes.
SpreadsheetApplet	Responsible for creating, showing, and hiding the SpreadsheetFrame that provides this applet's visual display.

Adding Scrollbars

As the spreadsheet applet stood at the end of Chapter 4, "Enhancing the Spreadsheet Applet," you couldn't look at any of the cells in the spreadsheet that didn't fit onscreen. This severely reduced the applet's usefulness, but this problem can be fixed by adding scrollbars. With horizontal and vertical scrollbars, you can scroll to the cell you want to view; therefore, the spreadsheet's full contents can be used.

Adding the Scrollbar Class

The AWT Scrollbar class is used to create vertical or horizontal scrollbars. A box at the center of the scrollbar represents the scrollbar's current position; this box has been called the *thumbtack*, the *thumb*, or *elevator*, but in this discussion "thumbtack" will be used. The thumbtack can be moved in line increments (when the scrollbar arrows are pressed) or in page increments (when the scrollbar area between the arrows is clicked). The thumbtack can also be dragged to a specific position.

A Scrollbar object can be created through a variety of constructors. The most useful constructor is one that takes five integer parameters. A good way to illustrate this constructor is to look at how the vertical and horizontal scrollbars are declared and created in the SpreadsheetFrame:

```
Scrollbar vScroll; // The vertical scrollbar
Scrollbar hScroll;  // The horizontal scrollbar
vScroll = new Scrollbar(Scrollbar.VERTICAL,1,1,1,numRows);
hScroll = new Scrollbar(Scrollbar.HORIZONTAL,1,1,1,numCols);
```

The first parameter refers to the scrollbar's orientation, which can be defined by using either the `Scrollbar.HORIZONTAL` or `Scrollbar.VERTICAL` constant. The former is a scrollbar set horizontally across the native container; the latter is displayed up the side. Figure 5.1 shows what the spreadsheet applet looks like after the scrollbars are added. The orientation of the scrollbar can be retrieved through the `getOrientation()` method.

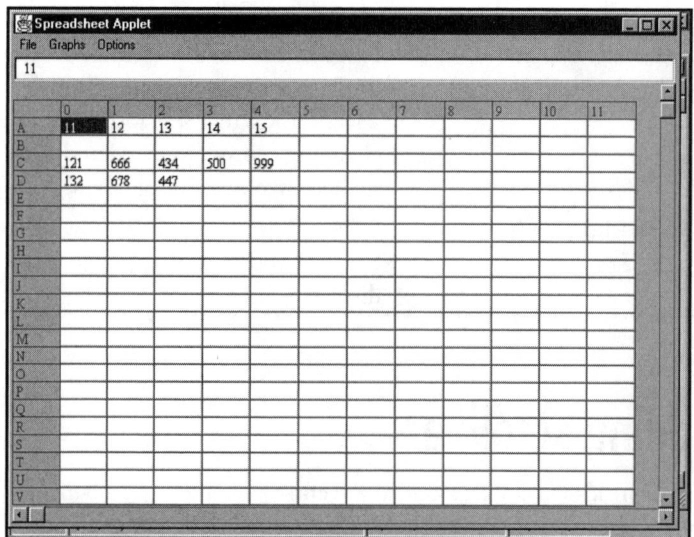

FIGURE 5.1.
The spreadsheet applet with scrollbars.

The next parameter specifies the initial value of the scrollbar. This must be between the minimum and maximum scrollbar values, specified in the last two parameters, respectively. In the case of the spreadsheet applet, the maximum value is the number of rows or columns supported by the spreadsheet. These are set at `26` and `40` in the SpreadsheetApplet class. The scrollbar's initial value of `1` indicates that the display begins at the top row and leftmost column of the spreadsheet.

The fourth parameter indicates the range of values that should be traversed when you click on the paging portion of the scrollbar. This corresponds to the visible portion of the scrollbar area. For example, if 10 rows are currently displayed on the screen, then the range is `10`. This range is also known as the *page increment* and can be set by the `setPageIncrement()` method. Since it is usually possible to resize a window that has scrollbars, you will need to modify the page increment on-the-fly. This can involve somewhat lengthy code, so it isn't used in the spreadsheet applet. There also seems to be a problem with the `setPageIncrement()` method in the version of AWT available at this time. Consequently, only the line increment and thumbtack drag aspects of scrollbars are set up for the spreadsheet applet.

Recall that the SpreadsheetFrame class uses GridBagLayout as its layout mechanism. How the scrollbars are added to the frame display provides another interesting example of using the complex GridBagLayout class. See this book's CD-ROM to find out how the scrollbars are added to the frame's GridBagLayout instance; this is defined in the file SpreadsheetApplet.java.

Handling Scrollbar Events

The next step in creating and using scrollbars is to catch events initiated by scrollbar actions. Five constants in the Event class are allocated for handling scrollbar events. These are listed in Table 5.2. The following code shows how the SpreadsheetFrame class traps these events:

```
public boolean handleEvent(Event evt) {
 switch(evt.id) {
case Event.SCROLL_LINE_UP:
         case Event.SCROLL_ABSOLUTE:
         case Event.SCROLL_LINE_DOWN:
         case Event.SCROLL_PAGE_UP:
         case Event.SCROLL_PAGE_DOWN:
           if (evt.target instanceof Scrollbar) {
               scrollbarAction((Scrollbar)evt.target);
            }  // end if
            return true;
```

Table 5.2. Scrollbar events.

Event	*Description*
`EVENT.SCROLL_LINE_UP`	User hit the line-up arrow.
`EVENT.SCROLL_LINE_DOWN`	User hit the line-down arrow.
`EVENT.SCROLL_PAGE_UP`	User hit the page-up arrow.
`EVENT.SCROLL_PAGE_DOWN`	User hit the page-down arrow.
`EVENT.SCROLL_ABSOLUTE`	User moved the thumbtack.

The event-handling code calls the `scrollbarAction()` method, which goes as follows:

```
// Handle scroll bar actions...
   void scrollbarAction(Scrollbar sb) {
      if (sb.getOrientation() == Scrollbar.VERTICAL)
         s.setNewTop(sb.getValue());
      else
         s.setNewLeft(sb.getValue());
   }
```

It checks to see whether a horizontal or vertical scrollbar has been selected by using the `getOrientation()` method of the target and comparing it to the Scrollbar constant value. The code then gets the current location of the thumbtack with the `getValue()` method. This returns a value between the minimum and maximum. If it is the minimum value, then the thumbtack is at the top or leftmost position of the scrollbar. The maximum value represents the bottom or rightmost position. This value is set to the appropriate method of the SpreadsheetContainer class.

This class is modified to support scrollbars by introducing two variables that indicate the top row and leftmost column to be displayed. When the scrollbar scrolls upward or downward, the display's top row is adjusted in the corresponding direction. Likewise, moving the scrollbar left or right adjusts the column of the spreadsheet drawn on the display's leftmost portion. The introduction of the `topCell` and `leftCell` integer variables are used to track where the row and column display begins.

Listing 5.1 provides the two SpreadsheetContainer methods called by the `scrollbarAction()` method shown above. These set the top row or leftmost column to be displayed. The SpreadsheetContainer then repaints itself, displaying the new selections. The following code shows how this display works.

Listing 5.1. Setting the top row and leftmost column of the SpreadsheetContainer object.

```
// Handle scrolling by setting new top...
   public void setNewTop(int newTop) {
      // Set top, taking into account headings and constraints...
      if (newTop < numRows)
         topCell = newTop;
```

```
      else
         topCell = numRows - 1;
      resetMarking();
      repaint();
   }

   // Set new leftmost column...
   public void  setNewLeft(int newLeft) {
      // Set new left, taking into account headings and constraints...
      if (newLeft < numColumns)
         leftCell = newLeft;
      else
         leftCell = numColumns - 1;
      resetMarking();
      repaint();
   }
```

Inside the SpreadsheetContainer Paint Methods

Listing 5.2 shows the code involved in painting the SpreadsheetContainer. These routines paint the row and column headers on the sides, then fill up the interior with the evaluated values of the SpreadsheetCell objects that fit in the painted region. This painting has as its origin the `topCell` variable as the top row to display and the `leftCell` variable as the first column of SpreadsheetCell objects to be displayed.

Listing 5.2. SpreadsheetContainer paint methods.

```
// Update message sent when repainting is needed...
   // Prevent paint from getting cleared out...
   public void update(Graphics g) {
      paint(g);
   }

// Draw the displayable spreadsheet contents...
public synchronized void paint (Graphics g) {
 // Go through the calculations of the paint while painting...
 calculatePaint(g,true,0,0);
}

// This goes through the motions of calculating what is on the
// screen and either calculates coordinates or paints...
// If it is not paint, returns cell that fits in hit region...
SpreadsheetCell calculatePaint(Graphics g,boolean bPaint,int xHit,int yHit) {
 // Get the current size of the display area...
 Dimension dm = size();
 Rectangle r = null;  //   The clipping rectangle...
 Rectangle cellRect = null; // The cell clipping rectangle...
 // Calculate the cell width and height
 // Cell should be wide enough to show 8 digits...
 if (bPaint == true) {
  cellWidth = g.getFontMetrics().stringWidth("12345.67");
```

continues

Listing 5.2. continued

```
 cellHeight = g.getFontMetrics().getHeight();
 r = g.getClipRect();
} // end if
// Figure out how many rows and cols can be displayed
int nCol = Math.min(numColumns,dm.width / cellWidth);
int nRow = Math.min((numRows + 1),dm.height / cellHeight);

// Draw the cells...
int index,i,x,j,y,currentRow,currentCol;
—nRow;
// Go across the rows...
// Show the headers and adjust for top and left cell...
for (currentRow = i = 0; i < nRow; ++i) {
 y = cellHeight + (i * cellHeight);
 // Go across the columns...
 for (currentCol = j = 0; j < nCol; ++j) {
  index = (currentRow * numColumns) + currentCol;
  x = (j * cellWidth);
  // Paint if told to...
  if (bPaint == true) {
              // See if it is in the intersection of the
              // clipping rectangle
              cellRect = new Rectangle(x,y,cellWidth,cellHeight);
              if (r.intersects(cellRect)) {
                // Paint if you are at a valid row...
                if ((currentRow < numRows) && (currentCol < numColumns)) {
                 matrix[index].paint(g,x,y,
                  cellWidth,cellHeight);
                } // end inner if
                else {  // Otherwise, fill it in with grey...
                  emptyCell.paint(g,x,y,cellWidth,cellHeight);
                } // end else
              } // end if
 } // end if
 else { // Otherwise, see if cell fits for highlight calculations…
  if ((currentRow < numRows) && (currentCol < numColumns)) {
    // See if it fits in the column...
    if ((xHit >= x) && (xHit < (x + cellWidth))) {
         // See if it fits in the row...
         if ((yHit >= y) && (yHit < (y + cellHeight))) {
                     paintIndex = index;
                     paintX = x;
                     paintY = y;
                     return matrix[index];
         } // end if
    } // end if
  } // end inner if
 } // end else
 // Adjust column display of cells
 if (j == 0)
       currentCol = leftCell;
 else
       ++currentCol;
}  // end column for
// Now start data cells at appropriate top...
if (i == 0)
```

```
         currentRow = topCell;
    else
         ++currentRow;
    } // end row for
    return null;  // Only used if paint is false...
}
```

The painting begins with the `update()` method. Recall that the earlier versions of the spreadsheet applet have a brief flicker of white when the spreadsheet area is repainted. This is because the `update()` method, by default, clears out the area before the `paint()` area is called; this clearing results in the flicker, which can be solved by overriding the `update()` method. In this case, it calls the `paint()` method directly. This method, in turn, calls the `calculatePaint()` method.

The `calculatePaint()` method is at the heart of the SpreadsheetContainer class. It is not only used for painting, but also is called by other routines to calculate where a cell is located. The second parameter of `calculatePaint()` indicates whether the method should repaint the region or simply calculate a value. The first part of the method calculates how many rows and columns of SpreadsheetCells can be displayed in the current canvas area. The `size()` method returns the area's size, and the `getFontMetrics()` methods are used to calculate the cell dimensions. Note that the dimensions will change when the font of the spreadsheet is resized, as discussed in the previous chapter's section on fonts.

The next step is to loop through all the rows and columns to be displayed. The `currentRow` and `currentCol` variables indicate which SpreadsheetCell is to be painted. These values are initially set to `0` so that the row and column headers are displayed. At the bottom of the `for` loops, these are adjusted to the top cell or leftmost column. In the ensuing iterations, the variables are simply incremented to get the new row or column.

If the mode of the `calculatePaint()` method is true, then the cells are to be painted. In this case, the code checks to see whether the item falls in the clipping rectangle, retrieved by the `getClipRect()` method. This actually represents the area to be painted. The clipping rectangle could be the whole screen or a single cell. The code that sets a highlighted cell or marks an area (to be discussed) only forces the area affected to be repainted. If it does fall in the region, the individual SpreadsheetCell is painted at the current coordinates. Recall that the cell has colors and a font associated with it. Highlighting or marking a cell is really nothing more than changing a SpreadsheetCell object's internal color variables and forcing it to be repainted. See the Chapter 3, "Building a Spreadsheet Applet," tutorial for how the SpreadsheetCell class works.

Painting affects only those objects that fall in the clipping rectangle. The `intersects()` method is used to see whether two Rectangle objects overlap. By painting only the cells that intersect the clipping region, the code saves some unnecessary processing.

If the method is not in painting mode, then the processing is used to check which cell an x-y coordinate belongs to. This is useful when the user clicks on a cell to be highlighted and when marking occurs.

By using a central routine for determining the locations of SpreadsheetCells, such activities as painting, scrolling, marking, and highlighting become relatively easy. If something goes wrong, it probably could be traced back to the `calculatePaint()` method.

Marking Cells

It is useful to mark cells to indicate that they are subject to some upcoming operation, such as cutting or copying, or, in this case, producing a graph. Marking is performed in this applet by clicking on a valid cell, holding the mouse key down, and dragging in a southeasterly direction. When the mouse is released, marking is complete. Figure 5.2 shows what a spreadsheet with some cells marked looks like.

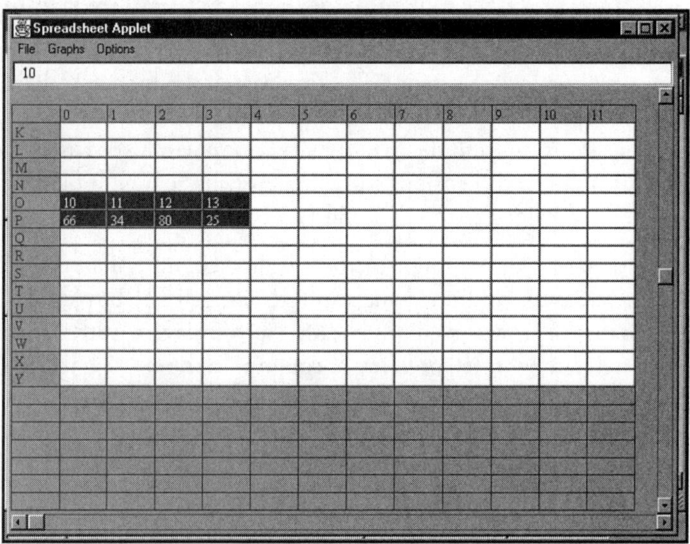

FIGURE 5.2.
A spreadsheet with cells marked.

Marking cells is actually a simple extension of the techniques that have been developed through the last three chapters. There are three key aspects to marking: tracking mouse movements, keeping track of the cells selected, and changing the color of the marked cells.

To track mouse movements, the SpreadsheetContainer `handleEvent()` method is modified to manage the mouse actions. The modified code is detailed in Listing 5.3.

Listing 5.3. SpreadsheetContainer event handler.

```
public boolean handleEvent(Event evt) {
 switch(evt.id) {
  // Mouse clicks. See whether you should highlight
  // cell on spreadsheet...
  case Event.MOUSE_DOWN:
```

```
      setMouseHighlight(evt.x,evt.y);
      // Handle cell marking...
      toggleMarking(evt.x,evt.y);
      return false;
   case Event.MOUSE_DRAG:
    // Select cells if marking...
    dragMarking(evt.x,evt.y);
    return false;
   case Event.MOUSE_UP:
    // If marking, then you are done!
    stopMarking(evt.x,evt.y);
    return false;
   }
   default:
    return false;
   }
  }
```

The marking code is too long and involved to list here; refer to the CD-ROM for the complete code. However, the general approach and highlights can be presented.

When you click the mouse over a valid cell (not a row or column header), the cell becomes the current focus and is highlighted. This is done through the `setMouseHighlight()` method, which calls `calculatePaint()` to find the reference of the selected SpreadsheetCell. After the cell is highlighted, the `toggleMarking()` method is called to either begin marking or to reset the marking if there were cells selected at the time of the mouse click. The `startMarking()` method begins tracking the mouse, and `resetMarking()` resets the marking state. SpreadsheetCell objects are set to their default colors through the `setNewColors()` method, which is used to set the normal and highlighted values of the spreadsheet. This method is called by the color dialog discussed in the previous chapter, and is called here with the current normal and highlighted colors as a simple way of resetting colors.

As the mouse is being dragged (which means the mouse key is still down), `MOUSE_DRAG` events are issued. If marking is on, the `dragMarking()` method checks to see whether the mouse has left the current cell; if it has, then new cells are marked. The `paintMarked()` method looks at the first cell marked and the last cell marked and figures out the rectangular area to be painted. It then sets the colors of each of the cells that are marked. The method then forces a limited repaint of the SpreadsheetContainer so that painting occurs quickly. The following code from `paintMarked()` takes the top-left and bottom-right areas that are marked and forces them to be repainted:

```
repaint(startX,startY,endX-startX,endY-startY);
```

When the paint message is processed, the marked cells are drawn in their new color. Cells outside the clipping rectangle issued by the `repaint()` method are not drawn.

When the mouse is released, the `stopMarking()` method is called, and the marking is finished. The marked areas can then be used for further operations.

Drawing Graphs

The last feature of the spreadsheet applet to be developed is drawing graphs from the marked cells. Most of the work is done in the `graphCanvas()` class. However, the graph is displayed inside a dialog object based on the GraphDialog class.

Two spreadsheet applets can produce two types of graphs: a line graph and a bar chart. The latter is shown in Figure 5.3. They are invoked by new menu items off the SpreadsheetFrame object. The menu items result in a call to the SpreadsheetFrame method `launchGraphicsDialog()`, which gets the currently marked data and then displays the graphics dialog box (which was instantiated in the frame's constructor). If nothing is marked, an error message in the status bar indicates that nothing was drawn.

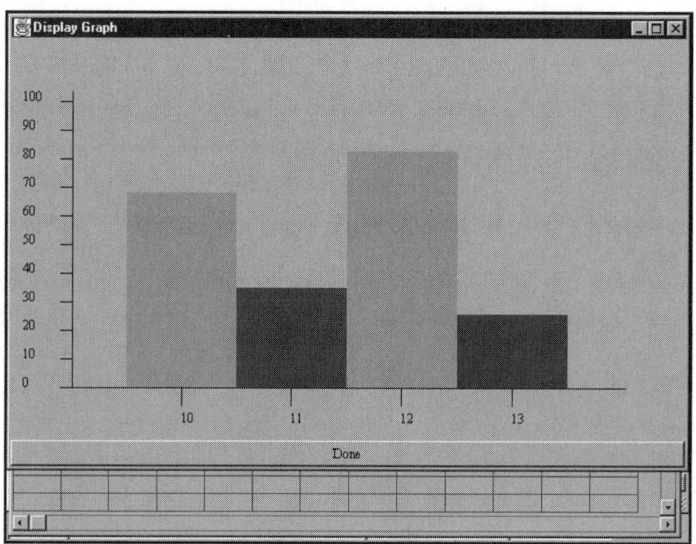

FIGURE 5.3.
Spreadsheet applet bar chart.

The GraphData class is an accessor class used to store the data to be displayed. It contains an array of double values representing the data to be plotted and an array of Strings used as the column labels. These arrays are prepared in the SpreadsheetContainer method `getGraphData()`, which is called by the frame's `launchGraphicsDialog()` method just discussed. The `getGraphData()` checks to see whether something is marked; if not, an IllegalArgumentException object is thrown. Otherwise, it stores the marked data in the GraphData object by moving across the columns. The bottom row marked is used to generate the data to be plotted and is placed in the double array. The top row is used to represent the column String headers. If only one row is marked, the cell headers (A1, A2, and so forth) are used as the column headers. The middle rows that are marked are ignored. As a further exercise, you can modify the graph-plotting algorithms to support multiple rows of data.

Once the graph data is collected, the GraphDialog is displayed. The dialog box is very simple, consisting of only two components: the GraphCanvas object for drawing the graph and a button for shutting down the dialog box. The only interesting code in the dialog box involves resizing the dialog box to take up most of the screen.

```
// Get the screen dimensions...
Dimension screen = Toolkit.getDefaultToolkit().getScreenSize();
// Get the font and use to calculate some margins...
FontMetrics fm = Toolkit.getDefaultToolkit().getFontMetrics(getFont());
resize(screen.width,screen.height - (4 * fm.getHeight()) );
```

This code uses the AWT Toolkit to get the screen size and the current font. The dialog box then resizes itself to take up the screen's full width and most of its height.

When the dialog box is shown, it first calls the GraphCanvas `prepareNewGraph()` method, which takes the GraphData and prepares it for presentation. When the dialog box appears and a paint event is issued, the GraphCanvas object draws the graph.

Listing 5.4 gives the full code for the GraphCanvas class. It uses two constants to indicate the two graph modes it supports: line or bar graph. When the canvas is constructed, it creates an array of six Color objects. This array is used to randomly generate colors for each bar chart or line so that they are more easily distinguished. When the `prepareNewGraph()` method is called, which must happen before painting occurs, the maximum value is calculated and stored in the `maxValue` variable. This is an important figure since it represents the range of values the data is plotted against. The maximum value is not the highest value in the data area, but actually is the highest value rounded up to the nearest power of 10. Therefore, if the top value is `66`, the maximum value will be set to `100`. Doing this makes it easy to divide the range of data values into intervals of one-tenth the maximum. The data in Figure 5.3 shows the plotting of values when the highest data value is `66` and the range is set from `0` to `100`.

Listing 5.4. The GraphCanvas class.

```
// Not a public class.  Imports are in GraphDialog class
// This paints a graph on a canvas...
class GraphCanvas extends Canvas {
    // Types of graphs...
   static final int LINE_GRAPH = 0;
   static final int BAR_GRAPH = 1;
   int graphMode;
   Color randomColors[];
   // This is the data for the display..
   GraphData gd;
   // Maximum scale of graph...
   int maxValue;

   // Constructor just inits data...
   public GraphCanvas() {
      gd = null;
      // Store the random colors...
      randomColors = new Color[6];
```

continues

Listing 5.4. continued

```
      randomColors[0] = Color.yellow;
      randomColors[1] = Color.red;
      randomColors[2] = Color.green;
      randomColors[3] = Color.magenta;
      randomColors[4] = Color.cyan;
      randomColors[5] = Color.blue;
   }
   // Set up graphics display...
   void prepareNewGraph(GraphData gphData,int graphMode) {
      // Store the data and string values...
      gd = gphData;
      this.graphMode = graphMode;
      // First calculate maximum value of graph...
      maxValue = calculateMaxValue();
   }

   // Calculate the maximum value of the graph...
   int calculateMaxValue() {
      double maximum = 0.0;
      double data;
      int temp,roundMax;
      // First get maximum figure...
      int length = gd.size();
      for (int i = 0; i < length; ++i) {
         data = gd.getData(i);
         if (data > maximum)
            maximum = data;
      } // end for
      // Now round it up to nearest power of 10
      roundMax = 1;
      for (temp = (int)maximum;temp > 0; temp /= 10)
         roundMax *= 10;
      return roundMax;
   }


   //  Draw the graph...
   public synchronized void paint (Graphics g) {
      if (gd == null)
         return;
      Dimension dm = size();

      // Calculate margins...
      int height = g.getFontMetrics().getHeight();
      int ymargin = 3 * height;
      int xmargin = g.getFontMetrics().stringWidth("1112345.67");
      int length = gd.size();

      // Select bottom-left origin
      Point origin = new Point(xmargin,dm.height - ymargin);

      // Draw X-Axis line
      int endx = dm.width - xmargin;
      g.drawLine(origin.x,origin.y,endx,origin.y);

      // Draw Y-Axis line
      g.drawLine(origin.x,ymargin,origin.x,origin.y);
```

```
        // Calculate how headers are spread out...
        int yIncrement = (origin.y - ymargin)/10;
        int xIncrement = (endx - origin.x) / (length + 1);

        // Draw horizontal axis headers
        int i,x;
        int yMarkStart = origin.y + height;
        int yTextStart = yMarkStart + height;
        for (i = 1; i < (length + 1); ++i) {
           // Draw marker...
           x = origin.x + (xIncrement * i);
           g.drawLine(x,yMarkStart,x,origin.y);
           // Print value header...
           g.drawString(gd.getHeading(i - 1),x,yTextStart);
        }

        // Draw vertical axis headers...
        int y;
        int inset = g.getFontMetrics().charWidth('W');
        int xMarkStart = origin.x - inset;
        int xTextStart = inset;
        int dataIncrement = maxValue / 10;
        String yHeader;
        for (i = 0; i <= 10; ++i) {
           // Draw marker...
           y = origin.y - (i * yIncrement);
           g.drawLine(xMarkStart,y,origin.x,y);
           // Print increment header...
           yHeader = String.valueOf(dataIncrement * i);
           g.drawString(yHeader,xTextStart,y);
        }

        // Call Graphic specific drawing..
        int vertLength = origin.y - ymargin;
        double dbLen = (double)randomColors.length;
        int index;
        int rectOffset = xIncrement / 2; // For bar graphs...
        Point lastPt = null;
        for (i = 1; i < (length + 1); ++i) {
           // Plot points, connecting points with lines...
           x = origin.x + (xIncrement * i);
           y = origin.y - (int)((gd.getData(i - 1)/maxValue) * vertLength);
           // Randomize colors...
           index = (int)(dbLen * Math.random());
           g.setColor(randomColors[index]);
           // If line graph, draw connecting lines...
           if (graphMode == LINE_GRAPH) {
                if (lastPt != null)
                    g.drawLine(lastPt.x,lastPt.y,x,y);
                lastPt = new Point(x,y);
           }
           // Otherwise, bar graph draw rectangle...
           else {
                g.fillRect(x - rectOffset,y,xIncrement,origin.y - y);
           }
        } // end for
    }
}
```

After the maximum value is determined, the graph is ready to be painted. This is surprisingly easy. The first step is to get the dimensions of the canvas area and to figure where the bottom-left origin of the graph should be; this is where the vertical line that marks the range of values and the horizontal line that provides the column headers will meet. The margins allow room at the sides and the bottom for displaying the range and column headers. These are calculated through the use of the FontMetrics class's `getHeight()` and `stringWidth()` methods. These margins make it easy to calculate the operations that follow. The next step is drawing the vertical and horizontal lines from the origin to the appropriate margin.

The column headers are next drawn underneath the horizontal line. The location of the headers is based on the length of the line divided by the number of columns. The horizontal range of values is calculated similarly, except that the locations are based on dividing the maximum value by ten and incrementing accordingly. The range values and headers are drawn through the `drawString()` method. The nearby `drawLine()` methods are used to make a small line marker indicating the range or header position.

The last step is to plot the graph. This is done in a `for` loop that moves across each column of data. For each column, a random color is chosen for the ensuing graph figure. This is done by using the `Math.random()` method, which returns a number between 0.0 and 1.0. The color is then set by calling the Graphics object's `setColor()` method. The data is then plotted based on its position in relation to the origin and the maximum value. If it is a line graph, a line is drawn from the endpoint of the last line drawn to the new value; the `drawLine()` method is used to do this. If it is a bar graph, a rectangle is drawn from the horizontal baseline to the plotted value with the `fillRect()` method of the Graphics class. Both the line and the interior of the bar rectangle will be the color just set by the random procedure.

Summary

This concludes the development of the spreadsheet applet. By going through this part of the book, you have learned most of the fundamental techniques needed to use the AWT package. You have also been exposed to exception handling, as well as the underlying principles of using input/output streams.

The next step is to tie these techniques in with some of Java's more advanced features, such as multithreading and sockets programming. With a good understanding of these new techniques, you can produce a network-enabled applet ready for prime-time use on the Internet!

III

Creating a Catalog Applet

6

Building a Catalog Applet

In this part of the book, a basic framework will be developed for creating catalog applications with general kiosk-like features. The application is described as "kiosk-like" because it emphasizes the use of images (rather than buttons and menus) to guide you through the various pages of the catalog. Consequently, the catalog will make heavy use of images, a primary subject of this part of the book.

Since images put a heavy load on the network, smarter methods are needed for loading them from the server to the client. Chapter 7, "Java and Images," introduces one of Java's most important features, multithreading, to illustrate some techniques for loading images before they are needed, thus making your application faster. The general overview of multithreading will form the foundations of thread programming, which will be used frequently in the rest of the book.

The kiosk will also make use of many of the features native to Java's applet classes. These classes make it easy to bring audio and images into your applet. They also give you a way to access features of the native browser, such as its status bar. One of the applet classes also provides a gateway for creating links to other HTML pages. The discussion of how this works will lead to the illustration of yet another component of Java, the URL classes. There will be an overview of how to open a stream to other URL objects, such as an image or text file residing on the server, and how to bring them into your client applet.

Basics of the Applet Class

This chapter's tutorial focuses on a variety of ways that the Applet class can be used to enhance the way your applet works. Recall that the Applet class provides the foundation for creating applets—Java applications that run in a browser environment. Besides launching your applet, the Applet class provides many useful services. It can be used to load image and audio files, work with URLs, and access the native browser environment. Since the Applet class is also a component of the AWT package (as was discussed in Part II, "Developing a Spreadsheet Applet with the AWT Package"), Applet objects provide many of the visual features that are part of the standard AWT repertoire, especially using the Graphics class for painting text, shapes, and images. Since the Applet class is a subclass of the AWT Component class, it can handle events such as mouse events and keystrokes.

Four often misunderstood Applet methods are overridden to manage the life cycle of an applet. None of these methods are required to be overridden, although their use will generally give you a more stable applet. These are the four methods:

- **`init()`** This is used to initialize an applet whenever it is loaded. You typically override this method to set up resources that will be used throughout an applet, such as fonts, or to initialize variables. This method is called once and only once during the lifetime of your applet. However, if the applet is reloaded for some reason or another, the `init()` method will be called again. Some Java literature may lead you to believe that you have to *always* override this method. This is not true! You need to override `init()` only when your applet's circumstances dictate that you should. A good example of this is initializing resources, such as AWT components.

- **`start()`** This is called whenever the HTML document on which an applet resides becomes the current page of a browser. When an applet is first run, the `start()` method is called after `init()`. Unlike the latter, however, `start()` will be called whenever the user visits the applet's page. Two very important types of activities should be located in the `start()` method. The `show()` method of instances of the Frame class are best called in the `start()` method. Since Frames occur outside the confines of an applet page, they will stay onscreen even after you have left the page. Consequently, they should be shown when you enter the page and hidden when you leave (see the `stop()` description method that follows). There will be an example in the upcoming listings. The `start()` method is also a good place to begin threads since their existence is also not confined to the page where they began.
- **`stop()`** This method is called whenever the user leaves a page—it is the converse of the `start()` method. Therefore, it's a good place to hide frames and terminate threads.
- **`destroy()`** The `destroy()` method is called whenever the applet is being shut down. Typically, this will occur when the browser is being closed, although there could be other circumstances that could lead to `destroy()` being invoked. This method is a good place to do some cleanup. However, since it's unpredictable when `destroy()` will be called, it should be used with some discretion.

The example that follows shows how these four methods work with the Frame class, providing an interesting insight into their behavior. Listing 6.1 shows code used to create a simple frame from an applet. The `init()` and `destroy()` methods print out their invocations to standard output so their behavior can be tracked.

Listing 6.1. An applet that creates Frames at initialization.

```
import java.awt.*;
import java.lang.*;
import java.applet.Applet;

// This applet illustrates how Frames work
// with basic Applet methods
public class AppletBasics extends Applet  {
   Frame f;
   // Called once and only once upon
   // applet initialization
   public void init() {
      System.out.println("In Applet init. Create frame!");
      // Create a frame and make it visible...
      f = new Frame("Applet Basics test!");
      f.resize(300,200);
      f.show();
   }
```

continues

Listing 6.1. continued

```
   // Applet destroyed.  Browser probably shutting down...
   public void destroy() {
    // Destroy the frame
    f.dispose();
    System.out.println("In applet destroy!");
   }
}
```

Frame's behavior is curious. If you leave the page where the Frame was created, the Frame will still be active and visible. This may or may not be the behavior you want. Furthermore, if you remove the `dispose()` method from the destroy call, you can get some downright undesirable behavior. In some browsers, you could create multiple instances of the frame by reopening its location reference. In Figure 6.1, three instances of the frame were created by going to its location several times.

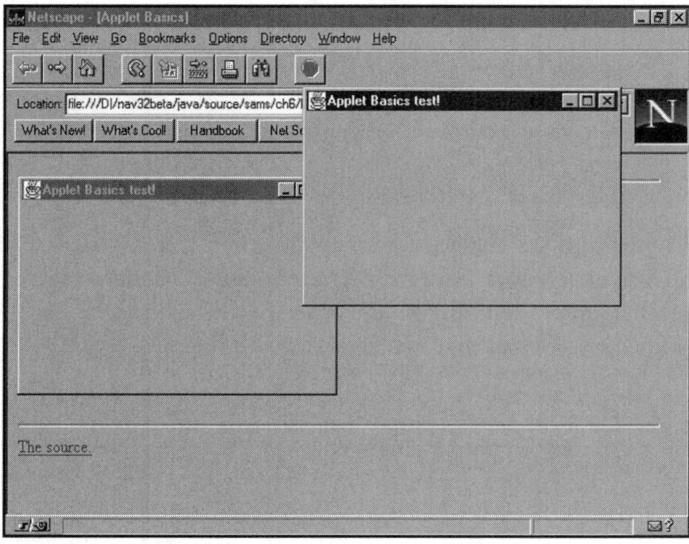

FIGURE 6.1.
Creating multiple frames by reloading its location.

Listing 6.2 gives the applet its desirable behavior of hiding the frame every time you leave the page and redisplaying it when you come back. It simply calls the `show()` method of the Frame class in an overridden Applet `start()` method and hides the Frame in an overridden `stop()` method.

Listing 6.2. An applet that displays the frame only when you are on the applet's page.

```
import java.awt.*;
import java.lang.*;
import java.applet.Applet;
```

```
// This applet illustrates how Frames work
// with basic Applet methods
public class AppletBasics extends Applet  {
   Frame f;
   // Called once and only once upon
   // applet initialization
   public void init() {
      System.out.println("In Applet init. Create frame!");
      // Create a frame and make it visible...
      f = new Frame("Applet Basics test!");
      f.resize(300,200);
   }

   // Move the show to the start method so the Frame
   // disappears when you leave the page...
   public void start() {
      System.out.println("In applet start!");
      f.show();
   }

   // Hide the frame when you leave the page...
   public void stop() {
      System.out.println("In applet stop!");
      f.hide();
   }

   // Applet destroyed.  Browser probably shutting down...
   public void destroy() {
      f.dispose();
      System.out.println("In applet destroy!");
   }
}
```

It is worth spending a few minutes playing around with this applet to get a full understanding of how these methods work. Try discarding or moving the code to see what will happen.

Applets and HTML

A special HTML tag is used for including applets within a Web page. The <APPLET> tag is used to indicate that an applet is to be run at the current location in the HTML. The typical syntax for the tag would be like the following:

```
<APPLET CODE="AppletTags" WIDTH=200 HEIGHT=60>
</APPLET>
```

The <APPLET> tag has required attributes, as this example shows. The CODE attribute states the name of the class file that runs the applet. The "AppletTags" class of this example will be a subclass of Applet. Java will look in the path specified in the `CLASSPATH` variable to find the class. The `WIDTH` and `HEIGHT` parameters describe the bounding region of the applet. These are also required and need to be set to the proper values if the applet is to look the way you want. Instances of the Window class, like frames, can appear outside this region. The </APPLET> tag is used to indicate the end of the HTML applet block.

An interesting characteristic of this <APPLET> tag pair is that any non-tagged text appearing within this block will appear in a browser that supports Java, but will not for non–Java-capable browsers. This feature can be used to indicate that a page is missing some functionality because the browser does not support Java. For example, the modifications of the previous lines

```
<APPLET CODE="AppletTags" WIDTH=200 HEIGHT=60>
You need to get a Java capable browser!
</APPLET>
```

will show the appropriate message for a browser that does not support Java.

The <APPLET> tag supports a couple of other optional attributes. The ALIGN attribute is used to control the alignment of the applet on the page. This attribute has about half a dozen possible values, including `LEFT`, `RIGHT`, `TOP`, `MIDDLE`, and so forth. The ALIGN attribute can be used to wrap text around an applet. The accompanying CD-ROM has a variation of the following example that uses the ALIGN attribute to right-align the text. (The file, which is in the Chapter 6 directory, is launched by `applettrighttags.html`.) The HSPACE and VSPACE attributes use the pixel values to control spacing between the applet and the text around it.

The CODEBASE attribute can be used to complement the CODE attribute. It specifies an alternative path where the class specified by CODE can be found.

Programmers will find the <PARAM> tag to be of the most interest. It is a separate tag from <APPLET>, although it appears within its block. The <PARAM> tag consists of NAME-VALUE attribute pairs that describe the name of a parameter variable and its corresponding value. It can appear multiple times with the <APPLET> block. This is illustrated with an example.

Figure 6.2 shows a page displaying a couple of strings of text. The first line is produced by the normal HTML text mechanism, but the second line is written out by an applet. Within the <APPLET> and </APPLET> tag pair are two parameters. The first one, with the NAME of "text," is used by the applet to display the second line of text, which is specified by the VALUE attribute. The second parameter, called "unused," is ignored but shows how multiple parameters can be included in the <APPLET> block.

Listing 6.3. An HTML listing of Figure 6.2 illustrating the use of <APPLET> and <PARAMETER> tags.

```
<TITLE>Applet Tags First Test</TITLE>
<HR>
<P> This is HTML text.
<P>
<P>
<APPLET CODE="AppletTags" WIDTH=200 HEIGHT=60>
<PARAM NAME=text VALUE="This is the AppletTags applet">
<PARAM NAME=unused VALUE="This doesn't matter">
You need to get a Java capable browser!
</APPLET>
<P>
<HR>
```

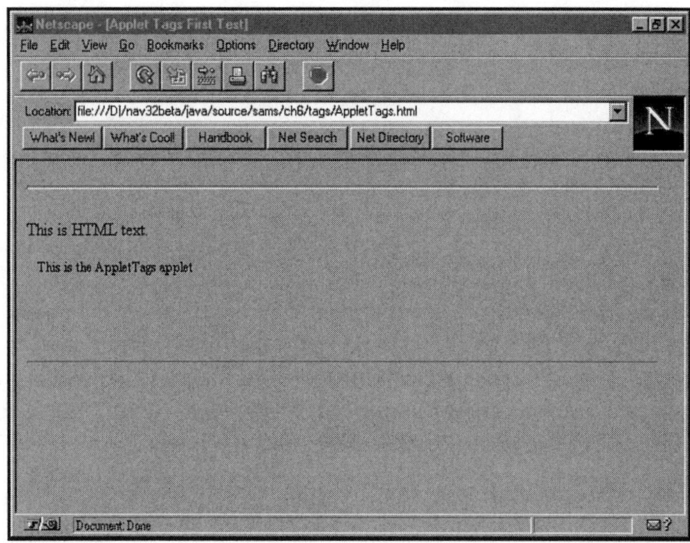

FIGURE 6.2.
An applet that uses the PARAMETER attribute to specify display text.

The Applet class uses the <PARAMETER> tags through the `getParameter()` method. This method takes a String indicating the NAME attribute and returns a String specifying the VALUE attribute. It will return null if the NAME attribute is not found. Listing 6.4 shows the code that uses the `getParameter()` method to display the second line of text in Figure 6.2.

Listing 6.4. Applet code of Figure 6.2 illustrating the use of parameters.

```
import java.awt.*;
import java.lang.*;
import java.applet.Applet;

// This applet takes an applet parameter
// and displays it...
public class AppletTags extends Applet  {
   String text;
   public void init() {
      // Get the text to be displayed from
      // the applet tag parameters...
      if ((text = getParameter("text")) == null)
            text = "Parameter not found!";
   }

   // Display the parameter text...
   public void paint(Graphics g) {
      g.drawString(text,10,10);
   }

}
```

The project at the end of this chapter makes extensive use of parameters and gives you a more involved illustration of how parameters can be constructed in the HTML and read in by the applet.

Applets and Images

The Applet class provides some basic methods for loading an image into memory. Both of these methods return an instance of an implementation of the Image class. The Image class is an abstract class providing methods that define the kind of behaviors an image should have. The underlying implementation of images in the JDK is somewhat complex. However, it isn't necessary to understand how this works to display images. Consequently, the internals of the Image and related classes will be postponed to later chapters. In this chapter, the focus will be on the basic mechanics of loading an image and displaying it.

The two forms of the `getImage()` method of the Applet class give you a simple way to load an image. Both these methods require an instance of a URL object. Although the specifics of the URL class will be discussed in more detail shortly, it's enough to say here that the URL class is used to encapsulate a URL. Typically, the URL object used in the `getImage()` method will be, in part, generated by one of two Applet class methods:

`getCodeBase()` Returns the URL of this Applet class (the one used to start the applet). This could be the value specified in the <APPLET> tag CODEBASE attribute or the directory of the HTML file in which this applet is embedded.

`getDocumentBase()` Returns the URL of the HTML containing this applet.

Perhaps the `getImage()` method you will find the most useful is the one that takes two arguments: a base URL and a String representing the path or filename in relation to the base. In the example that follows, the image is loaded from a subdirectory off where the applet HTML is located:

```
Image img = getImage(getDocumentBase(),"images/mail.gif");
```

The other `getImage()` method takes a URL object as its only parameter. This will have the full path and filename of the image. The multiple constructors of URL objects will be discussed shortly, but the construction of a URL object with a String is illustrated as follows:

```
Image img = getImage(new URL("http://AFakeServer.com/images/mail.gif"));
```

Once you get the image, it is ready to be drawn. When the `paint()` method is invoked, an image is drawn by calling the `drawImage()` method of the Graphics object:

```
g.drawImage(img,10,10,this);
```

This code draws the Image created in the previous example at an x, y coordinate. The last parameter refers to an implementation of the ImageObserver interface. This class is used for tracking the progress of an image as it is loaded and decoded. This makes it possible to show partial images as the full image is being constructed. The ImageObserver interface will be discussed in more detail later, along with its related classes and methods. For now, it's enough to say that the AWT Component class provides the basic methods necessary for managing this image display behavior. The "this" of the above `drawImage()` sample code refers to the component displaying the object.

Listing 6.5 and Figure 6.3 illustrate an applet that loads an image and displays it at different scales each time the applet receives a mouse click. The image is loaded in the applet `init()` method by using `getImage()`. The first time the image appears, it is at its normal size using the version of `drawImage()` previously discussed. When you click the mouse, it changes the image's scale and forces the applet to be redrawn. If the image is not at its normal scale, then it's displayed at its modified size with the following code:

```
int width = img.getWidth(this);
int height = img.getHeight(this);
g.drawImage(img,10,10,scale * width,scale * height,this);
```

The first two statements use methods of the Image class to get the width and height of the image. A different version of the `drawImage()` method is used to draw the image scaled to fit inside a bounding box specified by a width and height. The image is automatically scaled to fit tightly inside the box. In the case of this example, the width and height are multiplied by values of `2`, `3`, and `4`.

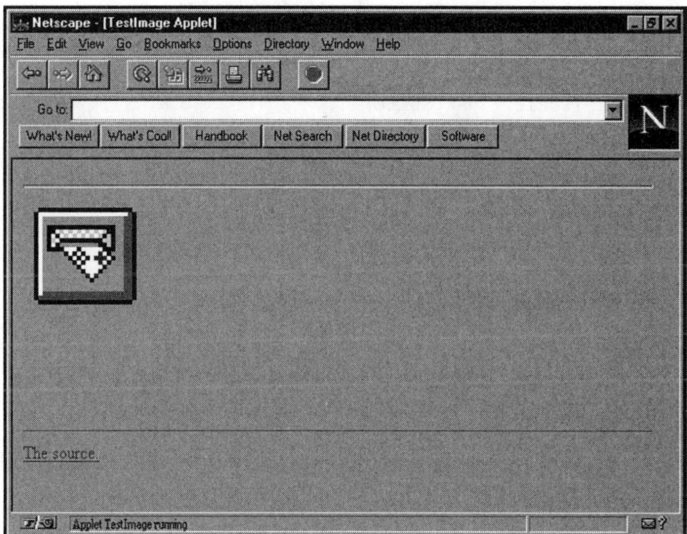

FIGURE 6.3.
Drawing a scaled Applet image.

Listing 6.5. Code for drawing scaled images.

```
import java.awt.*;
import java.lang.*;
import java.applet.Applet;

public class TestImage extends Applet {
   // Load the image off the document base...
   Image img;
   int scale = 1;
   public final int MAX_SCALE = 4;
   public void init() {
      img = getImage(getDocumentBase(),"images/mail.gif");
// Set toggle state...
   }

   // Paint the image at its normal size or at twice
   // its normal size...
   public void paint(Graphics g) {
      // Show at normal scale
      if (scale == 1) {
         g.drawImage(img,10,10,this);
      }
      // Or make bigger...
      else {
         int width = img.getWidth(this);
         int height = img.getHeight(this);
         g.drawImage(img,10,10,scale * width,
            scale * height,this);
      }
   }

   // Mouse clicks change the scale of the image
   public boolean mouseDown(Event ev, int x, int y) {
      ++scale;
      // If the max size of the image is reached, then
      // go back to normal size...
      if (scale > MAX_SCALE)
            scale = 1;
      // Force a repaint of the image...
      repaint();
      return true;
 };
}
```

An interesting thing to note is that the Toolkit class provides its own versions of `getImage()`. One takes a single URL parameter as in the Applet single parameter `getImage()` method; this Toolkit method is used in this chapter's project. The other version of `getImage()` takes a single String parameter that describes the file containing the image.

Applets and Audio

The Applet class has two simple methods for loading and playing an audio clip. These `play()` methods have two variations, as the `getImage()` method does: One takes a fully constructed URL of the desired audio clip; the other method takes a base URL, plus a String specifying additional directory and filename information. For example, the following code could be called to play a sound located off the HTML directory:

```
play(getDocumentBase(),"audio/song.au");
```

The only audio format currently supported by Java is the AU format, but this limitation will probably be relaxed in the near future.

Another way to play a sound is to create an AudioClip object. AudioClip is an interface implemented by the native environment Java is running on. Just like `play()` and `getImage()`, the Applet class offers two ways to get a reference to an AudioClip. The Applet class `getAudioClip()` method with a single URL parameter is one way of getting a reference to an AudioClip object:

```
import java.applet.AudioClip;
// ...
AudioClip sound = getAudioClip(new URL("http://AFakeServer.com/audio/song.au"));
```

Note that the AudioClip interface is actually located in the Applet package. You can also refer to an AudioClip by giving a URL and a String representing additional directory and filename information.

Once you have an AudioClip, it can be played with the `play()` method. This method takes no parameters and plays the clip only once. The `loop()` method plays the sound repeatedly:

```
sound.loop();
```

The `stop()` method is used to terminate the playing of the audio clip:

```
sound.stop();
```

It is important to remember to stop an audio clip when you leave the page that started the clip. The `stop()` method of the applet should, therefore, call the AudioClip `stop()` when appropriate.

Under the Applet Hood

It is worth spending a few moments to look at the underpinnings of the Applet class. Closely related to the Applet class is the AppletContext interface, which represents the underlying applet environment. This will typically be a browser, such as Netscape Navigator or HotJava. Therefore, the AppletContext provides a link to the resources of the browser. The Applet method `getAppletContext()` is used to return a reference to this underlying context.

Once you get access to the AppletContext object, it's possible to do all kinds of interesting things. One of the simplest and most useful things to do is to display a message on the browser's status bar:

```
getAppletContext().showStatus("This is a message");
```

The various projects throughout this book use this technique to display problems to the user. An interesting thing to do is to use this to show the results of an exception:

```
try {
 // … do something
}
// If exception, then show detail message to status bar…
catch (Exception e) {
   getAppletContext().showStatus(e.getMessage());
}
```

Since `getAppletContext()` is a method of the Applet context, this code needs to be called from within an Applet subclass. However, now that this has been explained, it needs to be pointed out that the Applet class has its own `showStatus()` method with the same function. Therefore, the first code fragment could just as easily have been the following:

```
showStatus("This is a message");
```

Actually, this code does little more than call the underlying AppletContext `showStatus()` method.

Another important thing that the AppletContext can do is return references of Applets running on the current HTML page. The `getApplet()` method takes a String name of an Applet and returns a reference to it. The `getApplet()` method enumerates the applets on the current page. Both of these are useful for inter-applet communication.

The AppletContext also ties in to one of the basic functions of a browser—dynamically linking to another HTML page. This can be done in one simple method call! The basic form of `showDocument()` takes a URL and makes it the current HTML of the browser. This implies that the `stop()` method of the current applet will be called, because its container page will no longer be current. This chapter's project will use `showDocument()` to link from one page to another. Here is a code fragment from the project:

```
try {
            URL u = new URL(URLBase,link);
            System.out.println("Show new doc: " + u);
            a.getAppletContext().showDocument(u);
}
catch (MalformedURLException e) {
           a.showStatus("Malformed URL: " + link);
}
catch (Exception e) {
           a.showStatus("Unable to go to link: " + e);
}
```

It creates a URL of the new page to be loaded and calls `showDocument()` to go to it. Note how the browser status bar is used to display any errors.

An alternative form of `showDocument()` takes a second String parameter that specifies the target frame or window to place the loaded page. This is useful for browsers that support framed pages. Note, however, that this method (like the other AppletContext methods) might not do anything if the native browser does not support the action.

Finally, a word should be said about the AppletStub interface. This interface is used to create a program to view applets. Consequently, any browser that supports Java will need to use the AppletStub interface to make the Applet class functional.

Creating and Reading a URL

Since the Uniform Resource Locator, or URL, is at the heart of the World Wide Web, it is only appropriate that an Internet language like Java has a URL class. Several examples of how to create and use a URL object have already been presented in this chapter. There are four different constructors of URL objects. Two of them should already be familiar. The simplest constructor takes a string and converts it to a URL:

```
URL u = new URL("http://AFakeServer.com/");
```

Another method should also be familiar. It takes a URL and a String representing a relative path and creates a new URL from it.

```
URL urlNew = new URL(u,"audio/sound.au");
```

Recall that a URL typically consists of a protocol, the name of the host computer, and a path to the location of the resource. A third URL constructor takes these as protocol, host, and file Strings, respectively, and returns a URL. The final constructor adds a String specifying the port as an additional parameter. However, protocols generally have a fixed port number (HTTP is 80), so this information is usually not needed.

A couple of methods can be used for deconstructing a URL. The following code prints the protocol, host, port, file, and finally the URL itself of the HTML of the applet:

```
System.out.println("Protocol: " + getDocumentBase().getProtocol());
System.out.println("Host: " + getDocumentBase().getHost());
System.out.println("Port: " + getDocumentBase().getPort());
System.out.println("File: " + getDocumentBase().getFile());
System.out.println("URL: " + getDocumentBase());
```

Once constructed, the URL can be used to open up a network connection to the URL. This is done through the `openStream()` method, which returns an instance of InputStream. You saw how InputStream classes worked in Chapter 4, "Enhancing the Spreadsheet Applet." The FilterInputStream subclasses can be constructed from this to create high-level interfaces to the streams. The DataInputStream class can be used to read in streams according to a specified data type, such as Strings. Listing 6.6 shows how to combine the URL and stream classes for a quick and easy printout of the contents of the HTML containing an applet.

Listing 6.6. Printing the contents of the applet's HTML.

```
void printSelf() {
    // Open up a stream to the document URL and
    // print its contents...
    try {
        DataInputStream dis = new DataInputStream(
            new BufferedInputStream(
               getDocumentBase().openStream() ) );
        String s;
        while ( (s = dis.readLine()) != null)
            System.out.println(s);
        System.out.println("EOF");
    }
    catch (IOException e) {
      System.out.println("URL read error");
    }
   }
```

The key to this is the first line in the `try` clause. The URL of the base document is taken from `getDocumentBase();` its `OpenStream()` method is then applied. Once the stream is open, an instance of the easy-to-use DataInputStream class is created. Each line of the HTML is then fetched by the `readLine()` method of DataInputStream and sent to standard output.

Chapter Project

This chapter's project begins the development of a kiosk-style online catalog. It has a couple of interesting characteristics. First of all, it uses HTML applet parameters to describe how each applet is constructed and operates. Each page in the catalog has images describing the current choices. Figure 6.4 shows the main menu of the catalog. The images are loaded and displayed by the applet, not the HTML. When a choice is made, the applet jumps to the next HTML and reloads the applet with the new parameters.

Since the applet makes extensive use of images, it poses certain problems. Images use much network bandwidth and so need to be used efficiently. The project works around this problem by creating a MediaLoader class that acts as a cache for images. In the next chapter, this class is improved by acting as a pre-loader of images before the next applet is retrieved.

Another notable feature of the project is its configurability. The same applet runs on every page of the catalog; its features are determined by <APPLET> tag parameters in the current HTML. Furthermore, it uses a URL stream to load in additional data to be displayed on the button. This data comes from a local text file, which can be edited outside the actual applet code.

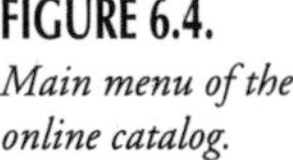

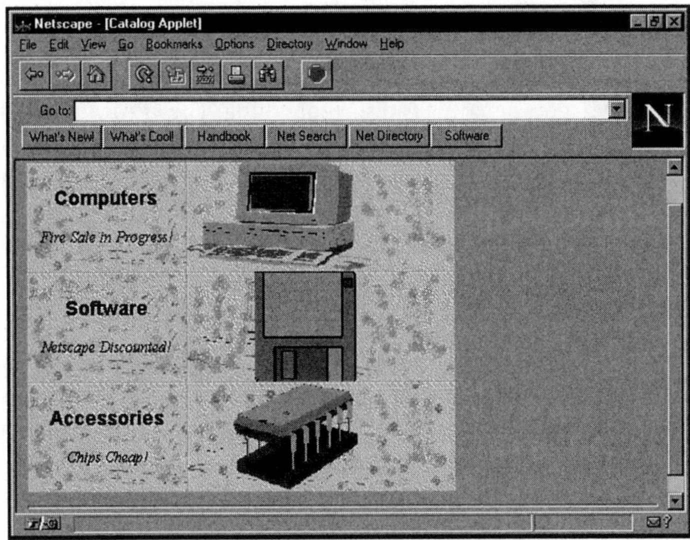

FIGURE 6.4.
Main menu of the online catalog.

Class Organization

Table 6.1 lists the classes used in this chapter's version of the catalog applet.

Table 6.1. Catalog project classes.

Class	*Description*
CacheEntry	Represents a single entry in the image cache maintained by the MediaLoader class.
Catalog	The Applet class that takes HTML parameters and constructs the components that represent the current choices.
CatalogButton	A image-based button that shows text representing a choice and links to another Catalog applet when selected.
MediaLoader	A class that actually loads the images and uses static methods to employ a cache that exists across Catalog applet invocations.
MediaLoaderException	An exception thrown by the MediaLoader when there is a problem.
SelectionCanvas	Displays a large image representing a possible choice of the user. Appears to the right of its companion CatalogButton.

Catalog HTML

Listing 6.7 shows the HTML of the catalog page displayed in Figure 6.4. As the listing shows, the HTML does not actually display anything. The <PARAM> tag fields actually tell the applet what to display. These are passed to the Catalog applet run for each page of the applet. It reads in the parameters to determine what images to display. There are three rows of display for each Catalog applet. On each row there is a field (also known as a CatalogButton, after its class) that appears on the left-hand side; it is effectively a button that appears as an image. The field is complemented by a larger image that appears on its right (called a SelectionCanvas, after its class).

The three <PARAM> tags whose NAME attribute begins with the "field" prefix specify the left-hand image buttons. The corresponding VALUE attribute has four subfields used to create the CatalogButton. The first subfield is the name appearing on the button. The second is the image to be displayed in the button's area. The third subfield is a style, which represents the size of the button. Although the MEDIUM style is the only one used in the sample applets, its existence gives you a way of customizing the applet. The last subfield specifies the URL that the applet goes to when you click the image button.

The three <PARAM> tags whose NAME attribute begins with the "image" prefix specify the SelectionCanvas objects that appear to the right of the fields. The VALUE attribute specifies the image to be displayed in the canvas area.

The <PARAM> tag with the NAME attribute of "data" specifies a URL containing text data that can be used to complement the display of the CatalogButton objects. This data would be such things as "On Sale" that would appear underneath the larger font name of the button.

Listing 6.7. The HTML of the main catalog page (index.html).

```
<title>Catalog Applet</title>
<hr>
<applet code="Catalog" width=400 height=300>
<param name=field1 value="Computers,catalog/field1.gif,MEDIUM,computer/main.html">
<param name=image1 value="catalog/selection1.gif">
<param name=field2 value="Software,catalog/field1.gif,MEDIUM,software/main.html">
<param name=image2 value="catalog/selection1.gif">
<param name=field3 value="Accessories,catalog/field1.gif,MEDIUM,accessory/
➥main.html">
<param name=image3 value="catalog/selection1.gif">
<param name=data value="catalog/data.txt">
</applet>
<hr>
```

The Catalog Class

Listing 6.7 gives the full listing of the Catalog class. This subclass of Applet represents the applet loaded for every page in the catalog project. The initialization of the applet has three steps. Its main job is to create the CatalogButton and SelectionCanvas objects by parsing out the parameters specified in the current HTML. However, it also traps for a mouse click on one of the CanvasButton objects in `handleEvent()`. When this occurs, it calls the CanvasButton `select()` method, which may result in the browser loading in a new URL representing a new page in the catalog.

After the Catalog applet initializes the fonts, it gets the applet parameter in the HTML that corresponds to the "data" NAME attribute. It does this through the `getParameter()` method, which will return either a String representation of the corresponding VALUE attribute, or a null value if the name cannot be found. The `getParameter()` method is used to get all the CatalogButton and SelectionCanvas parameters that follow.

After the "data" value is retrieved, it is used to derive a URL that contains the additional text data. This is performed in the applet's `loadURLData()` method. It creates a URL object by taking the path to the text data in relation to the base document of the current HTML:

```
u = new URL(getDocumentBase(),dataPath);
```

It uses this URL object to open up an input stream to the text file, then reads the data in by Strings delimited by newlines. This process is similar to the example discussed in the "Creating and Reading a URL" section above.

The last step in the applet's initialization is to create the three rows of CatalogButton and SelectionCanvas couplets. It uses the `getParameter()` method to get the information needed to create the canvas components. In the `createCatalogButton()` method, the parameter values are parsed with an instance of the StringTokenizer class. Given a set of delimiters (like commas), this class simply walks through and produces String tokens that appear between the delimiters.

The other thing that the Catalog class does is handle the painting of the applet. This is simple because it walks through the three rows and displays the components based on the size of their images.

Listing 6.7. The Catalog class.

```
import java.awt.*;
import java.lang.*;
import java.util.StringTokenizer;
import java.applet.*;
import java.net.URL;
import java.io.DataInputStream;
import java.io.BufferedInputStream;
import java.io.IOException;
import java.net.MalformedURLException;

// This is the main class that loads the parameters
// for the current applet and sets up the images
// fields.
```

continues

Listing 6.7. continued

```
public class Catalog extends Applet {
   CatalogButton button[] = new CatalogButton[3];
   SelectionCanvas drawing[] = new SelectionCanvas[3];
   // Three styles
   private static final int SMALL_STYLE = 0;
   private static final int MEDIUM_STYLE = 1;
   private static final int LARGE_STYLE = 2;
   private static final int DEFAULT_STYLE = MEDIUM_STYLE;
   Font styleFont[] = new Font[3];
   Font dataFont;
   String data[] = new String[3];

   // Initialize the graphic display...
   public void init() {
      // First create fonts...
      styleFont[0] = new Font("Helvetica",Font.PLAIN,16);
      styleFont[1] = new Font("Helvetica",Font.BOLD,18);
      styleFont[2] = new Font("Helvetica",Font.BOLD,24);
      dataFont = new Font("TimesRoman",Font.ITALIC,14);
      // Get the additional data from URL...
      loadURLData();

      // Add the components...
      addComponents();
      show();
   }

   // Add the components to the display...
   void addComponents() {
      // Create Font for buttons
      String fieldParam;
      String selectParam;
      // Add first row of field and display image...
      if (((fieldParam = getParameter("field1")) != null) &&
          ((selectParam = getParameter("image1")) != null) ) {
       button[0] = createCatalogButton(fieldParam,data[0]);
       drawing[0] = new SelectionCanvas(this,
         selectParam,getDocumentBase());
       button[0].resize(150,100);
       drawing[0].resize(250,100);
      } // end if
      else {
       getAppletContext().showStatus("Invalid parameter");
       button[0] = null;
      }

      // Add second row of field and display image...
      if (((fieldParam = getParameter("field2")) != null) &&
          ((selectParam = getParameter("image2")) != null) ) {
       button[1] = createCatalogButton(fieldParam,data[1]);
       drawing[1] = new SelectionCanvas(this,
         selectParam,getDocumentBase());
       drawing[1].resize(250,100);
       button[1].resize(150,100);
      } // end if
      else {
```

```
      getAppletContext().showStatus("Invalid parameter");
      button[1] = null;
     }

     // Add third row of field and display image...
     if (((fieldParam = getParameter("field3")) != null) &&
         ((selectParam = getParameter("image3")) != null) ) {
      button[2] = createCatalogButton(fieldParam,data[2]);
      drawing[2] = new SelectionCanvas(this,
        selectParam,getDocumentBase());
      button[2].resize(150,100);
      drawing[2].resize(250,100);
     } // end if
     else {
      getAppletContext().showStatus("Invalid parameter");
      button[2] = null;
     }
}

// Load additional data from URL...
void loadURLData() {
 // Get path to data from parameter...
 String dataPath = getParameter("data");
 if (dataPath == null) {
   System.out.println("No data variable found");
   return;
 } // end if
 // Create URL for data...
 URL u;
 try {
   u = new URL(getDocumentBase(),dataPath);
 }
 catch (MalformedURLException e) {
   System.out.println("Bad Data URL");
   return;
 }

 // Now load the data by opening up a stream
 // to the URL...
 try {
  DataInputStream dis = new DataInputStream(
   new BufferedInputStream(
      u.openStream() ) );
  // Read only the first three lines...
  int i;
  for (i = 0; i < 3; ++i) {
      data[i] = dis.readLine();
  } // end for
 }
 catch (IOException e) {
   System.out.println("URL read error");
 }
}

// Update message sent when repainting is needed...
// Prevent paint from getting cleared out...
public void update(Graphics g) {
```

continues

Listing 6.7. continued

```
      paint(g);
   }

   // Repaint all the canvas components...
   public synchronized void paint(Graphics g) {
     int i,x,y;
     Dimension dm;
     int defHeight = 150;

     // Go through the buttons...
     for (x = y = i = 0; i < 3; ++i) {
       if (button[i] != null) {
         button[i].paint(g,x,y);
         dm = button[i].size();
         x += dm.width;
         drawing[i].paint(g,x,y);
         x = 0;
         y += dm.height;
       }
       else
         y += defHeight;
     } // end for
   }

 public boolean mouseDown(Event ev, int x, int y) {
      // See if you clicked on any of the buttons...
      for (int i = 0; i < 3; ++i) {
         if ((button[i] != null) && (button[i].inside(x,y)) ) {
               System.out.println("Hit Button " + i);
               // Link to the button's selected field...
               button[i].select();
               break;
         }  // end if
      }
      return true;
 };

   // Parse a parameter and create catalog field...
   CatalogButton createCatalogButton(String param,String data) {
     // Set up defaults...
     String fieldName = "";
     String imageName = "";
     String style = "MEDIUM";
     String link = getDocumentBase().toString();
     // Parse out the string...
     StringTokenizer s = new StringTokenizer(param,",");
     if (s.hasMoreTokens()) {
      fieldName = s.nextToken();
      if (s.hasMoreTokens()) {
       imageName = s.nextToken();
       if (s.hasMoreTokens()) {
         style = s.nextToken();
         if (s.hasMoreTokens()) {
            link = s.nextToken();
         }
       } // end style if
```

```
            } // end image if
        } // end field if
        // Figure out the style. Convert it all to uppercase...
        style = style.toUpperCase();
        int styleType;
        if (style.equals("MEDIUM"))
            styleType = MEDIUM_STYLE;
        else if (style.equals("SMALL"))
            styleType = SMALL_STYLE;
        else if (style.equals("LARGE"))
            styleType = LARGE_STYLE;
        else
            styleType = DEFAULT_STYLE;

        // Create button according to these parameters...
        return new CatalogButton(this,
            imageName,fieldName,
            styleFont[styleType],getDocumentBase(),
            link,data,dataFont);
    }
}
```

The CatalogButton Class

The CatalogButton class is used to represent the choices you can make for each applet screen. It appears on the left-hand side of the applet and goes to another URL when the button is selected. This URL will represent another page in the catalog.

The CatalogButton constructor takes as input the main and sub text fields, the corresponding fonts, the background image, and a URL and relative path used to construct the URL the button will link to. One of the key things about the class is that its Image object is loaded through the MediaLoader class (described shortly) and not through the applet's `getImage()` method. This approach takes advantage of the caching techniques that will be developed in the MediaLoader throughout this chapter.

The `paint()` method is invoked by the Catalog class and passed the x-y coordinate where the image should be painted on the applet. It draws the image by using the `drawImage()` method. It then draws a title field in the center of the button. The FontMetrics are used to center the text. Finally, if an additional data field exists, it is drawn underneath the title in a smaller font.

If the button is selected, the CatalogButton object changes its text to white by setting an internal state variable and forcing a repaint. It then creates a URL object out of the base URL and its relative path. This URL represents the new catalog page in which to link. If the URL is successfully created, it links to the new page with the `showDocument()` method. If there is an error, then a message is displayed on the browser's status bar.

Listing 6.8. The CatalogButton class.

```
import java.awt.*;
import java.lang.*;
import java.net.*;
import java.applet.*;

// This class represents a button on the current page.
// It represents the lefthand element of a kiosk selection
// that has a background
// image and text describing what the button represents.
// The field has a link to the Web page it should go to
// if it is selected...
// Parent of button is responsible for sizing and setting
// correct position...
public class CatalogButton extends Canvas {
   String text; // What to display on left side...
   String data; // Additional data
   URL URLBase; // The base URL to link from...
   String link; // Where to link to relative to base...
   Image img; // Background image...
   Font f; // Font to paint with...
   Font dataFont;  // Font to paint data with...
   Applet a; // Use its ImageObserver...
   int lastX,lastY;  // Store last coordinates....
   // Store states of button
   private static final int NORMAL_STATE = 0;
   private static final int SELECTED_STATE = 1;
   int state;  // From above states...

   // Create the catalog button...
   public CatalogButton(Applet aIn,
     String backgroundImage,  String textIn, Font fIn,
      URL URLBaseIn, String linkIn, String dataIn,
      Font dataFontIn) {
         // Store parameters...
         a = aIn;
         text = textIn;
         f = fIn;
         URLBase = URLBaseIn;
         link = linkIn;
         lastX = lastY = -1;
         state = NORMAL_STATE;
         data = dataIn;
         dataFont = dataFontIn;
         // Now start loading the background image
         // through the Media Loader...
         try {
            img = MediaLoader.getMediaLoader().loadImage(URLBase,backgroundImage);
         }
         catch (MediaLoaderException e) {
            img = null;
            a.showStatus(e.getMessage());
         }
   }

   // Paint the image...
   public synchronized void paint(Graphics g,int x,int y) {
```

```
      // Kick out if internal image is bad...
      if (img == null)
            return;
      // Resize the image, if necessary...
      Dimension dm = size();
      g.drawImage(img,x,y,dm.width,dm.height,a);
      // Center font in image...
      int textX,textY;
      g.setFont(f);
      FontMetrics fm = g.getFontMetrics();
      if (state == NORMAL_STATE)
         g.setColor(Color.black);
      else
         g.setColor(Color.white);
      textX = x + ((dm.width - fm.stringWidth(text))/2);
      textY = y + ((dm.height - fm.getHeight())/2);
      g.drawString(text,textX,textY);

      // Show additional data...
      g.setFont(dataFont);
      fm = g.getFontMetrics();
      if (data != null) {
       textX = x + ((dm.width - fm.stringWidth(data))/2);
       textY += (2 * fm.getHeight());
       g.drawString(data,textX,textY);
      } // end if

      // Store the coordinates...
      lastX = x;
      lastY = y;
   }

   // See whether coordinates are inside this button...
   public synchronized boolean inside(int x,int y) {
      // Kick out if not ready yet...
      if ((lastX < 0) || (lastY < 0))
         return false;
      // Make clipping rectangles for comparions...
      Dimension dm = size();
      Rectangle thisRect,inRect;
      thisRect = new Rectangle(lastX,lastY,dm.width,dm.height);
      inRect = new Rectangle(x,y,0,0);
      // See rectangles overlap...
      if (thisRect.intersects(inRect))
         return true;
      return false;
   }

   // Button was selected...
   public synchronized void select() {
      state = SELECTED_STATE;
      // Force repaint to show selected state...
      Dimension dm = size();
      a.repaint(lastX,lastY,dm.width,dm.height);
      // Go to the next URL if there is a link...
      if ((link != null) && (link.length() > 0)) {
         try {
```

continues

Listing 6.8. continued

```
            URL u = new URL(URLBase,link);
            System.out.println("Show new doc: " + u);
            a.getAppletContext().showDocument(u);
         }
         catch (MalformedURLException e) {
           a.showStatus("Malformed URL: " + link);
         }
         catch (Exception e) {
           a.showStatus("Unable to go to link: " + e);
         }
      } // end if
   }
}
```

The SelectionCanvas Class

This class, shown in Listing 6.9, is really a simplified version of the CatalogButton. Like CatalogButton, it loads an Image from the MediaLoader. It paints the image at the specified applet parameters with the `drawImage()` method of the Graphics class.

Listing 6.9. The SelectionCanvas class.

```
import java.lang.*;
import java.awt.*;
import java.net.URL;
import java.applet.*;

// Shows visual cue as to what an item is...
public class SelectionCanvas extends Canvas {
   URL URLBase; // The base URL to link from...
   Image img; // Display image...
   Applet a; // Use its ImageObserver...
   // Create the canvas display...
   public SelectionCanvas(Applet aIn,
     String displayImage,URL URLBaseIn) {
        // Store parameters...
        a = aIn;
        URLBase = URLBaseIn;
        // Now start loading the background image
        // through the Media Loader...
        try {
           img = MediaLoader.getMediaLoader().loadImage(URLBase,displayImage);
        }
        catch (MediaLoaderException e) {
           img = null;
           a.getAppletContext().showStatus(e.getMessage());
        }
   }

   // Paint the image...
   public synchronized void paint(Graphics g,int x,int y) {
```

```
        // Kick out if internal image is bad...
        if (img == null)
             return;
        // Resize the image if necessary...
        Dimension dm = size();
        g.drawImage(img,x,y,a); // dm.width,dm.height,a);
    }
}
```

The MediaLoader Class

Listing 6.10 shows some of the code for the MediaLoader class. This class will be a focal point for developing the catalog project throughout this part of the book. Eventually, the MediaLoader class will pre-load images of possible catalog pages that may be viewed. It will be developed in the next chapter as a background thread, but in this chapter, it will be part of a single-task applet.

The MediaLoader also has an internal cache that keeps track of images that have been loaded; its major feature is that it needs to persist across applet invocations. So if you are on one page of the catalog, go to a Yahoo page, and then go to another catalog page, the MediaLoader cache should still persist and return any pre-loaded images that might be found.

To allow the MediaLoader to have a persistent cache, you need to prevent the MediaLoader from being instantiated by another object. Therefore, it has a private constructor. Its variables are static, so they exist for the class and not for a specific instantiation. The cache, a Hashtable object, is created once and only once for the MediaLoader. Therefore, the cache can persist whether a catalog page is present or not. The MediaLoader and the cache will exist until they are destroyed—probably by the browser being shut down.

The only public method of the MediaLoader is `loadImage()`. Like `getImage()`, it takes a URL and a relative path as its parameter. Eventually, the method calls `getImage()`—although it uses the Toolkit version of the method, as opposed to the applet version. It is structured to do this because the MediaLoader should not be tied to a specific applet; the Toolkit class, which also persists outside a specific applet, is, therefore, a good match. After creating the URL, the loader checks to see whether the Image object is in its cache. The cache is a Hashtable that takes URL objects as its key and a CacheEntry object as its data. The CacheEntry object is an instantiation of a simple accessor class that does nothing more than contain an Image and an age variable (the function of which will be discussed briefly). If the URL is found in the cache, the corresponding Image is returned. If it is not found, then the Toolkit's `getImage()` method is called. The returned image is then placed in the cache.

As shown in Listing 6.10, the age field is used for the MediaLoader's internal "garbage collector." A static integer counter called currentAge increases every time the `loadImage()` method is invoked. The cache entry of the Image returned is then set to an age that matches the currentAge. This way, it's possible to tell when an Image has not been used for a while. Occasionally, the loadImage() method will invoke a method called sweeper(). The role of this method is to remove any cache entries that have not been used for a while. It does this by enumerating the CacheEntry objects in the cache, sorting them by age, and removing any objects older than a certain limit. This limit is set to the size of the cache; the goal is to keep the number of entries in the cache to a number near its original size.

In the next chapter, the sweeper() method will be replaced by a background thread that runs independently of the MediaLoader.

Listing 6.10. The MediaLoader class.

```
// This class loads image media through URL commands and
// keeps a local cache of images. Each image has an
// address used for aging. When the image is too
// old, then it is removed from that cache.
public class MediaLoader {
   // The loader is static and so can be created only once
   private static MediaLoader loader = new MediaLoader();

   // Cache size is used for tracking age of URL
   static int cacheSize = 40;
   static int currentAge = 0;

   // Cache is hashtable...
   static Hashtable cache = new Hashtable(cacheSize);;

   // Private internal constructor: Create the cache...
   private MediaLoader() {
   }

   // Return reference to this MediaLoader object
   public static synchronized MediaLoader getMediaLoader() {
      return loader;
   }

   // Load an image through a URL
   // Check to see whether it is in the cache
   // If it isn't, then load it in, store in cache,
   // and return it
   public synchronized Image loadImage(URL base,String name) throws
➥MediaLoaderException {
      // Create a URL for the image...
      URL u;
      try {
           u = new URL(base,name);
      }
      catch (MalformedURLException e) {
           throw new MediaLoaderException("Malformed URL");
      }

      // See whether it is in the cache...
      ++currentAge;

      CacheEntry ce = (CacheEntry) cache.get(u);
      // If it's in the cache, update the age and
```

```
      // return image...
      if (ce != null) {
         ce.setAge(currentAge);
         System.out.println("MediaLoader: Cache hit URL " + u);
         return ce.getImage();
      }

      // See whether you need to run the sweeper...
      // Just run it every 20 fetches...
      if ((currentAge%20) == 0)
          sweeper();

      // Otherwise, get the Image...
      System.out.println("MediaLoader: Loading URL " + u);
      Image img = Toolkit.getDefaultToolkit().getImage(u);

      // Put in cache...
      cache.put(u,new CacheEntry(img,currentAge));
      return img;
   }

   // Removes any item from cache that has an
   // age that is too old...
   private synchronized void sweeper() {
      // Do nothing if cache is too small...
      if (cache.size() < cacheSize)
            return;
      CacheEntry ce;
      // Array for placing hashtable elements...
      int ages[] = new int[cache.size()];
      // First step is to go through and get all the ages...
      Enumeration em = cache.elements();
      for (int i = 0; em.hasMoreElements(); ++i) {
         ce = (CacheEntry)em.nextElement();
         ages[i] = ce.getAge();
      }
      // Next step is to get minimum age...
      // This is ugly since you have to perform
// a sort...
sort(ages);
      // Now get nTh element
      int minAge = ages[cacheSize - 1];
      // Do nothing if you have nothing that's old...
      if (minAge > (currentAge - cacheSize)) {
         System.out.println("Nothing is old enough. No cleaning necessary...");
         return;
      }
      System.out.println("Run Sweeper. Min Age = " + minAge);

      // Final step is to walk through and remove
      // old elements...
      em = cache.keys();
      URL u;
      while (em.hasMoreElements()) {
         u = (URL)em.nextElement();
         // Get cache entry...
         ce = (CacheEntry)cache.get(u);
```

continues

Listing 6.10. continued

```
            // See whether it's too old...
            if (ce.getAge() < minAge) {
                  System.out.println("Remove cache element: " + u);
                  cache.remove(u);
            }
         }
      }

      // The identifying String of the loader
      public String toString() {
         return ("MediaLoader ID: " + hashCode());
      }
}
```

The MediaLoaderException Class

Listing 6.11 shows the MediaLoaderException class. An instance of this class is thrown whenever there's a problem with the MediaLoader. The Exception will usually have a custom detailed message attached to it. Note that it is a subclass of the AWTException class, which is a hierarchy of Exceptions related to the AWT package.

Listing 6.11. The MediaLoaderException class.

```
import java.awt.AWTException;

// Create object for throwing MediaLoaderExceptions...
public class MediaLoaderException extends AWTException {
   public MediaLoaderException(String msg) {
      super(msg);
   }
}
```

Summary

In this chapter, you see the first steps for developing a catalog-style application. Its most interesting feature is a cache that uses static methods to persist across browser pages. This MediaLoader cache is expanded on in the next chapter to pre-load images from the next pages of the catalog. This added function is done in the context of introducing you to the world of multithreading. Not only will the loader run as a thread, but so will the "sweeper" that removes old images from the cache.

7

Java and Images

Images offer the best way to work with Java graphics; as a matter of fact, everything in the AWT seems centered on the concept of images. This chapter shows you how to use Java for generating images. It leads off with rendering and tracking a simple image and continues by explaining the fundamental model behind Java images. The chapter ends by writing a class to display image formats not directly supported by Java.

Displaying Images

Images are nothing more than a collection of colors and their layout, but they are useful because, with an auxiliary paint program, you can create sophisticated visual effects that can be captured and displayed in your applets.

Java arrives with built-in support for two types of images: GIF and JPEG. The GIF standard (Graphics Interchange Format) is maintained by CompuServe. It uses an excellent compression scheme (LZW) to represent a large image in a small file. JPEG (Joint Photographic Experts Group) is an international standard mainly used for photographic material. It uses a discrete cosine transform (DCT) to remove extraneous material your eye doesn't really notice, so a very efficient compression scheme can be used. The cosine transform is "lossy," meaning it loses some information when applied. LZW, on the other hand, is "lossless." It turns out that the information removed by a cosine transform is precisely the photographic detail that your eye does not see.

Loading Java Images

Both these formats can be easily loaded by your applets:

```
Image newImage = getImage(URL);
```

```
Image newImage = Toolkit.getDefaultToolkit().getImage(filename or URL);
```

The first line may be used only from a subclass of Applet, but line two can be called by either an applet or application. Each `getImage()` method returns immediately, without actually loading the image. To retrieve the image, you must try to display it; this is done to keep memory consumption down. For example, sometimes an applet might refer to an image, but not actually make use of it. Therefore, until the image is really needed, it will remain on the server.

> **NOTE**
>
> The `getImage()` method does not cause your image to be loaded. The image remains on the server until you try to display it.

The Applet class provides two versions of `getImage()`:

- `public Image getImage(URL imgLocation);`
- `public Image getImage(URL baseLocation, String filename);`

The second call is the one most commonly used because applets can load only from the server they originated on. The methods to get either the URL of the page or the applet code's URL can then be combined with the filename of the image to construct a complete path:

```
Image newImage = getImage(getDocumentBase(), "image.gif");
```

or

```
Image newImage = getImage(getCodeBase(), "image.gif");
```

The call you use depends on whether your image is grouped with the class files or the HTML Web pages on your server.

NOTE

You must be aware of the organization of your various data files on the server. If your images reside with your class files (/htdocs/classes/images), then use `getCodeBase()`; however, if your images reside with your HTML files (/htdocs/images), use `getDocumentBase()`. Many times, class files are grouped together with HTML files. In this case, both methods will return the same URL.

The Toolkit also provides two `getImage()` methods:

- `public Image getImage(URL imgLocation);`
- `public Image getImage(String filename);`

Although the Toolkit can retrieve a filename, applets can't use `getImage()` to read local files because they would cause a security exception. Remember, applets can read only from the server they originated on. Allowing applets to read from a local drive is definitely a security no-no.

Image Display

Once an Image object is instantiated, it can be displayed in an applet's `paint()` method by using the Graphics object passed to it:

```
g.drawImage(newImage, x, y, this);
```

Variables `x` and `y` contain the coordinates of the image's upper-left corner, and the final parameter is an ImageObserver object. This interface is implemented in the Component class that the applet is derived from, which is why you can pass the `this` pointer. You'll learn more about the ImageObserver interface in the next section.

There are four variations of `drawImage()` in the Graphics class:

- `public abstract boolean drawImage(Image img, int x, int y, ImageObserver observer);`
- `public abstract boolean drawImage(Image img, int x, int y, int width, int height, ImageObserver observer);`
- `public abstract boolean drawImage(Image img, int x, int y, Color bgcolor, ImageObserver observer);`
- `public abstract boolean drawImage(Image img, int x, int y, int width, int height, Color bgcolor, ImageObserver observer);`

The width and height parameters allow you to scale an image, which can be enlarged or reduced in either the x or y direction. The `bgcolor` parameter specifies which color to use for any transparent pixels in the image. Each `drawImage()` version returns `true` if the image was painted, `false` otherwise. The image will not paint if it hasn't been loaded yet. It will eventually display because the Component class will be notified of the load and will call your paint method when the image arrives.

Image Observers

The Component class accomplishes this because it implements the ImageObserver interface. Most of Java's image-manipulation routines are *asynchronous*, meaning they return immediately and notify you when they have completed their assignment. The notification, which flows through the ImageObserver interface, contains the following method:

- `public abstract boolean imageUpdate(Image img, int infoflags, int x, int y, int width, int height);`

The Component class uses this method, but you can override it to get information about your image. The `infoflags` parameter is a bit flag; the settings for the bits are shown in Table 7.1.

Table 7.1. `Infoflags` bit values for the ImageObserver interface.

Name	*Meaning*
WIDTH=1	Width is available and can be read from the width parameter.
HEIGHT=2	Height is available and can be read from the height parameter.
PROPERTIES=4	Image properties are now available. The `getProperty()` method can be used.
SOMEBITS=8	Additional pixels for drawing a scaled image are available. The bounding box of the pixels can be read from the x, y, width, and height parameters.
FRAMEBITS=16	A complete image frame has been built and can now be displayed.

Name	*Meaning*
ALLBITS=32	A complete static image has been built and can now be displayed.
ERROR=64	An error occurred. No further information will be available, and drawing will fail.
ABORT=128	Image processing has been aborted. Set at the same time as ERROR. If ERROR is not also set, then you may try to paint the object again.

The following routine is used to repaint the applet when a complete image arrives:

```
public boolean imageUpdate(Image whichOne, int flags, int x, int y, int w, int h)
{
    if ( (flags & (ERROR ¦ FRAMEBITS ¦ ALLBITS)) != 0 )
    {
        repaint();
        return false;
    }
    return true;
}
```

The return value specifies whether you would like to continue to get information on this image; returning `false` will stop future notifications.

Tracking Image Loading

Image loading can also be tracked by using the MediaTracker class. Unlike the ImageObserver interface, it will not call back when something completes. The client of a MediaTracker object must register images with the tracker, then ask for status. *Registration* involves passing an image and assigning a tracking number to it, which then is used to query for the image's status. The following methods are available for image registration:

- `public void addImage(Image image, int id);`
- `public void addImage(Image image, int id, int w, int h);`

If a width and height are specified, the image will be scaled to these values. You can assign the same ID to multiple images. All the status-check routines can work on several images at once.

NOTE

If you assign the same ID to two or more images, then you can't check on the individual status of each image. Only group status as a whole can be checked.

You can use the following routines to get status information:

- `public boolean checkAll();`
- `public boolean checkAll(boolean load);`
- `public void waitForAll();`
- `public boolean waitForAll(long timeout);`
- `public int statusAll(boolean load);`
- `public boolean checkID(int id);`
- `public boolean checkID(int id, boolean load);`
- `public void waitForID(int id);`
- `public boolean waitForID(int id, long timeout);`
- `public int statusID(int id, boolean load);`

The MediaTracker class can be passed a load parameter. If this parameter is `true`, then the image (or images) will start to load. Remember, `getImage()` does not actually load the image. MediaTracker can be used to preload an image before it is displayed. The methods returning a Boolean value will indicate `false` unless all eligible images are complete. Images that encounter an error are considered to be complete, so you have to check for errors with these routines:

- `public boolean isErrorAny();`
- `public Object[] getErrorsAny();`
- `public boolean isErrorID(int id);`
- `public Object[] getErrorsID(int id);`

The integer returned by `statusAll()` and `statusID()` uses a bit flag much like `imageUpdate()` does; the values for the bit flag are listed in Table 7.2. The wait methods will block until all images are complete. You can also specify a time-out in milliseconds that determines the maximum time to wait.

Table 7.2. Status bit values for MediaTracker.

Name	*Meaning*
LOADING=1	Some (or all) images are still loading.
ABORTED=2	Some (or all) images have aborted.
ERRORED=4	Some (or all) images have encountered an error.
COMPLETE=8	Some (or all) images have loaded.

The Consumer/Producer Model

In Java, the Image class is just the tip of the iceberg; beneath it stand the ImageConsumer and ImageProducer interfaces. Image data is originated in an object that adheres to the ImageProducer interface, which sends the data to an object using the ImageConsumer interface. Figure 7.1 illustrates this relationship.

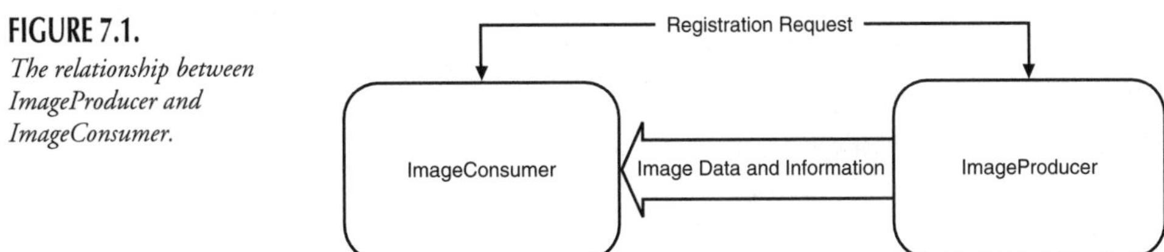

FIGURE 7.1.
The relationship between ImageProducer and ImageConsumer.

This model allows any type of object to both originate and receive image data. By creating the image subsystems as interfaces, Sun has freed image production from any specific object type. This is an important abstraction that you'll exploit in this chapter's project.

Java Color Models

As stated earlier, an image is a collection of colors and their layout. Much research has been done on how color is represented. Humans perceive color when combinations of wavelengths of visible light stimulate the retina. The number of wavelength combinations is infinite, but humans can see only a fixed subset as separate colors. Therefore, *color models* were invented to group human-visible colors into a working set. There are two predominant color models used to represent color information:

- The CMY (cyan-magenta-yellow) color model is used in subtractive color systems, such as printing.
- The RGB (red-green-blue) color model is used in additive color systems, such as television and computer screens.

Printing is a *subtractive system* because the perceived color is contained in wavelengths of light reflected from the paper. The absorbed colors are said to be "subtracted" from the perceived color. Conversely, an *additive color system* creates the light source containing the color. Therefore, you can watch television in the dark, but you can't read a magazine.

> **NOTE**
>
> If you're really curious, cyan absorbs red light, magenta absorbs green light, and yellow absorbs blue light. CMY color systems subtract RGB light and thus control the appearance of RGB color on a printed page.

Java encapsulates color information for an image in the ColorModel class. Using the model, pixel data is interpreted into a raw color component (red, green, blue, and alpha) for display. The ColorModel class has the following methods:

- `public static ColorModel getRGBdefault();`
- `public int getPixelSize();`
- `public int getRed(int pixel);`
- `public int getGreen(int pixel);`
- `public int getBlue(int pixel);`
- `public int getAlpha(int pixel);`
- `public int getRGB(int pixel);`

The lone static method returns the system default ColorModel.

Default RGB

Java uses the RGB color model for all its painting; all other models are eventually translated into this format. It has 8 bits of red, 8 bits of green, 8 bits of blue, and 8 bits of alpha. The alpha channel supplies transparency—255 is opaque (visible), and 0 is transparent. These add up to 32 bits of color information, which just happens to be the size of a Java integer. The format of colors within an integer is `0xAARRGGBB`.

To support images, Java supplies two other ColorModels: DirectColorModel and IndexColorModel.

Direct Color

The DirectColorModel is used when the underlying pixels in an image contain the RGB values directly. This is also known as "true color." There are two constructors—one with an alpha channel, one without. To create the model, you need to specify only the number of bits per pixel and which bits correspond to which color:

- `public DirectColorModel(int bits, int rmask, int gmask, int bmask);`
- `public DirectColorModel(int bits, int rmask, int gmask, int bmask, int amask);`

The mask values for Java's default RGB model are the following:

- `r = 0x00ff0000`
- `g = 0x0000ff00`
- `b = 0x000000ff`
- `a = 0xff000000`

Index Color

The IndexColorModel is used when the underlying pixels in an image represent an index into a color table. Most bitmaps fall into this category because the actual colors are contained in a color map somewhere in the file. The actual pixel data represent indexes into the color map instead of complete RGB values. There are five constructors for this model:

- `public IndexColorModel(int bits, int size, byte r[], byte g[], byte b[]);`
- `public IndexColorModel(int bits, int size, byte r[], byte g[], byte b[], int trans);`
- `public IndexColorModel(int bits, int size, byte r[], byte g[], byte b[], byte a[]);`
- `public IndexColorModel(int bits, int size, byte cmap[], int start, boolean hasalpha);`
- `public IndexColorModel(int bits, int size, byte cmap[], int start, boolean hasalpha, int trans);`

The parameter `bits` represents how many bits per pixel in the image, and `size` specifies the length of each color array. The colors themselves can be passed as individual arrays or packed into one large array (all reds, then all greens, and so forth). The parameter `hasalpha` signals the presence (or absence) of alpha information at the end of the packed array, and the `trans` parameter indicates which index is to be considered transparent, regardless of its alpha channel setting.

Chapter Project: Displaying a Windows BMP Image

Java has built-in support for GIF and JPEG format images, but what if you want to display an image using a different format? This chapter's project creates a class to display Windows BMP images. The principles involved in the display can be applied to almost any image format.

Using Image Types Not Supported by Java

The goal of this project is to create a class that accepts a URL and filename just as `getImage()` does. Although `getImage()` returns an image, the BmpImage class will return an ImageProducer. The caller of the class will have to use the producer to create an image:

```
producer = BmpImage.getImageProducer(getCodeBase(), "Forest.bmp");
myImage = createImage(producer);
```

NOTE

BmpImage could return an image, but the class would have had to be a component subclass to create an image. I didn't want to apply any restrictions to using BmpImage.

Memory Images

External image formats are most easily displayed by using the Java class MemoryImageSource, which allows an arbitrary array of pixels to be stored and used as the source for an ImageProducer. Because MemoryImageSource uses the ImageProducer interface, it can be used as the source for an image in the same way a GIF or JPEG image is used. The class has six different constructors:

- `public MemoryImageSource(int w, int h, ColorModel cm, byte pix[], int off, int scan);`
- `public MemoryImageSource(int w, int h, ColorModel cm, byte pix[], int off, int scan, Hashtable props);`
- `public MemoryImageSource(int w, int h, ColorModel cm, int pix[], int off, int scan);`
- `public MemoryImageSource(int w, int h, ColorModel cm, int pix[], int off, int scan, Hashtable props);`
- `public MemoryImage(int w, int h, int pix[], int off, int scan);`
- `public MemoryImage(int w, int h, int pix[], int off, int scan, Hashtable props);`

The first four pass in a ColorModel, but the final two do not. No ColorModel indicates that the passed pixel array uses the default RGB model. Hashtable `props` will be passed in the ImageConsumer call `setProperties(Hashtable)`. Normally, the props constructors are not used unless your image consumer uses the `setProperties()` method.

Now that you know how to create a suitable ImageProducer, the only remaining mystery is how to load and convert an arbitrary BMP image into the correct constructor arguments for MemoryImageSource.

Loading Foreign Images

Foreign images, such as BMP, are loaded by using the Java URL class. The following code snippet creates an input stream for a URL:

```
InputStream is = new URL(getCodeBase(), filename).openStream();
```

Once created, the input stream is read until all the information needed to create the image has been extracted.

BMP File Format

The Windows and OS/2 BMP formats are simple color map images; Figure 7.2 lays out the formats. All quantities are in Intel little-endian format. This means that all multibyte quantities, such as a 2-byte short, are stored as low byte, then high byte. Java uses big endian for all I/O reads (high byte, then low byte). You cannot use Java's `readShort()` or `readInt()` method to parse the file.

NOTE

The 2-byte quantity `0x1234` appears in memory differently depending on the system's endian order. In a little-endian system, the number would be stored in memory as 34, 12 (low byte first). Big-endian systems would store the number in memory as 12, 34 (high byte first).

Windows color maps are stored as 4 bytes per index. Each index consists of blue, green, red, and reserved bytes, in that order. The number of indexes is determined from either the number of colors specified in the header or the number of bits per pixel. If the number of colors in the header is zero, than bits per pixel is converted into number of colors. Images having 1, 4, or 8 bits per pixel use 2, 16, or 256 colors, respectively. OS/2 BMP images store colors as 3 bytes per index. Each OS/2 index consists of blue, green, and red bytes, in that order.

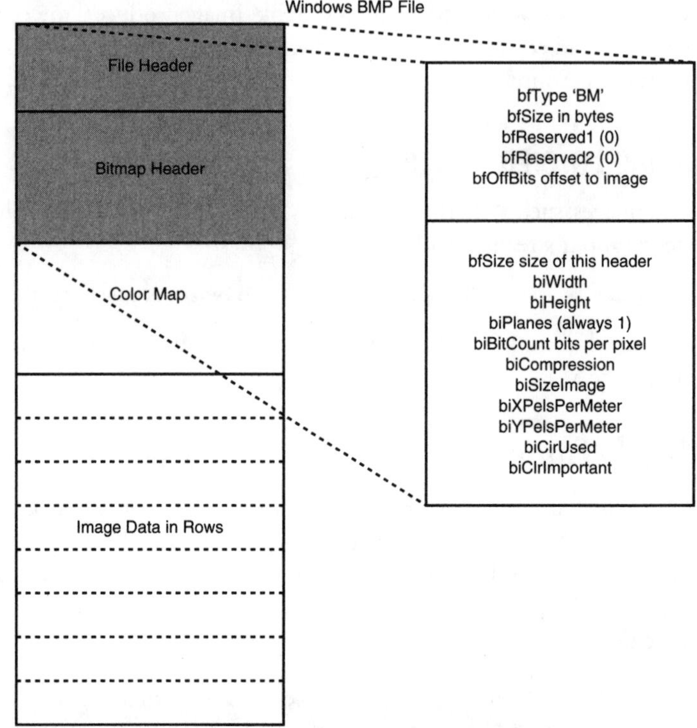

FIGURE 7.2.
Layout of Windows and OS/2 BMP files.

Reading Unsigned Binary in Java

I created a single method to read in a multibyte little-endian sequence:

```
/**
 * A private method for extracting little endian
 * quantities from a data input stream.
 * @param is contains the input stream
 * @param len is the number of bytes in the quantity
 * @returns the result as an integer
 */
private int pullVal(DataInputStream is, int len)
    throws IOException
{
    int value = 0;
    int temp;

    for ( int x = 0; x < len; x++ )
    {
        temp = is.readUnsignedByte();
        value += (temp << (x * 8));
    }
    return value;
}
```

Each byte is read as an unsigned quantity and shifted into the proper position before being added to the total. Little-endian values are stored in completely reversed format, so the routine shifts each byte in multiples of 8 bits.

> **NOTE**
>
> The Java method `readUnsignedByte()` returns an integer, not a byte. Java bytes are signed quantities, so a larger storage variable had to be used to contain the unsigned value.

Creating the Color Table

Since the colors are stored in RGB format, you will create separate arrays for each color. One large array could have been used, but managing it would have been more complex. Once the color arrays have been stored, they are used to create a ColorModel:

```
/**
 * A private method for extracting the color table from
 * a BMP type file.
 * @param is contains the input stream
 * @param numColors contains the biClrUsed (for Windows) or zero
 */
private void extractColorMap(DataInputStream is, int numColors)
    throws IOException, AWTException
{
    byte blues[], reds[], greens[];

    // if passed count is zero, then determine the
    // number of entries from bits per pixel.
    if ( numColors == 0 )
    {
        switch ( biBitCount )
        {
        case 1:  numColors =   2; break;
        case 4:  numColors =  16; break;
        case 8:  numColors = 256; break;
        case 24: numColors =   0; break;
        default: numColors =  -1; break;
        }
}
if ( numColors == -1 )
    throw new AWTException("Invalid bits per pixel: " + biBitCount);
else if ( numColors == 0 )
      colorModel = new DirectColorModel(24, 255 * 3, 255 * 2, 255);
else
{
      reds = new byte[numColors];
      blues = new byte[numColors];
      greens = new byte[numColors];
      for ( int x = 0; x < numColors; x++ )
      {
          blues[x] = is.readByte();
```

```
                greens[x] = is.readByte();
                reds[x] = is.readByte();
                if ( windowsStyle )
                    is.skipBytes(1);
            }
            colorModel = new IndexColorModel( biBitCount, numColors,
                                              reds, greens, blues );
        }
    }
```

DirectColorModel is used for true color BMP images; IndexColorModel, for all other representations.

Constructing the Image

The image data itself is stored differently depending on the number of bits per pixel and whether the data is compressed. BMPImage will only support uncompressed 4 and 8 bits per pixel, though it can easily be extended to support all other modes.

All modes store the image in rows from the bottom of the image to the top. Yes, this means that the image is stored upside down. For 8 bits per pixel, each row is stored as single bytes and padded to a 4-byte boundary. The following code block extracts uncompressed, 8-bits-per-pixel images:

```
/**
 * A private method for extracting 8 bit per pixel
 * image data.
 * @param is contains the input stream
 */
private void extract8BitData( DataInputStream is )
    throws IOException
{
    int index;

    if ( biCompression == 0 )
    {
        int padding = 0;
        int overage = biWidth % 4;
        if ( overage != 0 )
            padding = 4 - overage;
        pix = new int[biHeight * biWidth];
        for ( int y = biHeight - 1; y >= 0; y— )
        {
            index = y * biWidth;
            for ( int x = 0; x < biWidth; x++ )
            {
                pix[index++] = is.readUnsignedByte();
            }
            if ( padding != 0 ) is.skipBytes(padding);
        }
    }
    else
    {
    }
}
```

Storage for 4 bits per pixel is similar to 8 bits per pixel, except the data is stored two per byte. The next code block extracts 4 bits per pixel data:

```
private void extract4BitData( DataInputStream is )
    throws IOException
{
    int index, temp = 0;

    if ( biCompression == 0 )
    {
        int padding = 0;
        int overage = ((biWidth + 1)/ 2) % 4;
        if ( overage != 0 )
            padding = 4 - overage;
        pix = new int[biHeight * biWidth];
        for ( int y = biHeight - 1; y >= 0; y-- )
        {
            index = y * biWidth;
            for ( int x = 0; x < biWidth; x++ )
            {
                // if on an even byte, read new 8 bit quantity
                // use low nibble of previous read for odd bytes
                if ( (x % 2) == 0 )
                {
                    temp = is.readUnsignedByte();
                    pix[index++] = temp >> 4;
                }
                else
                    pix[index++] = temp & 0x0f;
            }
            if ( padding != 0 ) is.skipBytes(padding);
        }
    }
    else
    {
        throw new IOException("Compressed images not supported");
    }
}
```

The real complication occurs when figuring the padding bytes. If the rows have an odd number of columns, then the last pixel will take up an entire byte. To accommodate this, the width is bumped up by one before it is divided by two. This will force odd-numbered columns to yield the correct number of bytes; even-numbered columns are unaffected (see the following code lines for an example):

```
11 columns: 11 / 2 = 5 [incorrect], (11 + 1) / 2 = 6 [correct]
12 columns: 12 / 2 = 6 [correct],   (12 + 1) / 2 = 6 [correct]
```

Listing 7.1 displays the entire BmpImage class. At the bottom of the listing, you will see a static main function; it was added to allow testing of the class. This function allows the class to be invoked from the command line as follows:

```
java BmpImage Forest.bmp
```

Although the image won't be rendered, the entire image will be processed, and all the header contents will be displayed to the screen. In addition, any exceptions thrown during image extraction will be displayed.

Listing 7.1. The BMP display class.

```
import java.io.*;
import java.net.*;
import java.awt.*;
import java.awt.image.*;

public class BmpImage
{
    String bfName;
    boolean imageProcessed;
    boolean windowsStyle;
    ColorModel colorModel = null;
    int pix[];

    byte bfType[];
    int bfSize;
    int bfOffset;
    int biSize;
    int biWidth;
    int biHeight;
    int biPlanes;
    int biBitCount;
    int biCompression;
    int biSizeImage;
    int biXPelsPerMeter;
    int biYPelsPerMeter;
    int biClrUsed;
    int biClrImportant;

    public BmpImage(String name)
    {
        bfName = name;
        bfType = new byte[2];
        imageProcessed = false;
    }

    /**
     * A private method for extracting little endian
     * quantities from a input stream.
     * @param is contains the input stream
     * @param len is the number of bytes in the quantity
     * @returns the result as an integer
     */
    private int pullVal(DataInputStream is, int len)
        throws IOException
    {
        int value = 0;
        int temp = 0;

        for ( int x = 0; x < len; x++ )
        {
```

```
            temp = is.readUnsignedByte();
            value += (temp << (x * 8));
        }
        return value;
    }

    /**
     * A private method for extracting the file header
     * portion of a BMP file.
     * @param is contains the input stream
     */
    private void extractFileHeader(DataInputStream is)
        throws IOException, AWTException
    {
        is.read(bfType);
        if ( bfType[0] != 'B' || bfType[1] != 'M' )
            throw new AWTException("Not BMP format");
        bfSize = pullVal(is, 4);
        is.skipBytes(4);
        bfOffset = pullVal(is, 4);
    }

    /**
     * A private method for extracting the color table from
     * a BMP type file.
     * @param is contains the input stream
     * @param numColors contains the biClrUsed (for Windows) or zero
     */
    private void extractColorMap(DataInputStream is, int numColors)
        throws IOException, AWTException
    {
        byte blues[], reds[], greens[];

        // if passed count is zero, then determine the
        // number of entries from bits per pixel.
        if ( numColors == 0 )
        {
            switch ( biBitCount )
            {
            case 1:  numColors =   2; break;
            case 4:  numColors =  16; break;
            case 8:  numColors = 256; break;
            case 24: numColors =   0; break;
            default: numColors =  -1; break;
            }
        }
        if ( numColors == -1 )
            throw new AWTException("Invalid bits per pixel: " + biBitCount);
        else if ( numColors == 0 )
            colorModel = new DirectColorModel(24, 255 * 3, 255 * 2, 255);
        else
        {
            reds = new byte[numColors];
            blues = new byte[numColors];
            greens = new byte[numColors];
            for ( int x = 0; x < numColors; x++ )
            {
```

continues

Listing 7.1. continued

```
                blues[x] = is.readByte();
                greens[x] = is.readByte();
                reds[x] = is.readByte();
                if ( windowsStyle )
                    is.skipBytes(1);
            }
            colorModel = new IndexColorModel( biBitCount, numColors,
                                    reds, greens, blues );
        }
    }

    /**
     * A private method for extracting an OS/2 style
     * bitmap header.
     * @param is contains the input stream
     */
    private void extractOS2Style(DataInputStream is)
        throws IOException, AWTException
    {
        windowsStyle = false;
        biWidth = pullVal(is, 2);
        biHeight = pullVal(is, 2);
        biPlanes = pullVal(is, 2);
        biBitCount = pullVal(is, 2);
        extractColorMap(is, 0);
    }

    /**
     * A private method for extracting a Windows style
     * bitmap header.
     * @param is contains the input stream
     */
    private void extractWindowsStyle(DataInputStream is)
        throws IOException, AWTException
    {
        windowsStyle = true;
        biWidth = pullVal(is, 4);
        biHeight = pullVal(is, 4);
        biPlanes = pullVal(is, 2);
        biBitCount = pullVal(is, 2);
        biCompression = pullVal(is, 4);
        biSizeImage = pullVal(is, 4);
        biXPelsPerMeter = pullVal(is, 4);
        biYPelsPerMeter = pullVal(is, 4);
        biClrUsed = pullVal(is, 4);
        biClrImportant = pullVal(is, 4);
        extractColorMap(is, biClrUsed);
    }

    /**
     * A private method for extracting the bitmap header.
     * This method determines the header type (OS/2 or Windows)
     * and calls the appropriate routine.
     * @param is contains the input stream
     */
    private void extractBitmapHeader(DataInputStream is)
```

```
        throws IOException, AWTException
    {
        biSize = pullVal(is, 4);
        if ( biSize == 12 )
            extractOS2Style(is);
        else
            extractWindowsStyle(is);
    }

    /**
     * A private method for extracting 4 bit per pixel
     * image data.
     * @param is contains the input stream
     */
    private void extract4BitData( DataInputStream is )
        throws IOException
    {
        int index, temp = 0;

        if ( biCompression == 0 )
        {
            int padding = 0;
            int overage = ((biWidth + 1)/ 2) % 4;
            if ( overage != 0 )
                padding = 4 - overage;
            pix = new int[biHeight * biWidth];
            for ( int y = biHeight - 1; y >= 0; y-- )
            {
                index = y * biWidth;
                for ( int x = 0; x < biWidth; x++ )
                {
                    // if on an even byte, read new 8 bit quantity
                    // use low nibble of previous read for odd bytes
                    if ( (x % 2) == 0 )
                    {
                        temp = is.readUnsignedByte();
                        pix[index++] = temp >> 4;
                    }
                    else
                        pix[index++] = temp & 0x0f;
                }
                if ( padding != 0 ) is.skipBytes(padding);
            }
        }
        else
        {
            throw new IOException("Compressed images not supported");
        }
    }

    /**
     * A private method for extracting 8 bit per pixel
     * image data.
     * @param is contains the input stream
     */
    private void extract8BitData( DataInputStream is )
        throws IOException
```

continues

Listing 7.1. continued

```
{
    int index;

    if ( biCompression == 0 )
    {
        int padding = 0;
        int overage = biWidth % 4;
        if ( overage != 0 )
            padding = 4 - overage;
        pix = new int[biHeight * biWidth];
        for ( int y = biHeight - 1; y >= 0; y-- )
        {
            index = y * biWidth;
            for ( int x = 0; x < biWidth; x++ )
            {
                pix[index++] = is.readUnsignedByte();
            }
            if ( padding != 0 ) is.skipBytes(padding);
        }
    }
    else
    {
        throw new IOException("Compressed images not supported");
    }
}

/**
 * A private method for extracting the image data from
 * a input stream.
 * @param is contains the input stream
 */
private void extractImageData( DataInputStream is )
    throws IOException, AWTException
{
    switch ( biBitCount )
    {
    case 1:
        throw new AWTException("Unhandled bits/pixel: " + biBitCount);
    case 4:  extract4BitData(is); break;
    case 8:  extract8BitData(is); break;
    case 24:
        throw new AWTException("Unhandled bits/pixel: " + biBitCount);
    default:
        throw new AWTException("Invalid bits per pixel: " + biBitCount);
    }
}

/**
 * Given an input stream, create an ImageProducer from
 * the BMP info contained in the stream.
 * @param is contains the input stream to use
 * @returns the ImageProducer
 */
public ImageProducer extractImage( DataInputStream is )
    throws AWTException
{
```

```
    MemoryImageSource img = null;
    try
    {
        extractFileHeader(is);
        extractBitmapHeader(is);
        extractImageData(is);
        img = new MemoryImageSource( biWidth, biHeight, colorModel,
                                     pix, 0, biWidth );
        imageProcessed = true;
    }
    catch (IOException ioe )
    {
        throw new AWTException(ioe.toString());
    }
    return img;
}

/**
 * Describe the image as a string
 */
public String toString()
{
    StringBuffer buf = new StringBuffer("");
    if ( imageProcessed )
    {
        buf.append("       name: " + bfName + "\n");
        buf.append("       size: " + bfSize + "\n");
        buf.append(" img offset: " + bfOffset + "\n");
        buf.append("header size: " + biSize + "\n");
        buf.append("      width: " + biWidth + "\n");
        buf.append("     height: " + biHeight + "\n");
        buf.append(" clr planes: " + biPlanes + "\n");
        buf.append(" bits/pixel: " + biBitCount + "\n");
        if ( windowsStyle )
        {
            buf.append("compression: " + biCompression + "\n");
            buf.append(" image size: " + biSizeImage + "\n");
            buf.append("Xpels/meter: " + biXPelsPerMeter + "\n");
            buf.append("Ypels/meter: " + biYPelsPerMeter + "\n");
            buf.append("colors used: " + biClrUsed + "\n");
            buf.append("primary clr: " + biClrImportant + "\n");
        }
    }
    else
        buf.append("Image not read yet.");
    return buf.toString();
}

/**
 * A method to retrieve an ImageProducer for a BMP URL.
 * @param context contains the base URL (from getCodeBase() or such)
 * @param name contains the file name.
 * @returns an ImageProducer
 * @exception AWTException on stream or bitmap data errors
 */
public static ImageProducer getImageProducer( URL context, String name )
    throws AWTException
```

continues

Listing 7.1. continued

```
    {
        InputStream is = null;
        ImageProducer img = null;

        try
        {
            BmpImage im = new BmpImage(name);
            is = new URL(context, name).openStream();
            DataInputStream input = new DataInputStream( new
                                            BufferedInputStream(is) );
            img = im.extractImage(input);
        }
        catch (MalformedURLException me)
        {
            throw new AWTException(me.toString());
        }
        catch (IOException ioe)
        {
            throw new AWTException(ioe.toString());
        }
        return img;
    }

    /**
     * A method to retrieve an ImageProducer given just a BMP URL.
     * @param context contains the base URL (from getCodeBase() or such)
     * @returns an ImageProducer
     * @exception AWTException on stream or bitmap data errors
     */
    public static ImageProducer getImageProducer( URL context)
        throws AWTException
    {
        InputStream is = null;
        ImageProducer img = null;
        String name = context.toString();
        int index; // Make last part of URL the name
        if ((index = name.lastIndexOf('/')) >= 0)
            name = name.substring(index + 1);
        try {
            BmpImage im = new BmpImage(name);
            is = context.openStream();
            DataInputStream input = new DataInputStream( new
                                            BufferedInputStream(is) );
            img = im.extractImage(input);
        }
        catch (MalformedURLException me)
        {
            throw new AWTException(me.toString());
        }
        catch (IOException ioe)
        {
            throw new AWTException(ioe.toString());
        }
        return img;
    }

    /**
```

```
     * A public test routine (you must pass the filename as the 1st arg)
     */
    public static void main( String args[] )
    {
        try
        {
            FileInputStream inFile = new FileInputStream(args[0]);
            DataInputStream is = new DataInputStream( new
                                    BufferedInputStream(inFile) );
            BmpImage im = new BmpImage(args[0]);
            ImageProducer img = im.extractImage(is);
            System.out.println("Output:\n" + im);
        }
        catch ( Exception e )
        {
            System.out.println(e);
        }
    }
}
```

This class supports both Windows and OS/2 format bitmaps. OS/2 image data is identical to Windows image data, though OS/2 supports only uncompressed formats.

The concepts used to create the BMP image can also be applied to other image formats. The steps can be boiled down to the following list:

- Acquire the input stream for the image data.
- Parse the image data to extract and create a ColorModel.
- Extract the image data into an array that conforms to the ColorModel previously created.
- Use the model and data to create a MemoryImageSource object that acts as the ImageProducer for the image.

Listing 7.2 shows a simple applet that uses BmpImage to display a bitmap.

Listing 7.2. The SimpleBmp applet used to exercise the BmpImage class.

```
import java.applet.*;
import java.awt.*;
import java.awt.image.*;
import BmpImage;

public class SimpleBmp extends Applet
{
    private boolean init = false;
    Image myImage = null;

    /**
     * Standard initialization method for an applet
     */
    public void init()
```

continues

Listing 7.2. continued

```
    {
        ImageProducer producer;
        if ( init == false )
        {
            init = true;
            try
            {
                producer = BmpImage.getImageProducer(getCodeBase(),
                                                     "Forest.bmp");
                myImage = createImage(producer);
            }
            catch (AWTException ae)
            {
                System.out.println(ae.toString());
            }
        }
    }

    /**
     * Standard paint routine for an applet.
     * @param g contains the Graphics class to use for painting
     */
    public void paint(Graphics g)
    {
        g.drawImage(myImage, 0, 0, this);
    }
}
```

Summary

This chapter covers Java image concepts, including loading and display. Remember the image producer/consumer model; you'll see it recur whenever you deal with images. The Java color models—direct and indexed—are also important concepts. The producer/consumer and color models combine to enable you to render an almost infinite number of image types and formats. The chapter ends by demonstrating a class for reading and displaying image formats that Java doesn't directly support. Chapter 8, "Adding Threads to Applets," will explore image loading and tracking in more depth, so you can make use of the material covered in this chapter.

8

Adding Threads to Applets

Using images might make your applet look nicer, but it also slows the performance of your applet quite a bit. The biggest reason for this delay is that images are large compared to normal text documents, such as HTML files; consequently, images take longer to load from the network. Another reason for this delay is the time it takes to render some images. Most images are based on a graphics format that uses some type of compression algorithm. Although this compression can result in faster delivery, rendering the image will take additional time, even though this time delay may be minor.

In traditional programming, you would have no options for speeding up the image display. You would simply have to wait for each image to be downloaded, then wait for it to be rendered. However, this chapter ends Part III of this book by introducing *multithreading* as a way to make your applet run faster and more efficiently. No longer will you have to wait for each image to be downloaded and rendered. With multithreading, you can download images while other images are being displayed. The prospective user of your applet won't have to wait for all the images to be downloaded to make a decision. With multithreading, you can use a single image when it's ready instead of waiting for all images to be made available.

What Is a Thread?

A *thread* has many features of a standalone process. It has a beginning, a middle, and an ending. Technically speaking, a thread is a single sequential stream of execution. A thread can perform a task until it has run to its conclusion (such as a long calculation), or it can run indefinitely, waiting for requests to perform a service (such as a database server). In practical terms, a thread can do just about everything a process can.

So what is special about threads? The key thing to note is that a thread runs inside a process; to put it another way, a process can contain one or more threads (in an operating environment that supports multithreading). This means that one process can have a thread that performs a calculation, another thread that performs a service, and so forth. Furthermore, threads can create new threads. In Java, threads are everywhere. There are even threads you haven't explicitly created. The object garbage collector runs in the virtual machine as a thread. Even the Applet class that starts your applet is itself running as part of a thread.

There are other subtle differences between processes and threads. Multitasking operating systems, which have been around for a long time, allow multiple processes to run simultaneously. However, these processes are generally completely independent of each other; the only thing they share is the operating environment. Consequently, activities like getting processes to communicate with each other can be a little tricky. In a multithreading environment, however, programs that would traditionally be run as separate processes can be structured to run as separate threads within a common process. This allows the threads to share resources common to that process, such as objects and variables. Consequently, the threads of a process, though running separately, also work together to form a greater whole. Each thread can be seen as existing as part of a single, greater unit. For example, when the process dies, so do all its threads.

Creating a Thread with the Thread Class

Java offers a variety of tools for writing multithreaded programs. The most useful is the Thread class, which, as its name suggests, is used for creating a class that runs as a thread. You need to declare a subclass of Thread if you want to create a functional thread. After the subclass is created, you need to override Thread's `run()` method. This method is the key to making the Thread class perform as a thread; it defines your class's thread of execution. After the `run()` method is established and your class is instantiated, you can begin the thread with the `start()` method.

A simple example shows how easy it is to create a thread in Java. Figure 8.1 shows an applet with lines drawn randomly throughout its workspace. These lines are drawn by a thread using the code in Listing 8.1. The class LineThread is a subclass of Thread that loops indefinitely, randomly drawing lines on an applet. The applet is provided to LineThread through its constructor. Although the LineThread class has a custom constructor, Thread classes often do not have special constructors.

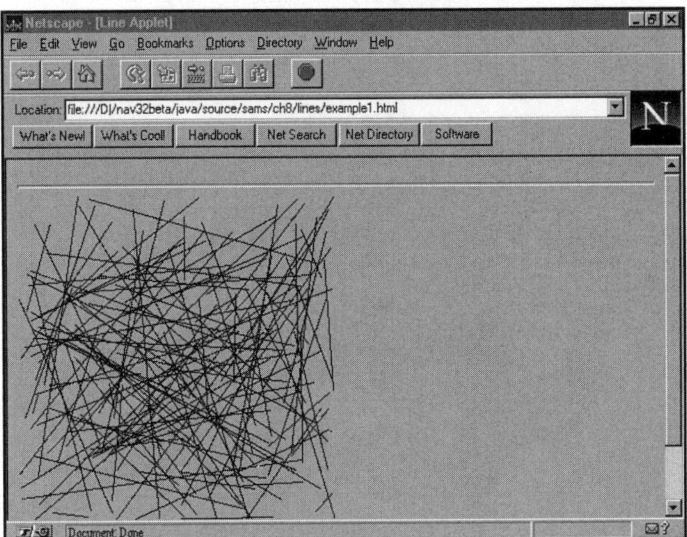

FIGURE 8.1.
An applet with lines drawn by a thread.

Listing 8.1. The source code for applet with lines drawn by a thread.

```
import java.awt.*;
import java.lang.*;
import java.applet.Applet;

// This is an applet that creates a Thread that
// randomly draws lines on its workspace...
public class LineApplet extends Applet  {
   Thread t;
   // Set the size of the applet, create the thread,
   // and start it...
```

continues

Listing 8.1. continued

```
    public void init() {
       resize(300,300);
       t = new LineThread(this);
       t.start();
    }

    // Click the mouse to kill the thread...
    public boolean mouseDown(Event ev, int x1, int x2) {

       if (t != null) {
          t.stop();
          t = null;
       }
       return true;
    };
}

// Thread that randomly draws lines all over a component...
class LineThread extends Thread {
   Applet a;  // Thread needs to know the applet...
   // Constructor simply stores the applet to paint...
   public LineThread(Applet a) {
    this.a = a;
   }

   // Run the thread. Lines everywhere!
   public void run() {
      // Get dimension data about the applet...
      double width = (double) a.size().width;
      double height = (double)a.size().height;
      // Loop and draw lines forever...
      while (true) {
         Graphics g = a.getGraphics();
         g.drawLine((int)(width * Math.random()),
            (int)(height * Math.random()),
            (int)(width * Math.random()),
            (int)(height * Math.random()) );
      }
   }
}
```

The `run()` method of LineThread provides the applet's threaded activity. After getting the applet's dimensions, the thread enters an indefinite `while` loop, randomly drawing lines on each iteration. (The Component class's `getGraphics()` method is a way of getting a Graphics object to draw on a component outside the `paint()` method.) The thread will run until the applet is terminated or until the thread is explicitly stopped.

After setting its own size and constructing a LineThread object, the Applet class, LineApplet, begins the line drawing by calling the `start()` method. This `start()` method call begins the thread and invokes the `run()` method of the LineThread class. The thread will not run until the `start()` method is applied.

The stop() method terminates a thread. In a general sense, stop() causes a thread to abruptly leave its run() method and, therefore, end its threaded activity. In this example, a mouse click on the applet causes the thread (and hence the line drawing) to stop.

Enhancing Your First Multithreaded Applet

A couple of things can be done to this applet to further illustrate the Thread class. Listing 8.2 gives the source code for the enhanced version of the applet. The threaded class, LineThread, was modified to delay a little between the line drawings by using the sleep() method, which causes the thread to "sleep" for a specific number of milliseconds; in this case, the delay is for a tenth of a second. Note how the sleep() method requires catching InterruptedException objects. This is meant for situations in which a thread has been interrupted by another thread. However, this capability doesn't seem to be active in the current version of the JDK. Consequently, you will see null handlers for InterruptedException objects throughout this book. Because it is annoying to have to have an exception handler every time you call sleep(), you might want to encapsulate sleep() and the exception handling in your own method. This technique appears in the code used elsewhere in this book.

Listing 8.2. Enhanced version of the line-drawing applet.

```
import java.awt.*;
import java.lang.*;
import java.applet.Applet;

// This is an applet that creates a Thread that
// randomly draws lines on its workspace...
public class LineApplet extends Applet  {
   Thread t;
   boolean running = false;
   // Set the size of the applet, create the thread
   // and start it...
   public void init() {
      resize(300,300);
      t = new LineThread(this);
      t.start();
      running = true;
   }

   // Click the mouse down to kill the thread...
   public boolean mouseDown(Event ev, int x1, int x2) {
      // If the thread is active, suspend the thread
      // and remove the lines...
      if (running) {
         running = false;
         t.suspend();
         repaint();  // Removes the lines...
      }
      // If thread is suspended, then reactivate it...
      else {
```

continues

Listing 8.2. continued

```
            running = true;
            t.resume();
         }
         return true;
      };

      // Destroy the thread when the applet shuts down...
      public void destroy() {
         // Stop the thread and wait for it to die...
         t.stop();
         try {
              t.join();
         }
         catch (InterruptedException e) { }
      }
}

// Thread that randomly draws lines all over a component...
class LineThread extends Thread {
   Applet a;  // Thread needs to know the applet...
   // Constructor simply stores the applet to paint...
   public LineThread(Applet a) {
    this.a = a;
   }

   // Run the thread. Lines everywhere!
   public void run() {
      // Get dimension data about the applet...
      double width = (double) a.size().width;
      double height = (double)a.size().height;
      // Loop and draw lines forever...
      while (true) {
         Graphics g = a.getGraphics();
         // Randomly select a color...
         Color c = new Color((int)(255.0 * Math.random()),
            (int)(255.0 * Math.random()),
            (int)(255.0 * Math.random()) );
         g.setColor(c);
         g.drawLine((int)(width * Math.random()),
            (int)(height * Math.random()),
            (int)(width * Math.random()),
            (int)(height * Math.random()) );
         // Sleep some...
         try {
            sleep(100);
         }
         catch (InterruptedException e) { }
      }
   }
}
```

A visual enhancement also was made to LineThread. It randomly creates a new Color object and uses it (with the Graphics class `setColor()` method) in each iteration. Figure 8.2 shows the enhancement.

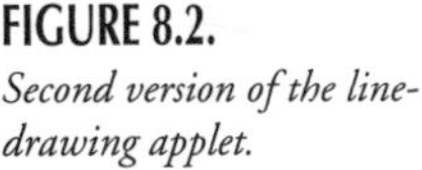

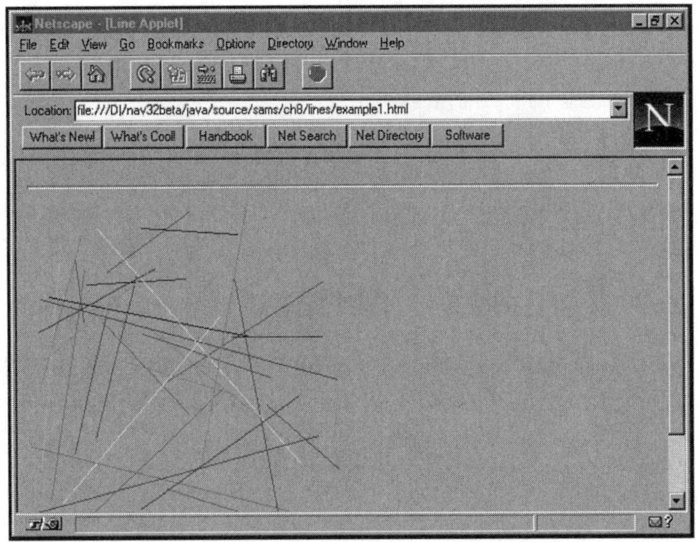

FIGURE 8.2.
Second version of the line-drawing applet.

Most of the changes occur in the Applet class LineApplet. The method that traps the mouse clicks, `mouseDown()`, is changed so it no longer stops the thread. It now toggles between pausing and resuming the thread's execution. The `suspend()` method suspends a thread's execution; when a thread is suspended, it will not continue its stream of execution until the complementary `resume()` method is invoked. In this example, suspending a thread is accompanied by clearing out the applet's drawing area through the `repaint()` method. (This clearing occurs because the applet does not override the `paint()` method.) The `running` variable is used to keep track of whether the thread is suspended; unfortunately, there is no method in the Thread class for determining this.

The last bit of code occurs in the newly added `destroy()` method, which is called when the applet shuts down. In this call, the `stop()` method terminates the thread. It is accompanied by a `join()` call, which forces the calling thread to wait until the victim thread is really "dead." This is important because stopping a thread does not cause an immediate (in the strict sense of the word) termination of the thread. There may be some delay due to time-slicing or some other reason. It is often dangerous not to wait for a thread to die. In some cases, the thread may run even after some of the objects it uses (like the applet) are no longer valid. This will cause an exception. Furthermore, an applet that has been stopped without waiting for its constituent threads to terminate could cause the applet to unexpectedly "hang." Consequently, it's good practice to follow `stop()` calls by a complementary call to `join()` to prevent this from happening. It should be noted that the Thread class has two additional versions of `join()` that take time-out flags. Use these if your applet has some severe time constraints and you cannot afford to wait indefinitely for a thread to end. The time-out values (like most time-outs in Java) are in milliseconds with an optional nanosecond precision value.

It is easy to modify the example to have multiple line-drawing threads. If you add the following code, there will be two threads drawing lines on the applet:

```
Thread t2 = new LineThread(this);
t2.start();
```

You should add corresponding `stop()` and `join()` methods to terminate the threads in the applet `destroy()` method.

The Runnable Interface

One thing may strike you as troubling in this discussion about how threads work. If you have to use the Thread class every time you need to run something as a thread, don't you lose the capability to inherit other classes? Because Java is a single-inheritance system, forcing a class to inherit the Thread class would seem to be overly restrictive because you couldn't, for example, run the Applet class as a thread. Fortunately, Java actually implements threads through an interface, thus allowing any class to use a thread's functions. The interface is called *Runnable* and has only one method, `run()`. The `run()` method of the Thread class is itself an implementation of Runnable.

The typical way of starting a class that implements Runnable as a thread is to call an alternate Thread constructor. This constructor takes a Runnable class as its target parameter. For example, if you have a Runnable object assigned to the variable `r`, you would pass it to the Thread constructor as follows:

```
t = new Thread(r);
```

When the thread's `start()` method is called after this, the `run()` method of the Runnable target is invoked. If you don't want to explicitly declare a `Thread` variable, you can start the Runnable target in a more concise manner:

```
new Thread(r).start();
```

A Thread object created with a Runnable target behaves similarly to the thread behavior discussed in the previous sections. The `stop()` method terminates the thread, `suspend()` and `resume()` are used to pause and restart the thread, and so on.

The line-drawing applet can be reworked to use the Runnable interface. In the example shown in Listing 8.3, the LineThread class is removed, and the Applet class (called LineRun, in this case) implements the Runnable interface. Therefore, there is only one class in the applet that both draws the lines and runs as a thread.

Listing 8.3. The line-drawing applet using the Runnable interface.

```
import java.awt.*;
import java.lang.*;
import java.applet.Applet;
```

```
// Runs the Applet as a Thread so that it can paint
// lines indefinitely...
public class LineRun extends Applet implements Runnable {
   Thread t;  // This is the thread!
   // Set the size of the applet...
   public void init() {
         resize(300,300);
   }

   // Entering the Applet. Start the thread...
   public void start() {
     if (t == null) {
      t = new Thread(this);
      t.start();
     } // end if
   }

   // Leaving the Applet. Stop the thread...
   public void stop() {
     if (t != null) {
      t.stop();
      try {
         t.join();
      }
      catch (InterruptedException e) { }
     } // end if
     t = null;
   }

   // Run the thread. Lines everywhere!
   public void run() {
      // Get dimension data about the applet...
      double width = (double)size().width;
      double height = (double)size().height;
      // Loop and draw lines forever...
      while (true) {
         Graphics g = getGraphics();
         // Randomly select a color...
         Color c = new Color((int)(255.0 * Math.random()),
            (int)(255.0 * Math.random()),
            (int)(255.0 * Math.random()) );
         g.setColor(c);
         g.drawLine((int)(width * Math.random()),
            (int)(height * Math.random()),
            (int)(width * Math.random()),
            (int)(height * Math.random()) );
         // Sleep some...
         try {
            t.sleep(100);
         }
         catch (InterruptedException e) { }
      }
   }
}
```

There are a couple of interesting things to note about this applet. It looks almost exactly like the example in the previous section. In fact, the `run()` method of Listing 8.3 is only slightly modified from that of the second version of the LineThread class; the only changes are the removal of the references to the Applet class and how the `sleep()` method is invoked.

The thread that runs the Runnable target is constructed in the `start()` method of the LineRun class. (Keep in mind that the `start()` method here is that of the Applet class and not the Thread class.) You must check whether the thread already exists because you might move back and forth from the line-drawing Web page to another page. If you leave the drawing page, the Applet `stop()` method kills the thread and waits for it to die. It will be restarted if you return to the page.

An interesting thing to note about classes that implement Runnable is that they are not "dead" if their `run()` method has been stopped. Even if the thread is dead, the other methods in a class using Runnable still can be invoked. For example, add the following code to the LineRun class:

```
// Toggle the running of the line-drawing thread...
public boolean mouseDown(Event ev, int x, int y) {
     // Stop the thread if it is running...
     if (t != null) {
         t.stop();
         try {
            t.join();
         }
         catch (InterruptedException e) { }
         t = null;
     }
     // If it is dead, then start a new thread...
     else {
         t = new Thread(this);
         t.start();
     }
     return true;
};
```

This code stops the thread if it is running and restarts it if the thread is stopped. Therefore, the LineRun object is alive regardless of whether the `run()` method is active. This example points out an advantage of using the Runnable interface over creating a subclass of Thread. When a Thread object's `run()` method is stopped, it cannot be restarted; you have to create a new Thread to have its `run()` method run again. On the other hand, an object using Runnable can have its `run()` method repeatedly started and stopped.

Another advantage of using the Runnable interface for your custom thread is that it does carry all the baggage of the Thread class, which supports over two dozen methods. It seems wasteful to subclass threads so that you can override only the `run()` method. On the other hand, the Thread class might be useful if your threaded class doesn't need to be a subclass of a complex class like Applet. In general, it's best to follow the design versus implementation rule: If your class is designed to be a special kind of thread, then use the Thread class; if it's designed to be something else (like an AWT component) but needs to implement threads, then use Runnable.

Synchronization

As you can see from the previous examples, writing threaded classes in Java is generally pretty easy, so you might wonder why, until recently, relatively few languages and programs have supported multithreading. The reason for this is that multithreading is not without risks. In particular, a class meant to run in a concurrent environment must be designed so that multiple threads can access an instance of the class without causing undesired behavior. An instance of the class must be as reliable in an environment with multiple threads of execution as it is within a single-threaded environment. In other words, the class must be *thread-safe*. You will now see an example of a class that's not thread-safe.

A TestStack Class That Is Not Thread-Safe

Listing 8.4 shows the code for a class that is a stack of Integer objects. It is a generally well-constructed class, showing good Java programming practices, such as handling errors (like an empty stack) by throwing exceptions. However, it is not thread-safe. Why is this? Look at the `push()` and `pop()` methods. They both use the `top` integer variable to indicate the current top of the stack. But what happens if one thread is calling `push()` at the same time another thread is calling `pop()`? In this situation, `push()` and `pop()` might behave in an undesired fashion.

Listing 8.4. A TestStack class that isn't thread-safe.

```
// Classes of stack exceptions...
class StackException extends Exception { }
class StackFullException extends StackException { }
class StackEmptyException extends StackException { }

// This class implements a simple stack as
// an array of integers...
class TestStack {
   Integer s[];  // The stack array of integer objects...
   int top; // The current top of the stack. Next item to place.
   // Construct a stack of the specified size...
   public TestStack(int size) {
      s = new Integer[size];
      top = -1;    // Empty stack...
   }
   // Push an item onto the stack...
   public void push(Integer item) throws StackFullException {
      // Throw exception if stack is full...
      if (top == s.length)
            throw new StackFullException();
      // Otherwise increment the top and add the item...
      ++top;
      s[top] = item;
   }

   // Pop the top item off the stack...
   public Integer pop() throws StackEmptyException {
```

continues

Listing 8.4. continued

```
      // Throw exception if stack is empty...
      if (top < 0)
            throw new StackEmptyException();
      // Otherwise, return the top item and decrement the top...
      Integer I = s[top];
      s[top] = null;
      —top;
      return I;
   }

   // List the contents of the stack...
   public void list() {
      for (int i = 0; i <= top; ++i)
            System.out.println(i + ": " + s[i]);
   }
}
```

It is important to note that threads generally function by *time-slicing*. What occurs in an environment that supports time-slicing is that threads share CPU time while executing their respective code. In effect, although the threads are said to be running simultaneously, there is really only one thread executing at a given moment in time. It just *seems* like the threads are running simultaneously. The speed of the computer and the small increments of time make it possible for the threads to look like they're performing simultaneously.

Suppose there are two threads, A and B. If thread A is executing a method, thread B could get a slice of time before A is finished with its method. If the method is thread-safe, it won't matter to thread A that one or more threads interrupts its processing. Regardless of the time-slicing sequence, a thread-safe thread A will get the desired results.

NOTE

Java works best in environments designed to support *preemptive* time scheduling. A preemptive scheduler gives running tasks (processes or threads) small portions of time to execute by using time-slicing, discussed in this section. UNIX and Windows 95 are two operating systems that support some form of preemptive scheduling. However, some platforms, such as Windows 3.1, support a more primitive form of scheduling, called *nonpreemptive*. In this form of scheduling, one task doesn't give another task a chance to run until it's finished or has manually yielded its time. This makes writing cooperative programs fairly difficult—especially those with long CPU-intensive operations. You basically have to code your application around the system being nonpreemptive; in certain portions of the code, you need to call some kind of yield method to let other threads execute. In preemptive scheduling environments, this kind of manual coding is not necessary.

With time-slicing in mind, it isn't difficult to expose the problem with the TestStack class. Think about what would happen if the `push()` and `pop()` code shared time slices in the following manner:

```
PUSH: ++top;
POP: Integer I = s[top];
POP: s[top] = null;
POP; —top;
PUSH: s[top] = item;
```

In this case, the `pop()` call would be in error because it would return a stack top that hasn't been assigned a value yet. In short, if the `push()` and `pop()` operations share slices of time, they will probably not work properly. The operations with the `top` variable need to be *atomic*, which effectively means that another thread cannot interrupt the execution of the operation until it's finished.

This issue of operations causing undesired behavior because of concurrency is often referred to as the *producer/consumer problem*. This problem is characterized by one thread producing data (in this case, pushing an item onto the stack), while a concurrent thread is consuming the data (popping the stack). The problem is one of *synchronization*: Consuming and producing operations cannot be interleaved indiscriminately; rather, the operations need to be synchronized to guarantee thread-safe behavior.

NOTE

Although a stack class was used in this example, note that there is a stack class available in the java.util package. The stack class written in this chapter is used strictly to illustrate problems with multithreading.

Also note that the Exception classes associated with the stack code of this section give you a good example of how to create a subhierarchy of Exception classes. In this case, a new hierarchy of stack exceptions was created, with StackException as the root.

Listing 8.5 provides Applet and Thread classes that use the TestStack class appearing throughout this discussion on synchronization. The Applet class, StackApplet, pushes an element onto the stack whenever you click the mouse. It follows this push with a listing of the current stack contents. The Thread class, called StackThread, loops indefinitely, looking for items on the stack. If one is found, its integer value is displayed to standard output. If not (indicated by a StackEmptyException object being thrown), the thread sleeps a little and tries again. The synchronization problem can be seen by clicking the mouse rapidly. The `push()`, `pop()`, and `list()` methods can then be interleaved. It is likely you'll see the listing appearing incorrectly if you click fast enough. In fact, the problem will be blatant: The output from the `pop()` method—which changes the `top` variable also used in `list()`—will occur in the middle of the `list()` method, thus undermining its results.

Listing 8.5. Applet and Thread classes that use the TestStack class.

```
import java.awt.*;
import java.lang.*;
import java.applet.Applet;

public class StackApplet extends Applet  {
   TestStack s;
   int counter = 0;  // For stack test data...
   Thread t; // The stack thread...
   // Create the stack at initialization...
   // Make a thread to read the stack...
   public void init() {
      s = new TestStack(20);
      t = new StackThread(s);
      t.start();
   }

   // Add an item to the stack whenever you click
   // on the mouse...
   public boolean mouseDown(Event ev, int x, int y) {
      try {
         s.push(new Integer(++counter));
         s.list();
      }
      catch (StackFullException e) {
         System.out.println("Stack full!");
      }
      return true;
   };

   // Kill the stack thread when leaving...
   public void destroy() {
      t.stop();
      try {
         t.join();
      }
      catch (InterruptedException e) { }
   }
}

// Thread that constantly reads the stack and prints out
// the current top...
class StackThread extends Thread {
   TestStack s;
   public StackThread(TestStack s) {
      this.s = s;
   }
   // Loop forever, looking at the top of the stack...
   public void run() {
      Integer Top;
      while (true) {
         // Print out top of stack, if stack isn't empty...
         try {
               Top = s.pop();
               System.out.println("Thread: Read " + Top);
         }
         // Sleep some if stack is empty...
```

```
            catch (StackEmptyException se) {
                    try {
                        sleep(250);
                    }
                    catch (InterruptedException e) { }
            }
        }
    }
}
```

Introducing the Synchronized Modifier

The developers of Java are aware of the synchronization problem described in the preceding section. They also know that synchronization is often dealt with by issuing many lines of code. Fortunately for Java developers, the Java architects took advantage of programming constructs introduced over 20 years ago that make creating thread-safe classes relatively easy. Java synchronization is based on the concept of *monitors*. The idea is that each class and object has its own monitor that functions as a lock on the item. For example, if one thread locks an object's monitor, then another thread cannot access that object until the monitor is released. A monitor can make a code fragment behave like a *critical section*, with a piece of code that should only have one thread in it at a given time.

The Java language's *synchronized* modifier is used to implement a monitor. The modifier can be applied on a method or a block of code. If a method is declared as synchronized, then a thread that invokes the method owns the monitor of the object or class until it leaves the method. If another thread tries to invoke the method while the other thread owns the monitor, then that calling thread will have to wait until the first thread is finished. When this occurs, the monitor is released, and the next thread can execute the method.

Placing the synchronized modifier in just three areas of the TestStack class is all that's needed to make that class thread-safe. To do this, the three method declarations of the class need to be redeclared, as follows:

```
public synchronized void push(Integer item) throws StackFullException
public synchronized Integer pop() throws StackEmptyException
public synchronized void list()
```

With that simple change, the TestStack class is now thread-safe!

Another way of using the synchronized modifier is to apply it to blocks of code. Specifically, the critical sections of code should be synchronized. The TestStack class can be modified to do this, as shown in Listing 8.6. The same methods from the previous declaration are modified to have blocks of the structure

```
synchronized(this) {
}
```

around their critical sections of code. The `this` of the synchronized statement refers to the instance of the TestStack class. The effect in this case is similar to that of synchronizing methods; no thread can enter synchronized code while another thread holds the monitor of the object. As in synchronizing methods, this version of the TestStack class is thread-safe. Note, however, that the code is a little more cumbersome and harder to read. In general, synchronizing methods is preferred over synchronizing code blocks for both readability and ease of use. Furthermore, method-based synchronization is considered more object-oriented because it more effectively "hides" the fact that the code is executing as a thread, thus allowing you to focus on the object's behavior and not on how it works in a concurrent atmosphere. On the other hand, synchronizing blocks is more efficient because the monitors are held for shorter periods of time. If your code has only a small section of code that is critical, then it might be best to synchronize that block of code. However, classes such as TestStack are probably best implemented with synchronized methods.

Listing 8.6. The TestStack class with synchronized code blocks.

```
// This class implements a simple stack as
// an array of integers...
class TestStack {
   Integer s[];  // The stack array of integer objects...
   int top; // The current top of the stack. Next item to place.
   // Construct a stack of the specified size...
   public TestStack(int size) {
      s = new Integer[size];
      top = -1;    // Empty stack...
   }
   // Push an item onto the stack...
   public void push(Integer item) throws StackFullException {
    synchronized(this) {
      // Throw exception if stack is full...
      if (top == s.length)
            throw new StackFullException();
      // Otherwise increment the top and add the item...
      ++top;
      s[top] = item;
    }
   }

   // Pop the top item off the stack...
   public Integer pop() throws StackEmptyException {
    Integer I;
    synchronized(this) {
      // Throw exception if stack is empty...
      if (top < 0)
            throw new StackEmptyException();
      // Otherwise, return the top item and decrement the top...
      I = s[top];
      s[top] = null;
      --top;
    }
    return I;
   }
```

```
   // List the contents of the stack...
   public void list() {
    synchronized(this) {
      for (int i = 0; i <= top; ++i)
            System.out.println(i + ": " + s[i]);
    }
   }
}
```

The code blocks in Listing 8.6 could just have easily been synchronized with the stack Integer array `s`. The results would be the same. However, you cannot synchronize with the integer variable `top`. The synchronized modifier works only with objects and classes; variables, such as integers, are not proper synchronization types.

Notify and Wait

Suppose that you wanted to change the TestStack class to be blocking. That is, if you are invoking the `pop()` method and there is nothing on the stack, then you should wait until some other thread adds an element to the stack. However, because the `pop()` method is synchronized, you cannot wait inside that method without locking out the thread that is going to add the element you need! What you would like to do is wait inside the `pop()` method but relinquish the TestStack object monitor so that other threads can use the stack.

Fortunately, the designers of Java come to your rescue again! The base Object class has several methods built into it for this situation. Because these methods are part of the base class, they are available for every class you create. The `wait()` method provides the behavior you need for the `pop()` problem just discussed. When it is called, the `wait()` method releases the Object's monitor and simply waits until it is notified. Notification occurs when another thread calls the same Object's `notify()` method. This causes the waiting thread to wake up and reacquire the monitor. If the thread finds what it needs, it can leave the method and release the lock; otherwise, it can call `wait()` again.

Listing 8.7 shows modified methods of the TestStack class that implement the blocking behavior just discussed. The `pop()` method no longer throws an exception if the stack is empty. It now waits until the `push()` method calls `notify()` to indicate that an item has been added to the stack. In this example, the `wait()` method will wait indefinitely for an item to be added to the stack. In the Queue class developed in this chapter's project, you will see the use of alternate `wait()` methods that have time-outs associated with them.

Listing 8.7. The TestStack class with a blocking `pop()` method.

```
// Push an item onto the stack...
   public synchronized void push(Integer item) throws StackFullException {
      // Throw exception if stack is full...
      if (top == s.length)
```

continues

Listing 8.7. continued

```
            throw new StackFullException();
      // Otherwise increment the top and add the item...
      ++top;
      s[top] = item;
      notify();   // Let pop know you got something...
   }

   // Pop the top item off the stack...
   public synchronized Integer pop() {
      // Wait indefinitely if stack is empty...
      while (top < 0) {
         try {
            wait();
         }
         catch (InterruptedException e) { }
      } // end while
      // Otherwise, return the top item and decrement the top...
      Integer I = s[top];
      s[top] = null;
      —top;
      return I;
   }
```

Listing 8.8 shows the StackThread class that is modified to use the blocking `pop()` method. The `run()` method is a lot simpler than before because it no longer has to sleep between invocations of `pop()`. This is done implicitly when it is waiting for the TestStack to change.

Listing 8.8. The StackThread class modified to use the blocking `pop()` method.

```
// Thread that constantly reads the stack and prints out
// the current top...
class StackThread extends Thread {
   TestStack s;
   public StackThread(TestStack s) {
      this.s = s;
   }
   // Loop forever, looking at the top of the stack...
   public void run() {
      Integer Top;
      while (true) {
         // Print out top of stack, if stack isn't empty...
         // Wait indefinitely if the stack is empty...
         Top = s.pop();
         System.out.println("Thread: Read " + Top);
      }
   }
}
```

If more than one thread is waiting on an object, the `notifyAll()` method can be used to tell all waiting threads of the change in the object's state. On the other hand, the `notify()` method will send a signal only to a single waiting thread. It should also be noted that the `notify()` and `wait()` methods can be called only from within a synchronized method and from the thread that currently owns the object's monitor. For example, if the StackApplet object tried to call the TestStack object's `notify()` method, an IllegalMonitorStateException would be thrown.

More About Threads

Suppose you need one of your objects to sleep for a while, but the object is not an instance of the Thread class. How can this be done? The Thread class has a static method, called `currentThread()`, that returns a reference to the Thread object currently being executed. If the code is structured as in the following example, you can get the Thread reference you need:

```
public class MyClass {    // Note it does not extend Thread
   public MyMethod() {
      // ...work for a while...
      // Now sleep for 2 seconds
      Thread.currentThread().sleep(2000);
      // ...back to work...
   }
}
```

With the reference returned from `currentThread()`, you can execute the Thread methods that your class needs to perform. If you engage in serious Java programming, you will find the method to be useful in a wide variety of situations.

Another feature of the Thread class is that threads can run at different priority levels. Recall that threads generally operate by using time-slicing. Setting the priority of a thread lets you establish how large a time-slice your thread will get in relation to other threads. For example, a high-priority thread will get larger slices of time to process than a low-priority thread will. The Thread class supplies three public variables that can be used to define a thread's priority:

- `MIN_PRIORITY` indicates the minimum priority value in which a thread can run. A thread set to this priority will receive little processing time. It is best used for low-priority activities whose rate of completion isn't important. In this context, it is worth noting that the Java garbage collector runs at low priority (although it may not be `MIN_PRIORITY`).
- `NORMAL_PRIORITY` indicates the default value in which a thread runs. Most threads you create will run at this priority.
- `MAX_PRIORITY` indicates the maximum priority value in which a thread can run. A thread running at this priority will take most of the available CPU time. This should be used only for short CPU-intensive tasks that need to finish quickly.

In general, these priorities are set at the values of `1`, `5`, and `10`, respectively. However, it is best not to code with this knowledge because these variable definitions exist to hide their underlying values.

A thread's priority can be set with the `setPriority()` method. This method takes an integer priority value as its sole parameter. It throws an IllegalArgumentException if the priority does not fall within the bounds of `MIN_PRIORITY` and `MAX_PRIORITY`, inclusively. For example, this code sets the priority of a thread to the minimum value:

```
// Create the thread...
myThread t;
t = new MyThread().
// Set the priority to minimum
try {
  t.setPriority(Thread.MIN_PRIORITY);
}
// This exception will not occur!
catch (IllegalArgumentException e) {
  System.out.println(e.getMessage());
}
// Start the thread at the low priority...
t.start();
```

The priority of a thread can be retrieved with the `getPriority()` method. Table 8.1 provides a summary of Thread class methods that you may find useful. Note that ThreadGroups and daemons will be discussed next.

Table 8.1. Summary of important methods of the Thread class.

Method	*Description*
`currentThread()`	Returns a reference to the currently executing Thread.
`getName()`	Gets the name of the Thread. Assigned manually or automatically in the constructor.
`getPriority()`	Returns the priority of a Thread.
`getThreadGroup()`	Returns the ThreadGroup of a thread.
`isAlive()`	Returns whether the Thread is alive; that is, it has been started but not stopped.
`join()`	Waits for a Thread to die.
`resume()`	Resumes the running of a suspended Thread.
`run()`	Establishes where the threaded activity occurs.
`setDaemon()`	Establishes the Thread as a daemon or user thread.
`setPriority()`	Sets the priority of a Thread.
`sleep()`	Causes a Thread to sleep for a specified amount of time.
`stop()`	Terminates the `run()` method of a Thread.
`suspend()`	Suspends the execution of a Thread.
`yield()`	Yields the currently scheduled time slice to another Thread.

ThreadGroups

The ThreadGroup class contains Threads and other ThreadGroups. This hierarchical structure allows a ThreadGroup method, such as `stop()`, to be applied recursively over the Threads and ThreadGroups it contains. In this case, the `stop()` method terminates all currently executing threads in the ThreadGroup hierarchy. This recursive nature of ThreadGroups also makes it easy to coordinate the activities of running threads in the group with a single method call. For example, a call to a ThreadGroup's `suspend()` method will recursively suspend all threads in the group; its `resume()` method will just as easily resume the execution of the group's threads.

The Java runtime environment organizes all Threads according to a hierarchical structure of ThreadGroups. Every Thread belongs to a ThreadGroup. In an applet, the Thread of the Applet class belongs to the top-level ThreadGroup. Other Threads can be placed into that top-level group or placed into a new ThreadGroup.

The ThreadGroup class has two constructors, both of which require a string name. The second constructor allows you to specify the ThreadGroup in which the group should belong. If the default is used, the new ThreadGroup will be placed in the ThreadGroup of the currently executing thread. The following code creates an owner ThreadGroup that belongs in the currently executing thread's ThreadGroup and an owned group that belongs in the owner group:

```
// This goes into the currently executing thread's ThreadGroup
ThreadGroup ownerGrp = new ThreadGroup("Owner Group"); // The naem
// Create the child group...
ThreadGroup ownedGrp = new ThreadGroup(ownerGrp,"Owned Group");
```

To add a Thread to a ThreadGroup, you need to create it as part of the specified ThreadGroup. If the default Thread constructor is used, the Thread is placed into the ThreadGroup of the currently executing thread. The following code creates a Thread that belongs to the owner ThreadGroup of the previous example:

```
Thread t = new Thread(ownerGrp, "My Thread");
```

Note that names are important to ThreadGroups. You can get the name of a Thread or ThreadGroup through the corresponding `getName()` method. A Thread's name can be set at any time with `setName()`. A thread can find out which ThreadGroup it belongs to by calling the Thread method `getThreadGroup()`. For example, the following code can be used at any time to see what group a non-thread object is running in:

```
ThreadGroup grp = Thread.currentThread().getThreadGroup();
```

The various `enumerate()` methods of the Thread and ThreadGroup classes can be used to list the active threads or groups in an instance of the class. For example, the following code lists active threads in the owner ThreadGroup of the previous examples:

```
Thread outArray[] = new Thread[ownerGrp.activeCount()];
int count = ownerGrp.enumerate(outArray);
for (int i = 0; i < count; ++i)
  System.out.println(outArray[i]);
```

The size of the output array is determined by the `activeCount()` method of the ThreadGroup class. This returns the number of active Threads in the group. Note that inactive threads will not appear in these `activeCount()` or `enumerate()` methods. This might be a problem in some situations, so you may need to keep a manual list of threads. The ThreadGroup method `activeGroupCount()` returns the number of active ThreadGroups in the group. It corresponds to an `enumerate()` method similar to the one shown earlier.

One of the primary roles ThreadGroups plays is related to Java security. In theory, the access of a Thread or ThreadGroup to another ThreadGroup is restricted according to their relationship to each other. For example, a ThreadGroup can change its child ThreadGroups, but not the other way around. The `checkAccess()` method of the Thread and ThreadGroup classes is used to see whether access to a ThreadGroup is allowed; if not, then a `SecurityException` object is thrown. Unfortunately, the security feature of ThreadGroups does not seem to have been fully implemented in the JDK at the time of this writing. However, the methods and structure are in place, so it may be worthwhile to test these mechanisms to see whether your version of the JDK supports the ThreadGroup security function.

Another role of ThreadGroups is to control the priority of the threads running in it. The `setMaxPriority()` method is used to set the maximum priority of all the threads (recursively) in a ThreadGroup. This method will not affect currently running threads until their priorities are changed manually; however, the new maximum will apply to any threads started after this call. For example, if the priority is set to a value below `NORMAL_PRIORITY` (the default priority), all new threads will have their priorities set to this new lower value. Any time a currently executing thread changes its priority to a value higher than that established by `setMaxPriority()`, the priority applied will be that set by the ThreadGroup.

A Thread or ThreadGroup can be set as a *daemon* thread or group, respectively, by using the corresponding `setDaemon()` method. A daemon differs from the default state (a *user* thread) by being independent of the group that created the daemon; it is typically used to run in the background as some kind of service provider, such as a file loader or a print spooler (when printing is supported in AWT). A daemon thread will run until it is manually terminated or until all user threads have stopped running. A daemon ThreadGroup will be destroyed when it no longer has any active threads or ThreadGroup objects. The `isDaemon()` method can be used to check whether a thread or group is a daemon or user.

Now that you have seen ThreadGroups and the Runnable interface, you are now ready to look at the list of the various constructors for the Thread class, as shown in Table 8.2. They use various combinations of ThreadGroups, Runnable targets, and string names. If a ThreadGroup is not specified, the Thread is assigned to the ThreadGroup of the currently executing thread. If a string name is not provided, one is automatically assigned.

Table 8.2. Thread constructors.

Constructor	*Description*
`Thread()`	Default constructor.
`Thread(Runnable)`	Constructs a thread with the provided Runnable object as the target of the `run()` method.
`Thread(ThreadGroup, Runnable)`	Same as the previous, except it is assigned to the specified ThreadGroup.
`Thread(String)`	Constructs a Thread with the specified name.
`Thread(ThreadGroup, String)`	Constructs a Thread with the specified name, assigned to the specified ThreadGroup.
`Thread(Runnable, String)`	Constructs a Thread with the specified name and Runnable target.
`Thread(ThreadGroup, Runnable, String)`	Constructs a Thread with the specified name and Runnable target, assigned to the specified ThreadGroup.

ThreadDeath

One of the interesting things about threads is how the `run()` method is terminated. From an external user standpoint, a thread is stopped by calling the `stop()` method. Internal to the Thread class, however, something more interesting is going on. The `stop()` method results in an instance of an Error subclass, called ThreadDeath, being thrown at the victim thread. Note that ThreadDeath is not an Exception because these are usually caught as part of good programming practice. However, because errors are generally not caught, the thrown ThreadDeath object will result in the termination of the `run()` method.

You can catch ThreadDeath as part of your `run()` method if some extraordinary cleanup needs to occur when the thread is terminated. However, if you do this, you will need to rethrow the ThreadDeath object to ensure that the thread is actually terminated. Although this practice of catching ThreadDeath is discouraged for its potential risk, an example is shown here to illustrate how it works:

```
public void run() {
 while (true) {
  try {
   // Do normal threaded loop processing here...
```

```
    }
    catch (Exception e) {
      // Normal exceptions are caught here...
    }
    // Catch thread death!
    catch (ThreadDeath e) {
       // Clean up here...
       // Then rethrow the object to guarantee thread termination
       throw e;
    }
  }
}
```

An alternative `stop()` method can be used to throw your own customized thread "death." The syntax of the method is as follows:

```
public final synchronized stop(Throwable o)
```

The parameter can be any Throwable object, including Exceptions. Suppose you create your own Exception subclass called MyThreadDeath. You can then stop your custom thread by calling the following:

```
t.stop(new MyThreadDeath());
```

Your `run()` method should then catch the Exception:

```
catch(MyThreadDeath e) {
  // Do some special cleanup here...
  // Then throw ThreadDeath to really kill the thread...
  throw new ThreadDeath();
}
```

Make sure to throw ThreadDeath to kill the thread or to set a flag to exit the `run()` method gracefully.

Given these two `stop()` methods, it is easy to see that the standard `stop()` does little more than call the other version of `stop()`, with ThreadDeath as the Throwable object.

Talking Threads: Pipes and Threads

One of the interesting problems of multithreaded programming is how to get two threads to exchange information. A common method is to specify a shared communication object. In this chapter's project, the main thread and the MediaLoader thread talk by using a shared queue object. When the main thread needs an image to be loaded, it places the request into the queue. When the loader thread has retrieved the image, it places the image reference into a shared cache object.

Another way to exchange information between two threads is to create a series of methods for sharing data. One thread can "put" data while another does a "get" on the data. This technique is problematic, however, because the calling thread needs to know when the "get" is complete.

By writing a shared object such as a queue or an instance of the TestStack class discussed earlier, you can solve the problem through a blocking mechanism that implements the `wait()` and `notify()` methods.

Another classical technique of interthread communication is the use of pipes. A *pipe* is a First-In First-Out (FIFO) mechanism best used by multiple threads. One thread exclusively writes to the pipe, but another exclusively reads from it. Blocking is easily implemented in pipes because the output (reader) thread can simply wait until an item is written to the pipe by the input thread.

This pipe model can be extended to work with the consumer-producer model. A consumer thread requests a service by writing to a pipe that the other thread constantly reads to see if it needs to produce something. Another pipe, with its input-output reversed, can be used to let the producer thread notify the consumer thread that the service request has been fulfilled. Figure 8.3 illustrates how this would work in a duplex pipe setup.

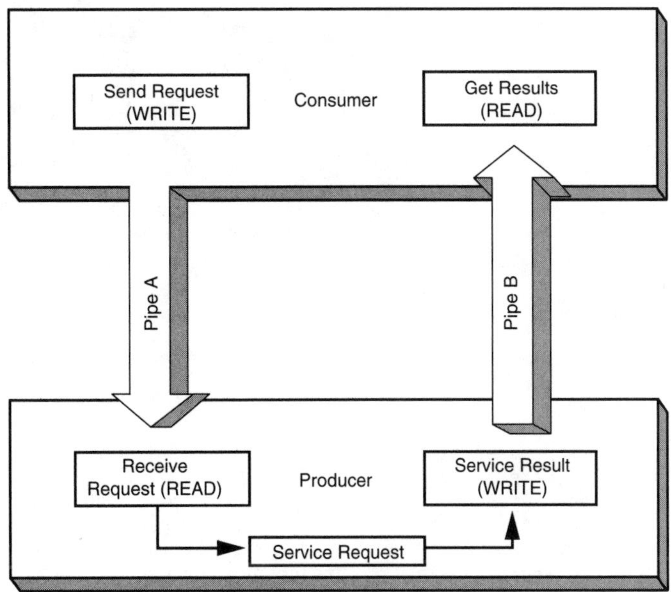

FIGURE 8.3.
Using pipes to implement a consumer-producer model.

The java.io package provides an easy-to-use mechanism for implementing pipes. An instance of the PipedOutputStream is used to write data to a pipe with the `write()` method. A PipedInputStream instance is connected to the same pipe by using the `read()` method. An example, shown in Figure 8.4, uses pipes to take a string specified in a TextField object and reverse its contents. The applet, appearing in Listing 8.9, creates two pipes and two threads. Whenever you enter a string into a TextField and press Enter, it sends the string to an output pipe. Another class, the ReverseThread, is a threaded object that waits on the applet's output pipe—which is an input to it—and reads in a string; the ReverseThread class is found in Listing 8.10. The thread reverses the string and sends it to its own output pipe. The applet has its own thread, which waits for input from the ReverseThread class. When the applet thread gets the reversed string, it sets it to the display Label at the bottom of the string. Figure 8.5 shows the data flow of this pipe example; note how it is similar to Figure 8.3.

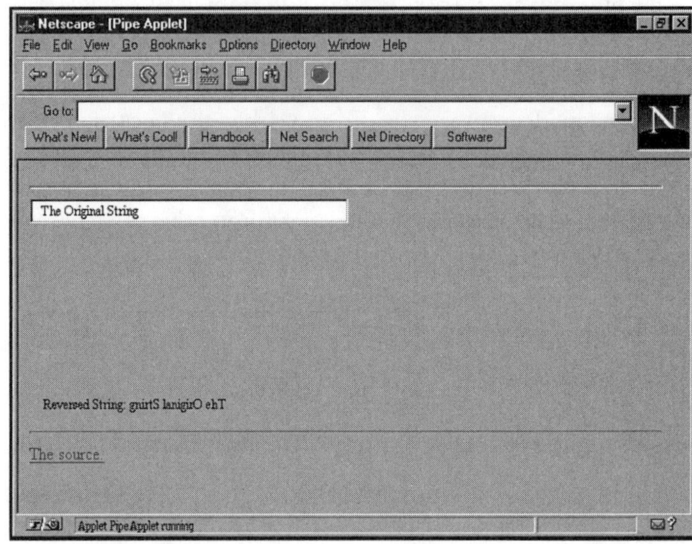

FIGURE 8.4.
An applet that uses pipes to reverse a string.

Listing 8.9. The applet code of the pipe program.

```
import java.awt.*;
import java.lang.*;
import java.applet.Applet;
import java.io.*;

// Applet that uses simple string reversal program
// to illustrate pipes...
public class PipeApplet extends Applet implements Runnable {
   TextField tf;  // You input the String to reverse here...
   Label reversed;  // Shows the reversed String...
   DataInputStream inPipe; // String request pipe...
   DataOutputStream outPipe; // String format...
   Thread t; // This thread
   ReverseThread r; // Thread to reverse Strings...

   // Create TextField to read text to reverse
   // and label to reverse it.
   public void init() {
      // Set up the components...
      setLayout(new BorderLayout());
      add("North",(tf = new TextField()));
      add("South",(reversed = new Label("Reversed String: ")) );
   }
```

```
// Catch a text entry and write to a pipe...
public boolean action(Event e,Object o) {
  // Take text field entry and stick in output pipe...
  if (e.target instanceof TextField) {
      try {
        outPipe.writeBytes(tf.getText()+"\n");
      }
      catch (IOException eio) {
        System.out.println("Applet Pipe Write Error: " + eio.getMessage());
      }
      tf.setText("");
  }
  return true;
}

// Main thread. Look for output from String Reverse pipe
// and write to label...
public void run() {
   String s;
   while (true) {
         try {
          // Print out reversed string to label...
          s = inPipe.readLine();
          reversed.setText("Reversed String: " + s);
         }
         catch (IOException eio) {
            System.out.println("Applet: Read error " + eio.getMessage());
         }
   }
}

// Entering Applet. Start the threads...
// Create communication pipes between the threads...
public void start() {
  if (t == null) {
   // Create the pipes...
   PipedOutputStream out;
   outPipe = new DataOutputStream(
       (out = new PipedOutputStream()));
   PipedInputStream in;
   inPipe = new DataInputStream(
       (in = new PipedInputStream()));
   // Create the thread objects...
   t = new Thread(this);
   r = new ReverseThread(in,out);
   // Start the threads...
   t.start();
   r.start();
  } // end if
}

// Leaving the Applet. Stop the threads...
public void stop() {
  if (t != null) {
   t.stop();
   r.stop();
   try {
```

continues

Listing 8.9. continued

```
         t.join();
         r.join();
      }
      catch (InterruptedException e) { }
    } // end if
    t = null;
  }
}
```

Listing 8.10. The thread code of the pipe program.

```
// Thread that looks into pipe for strings to reverse...
class ReverseThread extends Thread {
   DataInputStream inPipe;  // Request stream...
   DataOutputStream outPipe;  // Send out reversed string here...
   // Construct with the pipes to use...
   public ReverseThread(PipedInputStream in, PipedOutputStream out) {
       try {
        inPipe = new DataInputStream(
            new PipedInputStream(out));
        outPipe = new DataOutputStream(
            new PipedOutputStream(in));
       }
       catch (IOException eio) {
         System.out.println("Thread: " + eio.getMessage());
       }
   }

   // Loop looking for threads to reverse...
   public void run() {
      String s;  // Input String
      StringBuffer rev; // The reverse string...
      while (true) {
            try {
             // Get a string to reverse...
             s = inPipe.readLine();
             // Create the reversal of the string
             rev = new StringBuffer();
             for (int i = (s.length() - 1); i >= 0; —i)
                     rev.append(s.charAt(i));
             // Send the reversed string to the caller!
             outPipe.writeBytes(rev + "\n");
            }
            catch (IOException eio) {
               System.out.println("Thread: Read error " + eio.getMessage());
            }
      }
   }
}
```

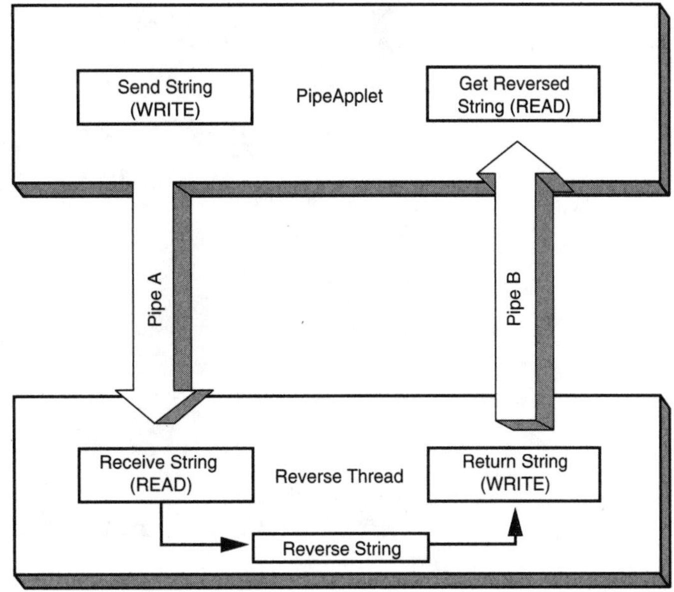

FIGURE 8.5.
The data flow of the pipe's example.

Chapter Project

Part III of this book concludes by adding a background media loader to the catalog applet developed in Chapter 6, "Building a Catalog Applet." This loader runs as a thread and retrieves images that are either to be used as soon as possible or are "preloaded" in anticipation of your going to another page in the catalog. This preloading feature improves the speed of your applet by loading images into memory *before* they are needed. Running the loader as a thread also improves performance because you can display a page of the catalog while the background thread is loading and preparing the images it needs.

Another thread that runs in the applet is a *sweeper* thread. This thread checks to see whether any items in the image cache have not been used for a while and so have aged beyond a useful time, therefore needing to be discarded. In the original version of this project in Chapter 6, the sweeper ran synchronously with the applet; when the sweeper was running, the applet would have to wait. In this version, the sweeper thread runs nonintrusively in the background. It is a low-priority thread, so its existence will probably go unnoticed.

The last enhancement to the catalog applet is linking in the BMP image producer discussed in the chapter project of Chapter 7, "Java and Images." The media loader thread checks to see the format of the image coming down; if it is a BMP file, it will use the BMP image producer. This makes the media loader act as a kind of "content handler," handling multiple kinds of content; at the very least, it is a first step toward having a real dynamic content handler as in HotJava.

The main menu of the catalog application is shown in Figure 8.6.

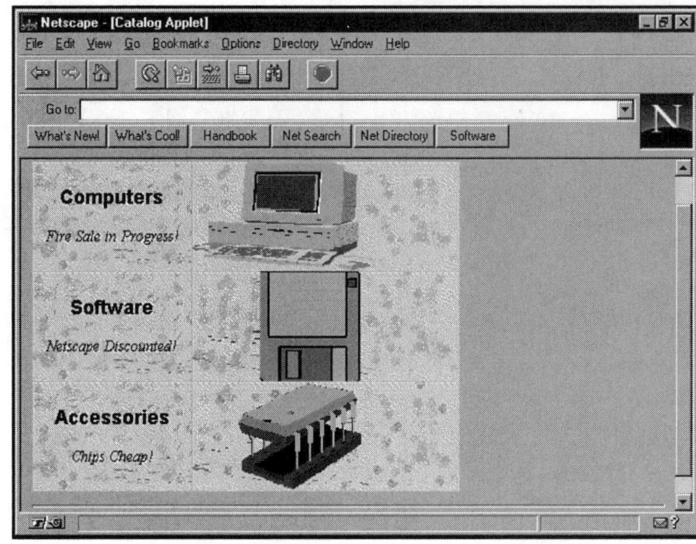

FIGURE 8.6.
Main menu of the online catalog.

Class Organization

Table 8.3 lists the classes used in this chapter's version of the catalog applet. Because many of these classes were created in the previous chapters, the new classes are delimited by having their names appear in boldface type. The classes that were modified have their names italicized.

Table 8.3. Catalog project classes.

Class	*Description*
BMPImage	Used to produce Images based on the BMP format.
CacheEntry	Represents a single entry in the image cache maintained by the MediaLoader class.
Catalog	The Applet class that takes HTML parameters and constructs the components representing the current choices. Adds images to be preloaded from the MediaLoader.
CatalogButton	An image-based button that shows text representing a choice and links to another Catalog applet when selected.
MediaLoader	A class used to maintain a cache of images. It starts and sends requests to an instance of MediaLoaderThread to actually get the images and starts a MediaSweeper thread to remove any old images from the cache.
MediaLoaderException	An exception thrown by the MediaLoader when there is a problem.

Class	*Description*
MediaLoaderThread	A background thread that loads normal or BMP images as they are requested. It gets requests for images from a Queue object and adds loaded images to the image cache.
MediaObserver	Used to track whether the loading of an image is complete.
MediaSweeper	A background thread that removes any old images from the image cache.
Queue	A generic class for reading or writing objects to a queue.
SelectionCanvas	Displays a large image representing a possible choice of the user. Appears to the right of its companion CatalogButton.

Catalog HTML and Preload File

A new parameter is added to the catalog HTML file. The `<PARAM>` tag with the name `preload` specifies the file that contains images that should be loaded by the background MediaLoader thread after all of the images needed by the current catalog page have been loaded. Listing 8.11 shows the HTML of the main catalog page, with the preload parameter set in bold. Notice that the data associated with the parameter is now a bitmap file. Reading in this format is automatically handled by the BMPImage class.

Listing 8.11. HTML of main catalog page (index.html).

```
<title>Catalog Applet</title>
<hr>
<applet code="Catalog" width=400 height=300>
<param name=field1 value="Computers,catalog/field1.gif,MEDIUM,computer/main.html">
<param name=image1 value="catalog/selection1.gif">
<param name=field2 value="Software,catalog/field1.gif,MEDIUM,software/main.html">
<param name=image2 value="catalog/selection2.gif">
<param name=field3 value="Accessories,catalog/field1.gif,MEDIUM,accessory/
➥main.html">
<param name=image3 value="catalog/selection3.bmp">
<param name=data value="catalog/data.txt">
<param name=preload value="preload">
</applet>
<hr>
```

Listing 8.12 displays the contents of the preload file that is tied to the HTML just listed. The entries of the preload file consist of a series of lines that list the following: the relative path and filename of the image to be preloaded, the style (for example, dimensions) of the file, and whether it goes on a CatalogButton object or a SelectionCanvas.

Listing 8.12. Preload file of the main catalog page.

```
computer/selection1.gif, MEDIUM, CANVAS
computer/field1.gif, MEDIUM, BUTTON
computer/selection3.gif, MEDIUM, CANVAS
software/softsel1.gif, MEDIUM, CANVAS
software/softsel3.gif, MEDIUM, CANVAS
```

The MediaLoaderThread and MediaObserver Classes

The MediaLoaderThread class, shown in Listing 8.13, is a background thread responsible for loading images that are requested in a shared instance of the Queue class. The heart of the class is its `run()` method. The thread waits indefinitely for input to appear in the input queue; as described later, the queue `get()` method is blocking, so the thread will do nothing until something is placed in the queue. When the appropriate data is found, the thread checks to see if the image is a BMP format or a standard image handled by Java. If it is the former, the BMPImage class is to produce an image based on the BMP format. If it is not a BMP file, then the Toolkit class is used to get an instance of the Image class. In either case, a MediaObserver object is created that is passed to the Toolkit's `prepareImage()` method. This forces the image to start being loaded. The MediaObserver will then track the progress of the image as it is being brought in. When the whole image is retrieved, the observer's complete flag is set. The MediaObserver class is shown in Listing 8.14. The ImageObserver interface on which it is based was described in the two previous chapters.

Listing 8.13. The MediaLoaderThread class.

```
// The MediaLoaderThread loads all images that appear in its
// input queue.  It works with the MediaObserver to track whether
// or not a standard image has been fully loaded.
public class MediaLoaderThread extends Thread {
   Queue inQueue;
   Hashtable cache;
   public static final int WAIT = 1;
   public static final int NO_WAIT = 2;
   public static final int LOAD_AND_WAIT = 3;
   static boolean debug = false;

   // Construct thread by giving it the cache hashtable
   // and the input queue
   public MediaLoaderThread(Hashtable cache,Queue q) {
      // Store the input queue...
      inQueue = q;
      this.cache = cache;
   }
```

```
// Run the thread until it gets an orderly shutdown...
public void run() {
   URL u;
   String s; // URL string from queue...
   int width,height,wait;
   boolean status;
   Image img;
   MediaObserver mo;
   ImageProducer producer;
   Integer I;
   while(true) {
      // See if there is something in the queue....
         s = (String) inQueue.get();
         debugString("Queue input: " + s);
         I = (Integer)inQueue.get();
         width = I.intValue();
         debugString("Queue input:  W = " + width);
         I = (Integer)inQueue.get();
         height = I.intValue();
         debugString("Queue input: H = " + height);
         I = (Integer)inQueue.get();
         wait = I.intValue();
         debugString("Queue input: Wait = " + wait);

      // Start loading the image....
      // Create a URL for the image...
      try {
           u = new URL(s);
           // See what type the image is.
           // BMPs are a special case...
           if (s.toUpperCase().endsWith(".BMP")) {
               debugString("Thread: Load Bitmap...");
               producer = BmpImage.getImageProducer(u);
               img = Toolkit.getDefaultToolkit().createImage(producer);
           } // end if
           // Handle normal images (JPEG or GIF)
           else {
              debugString("Thread: Load and prepare image...");
              img = Toolkit.getDefaultToolkit().getImage(u);
              img.flush();
           } // end else
           // Create MediaObserver and prepare image...
           mo = new MediaObserver(img,width,height);
           Toolkit.getDefaultToolkit().prepareImage(img,width,
                height,mo);
           // If load and wait, stick in cache right away...
           if (wait == LOAD_AND_WAIT)
            cache.put(u,new CacheEntry(img,Integer.MAX_VALUE));
           // Loop until complete. BMPs won't go through here...
           if ((wait != NO_WAIT) && (mo != null)) {
            debugString("Thread: Start waiting...");
            while (true) {
               if (mo.isComplete())
                     break;
               // If not complete, sleep a little...
               try {
                  sleep(100);
```

continues

Listing 8.13. continued

```
                }
                catch (InterruptedException e) { }
              }  // end while
            }  // end wait if
            debugString("Thread: Done loading");
            // Finished! Write to cache. High age prevents
            // premature garbage collection...
            if (wait != LOAD_AND_WAIT)
             cache.put(u,new CacheEntry(img,Integer.MAX_VALUE));
       }
       catch (MalformedURLException e) {
            System.out.println("Malformed URL");
       }
       catch (AWTException e) {
            System.out.println("AWTException: " + e);
       }
    } // end while
   }

   // See if we should print out debug strings...
   private void debugString(String s) {
      if (debug)
         System.out.println(s);
   }
}
```

Listing 8.14. The MediaObserver class.

```
// Observes an image as it's being loaded and tracks
// whether its loading is complete...
class MediaObserver implements ImageObserver {
   Image img;
   Boolean complete;
   static boolean debug = false;
   // Get image and dimensions...
   public MediaObserver(Image img,int width,int height) {
      this.img = img;
      complete = new Boolean(false);
   }

   // The complete flag needs to be synchronized...
   public boolean isComplete() {
      boolean status;
      synchronized(complete) {
            status = complete.booleanValue();
      }
      return status;
   }

   // Automatically called when an image is updated...
   public boolean imageUpdate(Image imgIn, int info,
      int x, int y, int width, int height) {
      if ((info & (ALLBITS | FRAMEBITS)) != 0) {
```

```
            synchronized(complete) {
               complete = new Boolean(true);
               if (debug)
                  System.out.println("COMPLETE!!!");
            }
         }
         return true;
      }
}
```

The MediaLoaderThread class indicates that an image is prepared by adding it to the image Hashtable cache shared by the parent class (MediaLoader). When the image is added to the cache depends on the class's wait mode, of which it has three variations. If the mode is `WAIT`, the image is not entered into the cache until it has been fully loaded, indicated by the complete flag of the MediaObserver. (Recall that the `getImage()` method returns immediately and only creates an instance of the Image class; the image data is not loaded until a request is made for it by a method such as `prepareImage()`.) If the mode is `NO_WAIT`, the image reference is placed immediately into the cache. For the `LOAD_AND_WAIT` mode, the image is placed immediately into the cache, but the next image request is not read until the image is fully loaded. This latter mode will be used for prefetching images. This mode of operation will work well in cases where the thread is in the middle of preloading an image that becomes immediately needed because you have moved to the page of the catalog in which the image appears.

Many enhancements can be made to these two classes. In particular, the MediaObserver can use the ImageObserver interface's `ABORT` flag to stop the loading of an image; the MediaLoaderThread class would also have to be adjusted. You might want to abort a load if you are moving to a new page of the catalog and you need its images loaded immediately. However, it is questionable whether this is actually worth while. Suppose that the image is 90 percent loaded, and you abort it. If the image is needed again shortly, network resources will have been wasted. Because this is a tough decision to make, the default procedure of letting the current load go through to completion was chosen.

The MediaLoader Class

The MediaLoader class was changed drastically from its original incarnation in Chapter 6. Consequently, its new design appears in Listing 8.15. The major change is that the actual loading of the images was moved into the MediaLoaderThread class, and the cleanup routines were placed into the MediaSweeper class. Both of these classes run as threads, which are created and started in the `start()` method. This is called once and only once by the private constructor. The `start()` method is also responsible for creating the Queue object that is used to place requests to the MediaLoaderThread object.

Listing 8.15. The MediaLoader class.

```
// This class loads image media via URL commands and
// keeps a local cache of images. Each image has an
// address that is used for aging. When the image is too
// old then it is removed from that cache.
public class MediaLoader {
   public static final int WAIT = MediaLoaderThread.WAIT;
   public static final int NO_WAIT =MediaLoaderThread.NO_WAIT;
   public static final int LOAD_AND_WAIT =MediaLoaderThread.LOAD_AND_WAIT;

   // Cache size is used for tracking age of URL
   static int cacheSize = 40;
   static int currentAge = 0;

   // Cache is hashtable...
   static Hashtable cache = new Hashtable(cacheSize);

   // The loader is static and so can be created only once
   private static MediaLoader loader = new MediaLoader();

   // Private internal constructor: Create the cache
   // abdstart the loaded thread...
   private MediaLoader() {
      System.out.println("Media Loader: CONSTRUCTOR!");
      start();
   }

   // Return reference to this MediaLoader object
   public static synchronized MediaLoader getMediaLoader() {
      return loader;
   }

   // Keeps track of whether or not it has started or
   // stopped the MediaLoaderThread object
   static boolean running = false;
   static MediaLoaderThread t;
   static MediaSweeper sweeper;
   static Queue reqQueue;


   // If not started yet, create output queue and
   // then start the media loader thread...
   public synchronized void start() {
      if (!running) {
         // Create request queue...
         reqQueue = new Queue(cacheSize * 4);
         // Start the media loader stream...
         t = new MediaLoaderThread(cache,reqQueue);
         t.start();
         // Start the sweeper. Try to keep cacheSize around
         // initial values...
         sweeper = new MediaSweeper(cache,cacheSize,cacheSize + 10);
         sweeper.start();
         running = true;
      }
   }
```

```
// If running, shutdown the thread and wait for it to die...
public synchronized void stop() {
   // Kill the thread if running...
   if (running) {
      // Orderly shutdown...
      t.stop();
      sweeper.stop();
      // Wait for thread to die...
      try {
         t.join();
         sweeper.join();
      }
      catch (InterruptedException e) { }
      // It's dead, Jim!
      running = false;
   }
}

// Get image via URL set for specified coordinates....
// Will send this into the output queue that the media
// thread reads...
public synchronized Image getImage(URL base,String name,
 int width,int height,int wait) throws MediaLoaderException  {
   // Create a URL for the image...
   URL u;
   try {
        u = new URL(base,name);
   }
   catch (MalformedURLException e) {
        throw new MediaLoaderException("Malformed URL");
   }

   // See if it is in the cache...
   showStatus("Get image " + u + "...");
   ++currentAge;
   CacheEntry ce = (CacheEntry) cache.get(u);
   // If its in the cache, update the age and
   // return image...
   if (ce != null) {
      ce.setAge(currentAge);
      showStatus("Image found in cache...");
      return ce.getImage();
   }

   // Now write the URL and dimensions to the request array...
   reqQueue.put(u.toString());
   reqQueue.put(new Integer(width));
   reqQueue.put(new Integer(height));
   reqQueue.put(new Integer(wait));

   // The running thread determines the wait flag...
   // It either sets the Image object right away
   // or it waits for it...
   while (true) {
      ce = (CacheEntry) cache.get(u);
      if (ce != null)
            break;
```

continues

Listing 8.15. continued

```
         try {
            Thread.currentThread().sleep(100);
         }
         catch (InterruptedException e) { }
      }  // end while
      showStatus("Image " + name + " retrieved...");
      ce.setAge(currentAge);
      return ce.getImage();
   }


   // Applet is used for updating status bar...
   Applet a = null;

   // Called when a new applet has been loaded...
   public synchronized void enter(Applet a) {
      this.a = a;
   }

   // Called when the current applet is leaving...
   public synchronized void leave(Applet a) {
      this.a = null;
      // Clear the queue...
      reqQueue.reset();
   }

   // Show status of load...
   public void showStatus(String msg) {
      System.out.println("MediaLoader: " + msg);
      if (a != null)
         a.showStatus(msg);
   }

   // The identifying String of the loader
   public String toString() {
      return ("MediaLoader ID: " + hashCode());
   }
}
```

The `getImage()` method has the same parameters as before, except for one that indicates how to wait. The wait flags correspond to the discussion in the previous section. Internally, the `getImage()` method is greatly simplified. It checks to see if the image requested appears in the cache; if so, then it updates its age and returns it immediately. Otherwise, it places a request for the image to the loader thread via the shared Queue object. The MediaLoader does not release control until the image is placed into the cache; when this occurs implicitly depends on the wait flag.

The other thing worth noting in the MediaLoader class is the `enter()` and `leave()` methods. These are used for tracking the current applet; a reference to the applet allows the loader to update the browser's status bar with the current state of a request. When you leave a page of the catalog, the `leave()` method clears out the request queue of any pending image preloads.

The loader thread will therefore finish only the current preload it is working on; it will then be free for any immediate requests needed for the new page.

The MediaSweeper Class

The MediaSweeper class is a low-priority thread that removes images from the MediaLoader cache whose age has grown beyond a certain acceptable value. This value is set by a desired cache size (the `desiredSize` variable). Whenever the size of the cache has grown bigger than a predetermined size (the `cleanSize` variable), the cache removes as many of the oldest cache entries as is necessary to get down to the desired size.

When the sweeper is constructed, it sets its priority to a low value by using the Thread class `setPriority()` method. When the sweeper thread is running, the `run()` method repeatedly checks to see whether the cache is bigger than the clean size, cleans if necessary, and then has a long sleep. If the cache is too big, the `sweeper()` method is called. This method, developed in Chapter 6, is only slightly changed to run inside the sweeper thread.

The contents of the MediaSweeper class appear in Listing 8.16.

Listing 8.16. The MediaSweeper class.

```
// Removes any item from cache that has an
// age that is too old...
   private void sweeper() {
      CacheEntry ce;
      // Array for placing hashtable elements...
      int ages[] = new int[cache.size()];
      // First step is to go through get all the ages...
      Enumeration em = cache.elements();
      for (int i = 0; em.hasMoreElements(); ++i) {
         ce = (CacheEntry)em.nextElement();
         ages[i] = ce.getAge();
      }
      // Next step is to get minimum age...
      // This is gross since we have to perform
      // a sort...
      sort(ages);
      // Now get nTh element
      int index = ages.length - desiredSize;
      int minAge = ages[index];
      int currentAge = ages[ages.length - 1];
      // Do nothing if we have nothing that's old...
      if (minAge > (currentAge - desiredSize)) {
         return;
      }

      // Final step is to walk through and remove
      // old elements...
      em = cache.keys();
      URL u;
      while (em.hasMoreElements()) {
```

continues

Listing 8.16. continued

```
            u = (URL)em.nextElement();
            // Get cache entry...
            ce = (CacheEntry)cache.get(u);
            // See if its too old...
            if (ce.getAge() < minAge) {
                  cache.remove(u);
            }
         }
      }

      // Sort an integer array...
      // I didn't have enough time to write quick sort
      // so here is a lame bubble sort...
      void sort(int data[]) {
         int N = data.length - 1;
         int i,j,t;
         for (i = N; i >= 0; —i) {
            for (j = 1; j <= i; ++j) {
               if (data[j - 1] > data[j]) {
                  t = data[j - 1];
                  data[j - 1] = data[j];
                  data[j] = t;
               } // end swap if
            } // end j if
         } // end i if
      }
   }
```

The Queue Class

The Queue class implements a standard circular queue that uses objects as entries. The tail of the queue marks the index of the next entry in queue; the head is the last item read from the queue. Like a dog, the head chases the tail. If the head is equal to the tail, the queue is empty.

The most notable thing about the queue, shown in Listing 8.17, is that the `put()` and `get()` methods are blocking. If you try to put an element in a queue that is full, the method will wait until an element has been removed from the queue; it does this through the object `wait()` and `notify()` methods discussed earlier in this chapter. Similarly, the `get()` method blocks until there is an element in the queue to read. The `put()` and `get()` methods can be called with an indefinite time-out (value `0`) or a millisecond timeout.

Listing 8.17. The Queue class.

```
// Generic class for holding a Queue of Objects...
// Uses synchronization and wait/notify methods to
// indicate when the Queue has something to read or
// is ready to accept a new entry...
public class Queue {
 Object Q[];
 int head,tail;
```

```
// Create Queue of specified size....
public Queue(int size) {
  Q = new Object[size];
  head = tail = 0;
}

// Add an element to the Queue.  If it is full then wait
// until something has been read or it times out.
// Timeout 0 means wait forever....
public synchronized void put(Object o,long timeout)
 throws QueueTimeoutException {
  // Add the element to the queue...
  Q[tail] = o;
  int newTail = tail + 1;  // Increment tail...
  // Wrap around if the end is reached...
  if (newTail >= Q.length)
     newTail = 0;
  // See if the queue is full and so we have to wait...
  if (newTail == head) {
     System.out.println("Q Full. Wait...");
     try {
        wait(timeout);
     }
     catch (InterruptedException e) { }
     // Throw exception if we timed out...
     if (head == tail)
           throw new QueueTimeoutException();
  } // end if
  tail = newTail;
  notify();
}

// Default put: Wait forever...
public void put(Object o) {
  try {
     put(o,0);
  }
  // This shouldn't happen...
  catch (QueueTimeoutException e) { }
}

// Get an element from the queue... Wait if queue
// is empty. If empty, then wait until timeout,
// where 0 means wait forever...
public synchronized Object get(long timeout)
 throws QueueTimeoutException {
  // See if Queue is empty...
  if (head == tail) {
     System.out.println("Nothing in Q. Wait...");
     try {
        wait(timeout);
     }
     catch (InterruptedException e) { }
     // Throw exception if we timed out...
     if (head == tail)
           throw new QueueTimeoutException();
  } // end if
  // Get the Object at the head of the Queue...
```

continues

Listing 8.17. contined

```
    Object o = Q[head];
    // Reset the Q entry...
    Q[head] = null;
    // Set the new head...
    ++head;
    if (head >= Q.length)
          head = 0;
    notify();
    return o;
  }

  // Default put: Wait forever...
  public Object get() {
    try {
       return get(0);
    }
    // This shouldn't happen...
    catch (QueueTimeoutException e) {
       return null;
    }
  }

  // Reset the queue to be empty....
  public synchronized void reset() {
    head = tail = 0;
  }

  // List the Q elements....
  public synchronized void list() {
   for (int i = 0; i < Q.length; ++i)
       System.out.println(i + ": " + Q[i]);
  }
}
```

The BMPImage Class

The BMPImage class constructed in Chapter 7 needed two new methods to handle the requirements of the catalog applet. The `extract4BitData()` method is used to handle additional bitmap formats (see the CD-ROM for its code). Listing 8.18 includes an additional constructor for the BMPImage class. Unlike the other constructor, it takes only a full URL as its sole parameter.

Listing 8.18. An additional constructor for the BMPImage class.

```
/**
     * A method to retrieve an ImageProducer given just a BMP URL.
     * @param context contains the base URL (from getCodeBase() or such)
     * @returns an ImageProducer
     * @exception AWTException on stream or bitmap data errors
     */
```

```
    public static ImageProducer getImageProducer( URL context)
        throws AWTException
    {
        InputStream is = null;
        ImageProducer img = null;
        String name = context.toString();
        int index; // Make last part of URL  the name
        if ((index = name.lastIndexOf('/')) >= 0)
            name = name.substring(index + 1);
        try {
            BmpImage im = new BmpImage(name);
            is = context.openStream();
            DataInputStream input = new DataInputStream( new
                                              BufferedInputStream(is) );
            img = im.extractImage(input);
        }
        catch (MalformedURLException me)
        {
            throw new AWTException(me.toString());
        }
        catch (IOException ioe)
        {
            throw new AWTException(ioe.toString());
        }
        return img;
    }
```

The Catalog Class

The `start()` method of the Catalog class is modified to notify the MediaLoader that a new catalog page is loaded, via the `enter()` method. It also starts the preload of images. This occurs in the `preload()` method. It reads in the file specified by the "preload" parameter and sends each entry as an image request to the MediaLoader. The `LOAD_AND_WAIT` flag tells the loader not to start loading any new requests until the current request is completely satisfied.

The `stop()` method tells the MediaLoader that you are leaving the current Catalog page by invoking its `leave()` method. This results in the clearing of the preload request queue. The changes to the Catalog class are shown in Listing 8.19.

Listing 8.19. Changes to the Catalog class.

```
// Begin preloading data...
   public void start() {
      // Let the loader know a new page has been loaded...
      MediaLoader.getMediaLoader().enter(this);
      // Start the preload of images...
      preload();
   }

   // Stop preload when leaving page...
   public void stop() {
```

continues

Listing 8.19. continued

```
      MediaLoader.getMediaLoader().leave(this);
   }

// Start preloading images if specified...
   public void preload() {
    // Get path to data from parameter...
    String dataPath = getParameter("preload");
    if (dataPath == null) {
      System.out.println("No preload variable found");
      return;
    } // end if
    // Create URL for data...
    URL u;
    try {
      u = new URL(getDocumentBase(),dataPath);
    }
    catch (MalformedURLException e) {
      System.out.println("Bad Data URL");
      return;
    }

    // Now load the data by opening up a stream
    // to the URL...
    try {
     DataInputStream dis = new DataInputStream(
      new BufferedInputStream(
         u.openStream() ) );
     // Read each line and put in MediaLoader queue...
     int i;
     String fetchLine, fileDir, tempStyle, tempType;
     while ((fetchLine = dis.readLine()) != null) {
         System.out.println("Prefetch: " + fetchLine);
         // Parse out the string...
         StringTokenizer s = new StringTokenizer(fetchLine,",");
         if (s.hasMoreTokens()) {
            fileDir = s.nextToken().trim();
            if (s.hasMoreTokens()) {
             tempStyle = s.nextToken().trim();
             // If we get past here, then all the fields are present
             // and we can start to preload the image...
             if (s.hasMoreTokens()) {
              tempType = s.nextToken().trim();
              // Right now only the Medium style is supported...
              try {
                 if (tempType.equalsIgnoreCase("button"))
                     MediaLoader.getMediaLoader().getImage(
                        getDocumentBase(),fileDir,150,100,
                        MediaLoader.LOAD_AND_WAIT);
                 else
                     MediaLoader.getMediaLoader().getImage(
                        getDocumentBase(),fileDir,250,100,
                        MediaLoader.LOAD_AND_WAIT);
              }
              // Just ignore errors....
              catch (MediaLoaderException e) {
                    System.out.println(e.getMessage());
```

```
            }
          } // end innermost if
        }
      }
    } // end while
  }
  catch (IOException e) {
    System.out.println("URL read error");
  }
}
```

The CatalogButton Class

The constructor of the CatalogButton class was changed to use the new MediaLoader `getImage()` format, as shown in Listing 8.20. The wait flag is, oddly enough, `NO_WAIT`. This causes the MediaLoader to continue as soon as the Image object is created and not to wait until the image is fully loaded. This allows painting to occur as soon as possible, and the image to be rendered as it is loaded. It is worth seeing what happens when the flag of this class and SelectionCanvas is set to `WAIT`. Nothing will appear until everything is loaded. However, the images are shown in their full form, not partially rendered.

Listing 8.20. Changes to the CatalogButton constructor.

```
// Create the catalog button...
   public CatalogButton(Applet aIn,
     String backgroundImage,  String textIn, Font fIn,
      URL URLBaseIn, String linkIn, String dataIn,
      Font dataFontIn) {
         // Store parameters...
         a = aIn;
         text = textIn;
         f = fIn;
         URLBase = URLBaseIn;
         link = linkIn;
         lastX = lastY = -1;
         state = NORMAL_STATE;
         data = dataIn;
         dataFont = dataFontIn;
         // Now start loading the background image
         // via the Media Loader...
         try {
              img = MediaLoader.getMediaLoader().getImage(
               URLBase,backgroundImage,150,100,
               MediaLoader.NO_WAIT);
         }
         catch (MediaLoaderException e) {
            img = null;
            a.showStatus(e.getMessage());
         }
   }
```

The SelectionCanvas Class

The constructor of this class is modified in a manner similar to the CatalogButton class. The wait flag of the `getImage()` call to the MediaLoader is also set to `NO_WAIT`, as shown in Listing 8.21.

Listing 8.21. Changes to the SelectionCanvas constructor.

```
// Create the canvas display...
   public SelectionCanvas(Applet aIn,
     String displayImage,URL URLBaseIn) {
         // Store parameters...
         a = aIn;
         URLBase = URLBaseIn;
         // Now start loading the background image
         // via the Media Loader...
         try {
            img = MediaLoader.getMediaLoader().getImage(
               URLBase,displayImage,250,100,
               MediaLoader.NO_WAIT);
         }
         catch (MediaLoaderException e) {
            img = null;
            a.getAppletContext().showStatus(e.getMessage());
         }
   }
```

Summary

This part of the book has emphasized how to use images for tasks like animation or smart image loading through a loader thread. The catalog applet developed in this chapter forms just the foundation for creating a serious online application. The media loader will need to be optimized to fit your particular needs, such as when to abort a load and how to use the wait flag to control how an image is displayed. But most of all, the catalog will probably need data from the server to show prices and other runtime information. This dynamic data loading is the subject of Part IV, "Managing Live Data"; in this part, you will develop an applet that dynamically reads in election night returns as they are fed in from a back-end server.

IV

Managing Live Data

9

Java Socket Programming

To demonstrate full Java client/server applet connectivity, an applet server is necessary. This chapter initiates the development of a Java HTTP server. Before beginning the server, however, you need some background knowledge of socket programming. This chapter begins with a socket overview and is followed by an exploration of Java's socket classes. The remainder of the chapter will delve into constructing a Java HTTP Web server and a client/server applet.

After reading this chapter, you should be able to do the following:

- Understand the socket abstraction
- Know the different modes of socket operation
- Have a working knowledge of the HTTP protocol
- Be able to apply the Java socket classes
- Understand applet socket use and limitations
- Comprehend the HTTP Java server

An Introduction to Sockets

The computers on the Internet are connected by the TCP/IP protocol. In the 1980s, the Advanced Research Projects Agency (ARPA) of the U.S. government funded the University of California at Berkeley to provide a UNIX implementation of the TCP/IP protocol suite. What was developed was termed the *socket interface*, although you might hear it called the Berkeley-socket interface or just Berkeley sockets. Today, the socket interface is the most widely used method for accessing a TCP/IP network.

A socket is nothing more than a convenient abstraction. It represents a connection point into a TCP/IP network, much like the electrical sockets in your home provide a connection point for your appliances. When two computers want to converse, they each use a socket. One computer is termed the server—it opens a socket and listens for connections. The other computer is termed the client; it calls the server socket to start the connection. To establish a connection, all that's needed is a destination address and a port number.

Each computer in a TCP/IP network has a unique address. *Ports* represent individual connections within that address. This is analogous to corporate mail—each person within a company shares the same address, but a letter is routed within the company by the person's name. Each port within a computer shares the same address, but data is routed within each computer by the port number. When a socket is created, it must be associated with a specific port—this is known as binding to a port.

Socket Transmission Modes

Sockets have two major modes of operation: *connection-oriented* and *connectionless*. Connection-oriented sockets operate like a telephone; they must establish a connection and a hang up.

Everything that flows between these two events arrives in the same order it was sent. Connectionless sockets operate like the mail—delivery is not guaranteed, and multiple pieces of mail may arrive in a different order than they were sent.

Which mode to use is determined by an application's needs. If reliability is important, then connection-oriented operation is better. File servers need to have all their data arrive correctly and in sequence. If some data was lost, the server's usefulness would be invalidated. Some applications—a time server, for example—send discrete chunks of data at regular intervals. If the data became lost, the server would not want the network to retry until the data was sent. By the time the data arrived, it would be too old to have any accuracy. When you need reliability, be aware that it does come with a price. Ensuring data sequence and correctness requires extra processing and memory usage; this extra overhead can slow down the response times of a server.

Connectionless operation uses the User Datagram Protocol (UDP). A datagram is a self-contained unit that has all the information needed to attempt its delivery. Think of it as an envelope—it has a destination and return address on the outside and contains the data to be sent on the inside. A socket in this mode does not need to connect to a destination socket; it simply sends the datagram. The UDP protocol promises only to make a best-effort delivery attempt. Connectionless operation is fast and efficient, but not guaranteed.

Connection-oriented operation uses the Transport Control Protocol (TCP). A socket in this mode needs to connect to the destination before sending data. Once connected, the sockets are accessed using a streams interface: open-read-write-close. Everything sent by one socket is received by the other end of the connection in exactly the same order it was sent. Connection-oriented operation is less efficient than connectionless, but it's guaranteed.

Sun Microsystems has always been a proponent of internetworking, so it isn't surprising to find rich support for sockets in the Java class hierarchy. In fact, the Java classes have significantly reduced the skill needed to create a sockets program. Each transmission mode is implemented in a separate set of Java classes. The connection-oriented classes will be discussed first.

Java Connection-Oriented Classes

The connection-oriented classes within Java have both a client and a server representative. The client half tends to be the simplest to set up, so it will be covered first.

Listing 9.1 shows a simple client application. It requests an HTML document from a server and displays the response to the console.

Listing 9.1. A simple socket client.

```
import java.io.*;
import java.net.*;

/**
 * An application that opens a connection to a Web server and reads
```

continues

Listing 9.1. continued

```
 * a single Web page from the connection.
 * NOTE: "merlin" is the name of my local machine.
 */
public class SimpleWebClient {
    public static void main(String args[])
    {
        try
        {
            // Open a client socket connection
            Socket clientSocket1 = new Socket("merlin", 80);
            System.out.println("Client1: " + clientSocket1);

            // Get a Web page
            getPage(clientSocket1);
        }
        catch (UnknownHostException uhe)
        {
            System.out.println("UnknownHostException: " + uhe);
        }
        catch (IOException ioe)
        {
            System.err.println("IOException: " + ioe);
        }
    }

    /**
     * Request a Web page using the passed client socket.
     * Display the reply and close the client socket.
     */
    public static void getPage(Socket clientSocket)
    {
        try
        {
            // Acquire the input and output streams
            DataOutputStream outbound = new DataOutputStream(
                clientSocket.getOutputStream() );
            DataInputStream inbound = new DataInputStream(
                clientSocket.getInputStream() );

            // Write the HTTP request to the server
            outbound.writeBytes("GET / HTTP/1.0\r\n\r\n");

            // Read the response
            String responseLine;
            while ((responseLine = inbound.readLine()) != null)
            {
                // Display each line to the console
                System.out.println(responseLine);

                // This code checks for EOF.  There is a bug in the
                // socket close code under Win 95.  readLine() will
                // not return null when the client socket is closed
                // by the server.
                if ( responseLine.indexOf("</HTML>") != -1 )
                    break;
            }
```

```
            // Clean up
            outbound.close();
            inbound.close();
            clientSocket.close();
        }
        catch (IOException ioe)
        {
            System.out.println("IOException: " + ioe);
        }
    }
}
```

NOTE

The examples in this chapter are coded as applications so as to avoid security restrictions. Run the code from the command line `java ClassName`.

Recall that a client socket issues a connect to a listening server socket. Client sockets are created and connected by using a constructor from the Socket class. The following line creates a client socket and connects it to a host:

```
Socket clientSocket = new Socket("merlin", 80);
```

The first parameter is the name of the host you want to connect to; the second parameter is the port number. A host name specifies only the destination computer. The port number is required to complete the transaction and allow an individual application to receive the call. In this case, 80 was specified, the well-known port number for the HTTP protocol. Other well-known port numbers are shown in Table 9.1. Port numbers are not mandated by any governing body, but are assigned by convention—this is why they are said to be "well known."

Table 9.1. Well-known port numbers.

Service	*Port*
echo	7
daytime	13
ftp	21
telnet	23
smtp	25
finger	79
http	80
pop3	110

Because the Socket class is connection oriented, it provides a streams interface for reads and writes. Classes from the java.io package should be used to access a connected socket:

```
DataOutputStream outbound = new DataOutputStream( clientSocket.getOutputStream() );
DataInputStream inbound = new DataInputStream( clientSocket.getInputStream() );
```

Once the streams are created, normal stream operations can be performed:

```
outbound.writeBytes("GET / HTTP/1.0\r\n\r\n);
String responseLine;
while ( (responseLine = inbound.readLine()) != null)
{
    System.out.println(responseLine);
}
```

The above code snippet requests a Web page and echoes the response to the screen. When the program is done using the socket, the connection needs to be closed:

```
outbound.close();
inbound.close();
clientSocket.close();
```

Notice that the socket streams are closed first. All socket streams should be closed before the socket is closed. This application is relatively simple, but all client programs follow the same basic script:

1. Create the client socket connection.
2. Acquire read and write streams to the socket.
3. Use the streams according to the server's protocol.
4. Close the streams.
5. Close the socket.

Using a server socket is only slightly more complicated, as explained in the following section.

Server Sockets

Listing 9.2 is a partial listing of a simple server application. The complete server example can be found on the CD-ROM in SimpleWebServer.java.

Listing 9.2. A simple server application.

```
/**
 * An application that listens for connections and serves a simple
 * HTML document.
 */
class SimpleWebServer {
    public static void main(String args[])
    {
        ServerSocket serverSocket = null;
        Socket clientSocket = null;
        int connects = 0;
        try
        {
```

```
            // Create the server socket
            serverSocket = new ServerSocket(80, 5);

            while (connects < 5)
            {
                // Wait for a connection
                clientSocket = serverSocket.accept();

                //Service the connection
                ServiceClient(clientSocket);
                connects++;
            }
            serverSocket.close();
        }
        catch (IOException ioe)
        {
            System.out.println("Error in SimpleWebServer: " + ioe);
        }
    }

    public static void ServiceClient(Socket client)
        throws IOException
    {
        DataInputStream inbound = null;
        DataOutputStream outbound = null;
        try
        {
            // Acquire the streams for IO
            inbound = new DataInputStream( client.getInputStream());
            outbound = new DataOutputStream( client.getOutputStream());

            // Format the output (response header and tiny HTML document)
            StringBuffer buffer = PrepareOutput();

            String inputLine;
            while ((inputLine = inbound.readLine()) != null)
            {
                // If end of HTTP request, send the response
                if ( inputLine.equals("") )
                {
                    outbound.writeBytes(buffer.toString());
                    break;
                }
            }
        }
        finally
        {
            // Clean up
            System.out.println("Cleaning up connection: " + client);
            outbound.close();
            inbound.close();
            client.close();
            client.close();
        }
    }
```

Servers do not actively create connections. Instead, they passively listen for a client connect request and then provide their services. Servers are created with a constructor from the ServerSocket class. The following line creates a server socket and binds it to port 80:

```
ServerSocket serverSocket = new ServerSocket(80, 5);
```

The first parameter is the port number on which the server should listen. The second parameter is optional. The API documentation indicates that this parameter is a listen time, but in traditional sockets programming the listen function's second parameter is the listen stack depth. As it turns out, this is also true for the second constructor parameter. A server can receive connect requests from many clients at the same time, but each call must be processed one at a time. The *listen stack* is a queue of unanswered connect requests. The above code instructs the socket driver to maintain the last five connect requests. If the constructor omits the listen stack depth, a default value of `50` is used.

Once the socket is created and listening for connections, incoming connections are created and placed on the listen stack. The `accept()` method is called to lift individual connections off the stack:

```
Socket clientSocket = serverSocket.accept();
```

This method returns a connected client socket used to converse with the caller. No conversations are ever conducted over the server socket itself. Instead, the server socket will spawn a new socket in the `accept()` method. The server socket is still open and queuing new connection requests.

Like the client socket, the next step is to create an input and output stream:

```
DataInputStream inbound = new DataInputStream( clientSocket.getInputStream() );
DataOutputStream outbound = new DataOutputStream( clientSocket.getOutputStream() );
```

Normal I/O operations can now be performed by using the newly created streams. This server waits for the client to send a blank line before sending its response. When the conversation is finished, the server closes the streams and the client socket. At this point, the server tries to accept more calls. What happens when there are no calls waiting in the queue? The method will wait for one to arrive. This behavior is known as *blocking*. The `accept()` method will block the server thread from performing any other tasks until a new call arrives. When five connects have been serviced, the server exits by closing its server socket. Any queued calls will be canceled.

All servers follow the same basic script:

1. Create the server socket and begin listening.
2. Call the `accept()` method to get new connections.
3. Create input and output streams for the returned socket.
4. Conduct the conversation based on the agreed protocol.

5. Close the client streams and socket.
6. Go back to step 2, or continue to step 7.
7. Close the server socket.

Figure 9.1 summarizes the steps needed for client/server connection-oriented applications.

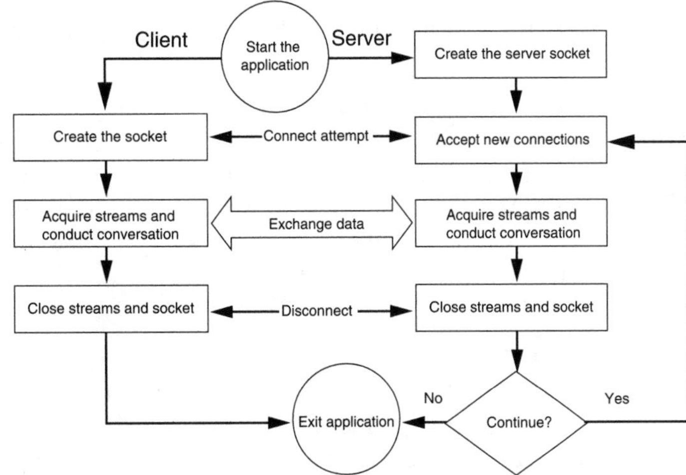

FIGURE 9.1.
Client and server connection-oriented applications.

Iterative and Concurrent Servers

The application just presented is known as an *iterative server* because the code accepts a client connection and completely processes it before it will accept another connection. More complex servers are concurrent. Instead of accepting connections and immediately processing them, a *concurrent server* spawns a new thread to process each new request, so it seems as though the server is processing many requests simultaneously. All commercial Web servers are concurrent servers.

Java Datagram Classes

Unlike connection-oriented classes, the datagram versions of the client and server behave in nearly identical manners—the only difference occurs in implementation. The same class is used for both client and server halves. The following lines create client and server datagram sockets:

```
DatagramSocket serverSocket = new DatagramSocket( 4545 );
DatagramSocket clientSocket = new DatagramSocket();
```

The server specifies its port using the lone constructor parameter `4545`. Since the client will call the server, the client can use any available port. The omitted constructor parameter in the second call instructs the operating system to assign the next available port number. The client could have requested a specific port, but the call would fail if some other socket had already bound itself to that port. It's better not to specify a port unless the intent is to be a server.

Since streams can't be acquired for communication, how do you talk to a DatagramSocket? The answer lies in the DatagramPacket class.

Receiving Datagrams

The DatagramPacket class is used to receive and send data over DatagramSocket classes. The packet class contains connection information as well as the data. As was explained earlier, datagrams are self-contained transmission units. The DatagramPacket class encapsulates these units. The following lines receive data from a datagram socket:

```
DatagramPacket packet = new DatagramPacket(new byte[512], 512);
clientSocket.receive(packet);
```

The constructor for the packet needs to know where to place the received data. A 512-byte buffer was created and passed to the constructor as the first parameter. The second constructor parameter was the size of the buffer. Like the `accept()` method in the ServerSocket class, the `receive()` method will block until data is available.

Sending Datagrams

Sending datagrams is really very simple; all that's needed is a complete address. Addresses are created and tracked by using the InetAddress class. This class has no public constructors, but it does contain several static methods that can be used to create an instance of the class. The following list shows the public methods that create InetAddress class instances:

Public InetAddress Creation Methods

```
InetAddress getByName(String host);
InetAddress[] getAllByName(String host);
InetAddress getLocalHost();
```

Getting the local host is useful for informational purposes, but only the first two methods are actually used for sending packets. Both `getByName()` and `getAllByName()` require the name of the destination host. The first method merely returns the first match it finds. The second method is needed because a computer can have more than one address. When this occurs, the computer is said to be *multi-homed.* The computer has one name, but multiple ways to reach it.

All the creation methods are marked as static. They must be called as follows:

```
InetAddress addr1 = InetAddress.getByName("merlin");
InetAddress addr2[] = InetAddress.getAllByName("merlin");
InetAddress addr3 = InetAddress.getLocalHost();
```

Any of these calls can throw an UnknownHostException. If a computer is not connected to a Domain Name Server (DNS) or if the host is really not found, an exception will be thrown. If a computer does not have an active TCP/IP configuration, then `getLocalHost()` is likely to fail with this exception as well.

Once an address is determined, datagrams can be sent. The following lines transmit a String to a destination socket:

```
String toSend = "This is the data to send!");
byte[] sendbuf = new byte[ toSend.length() ];
toSend.getBytes( 0, toSend.length(), sendbuf, 0 );
DatagramPacket sendPacket = new DatagramPacket( sendbuf, sendbuf.length, addr,
port);
clientSocket.send( sendPacket );
```

First, the string must be converted to a byte array. The `getBytes()` method takes care of the conversion. Next, a new DatagramPacket instance must be created. Notice the two extra parameters at the end of the constructor. Since this will be a send packet, the address and port of the destination must also be placed into the packet. An applet may know the address of its server, but how does a server know the address of its client? Remember that a datagram is like an envelope—it has a return address. When any packet is received, the return address can be extracted from the packet by using `getAddress()` and `getPort()`. This is how a server would respond to a client packet:

```
DatagramPacket sendPacket = new DatagramPacket( sendbuf, sendbuf.length,
    recvPacket.getAddress(), recvPacket.getPort() );
serverSocket.send( sendPacket );
```

Unlike connection-oriented operation, datagram servers are actually less complicated than the datagram client.

Datagram Servers

The basic script for datagram servers is as follows:

1. Create the datagram socket on a specific port.
2. Call receive to wait for incoming packets.
3. Respond to received packets according to the agreed protocol.
4. Go back to step 2, or continue to step 5.
5. Close the datagram socket.

Listing 9.3 shows a simple datagram echo server. It will echo back any packets it receives.

Listing 9.3. A simple datagram echo server.

```
import java.io.*;
import java.net.*;

public class SimpleDatagramServer
{
    public static void main(String[] args)
    {
        DatagramSocket socket = null;
        DatagramPacket recvPacket, sendPacket;
```

continues

Listing 9.3. continued

```
        try
        {
            socket = new DatagramSocket(4545);
            while (socket != null)
            {
                recvPacket= new DatagramPacket(new byte[512], 512);
                socket.receive(recvPacket);
                sendPacket = new DatagramPacket(
                    recvPacket.getData(), recvPacket.getLength(),
                    recvPacket.getAddress(), recvPacket.getPort() );
                socket.send( sendPacket );
            }
        }
        catch (SocketException se)
        {
            System.out.println("Error in SimpleDatagramServer: " + se);
        }
        catch (IOException ioe)
        {
            System.out.println("Error in SimpleDatagramServer: " + ioe);
        }
    }
}
```

Datagram Clients

The corresponding client uses the same process with one exception: A client must initiate the conversation. The basic recipe for datagram clients is as follows:

1. Create the datagram socket on any available port.
2. Create the address to send to.
3. Send the data according to the server's protocol.
4. Wait for receive data.
5. Go to step 3 (send more data), 4 (wait for receive), or 6 (exit).
6. Close the datagram socket.

Figure 9.2 summarizes the steps needed for client/server datagram applications. The symmetry between client and server is evident from this picture; compare Figure 9.2 with Figure 9.1.

Listing 9.4 shows a simple datagram client. It reads user input strings and sends them to the echo server from Listing 9.3. The echo server will send the data right back, and the client will print the response to the console.

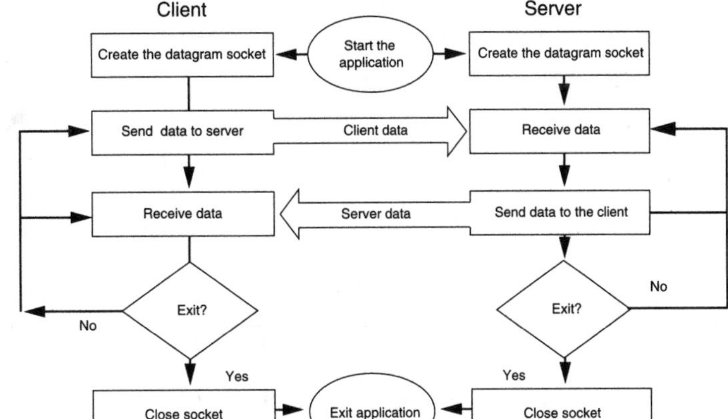

FIGURE 9.2.
Client and server datagram applications.

Listing 9.4. A simple datagram client.

```
import java.io.*;
import java.net.*;

public class SimpleDatagramClient
{
    private DatagramSocket socket = null;
    private DatagramPacket recvPacket, sendPacket;
    private int hostPort;

    public static void main(String[] args)
    {
        DatagramSocket socket = null;
        DatagramPacket recvPacket, sendPacket;
        try
        {
            socket = new DatagramSocket();
            InetAddress hostAddress = InetAddress.getByName("merlin");
            DataInputStream userData = new DataInputStream( System.in );
            while (socket != null)
            {
                String userString = userData.readLine();
                if (userString == null || userString.equals(""))
                    return;
                byte sendbuf[] = new byte[ userString.length() ];
                userString.getBytes(0, userString.length(), sendbuf, 0);
                sendPacket = new DatagramPacket(
                    sendbuf, sendbuf.length, hostAddress, 4545 );
                socket.send( sendPacket );
                recvPacket= new DatagramPacket(new byte[512], 512);
                socket.receive(recvPacket);
                System.out.write(recvPacket.getData(), 0,
                    recvPacket.getLength());
                System.out.print("\n");
            }
```

continues

Listing 9.4. continued

```
        }
        catch (SocketException se)
        {
            System.out.println("Error in SimpleDatagramClient: " + se);
        }
        catch (IOException ioe)
        {
            System.out.println("Error in SimpleDatagramClient: " + ioe);
        }
    }
}
```

All the examples so far have been Java applications. Running these in an applet presents an extra complication: security.

Applet Security and Sockets

When writing applications, you don't need to be concerned with security exceptions. This changes when the code under development is executed from an applet. Netscape Navigator 2.0 uses very stringent security measures where sockets are concerned. An applet may open a socket only back to the host name from which it was loaded. If any other connection is attempted, a SecurityException will be thrown.

Datagram sockets don't open connections, so how is security ensured for these sockets? When an inbound packet is received, the host name is checked. If the packet did not originate from the server, a SecurityException is immediately thrown. Obviously, sending comes under the same scrutiny. If a datagram socket tries to send to any destination except the server, a SecurityException is thrown. These restrictions apply only to the address, not the port number. Any port number on the host may be used.

All the socket techniques demonstrated so far will be developed further in this chapter's project.

Chapter Project: HTTP Server Application and Client Applet

This project at first glance seems a bit ambitious, but writing a rudimentary Web server is not as hard as it sounds. Client applets need an HTTP Web server so they can open sockets. If an applet is loaded into Netscape from a hard drive, then no socket activity is allowed to take place. A simple solution is to write an HTTP server application. Once written, additional server threads can be added to provide all types of back-end connectivity. This project will add a multipurpose datagram protocol that will be used for live data in both Chapter 10, "Native Methods and Java," and 11, "Building a Live Data Applet."

HTTP Primer

Before diving into the project, you need some background information on the HTTP protocol. The Hypertext Transfer Protocol (HTTP) has been in use on the World Wide Web since 1990. All applet-bearing Web pages are sent over the net with HTTP. The server will support a subset of version 1.0 in that only file requests will be handled. As long as Netscape page requests can be fulfilled, the server will have accomplished its goal.

HTTP uses a stream-oriented (TCP) socket connection. Typically, port 80 is used, but other port numbers can be substituted. All the protocol is sent in plain-text format. An example of a conversation was demonstrated in Listings 9.1 and 9.2. The server listens on port 80 for a client request, which takes this format:

```
GET FILE HTTP/1.0
```

The first word is referred to as the "method" of the request. Table 9.2 lists all the request methods for HTTP/1.0.

Table 9.2. HTTP/1.0 request methods.

Method	*Use*
GET	Retrieve a file
HEAD	Retrieve only file information
POST	Send data to the server
PUT	Send data to the server
DELETE	Delete a resource
LINK	Link two resources
UNLINK	Unlink two resources

The second parameter of a request is a file path. Each of the following URLs is followed by the request that will be formulated and sent:

```
HTTP://www.qnet.com/
GET / HTTP/1.0

HTTP://www.qnet.com/index.html
GET /index.html HTTP/1.0

HTTP://www.qnet.com/classes/applet.html
GET /classes/applet.html HTTP/1.0
```

The request does not end until a blank line containing only a carriage return (\r) and a line feed (\n) is received. After the method line, a number of optional lines can be sent. Netscape Navigator 2.0 will produce the following request:

```
GET / HTTP/1.0
Connection: Keep-Alive
User-Agent: Mozilla/2.0 (Win95; I)
Host: merlin
Accept: image/gif, image/x-xbitmap, image/jpeg, image/pjpeg, */*
```

Responses use a header similar to the request:

```
HTTP/1.0 200 OK
Content-type: text/html
Content-Length: 128
```

Like the request, the response header is not complete until a blank line is sent containing only a carriage return and a line feed. The first line contains a version identification string, followed by a status code indicating the results of the request. Table 9.3 lists all the defined status codes. The server will send only two of these: 200 and 404. The text that follows the status code is optional. It may be omitted, or, if present, it might not match the definitions given in the table.

Table 9.3. HTTP response status codes.

Status Code	*Optional Text Description*
200	OK
201	Created
202	Accepted
204	No Content
300	Multiple Choices
301	Moved Permanently
302	Moved Temporarily
304	Not Modified
400	Bad Request
401	Unauthorized
403	Forbidden
404	Not Found
500	Internal Server Error
501	Not Implemented
502	Bad Gateway
503	Service Unavailable

Immediately after the response header, the requested file is sent. When the file is completely transmitted, the socket connection is closed. Each request-response pair consumes a new socket connection.

That's enough information to construct a basic Web server. Full information on the HTTP protocol can be retrieved from `HTTP://www.w3.org/`.

Basic Web Server

The basic Web server will follow the construction of the SimpleWebServer from Listing 9.2. Many improvements will have to be made to method and response handling. The simple server does not parse or store the request header as it arrives. The new Web server will have to parse and store the requests for later processing. To do this, you need a class to contain an HTTP request.

HTTPrequest Class

Listing 9.5 shows the complete HTTPrequest class. The class must contain all the information that could be conveyed in a request header.

Listing 9.5. The HTTPrequest class.

```
import java.io.*;
import java.util.*;
import java.net.*;
import NameValue;

/**
 * This class maintains all the information from an HTTP request
 */
public class HTTPrequest
{
    public String version;
    public String method;
    public String file;
    public Socket clientSocket;
    public DataInputStream inbound;
    public NameValue headerpairs[];

    /**
     * Create an instance of this class
     */
    public HTTPrequest()
    {
        version = null;
        method = null;
        file = null;
        clientSocket = null;
        inbound = null;
        headerpairs = new NameValue[0];
    }
```

continues

Listing 9.5. continued

```
    /**
     * Add a name/value pair to the internal array
     */
    public void addNameValue(String name, String value)
    {
        try
        {
            NameValue temp[] = new NameValue[ headerpairs.length + 1 ];
            System.arraycopy(headerpairs, 0, temp, 0, headerpairs.length);
            temp[ headerpairs.length ] = new NameValue(name, value);
            headerpairs = temp;
        }
        catch (NullPointerException npe)
        {
            System.out.println("NullPointerException while adding name-value: " +
➥npe);
        }
    }

    /**
     * Renders the contents of the class in String format
     */
    public String toString()
    {
        String s = method + " " + file + " " + version + "\n";
        for (int x = 0; x < headerpairs.length; x++ )
             s += headerpairs[x] + "\n";
        return s;
    }
}
```

The NameValue class simply stores two strings: name and value. You can find the source code for it on the CD-ROM in NameValue.java. When a new pair needs to be added, a new array is allocated. The new array receives a copy of the old array as well as the new member. The old array is then replaced with the newly created entity.

Two data fields in the class are not directly part of an HTTP request. The `clientSocket` member allows response routines to get an output stream, and the `inbound` member allows easy closure after a request has been processed. The remaining members are all part of an HTTP request. The method `toString()` allows class objects to be printed using "plus notation." The following line will display the contents of a request by invoking the `toString()` method:

```
System.out.println("Request: " + request);
```

Now that the request container is finished, it's time to populate it.

BasicWebServer Class

This is the main class for the server. It can be broken down into request and response routines. Since this is a server, the request routines will be activated first. After some validation, the response routines will be called. Listing 9.6 provides the routines to parse an HTTP request.

Listing 9.6. HTTP request routines.

```
/**
 * Read an HTTP request into a continuous String.
 * @param client a connected client stream socket.
 * @return a populated HTTPrequest instance
 * @exception ProtocolException If not a valid HTTP header
 * @exception IOException
 */
public HTTPrequest GetRequest(Socket client)
    throws IOException, ProtocolException
{
    DataInputStream inbound = null;
    HTTPrequest request = null;
    try
    {
        // Acquire an input stream for the socket
        inbound = new DataInputStream(client.getInputStream());

        // Read the header into a String
        String reqhdr = readHeader(inbound);

        // Parse the string into an HTTPrequest instance
        request = ParseReqHdr(reqhdr);

        // Add the client socket and inbound stream
        request.clientSocket = client;
        request.inbound = inbound;
    }
    catch (ProtocolException pe)
    {
        if ( inbound != null )
            inbound.close();
        throw pe;
    }
    catch (IOException ioe)
    {
        if ( inbound != null )
            inbound.close();
        throw ioe;
    }
    return request;
}

/**
 * Assemble an HTTP request header String
 * from the passed DataInputStream.
 * @param is the input stream to use
 * @return a continuous String representing the header
 * @exception ProtocolException If a pre HTTP/1.0 request
 * @exception IOException
 */
private String readHeader(DataInputStream is)
    throws IOException, ProtocolException
{
    String command;
    String line;
```

continues

Listing 9.6. continued

```
        // Get the first request line
        if ( (command = is.readLine()) == null )
            command = "";
        command += "\n";

        // Check for HTTP/1.0 signature
        if (command.indexOf("HTTP/") != -1)
        {
            // Retrieve any additional lines
            while ((line = is.readLine()) != null  &&  !line.equals(""))
                command += line + "\n";
        }
        else
        {
            throw new ProtocolException("Pre HTTP/1.0 request");
        }
        return command;
    }

    /**
     * Parsed the passed request String and populate an HTTPrequest.
     * @param reqhdr the HTTP request as a continous String
     * @return a populated HTTPrequest instance
     * @exception ProtocolException If name,value pairs have no ':'
     * @exception IOException
     */
    private HTTPrequest ParseReqHdr(String reqhdr)
        throws IOException, ProtocolException
    {
        HTTPrequest req = new HTTPrequest();

        // Break the request into lines
        StringTokenizer lines = new StringTokenizer(reqhdr, "\r\n");
        String currentLine = lines.nextToken();

        // Process the initial request line
        // into method, file, version Strings
        StringTokenizer members = new StringTokenizer(currentLine, " \t");
        req.method = members.nextToken();
        req.file = members.nextToken();
        if (req.file.equals("/")) req.file = "/index.html";
        req.version = members.nextToken();

        // Process additional lines into name/value pairs
        while ( lines.hasMoreTokens() )
        {
            String line = lines.nextToken();

            // Search for separating character
            int slice = line.indexOf(':');

            // Error if no separating character
            if ( slice == -1 )
            {
                throw new ProtocolException(
                    "Invalid HTTP header: " + line);
```

```
            }
            else
            {
                // Separate at the slice character into name, value
                String name = line.substring(0,slice).trim();
                String value = line.substring(slice + 1).trim();
                req.addNameValue(name, value);
            }
        }
        return req;
    }
```

The method `readHeader()` interrogates the inbound socket stream searching for the blank line. If the request is not in HTTP/1.0 format, this method will throw an exception. Otherwise, the resulting String is passed to `parseReqHdr()` for processing.

These routines will reject any improperly formatted requests, including requests made in the older HTTP/0.9 format. Parsing makes heavy use of the StringTokenizer class found in the java.util package.

Normally, it would be preferable to close the inbound stream as soon as the request has been completely read. If this is done, then subsequent output attempts will fail with an IOException. This is why the inbound stream is placed into the HTTPrequest instance. When the output has been completely sent, both the output and the input streams will be closed.

CAUTION

Do not be tempted to close an inbound stream after all input has been read. Closing the input stream will cause subsequent output attempts to fail with an IOException. Close both streams only after all socket operations are finished.

Currently, the server makes no use of the additional lines in an HTTP request header. The HTTPrequest class does save them in an array, however, so they can be used in future enhancements. Wherever possible, the server has been written with future enhancements in mind.

Once you've built the request, you need to form a response. Listing 9.7 presents the response routines used by the server.

Listing 9.7. HTTP response routines.

```
    /**
     * Respond to an HTTP request
     * @param request the HTTP request to respond to.
     * @exception ProtocolException If unimplemented request method
     */
    private void implementMethod(HTTPrequest request)
        throws ProtocolException
```

continues

Listing 9.7. continued

```
    {
        try
        {
            if (debug && level < 4)
                System.out.println("DEBUG: Servicing:\n" + request);
            if ( (request.method.equals("GET") ) ||
                 (request.method.equals("HEAD")) )
                ServicegetRequest(request);
            else
            {
                throw new ProtocolException("Unimplemented method: " +
➥request.method);
            }
        }
        catch (ProtocolException pe)
        {
            sendNegativeResponse(request);
            throw pe;
        }
    }

    /**
     * Send a response header for the file and the file itself.
     * Handles GET and HEAD request methods.
     * @param request the HTTP request to respond to
     */
    private void ServicegetRequest(HTTPrequest request)
        throws ProtocolException
    {
        try
        {
            if (request.file.indexOf("..") != -1)
                throw new ProtocolException("Relative paths not supported");
            String fileToGet = "htdocs" + request.file;
            FileInputStream inFile = new FileInputStream(fileToGet);
            if (debug & level < 4)
            {
                System.out.print("DEBUG: Sending file ");
                System.out.print(fileToGet + " " + inFile.available());
                System.out.println(" Bytes");
            }
            sendFile(request, inFile);
            inFile.close();
        }
        catch (FileNotFoundException fnf)
        {
            sendNegativeResponse(request);
        }
        catch (ProtocolException pe)
        {
            throw pe;
        }
        catch (IOException ioe)
        {
            System.out.println("IOException: Unknown file length: " + ioe);
            sendNegativeResponse(request);
        }
```

```
}

/**
 * Send a negative (404 NOT FOUND) response
 * @param request the HTTP request to respond to.
 */
private void sendNegativeResponse(HTTPrequest request)
{
    DataOutputStream outbound = null;

    try
    {
        // Acquire the output stream
        outbound = new DataOutputStream(
            request.clientSocket.getOutputStream());

        // Write the negative response header
        outbound.writeBytes("HTTP/1.0 ");
        outbound.writeBytes("404 NOT_FOUND\r\n");
        outbound.writeBytes("\r\n");

        // Clean up
        outbound.close();
        request.inbound.close();
    }
    catch (IOException ioe)
    {
        System.out.println("IOException while sending -rsp: " + ioe);
    }
}

/**
 * Send the passed file
 * @param request the HTTP request instance
 * @param inFile the opened input file stream to send\
 */
private void sendFile(HTTPrequest request, FileInputStream inFile)
{
    DataOutputStream outbound = null;

    try
    {
        // Acquire an output stream
        outbound = new DataOutputStream(
            request.clientSocket.getOutputStream());

        // Send the response header
        outbound.writeBytes("HTTP/1.0 200 OK\r\n");
        outbound.writeBytes("Content-type: text/html\r\n");
        outbound.writeBytes("Content-Length: " + inFile.available() + "\r\n");
        outbound.writeBytes("\r\n");

        // Added to allow Netscape to process header properly
        // This is needed because the close is not recognized
        sleep(500);

        // If not a HEAD request, send the file body.
        // HEAD requests solicit only a header response.
```

continues

Listing 9.7. continued

```
            if (!request.method.equals("HEAD"))
            {
                byte dataBody[] = new byte[1024];
                int cnt;
                while ((cnt = inFile.read(dataBody)) != -1)
                    outbound.write(dataBody, 0, cnt);
            }

            // Clean up
            outbound.flush();
            outbound.close();
            request.inbound.close();
        }
        catch (IOException ioe)
        {
            System.out.println("IOException while sending file: " + ioe);
        }
    }
```

Only `GET` and `HEAD` requests are honored. The primary goal is to provide an applet server, not a full-featured Web server. File requests are all that's needed for applet loading, though additional handlers can certainly be added for other request methods. The `serviceGetRequest()` function handles all responses. When the input stream for a file is acquired, the file is opened. At this point, the routine knows whether the file exists and its size. Once a valid file is found, the `sendFile()` function can be called. The file is read and sent in 1K blocks. This keeps memory usage down while seeking to balance the number of disk accesses attempted. Negative responses are sent only for errors occurring after the request has been built. As a consequence, improperly formatted requests will generate no response.

The response routines rely on ProtocolExceptions to signal error conditions. When one of these exceptions reaches the `implementMethod()` function, a negative response is sent. Notice the catch clause in `serviceGetRequest()`. The ProtocolException must be caught and thrown again, or the following IOException will catch the event. This is because ProtocolException is a child class of IOException. If it had been placed after the IOException, the compiler would have generated an error:

```
BasicWebServer.java:303: catch not reached.
```

The remainder of the BasicWebServer application can be found on the CD-ROM. The remaining code calls the input routine `getRequest()` and then the output routine `implementMethod()` for each client connection.

The next section develops a client applet that will be loaded with the server just constructed. Another service thread will be added to the server to conduct a datagram socket protocol with the client.

Client Datagram Applet

Applets need to communicate with a server for a variety of applications. What is needed is a generic protocol that any applet can use to communicate with its server. This protocol should not be connection oriented because of the additional load that would be placed on a server. Datagrams present a lighter load and allow the same socket to be used no matter how many actual connections are being serviced. What is envisioned is a broadcast capability for data. It isn't reasonable for applets to query a server every five seconds to see whether data has changed. The server should be able to send to all of its connections whenever the data changes. With this in mind, the Datagram Transfer Protocol (DGTP) was developed. The primary requirements of this protocol were as follows:

- Use datagrams to lessen server socket use.
- Implement a hook-in and an unhook mechanism.
- Allow generic data of any type to be transferred.
- Allow any object type to use DGTP services.
- Provide a broadcast capability.

Figure 9.3 shows a client applet using DGTP to communicate with a server. Notice how the HTTP data connection does not extend to the applet. The browser spawns the applet from the data received from the server.

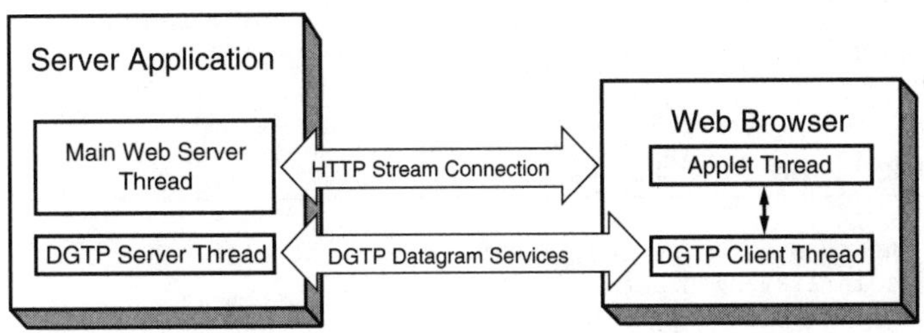

FIGURE 9.3.
DGTP communication in the client/server model.

The DGTP protocol uses a header much like HTTP; its basic methods are `REGISTER`, `UNREGISTER`, `DATA`, `PING`, and `PONG`. The two register methods accomplish hooking and unhooking. `PING` and `PONG` are currently unused, but could provide a mechanism to periodically check the connection list. The `DATA` method facilitates the transfer capability. To allow any object to use DGTP services, a standard interface was developed. These interfaces specify the set of functions that an object must use to communicate with DGTP service threads. Listing 9.8 shows the client and server interfaces.

Listing 9.8. DGTP client and server interfaces.

```
public interface LiveDataNotify
{
```

continues

Listing 9.8. continued

```
    public String getDestHost();
    public int getDestPort();
    public void recvNewData(byte[] newDataBlock);
    public void connectRefused();
}

public interface LiveDataServer
{
    public boolean ValidateRegistrant(ClientAddr user);
    public void NewRegistrant(ClientAddr user);
    public void DropRegistrant(ClientAddr user);
    public void recvNewData(byte[] newDataBlock, DatagramPacket fromWho);
}
```

Notice that both the client and the server have a method to receive blocks of data. The client has methods to specify the destination host and port, and the server has methods to validate and register new connections. The DGTP client is covered first.

DGTP Client

Since listening for receive will block until there is data, the registration requests will have to be sent using a different thread. The first thing the client's `run()` method does is to start the registration thread. At that point, it can begin receiving data. Listing 9.9 displays a partial listing of the DGTP client. The complete source code for the client and the registration threads is on the CD-ROM in DGTPClient.java.

Listing 9.9. The DGTPClient class.

```
/**
 * The runmethod for the client.  Start the register thread and
 * begin listening for incoming packets.
 */
public void run()
{
    DatagramPacket packet = null;
    try
    {
        regThread.start();
        while (socket != null)
        {
            packet = new DatagramPacket(new byte[512], 512);
            socket.receive(packet);
            try
            {
                parsePacketData(packet);
            }
            catch (ProtocolException pe)
            {
                System.out.println("ProtocolException: " + pe);
            }
```

```
            }
        }
        catch (IOException ioe)
        {
            System.out.println("IOException: in DGTPClient: " + ioe);
        }
    }

    /**
     * Handle a DGTP incoming header
     * @param packet the incoming packet to parse
     * @exception ProtocolException
     * @exception IOException
     */
    public void parsePacketData(DatagramPacket packet)
        throws IOException, ProtocolException
    {
        String command = null;
        ByteArrayInputStream barray = null;
        DataInputStream is = null;

        barray = new ByteArrayInputStream(
            packet.getData(), 0, packet.getLength() );
        is = new DataInputStream( barray );
        command = readHeader(is);

        StringTokenizer lines, cmds;
        lines = new StringTokenizer(command, "\r\n");
        cmds = new StringTokenizer(lines.nextToken(), " \t");
        String ver = cmds.nextToken();
        String cmd = cmds.nextToken();
        if ( cmd.equals("PING") )
            send("PONG" + cmds.nextToken());
        else if ( cmd.equals("REGISTER") )
        {
            lastResponse = cmds.nextToken();
            registered = true;
            if ( !lastResponse.equals("CONFIRM") )
            {
                dataClient.connectRefused();
                socket.close();
                socket = null;
            }
        }
        else if ( cmd.equals("UNREGISTER") )
        {
            lastResponse = cmds.nextToken();
            if ( lastResponse.equals("CONFIRM") )
            {
                registered = false;
                socket.close();
                socket = null;
            }
        }
        else if ( cmd.equals("DATA") )
        {
            int length = Integer.valueOf(cmds.nextToken()).intValue();
            byte[] data = new byte[length];
```

continues

Listing 9.9. continued

```
            try
            {
                is.readFully(data);
                dataClient.recvNewData(data);
            }
            catch (EOFException eof)
            {
                throw new ProtocolException(
                    "Server packet too short: " + eof);
            }
            catch (IOException ioe)
            {
                throw new ProtocolException(
                    "While reading server data: " + ioe);
            }
        }
        else
        {
            throw new ProtocolException(
                "Unknown DGTP command: " + cmd);
        }
        is.close();
    }

    /**
     * Unregister the DGTPClient
     */
    public void terminate()
    {
        unregThread = new ClientUnregistration(this);
        unregThread.start();
    }
```

The read routines are largely the same as the HTTP server's. What is significant is the translation of the packet data to stream format. Once that is done, the header can be parsed in the same manner as an HTTP request. To perform the translation, ByteArrayInputStream is used; this class is extremely useful when working with byte arrays. Once the array is in a stream format, it can be turned into a DataInputStream—the same format the BasicWebServer used to read its requests.

The `terminate()` function spawns a new thread to send the `UNREGISTER` command because the main client thread is blocked in a receive call.

DGTP Server Class

Since DGTP is a datagram protocol, the server will be very similar to the client. There are two main changes, the largest of which occurs in the `parsePacketData()` handler function. Listing 9.10 shows the data parse function for the DGTPServer class. The complete source code can be found on the CD-ROM in DGTPServer.java.

Listing 9.10. DGTPServer data parsing routine.

```
/**
 * Process all incoming packets
 * @param packet contains the DGTP request
 * @exception ProtocolException
 * @exception IOException
 */
public void ParsePacketData(DatagramPacket packet)
    throws IOException, ProtocolException
{
    String command = null;
    ByteArrayInputStream barray = null;
    DataInputStream is = null;
    String cmd = null;

    barray = new ByteArrayInputStream(
        packet.getData(), 0, packet.getLength() );
    is = new DataInputStream( barray );
    command = readHeader(is);

    try
    {
        StringTokenizer lines = new StringTokenizer(command, "\r\n");
        StringTokenizer cmds = new StringTokenizer(lines.nextToken(), " \t");
        String ver = cmds.nextToken();
        cmd = cmds.nextToken();
        if ( cmd.equals("PING") )
        {
            ClientAddr addr = new ClientAddr(
                packet.getAddress(), packet.getPort());
            send(addr, "PONG" + cmds.nextToken());
        }
        else if ( cmd.equals("REGISTER") )
        {
            ClientAddr addr = new ClientAddr(
                packet.getAddress(), packet.getPort());
            if (!Clients.containsKey(addr))
            {
                if ( dataServer.ValidateRegistrant(addr) )
                {
                    Clients.put(addr, addr);
                    send(addr, "REGISTER CONFIRM");
                    dataServer.NewRegistrant(addr);
                }
                else
                {
                    send(addr, "REGISTER DENIED");
                }
            }
            else
            {
                send(addr, "REGISTER CONFIRM");
            }
        }
        else if ( cmd.equals("UNREGISTER") )
        {
```

continues

Listing 9.10. continued

```
            int port = Integer.valueOf(cmds.nextToken()).intValue();
            dumpUser( new ClientAddr(packet.getAddress(), port) );
        }
        else if ( cmd.equals("DATA") )
        {
            int length = Integer.valueOf(cmds.nextToken()).intValue();
            byte[] data = new byte[length];
            try
            {
                is.readFully(data);
                dataServer.recvNewData(data, packet);
            }
            catch (EOFException eof)
            {
                throw new ProtocolException(
                    "Client packet too short: " + eof);
            }
            catch (IOException ioe)
            {
                throw new ProtocolException(
                    "While reading client data: " + ioe);
            }
        }
        else
        {
            throw new ProtocolException(
                "Unknown DGTP command: " + cmd);
        }
    }
    catch (NoSuchElementException ne)
    {
        throw new ProtocolException(
            "Command arg mismatch: " + cmd);
    }
    is.close();
}
```

The changes occur when adding new users. The server thread will receive a `REGISTER` request, which it will pass to the interface object for validation. If the interface object accepts the new user, a `REGISTER CONFIRM` response is sent, and the interface object is alerted to the addition. If the user is rejected, a `REGISTER DENIED` response is sent. The second change is one of omission. The `run()` method for the server will not spawn a registration thread. Otherwise, it is identical to the client's `run()` method.

The server keeps track of user connections in a Hashtable. The ClientAddr class object encapsulates the address and port as well as providing a hash key. This allows the server to add a new user quickly. The code for the `REGISTER` method creates the address and checks to see whether it's already present. Multiple `REGISTER` requests may have been sent before the `REGISTER CONFIRM` packet could travel back to the sender. If the server doesn't have this connection yet, it adds the address to the Clients list. Listing 9.11 shows the ClientAddr class. Pay particular attention to the `hashCode()` and `equals()` functions; they allow the object to act as a hash key.

Listing 9.11. The ClientAddr class.

```
import java.net.InetAddress;

public class ClientAddr
{
    public InetAddress address;
    public int port;

    ClientAddr(InetAddress addr, int hostPort)
    {
        address = addr;
        port = hostPort;
    }

    public int hashCode()
    {
        int result = address.hashCode();
        result += port;
        return result;
    }

    public boolean equals(Object obj)
    {
        return (obj != null) && (obj instanceof ClientAddr) &&
           (address.equals(((ClientAddr)obj).address)) &&
           (port == ((ClientAddr)obj).port);
    }
}
```

Since this is a broadcast server, there is a varied array of send methods embedded in the class. The DGTP server has two main send routines:

```
sendData(ClientAddr dest, byte[] data, int srcOffset, int length);
send(ClientAddr dest, String toSend);
```

The first routine sends the byte array as a DGTP DATA block. The second routine sends the passed String as a DGTP command header. All the remaining send routines call `sendData()` to do the actual transmission. This is the code for one version of `sendToUsers()`:

```
public void sendToUsers(byte[] data, int srcOffset, int length)
{
     for (Enumeration e = Clients.elements(); e.hasMoreElements();)
         sendData((ClientAddr)e.nextElement(), data, srcOffset, length);
}
```

This routine uses an Enumeration object to loop through the client hashtable and send to each member. All the remaining send methods are variations on this theme. Some send to all users; some send to a specific subset of users. These are all the public send methods:

Public Send Methods in DGTPServer

```
sendToUsers(String toSend);
sendToUsers(byte[] data, int Offset, int length);
```

continues

Public Send Methods in DGTPServer

```
sendToUsers(ClientAddr[] users, String toSend);
sendToUsers(ClientAddr[] users, byte[] data, int Offset, int length);
sendData(ClientAddr addr, String block);
sendData(ClientAddr dest, byte[] data, int srcOffset, int length);
send(ClientAddr dest, String toSend);
```

Now that the threads are in place, it's time to apply them in the actual client/server applet.

Client Applet

The client applet will be simple in appearance. The emphasis here will be on using the DGTP protocol. Figure 9.4 shows the applet in action.

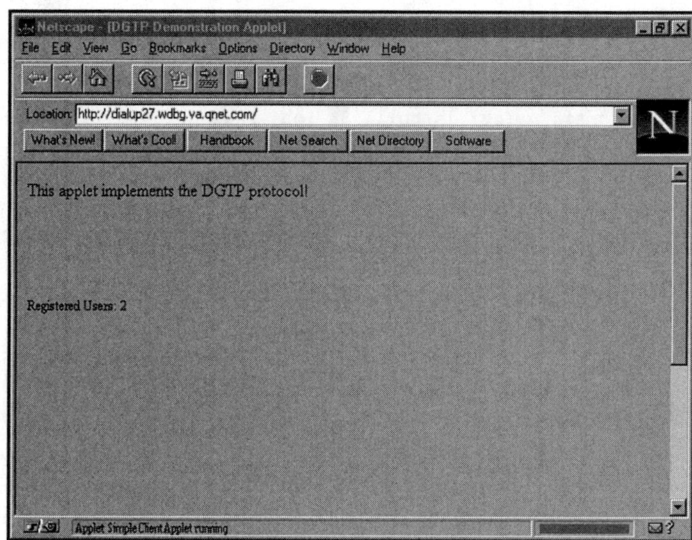

FIGURE 9.4.
A simple client applet display.

The purpose of this applet is to display the number of active connections to this page. Whenever a new user connects, the display will automatically update to reflect the new count. Likewise, when a user disconnects, the count will update. Listing 9.12 shows the client applet class.

Listing 9.12. A client applet.

```
import java.applet.*;
import java.awt.*;
import java.net.*;
import java.io.*;
import java.util.*;
import DGTPClient;
```

```
public class SimpleClientApplet extends Applet
    implements LiveDataNotify
{
    private boolean init = false;
    DGTPClient ct = null;
    int destPort;
    String destHost = null;
    String numUsers = "Unknown at this time";
    String users = null;

    public void init()
    {
        if ( init == false )
        {
            init = true;
            resize(500,500);
            String strPort = getParameter("PORT");
            if ( strPort == null )
            {
                System.out.println("ERROR: PORT parameter is missing");
                strPort = "4545";
            }
            destPort = Integer.valueOf(strPort).intValue();
            destHost = getDocumentBase().getHost();
        }
    }

    public void paint(Graphics g)
    {
        g.drawString("Registered Users: " + getUsers(), 0, 100);
    }

    public String getDestHost()
    {
        return destHost;
    }

    public int getDestPort()
    {
        return destPort;
    }

    public synchronized void recvNewData(byte[] newDataBlock)
    {
         users = new String(newDataBlock, 0);
         repaint();
    }

    public synchronized String getUsers()
    {
        if (users != null)
        {
            StringTokenizer cmds = new StringTokenizer(users, " \t");
            if (cmds.nextToken().equals("CLIENTS"))
                numUsers = cmds.nextToken();
        }
        return numUsers;
```

continues

Listing 9.12. continued

```
    }

    public void start()
    {
        ct = new DGTPClient(this);
        ct.start();
    }

    public void stop()
    {
        System.out.println("SimpleClientApplet.stop()");
        ct.terminate();
    }

    public void connectRefused()
    {
    }
}
```

The applet layers a simple protocol on top of DGTP. Whenever the server detects a change in the number of users, it sends a DATA block with the following text:

```
CLIENTS number CRLF
```

The applet receives the new DATA block and converts it to a String in `recvNewData()`. Note that this routine as well as `getUsers()` is marked as synchronized. This prevents the applet from attempting to read the String while DGTP is updating it.

The applet uses an applet parameter to know which port the server is monitoring. The following line reads the PORT parameter:

```
String strPort = getParameter("PORT");
```

The server host name is retrieved from the document itself:

```
destHost = getDocumentBase().getHost();
```

This is all the information needed to establish a server connection.

USING `getHost()` OVER A DIAL-UP CONNECTION

If you connect to the Internet through a dial-up account, then you might have trouble with this application because of a host name issue. Specifically, when a dial-in PPP connection is made, your computer is assigned an IP address by the provider. This address is displayed by the server when it is started. Users on the Internet can now reach your server by typing in your IP address:

```
HTTP://xxx.xxx.xxx.xxx/
```

This will access your server, and pages can be sent. The trouble arises when your applet attempts to receive data from your server. The call to `getDocumentBase().getHost()` will return the IP address that the user typed in to reach your server:

`"xxx.xxx.xxx.xxx"`

In reality, your service provider has already assigned your connection a name:

`"dialup_xx.internet.service.provide.com"`

When the server sends data to the applet, the host name on the data will be that of the service provider. Netscape will flag this as a security violation and raise the dreaded SecurityException. The solution is to enter the actual connection name into the initial URL, but determining this name is a problem. The easiest method I've found is to go ahead and use the IP address initially. When the exception is raised, open the Java console to discover the actual connection name. Use this name instead, and your applet will work wonderfully.

The `PORT` parameter needs to be coded into the HTML applet file so the applet knows on which port the server is listening. The HTML tag for this applet looks like this:

```
<applet
  codebase="/classes"
  code="SimpleClientApplet.class"
  width=500
  height=500
>
<param name="PORT" value="4545">
</applet>
```

Adding the DGTP Server Thread

Because the BasicWebServer project was written in Java, it's trivial to add an instance of the DGTPServer. The problem is that some object needs to implement the LiveDataServer interface. The base server class could be changed to add this behavior, but then it would have to be rewritten any time you wanted a new service thread. A better solution is to create a separate thread whose only purpose is to spawn and communicate with the DGTPServer. To this end, the NumUsersServer class was created. It really doesn't do much, but it does create the needed interface and enable simple integration with the Web server. Listing 9.13 shows the NumUsersServer.

Listing 9.13. The NumUsersServer class.

```
import java.lang.Thread;
import java.net.DatagramPacket;
import DGTPServer;
import LiveDataServer;
import ClientAddr;
```

continues

Listing 9.13. continued

```
public class NumUsersServer extends Thread
    implements LiveDataServer
{
    private DGTPServer servThread = null;

    public NumUsersServer(int hostPort)
    {
        servThread = new DGTPServer(this, hostPort);
    }

    public void run()
    {
        servThread.start();
        while(true) yield();
    }

    public boolean ValidateRegistrant(ClientAddr user)
    {
        return true;
    }

    public void NewRegistrant(ClientAddr user)
    {
         servThread.sendToUsers("CLIENTS " + servThread.Clients.size());
    }

    public void DropRegistrant(ClientAddr user)
    {
         servThread.sendToUsers("CLIENTS " + servThread.Clients.size());
    }

    public void recvNewData(byte[] newDataBlock, DatagramPacket fromWho)
    {
        System.out.println("Receive data block...discarding");
    }
}
```

The `run()` method starts the DGTP server and then enters into an infinite `while` loop. It calls the `yield()` function to avoid interfering with other active threads.

The thread is now added to the BasicWebServer class in the `start()` method:

```
// Create the server socket
serverSocket = new ServerSocket(HTTP_PORT, 5);

// Create and start any additional
// server thread services here
st = new NumUsersServer(4545);
st.start();
```

The project is now finished, so compile all the source code and start the server. If you maintained the directory structure of the CD-ROM, you should be able to start the server and connect to it. The client applet classes are under htdocs/classes. The default HTML document is in htdocs/index.html.

Summary

In this chapter, you have learned about socket abstraction as well as the Java implementation of sockets. After some basic client/server applications, a full HTTP server is undertaken. You should have a working knowledge of HTTP and an appreciation for socket applet security. The last part of the chapter introduces the DGTP protocol for applet/server interaction. This protocol will be reused in Chapter 11, "Building a Live Data Applet," as the basis for a live data server, but first, you must learn to work with native methods for database access.

10

Native Methods and Java

This chapter builds on the concepts of Chapter 9, "Java Socket Programming," to construct a sophisticated database server. The server reads from a back-end database in real time. Since the standard Java classes do not, as yet, provide a database interface, native methods must be used to read the tables. A native interface library is developed and used to read a sample database. Along the way, you will learn the following:

- Calling C methods from Java
- Creating C libraries that can be called from Java
- Handling Java types as arguments to C functions
- Accessing Java class members from C functions
- Calling Java methods from C functions
- Throwing Java exceptions from a C function

Deciding to Use Native Methods

The decision to use native methods comes with a heavy cost. Any classes that load native methods cannot be used in an applet! There aren't any browsers available that allow applets to call native methods. The reason for this restriction is security. The Java security manager can't protect against malicious attacks from within a native method. The only solution is to not allow native methods to be called.

Another disadvantage is the lost portability of your applications. One of the chief benefits of using Java is the portability of the resulting code between disparate platforms. A small industry has developed trying to provide truly portable application frameworks. For all their refinement, you are still left recompiling a version for each platform. Java steps into the fray with an intermediate format that enables you to compile once and execute everywhere. When you choose to use native methods, you lose this capability. Once again, you will be relegated to coding a separate library for each platform that runs Java.

Now that the downside to native methods is clear, why use them at all? The single best reason to resort to native methods is to add functions not present in the standard classes. Maybe you want to interface with a specific piece of hardware or use a new network driver. Whatever the reason, native methods supply the capability. Because Java is portable, it cannot take advantage of operating specific features. The Java developers endeavored to supply the standard classes with all needed functionality, but this is an impossible task. The ability to call native C methods supplies a way to use features not available through the Java classes. Most of the functions in the standard classes themselves have to resort to native method calls to accomplish their tasks.

Native Methods from the Java Side

Native methods within a Java class are very simple. Any Java method can be transformed into a native method—simply delete the method body, add a semicolon at the end, and prefix the `native` keyword. The following Java method

```
public int myMethod(byte[] data)
{
    ...
}
```

becomes

```
public native int myMethod(byte[] data);
```

Where does the method body get implemented? In a Java-called native library that gets loaded into Java at runtime. The class of the above method would have to cause the library to be loaded. The best way to accomplish the load is to add a static initializer to the class:

```
static
{
   System.loadLibrary("myMethodLibrary");
}
```

Static code blocks are executed once by the system when the class is first introduced. Any operations may be specified, but library loading is the most common use. If the static block fails, the class will not be loaded. This ensures that no native methods are executed without the underlying libraries.

That's all there is to Java-side native methods. All the complexity is hidden within the native library. A native method appears to Java like all other real Java methods. In fact, all the Java modifiers (public, private, and so forth) apply to native methods as well.

Writing Native Methods

The Java runtime was implemented in the C programming language, so currently the only native language supported is C. The entry points into a C library that can be called from Java are called *stubs*. When you execute a native method call, a stub is entered. Java tries to ease the transition into native code by supplying a tool to generate a C header file and stub module.

NOTE

Any language that can link with and be called by C can be used to implement a native method. The C language is needed only to provide the actual interface with Java. Any additional, non-Java processing could be done in another language, such as Pascal.

Using Javah

Javah is the tool used to generate C files for Java classes; here's how you use it:

```
javah [options] class
```

Table 10.1 briefly lists the options available. By default, javah will create a C header (.h) file in the current directory for each class listed on the command line. Class names are specified without the trailing .class. Therefore, to generate the header for SomeName.class, use the following command:

```
javah SomeName
```

Table 10.1. Javah options.

Option	*Description*
-verbose	Causes progress strings to be sent to stdout
-version	Prints the version of javah
-o *outputfile*	Overrides default file creation;uses only this file
-d *directory*	Overrides placement of output in current directory
-td *tempdirectory*	Overrides default temp directory use
-stubs	Creates C code module instead of header module
-classpath *path*	Overrides default classpath

NOTE

If the class you want is within a package, then the package name must be specified along with the class name: javah java.net.Socket. In addition, javah will prefix the package name to the output filename: java_net_Socket.h.

Listing 10.1 is a simple class with native methods. The class was chosen because it uses most of the Java types. Compile this class and pass it to javah.

Listing 10.1. A simple class using native methods.

```
public class Demonstration
{
    public String publicName;
    private String privateName;
    public static String publicStaticName;
    private static String privateStatucName;
```

```
    public native void method1();
    public native int method2(boolean b, byte by, char c, short s);
    public native byte[] method3(byte data[], boolean b[]);
    public native String[] method4(int num, long l, float f, double d);

    static
    {
        System.loadLibrary("Demonstration");
    }
}
```

The javah output of the above class is in Listing 10.2.

Listing 10.2. Javah output header of Demonstration class.

```
/* DO NOT EDIT THIS FILE - it is machine generated */
#include <native.h>
/* Header for class Demonstration */

#ifndef _Included_Demonstration
#define _Included_Demonstration
struct Hjava_lang_String;

typedef struct ClassDemonstration {
    struct Hjava_lang_String *publicName;
    struct Hjava_lang_String *privateName;
/* Inaccessible static: publicStaticName */
/* Inaccessible static: privateStatucName */
} ClassDemonstration;
HandleTo(Demonstration);

#ifdef __cplusplus
extern "C" {
#endif
__declspec(dllexport) void Demonstration_method1(struct HDemonstration *);
__declspec(dllexport) long Demonstration_method2(struct HDemonstration *,/
*boolean*/ long,
             char,unicode,short);
__declspec(dllexport) HArrayOfByte *Demonstration_method3(struct HDemonstration *,
             HArrayOfByte *,HArrayOfInt *);
__declspec(dllexport) HArrayOfString *Demonstration_method4(struct HDemonstration
*,long,
             int64_t,float,double);
#ifdef __cplusplus
}
#endif
#endif
```

The class has been transformed into a C structure. Each class member is represented, except for static fields. Representation in a structure has an interesting side effect. Native methods have access to all non-static fields, including private class members. You are free to read and alter any member of the class.

Now focus your attention on the four native method prototypes. Each method has been renamed by prefixing the class name to the method name. Had this class been contained in a package, the package name also would have been added. Each method has an additional argument. All native methods have a `this` pointer that allows the function to access the variables of its associated class. This argument is often referred to as an "automatic" parameter. Java will add this parameter to your methods automatically.

The final piece to the puzzle is the `HandleTo()` macro. Every object in Java is represented in a structure called a JHandle. The format of this structure for the Demonstration class is as follows:

```
struct HDemonstration
{
    ClassDemonstration *obj;
    methodtable *methods;
}
```

The `HandleTo()` macro names the JHandle by adding an *H* to the passed name. To access any member of a JHandle class, you must dereference it with the `unhand()` macro. This macro has the opposite effect of `HandleTo()`. The following line retrieves a string member from the Demonstration class:

```
Hjava_lang_String str = unhand(demoPtr)->publicName;
```

The code for the `unhand()` macro shows the conversion:

```
#define unhand(o)  ((o)->obj)
```

Structure member `obj` is obviously the class structure, but what of the other structure member?

Typically, structure member methods will contain a pointer to an internal Java runtime structure that represents all the information on a class. This includes the Java byte codes, the exception table, any defined constants, and the parent class. There are times, however, when the variable is not a pointer at all. Java has reserved the lower 5 bits of the pointer for flags. If all 5 bits are zero, then the value is a pointer. If the lower 5 bits are non-zero, then the methods field becomes a typecode. You will encounter typecodes whenever you handle arrays.

Java Arrays

Arrays are handled uniquely in Java. They are considered objects, though they have no methods. Arrays occupy the realm somewhere between basic runtime types, such as `int` or `long`, and formal class objects. In Java, basic types are represented in a compact form. It would be inefficient to have all the class baggage carried around with something simple like an integer. When you need to represent an `int` as an object, you use a wrapper class, such as class Integer. This is why the "wrapper" classes are necessary. Arrays are much more complicated than numbers because they have variable length and multiple members. Like class objects, their storage is best represented by a C structure. Unlike class objects, arrays don't have methods. It was decided that the `methodtable` pointer could be better used as a scalar quantity for arrays.

The upper 27 bits of the pointer represent the length of the array, and the lower 5 bits represent the type of data the array contains. All the runtime types are actually represented in the lower 4 bits. The fifth bit is reserved for compiler usage. Table 10.2 shows the encoding of the lower 4 flag bits and their meanings.

Table 10.2. Type encoding.

Encoding	*Type*
0000	T_NORMAL_OBJECT
0001	Unused
0010	T_CLASS
0011	Unused
0100	T_BOOLEAN
0101	T_CHAR
0110	T_FLOAT
0111	T_DOUBLE
1000	T_BYTE
1001	T_SHORT
1010	T_INTEGER
1011	T_LONG

There are macros to help you read both the type bits and the length. The `obj_flags()` macro will return the flag bits, and `obj_length()` will return the array length. Both must be passed a JHandle pointer:

```
if ( obj_flags( demoPtr ) != T_NORMAL_OBJECT )
   length = obj_length( demoPtr );
```

In practice, you will not need to check the type bits because Java will create and pass one of the standard array structures. You can see this in `Demonstration_method3()`. The parameter `byte[]` has been passed as an HArrayOfByte pointer. All the standard array structures have a single member: `body[1]`. Table 10.3 lists all the array structures and their contents. To access an array member, dereference the JHandle and index into the body array. The following line reads the fifth byte from a Java byte array:

```
char fifthByte = unhand(hByte)->body[4];
```

As you can see, Java arrays are zero-based just like C arrays.

Table 10.3. Standard array structures.

Structure	*Contents*
ArrayOfByte	char body[1]
ArrayofChar	unicode body[1]
ArrayOfShort	signed short body[1]
ArrayOfInt	long body[1]
ArrayOfLong	int64_t body[1]
ArrayOfFloat	float body[1]
ArrayOfDouble	double body[1]
ArrayOfArray	JHandle *(body[1])
ArrayOfObject	HObject *(body[1])
ArrayOfString	HString *(body[1])

In contrast to JHandle and array pointers, the Java basic types are passed and referenced as direct C types. Table 10.4 displays all the basic Java types and their corresponding C representation.

Table 10.4. C representation of Java basic types in Windows 95.

Java Type	*C Representation*
`boolean`	long
`char`	unicode
`short`	short
`int`	long
`long`	int64_t
`float`	float
`double`	double

NOTE

All the type information in this chapter is specific to Windows 95. The Java type representations may be different on another platform. It is best to run `javah` on the Demonstration class to verify the C representations when working on a different platform. In addition, all the macros and structures discussed can be found in the Java header files in the Java/include directory. These files are specific to a given platform and, as such, should be consulted when performing native method work.

Now that you understand the C side of Java data, it's time to generate the code that interfaces Java to C.

The Stubs Code

Run the following command on the Demonstration class:

```
javah -stubs Demonstration
```

The output will be a C file in the current directory. Listing 10.3 shows the result.

Listing 10.3. The output of `javah -stubs Demonstration`.

```
/* DO NOT EDIT THIS FILE - it is machine generated */
#include <StubPreamble.h>

/* Stubs for class Demonstration */
/* SYMBOL: "Demonstration/method1()V", Java_Demonstration_method1_stub */
declspec(dllexport) stack_item *
 Java_Demonstration_method1_stub(stack_item *_P_,struct execenv *_EE_) {
            extern void Demonstration_method1(void *);
            (void) Demonstration_method1(_P_[0].p);
            return _P_;
}
/* SYMBOL: "Demonstration/method2(ZBCS)I", Java_Demonstration_method2_stub */
declspec(dllexport) stack_item *
 Java_Demonstration_method2_stub(stack_item *_P_,struct execenv *_EE_) {
            extern long Demonstration_method2(void *,long,long,long,long);
            _P_[0].i = Demonstration_method2(_P_[0].p,((_P_[1].i)),
                                             ((_P_[2].i)),((_P_[3].i)),
                                             ((_P_[4].i)));
            return _P_ + 1;
}
/* SYMBOL: "Demonstration/method3([B[Z)[B", Java_Demonstration_method3_stub */
declspec(dllexport) stack_item *
 Java_Demonstration_method3_stub(stack_item *_P_,struct execenv *_EE_) {
            extern long Demonstration_method3(void *,void *,void *);
            _P_[0].i = Demonstration_method3(_P_[0].p,((_P_[1].p)),((_P_[2].p)));
            return _P_ + 1;
}
/* SYMBOL: "Demonstration/method4(IJFD)[Ljava/lang/String;",
Java_Demonstration_method4_stub */
declspec(dllexport) stack_item *
 Java_Demonstration_method4_stub(stack_item *_P_,struct execenv *_EE_) {
            Java8 _t2;
            Java8 _t4;
```

continues

Listing 10.3. continued

```
        extern long Demonstration_method4(void *,long,int64_t,float,double);
        _P_[0].i = Demonstration_method4(_P_[0].p,
                                         ((_P_[1].i)),
                                          GET_INT64(_t2, _P_+2),
                                         ((_P_[4].f)),
                                          GET_DOUBLE(_t5, _P_+5));
        return _P_ + 1;
}
```

This file contains the stub functions for each of the four native methods. It is the stub's job to translate Java data structures into a C format. Once this is done, the stub will then enter your C function. Sometimes the stub will have to do a little extra work to make the transition. For example, take a look at `method4`'s stub. The Java stack is made up of 32-bit words. Java data types `long` and `double` each command 64 bits of storage. The stub code calls "helper" functions to extract the data from the Java stack. The stubs will perform all the work necessary, no matter how complex, to interface the Java stack to C.

The other interesting feature of the stub module is the `SYMBOL` comment at the top of each method. Java uses a system of method "signatures" to identify functions. The signature contains the method arguments and the return type; the symbols are explained in Table 10.5.

Table 10.5. Method signature symbols.

Type	*Signature Character*
`byte`	B
`char`	C
`class`	L
`end of class`	;
`float`	F
`double`	D
`function`	(
`end of function`	)
`int`	I
`long`	J
`short`	S
`void`	V
`boolean`	Z

Signatures are important because they enable you to make calls back into the Java system. If you know the class, name, and signature of a method, then these elements can be used to invoke the Java method from within a C library. The format of a signature is as follows:

```
"package_name/class_name/method_name(args*)return_type"
```

Arguments can be any combination of the characters in Table 10.5. Class name arguments are written like this:

```
Lclass_name;
```

The semicolon signals the end of the class name, just as the right (closing) parenthesis signals the end of an argument list. Arrays are followed by the array type:

```
[B for an array of bytes
[Ljava/langString; for an array of objects (in this case, Strings)
```

The Demonstration class is not actually going to be used; it's merely a convenient tool to demonstrate the C features of Java's runtime environment. Now it's time to move on to the chapter project and some actual native method code.

Chapter Project: A Database Interface Library Using ODBC

The goal of this project is to be able to read from a database. Although this project uses ODBC for its database access layer, any embedded SQL routines could be used. The database query routine has been separated from the Java return logic within the native method. Any database access method could easily be substituted. In fact, if you don't have ODBC installed, a synthetic query routine is supplied on the CD-ROM in the file FakeDatabaseImpl.c.

The project will consist of two classes and an interface library. A container class will be used to house the query statement and resulting data, and a second class called Database will perform all the native methods.

Listing 10.4 lays out the SQLStmt class. The native method library reads and writes directly to the variables in this container class.

Listing 10.4. The SQLStmt class.

```
import java.io.*;
import java.lang.*;
import DBException;

/**
 * Class to contain an SQL statement and resulting data
 */
```

continues

Listing 10.4. continued

```
public class SQLStmt
{
    // The query string
    public String sqlStmt = null;

    // The actual data from the query
    private String result[][];
    private int nRows, nCols;

    // True if the query is successful
    private boolean query = false;

    /**
     * The lone constructor, you must supply a query
     * string to use this constructor
     * @param stmt contains the query to execute
     */
    SQLStmt(String stmt)
    {
        sqlStmt = stmt;
        System.out.println("Statement: " + stmt);
    }

    /**
     * Return the number of rows in a query data set
     * @exception DBException if no query has been made
     */
    public int numRows()
        throws DBException
    {
        if ( !query )
            throw new DBException("No active query");
        return nRows;
    }

    /**
     * Return the number of cols in a query data set
     * @exception DBException if no query has been made
     */
    public int numCols()
        throws DBException
    {
        if ( !query )
            throw new DBException("No active query");
        return nCols;
    }

    /**
     * Retreive the contents of a row.  Each column
     * is separated from the others by a pipe '¦' character.
     * @param row is the row to retreive
     * @exception DBException if invalid row
     */
    public String getRow(int row)
        throws DBException
    {
        if ( !query )
```

```
            throw new DBException("No active query");
        else if ( row >= nRows )
            throw new DBException("Row out of bounds");
        String buildResult = new String("");

        for ( int x = 0; x < nCols; x++ )
            buildResult += (result[row])[x] + " |";
        return buildResult;
    }

    /**
     * Retreive the contents of a column.
     * @param row, col is the column to retreive
     * @exception DBException if invalid row or column
     */
    public String getColumn(int row, int col)
        throws DBException
    {
        if ( !query )
            throw new DBException("No active query");
        else if ( row >= nRows )
            throw new DBException("Row out of bounds");
        else if ( col >= nCols )
            throw new DBException("Column out of bounds");
        return result[row][col];
    }

    public void allDone(String str)
    {
        System.out.println(str);
    }

    /**
     * Display the contents of the statement
     */
    public String toString()
    {
        String s = new String();

        if ( query == false )
        {
            s += sqlStmt;
        }
        else
        {
            try
            {
                for ( int x = 0; x < nRows; x++ )
                    s += getRow(x) + "\n";
            }
            catch (DBException de)
            {
                System.out.println(de);
            }
        }
        return s;
    }
}
```

The SQLStmt class has public methods to enable extracting query data in an orderly manner: `numRows()`, `numCols()`, `getRow()`, and `getColumn()`. SQLStmts are two-way objects—they hold both the input and the output data. The output is contained in a two-dimensional array of Strings. This scheme forces the database interface library to translate all table columns into String format.

A new exception has been defined with this class. It can be found on this book's CD-ROM in the file DBException.java. This exception is thrown by the SQLStmt class when a request is made, but no query has been attempted. The Database class, discussed in the following paragraphs, also throws DBExceptions.

The method `allDone()` will be called by the native library and gives the library a convenient way to print. It serves no other purpose.

Although the SQLStmt class contains all the database information, it does not actually interface with the native library. For this task, the Database class is used. This class is much simpler than the data container; its chief role is to interface with the native methods. Listing 10.5 shows the Database class.

Listing 10.5. The Database class.

```
import java.lang.*;
import java.io.*;
import SQLStmt;
import DBException;

/**
 * Class to allow access to the database library
 */
public class Database
{
    // Table name to use (ODBC data source)
    public String tableName;

    /**
     * Lone constructor.  A data source must be passed.
     * @param s holds the name of the data source to use
     */
    Database(String s)
    {
        tableName = s;
    }

    /**
     * Native method query
     * @param stmt holds the SQLStmt class to use
     * @exception DBException is thrown on any error
     */
    public synchronized native void query(SQLStmt stmt)
        throws DBException;
```

```
    public synchronized native SQLStmt sql(String stmt)
        throws DBException;

    static
    {
        System.loadLibrary("Database");
    }
}
```

The first native method uses an SQLStmt object for both input and output, and the second native method uses a String input and returns an SQLStmt object as output. It is the native library's task to create and fill the output object. Both native methods are marked as synchronized because the library implementation is single-threaded. Nothing in Java precludes making re-entrant native libraries, but the database library uses global variables for storage. This makes it necessary to protect the library from being entered by more than one thread at a time.

As with the Demonstration class, the first step is to compile the classes and pass them to the `javah` tool:

```
javac SQLStmt.java Database.java
javah SQLStmt Database
```

Here is the output for the SQLStmt class:

```
/* DO NOT EDIT THIS FILE - it is machine generated */
#include <native.h>
/* Header for class SQLStmt */

#ifndef _Included_SQLStmt
#define _Included_SQLStmt
struct Hjava_lang_String;

typedef struct ClassSQLStmt {
    struct Hjava_lang_String *sqlStmt;
    struct HArrayOfArray *result;
    long nRows;
    long nCols;
    /*boolean*/ long query;
} ClassSQLStmt;
HandleTo(SQLStmt);

#ifdef __cplusplus
extern "C" {
#endif
#ifdef __cplusplus
}
#endif
#endif
```

Notice how the two-dimensional array has been translated into HArrayOfArray. SQLStmt doesn't have any native methods, though the `javah` tool still places the surrounding `ifdef cplusplus` statements where native methods would normally appear.

Here is the output for the Database class:

```
/* DO NOT EDIT THIS FILE - it is machine generated */
#include <native.h>
/* Header for class Database */

#ifndef _Included_Database
#define _Included_Database
struct Hjava_lang_String;

typedef struct ClassDatabase {
    struct Hjava_lang_String *tableName;
} ClassDatabase;
HandleTo(Database);

#ifdef __cplusplus
extern "C" {
#endif
struct HSQLStmt;
__declspec(dllexport) void Database_query(struct HDatabase *,struct HSQLStmt *);
__declspec(dllexport) struct HSQLStmt *Database_sql(struct HDatabase *,struct
Hjava_lang_String *);
#ifdef __cplusplus
}
#endif
#endif
```

The two native methods appear at the bottom of the header. Since this file has native methods, it needs to have stub code generated for it. The next step is to execute the `javah` tool with the stubs option:

```
javah -stubs Database
```

NOTE

There is no rule about what the stub module must be called. You can use the `-ofilename` option to override `javah`'s default naming convention. This option is also useful for forcing the output from multiple classes into a single stubs file: `javah -stubs -ostubs.c class1 class2 class3`. This can be done as long as all the native methods for classes 1, 2, and 3 will appear in the same native library.

Here is the stub module for the Database class:

```
/* DO NOT EDIT THIS FILE - it is machine generated */
#include <StubPreamble.h>

/* Stubs for class Database */
/* SYMBOL: "Database/query(LSQLStmt;)V", Java_Database_query_stub */
declspec(dllexport) stack_item *Java_Database_query_stub(stack_item *_P_,
                                                          struct execenv *_EE_) {
    extern void Database_query(void *,void *);
    (void) Database_query(_P_[0].p,((_P_[1].p)));
```

```
    return _P_;
}
/* SYMBOL: "Database/sql(Ljava/lang/String;)LSQLStmt;", Java_Database_sql_stub */
declspec(dllexport) stack_item *Java_Database_sql_stub(stack_item *_P_,
                                                        struct execenv *_EE_) {
    extern long Database_sql(void *,void *);
    _P_[0].i = Database_sql(_P_[0].p,((_P_[1].p)));
    return _P_ + 1;
}
```

All that's left to do is to write the implementation module for the Database stub. In the interest of having a comprehensible project layout, the name of this module will be DatabaseImpl.c. Listing 10.6 shows only the code that manipulates the Java structures. The entire source code for DatabaseImpl, including the ODBC calls, can be found on the CD-ROM.

Listing 10.6. Java interface functions from DatabaseImpl.c.

```
#include <StubPreamble.h>
#include <javaString.h>
#include "Database.h"
#include "SQLStmt.h"
#include <stdio.h>
#include <sql.h>

#define MAX_WIDTH     50
#define MAX_COLS      20
#define MAX_ROWS      200

static SQLSMALLINT nRows, nCols;
static SQLINTEGER namelen[ MAX_COLS ];
static char *cols[ MAX_COLS ];
static char *rows[ MAX_ROWS ][ MAX_COLS ];

bool_t throwDBError(char *description)
{
    SignalError(0, "DBException", description);
    return FALSE;
}

/*
 * Extract from local storage into the passed String array.
 */
void getTableRow(struct HDatabase *db,
                    HArrayOfString *result,
                    long row)
{
    int col;
    char *st;

    for ( col = 0; col < nCols; col++ )
    {
        st = rows[row][col];
        unhand(result)->body[col] = makeJavaString(st, strlen(st));
    }
```

continues

Listing 10.6. continued

```
}

/*
 * Perform a database lookup using the passed HSQLStmt.
 */
void Database_query(struct HDatabase *db,
                    struct HSQLStmt *stmt)
{
    int x;
    HArrayOfArray *all;
    HString *s;

    /* Read from the database into local storage */
    if ( doQuery(db, stmt) == FALSE )
        freeStorage();

    /* If we have data, store it in the class */
    if ( nRows != 0 && nCols != 0 )
    {
        /* Allocate the row array (1st dimension) */
        all = (HArrayOfArray *)ArrayAlloc(T_CLASS, nRows);
        if ( !all )
        {
            freeStorage();
            unhand(stmt)->query = FALSE;
            throwDBError("Unable to allocate result array");
            return;
        }
        /* Set the array into the HSQLStmt class object */
        unhand(stmt)->result = all;

        /* For each row, store the result strings */
        for ( x = 0; x < nRows; x++ )
        {
            /* Allocate the columns (2nd dimension) */
            all->obj->body[x] = ArrayAlloc(T_CLASS, nCols);

            /* Extract the data from local storage into the
             * HSQLStmt object.
             */
            getTableRow(db, (HArrayOfString *)all->obj->body[x], x);
        }
        /* Set final variables in the object to reflect the query */
        unhand(stmt)->query = TRUE;
        unhand(stmt)->nRows = nRows;
        unhand(stmt)->nCols = nCols;

        /* Print the results of the query by calling
         * allDone( HSQLStmt.toString() );
         */
        s = (HString *)execute_java_dynamic_method(0, (HObject *)stmt,
            "toString",
            "()Ljava/lang/String;");
```

```
        execute_java_dynamic_method(0, (HObject *)stmt, "allDone",
            "(Ljava/lang/String;)V", s);
    }
    else
        unhand(stmt)->query = FALSE;
}

/*
 * Create a HSQLStmt class object and pass it to the
 * query routine.
 */
struct HSQLStmt *Database_sql(struct HDatabase *db,
                               struct Hjava_lang_String *s)
{
    HObject *ret;

    /* Create the object by calling its constructor */

    ret = execute_java_constructor(0, "SQLStmt",
              FindClass( 0, "SQLStmt", TRUE),
              "(Ljava/lang/String;)", s);
    if ( !ret ) return NULL;

    Database_query(db, (HSQLStmt *)ret);
    return (HSQLStmt *)ret;
}
```

The `doQuery()` function merely uses ODBC to read a sample database into the local two-dimensional array: rows. The storage for the array is allocated as needed, though the total possible size is limited by the constants `MAX_ROWS` and `MAX_COLS`. The `doQuery()` function also fills in the variables `nRows` and `nCols` to reflect the storage allocated in the local array. Once the data has been extracted from the database, it's time to move it into the SQLStmt container object.

The native method `Database_query()` performs most of the interesting work. After making sure that `doQuery()` returns some data, the function first allocates a Java array to store the rows:

```
all = (HArrayOfArray *)ArrayAlloc(T_CLASS, nRows);
```

Unlike C, Java two-dimensional arrays are not allocated together. In Java, a two-dimensional array is actually an array of an array. The Java function `ArrayAlloc()` is used to make an array. The first parameter is the type of data that the array will contain; the second parameter is the array length. A JHandle pointer is returned. Since this is the first dimension of a two-dimensional array, it will contain arrays. `T_CLASS` represents any object, including arrays. It signals that the array contains JHandles.

NOTE

The rows of a two-dimensional Java array do not have to contain the same number of columns. Some rows could even be NULL. You should be aware of this when dealing with multidimensional arrays. The database library will make sure that the number of columns is consistent throughout the array.

Assuming everything allocated successfully, the JHandle is placed into the SQLStmt class with the following line:

```
unhand(stmt)->result = all;
```

If there is an error, the native method will throw a DBException by using the function `throwDBError()`. A Java function called `SignalError()` is used to throw the actual exception:

```
SignalError(0, "DBException", description);
```

The first parameter is a structure called `execenv`. Zero is substituted to cause the current environment to be used. The next parameter is the name of the exception, and the final parameter is the exception description. The preceding code line is equivalent to the Java line:

```
throw new DBException(description);
```

NOTE

Whenever the `execenv` structure (or `ExecEnv`) is called for, you may substitute NULL or 0. This causes the Java runtime to use the current environment. The actual environment pointer is supplied to the stub methods as parameter `_EE_`, but it is not passed into the native implementations.

An additional array is allocated for each row; this second dimension array has `nCols` members. The array will contain String objects, so `T_CLASS` is again passed into `ArrayAlloc()`. The created array is passed into `getTableRow()` to be filled in with the table data.

The `getTableRow()` function creates a Java String object for each column's data:

```
unhand(result)->body[col] = makeJavaString(st, strlen(st));
```

The Java function `makeJavaString()` takes a C `char` pointer and the string length as parameters. It returns a JHandle to an equivalent Java String, then the created String is stored. There is a corollary function for `makeJavaString()`:

```
char *makeCString(Hjava_lang_String *s);
```

This function converts a Java String back into a C string. Storage for the string is allocated from the Java heap. You should keep the pointer in a Java class variable somewhere to prevent the C string from being garbage-collected. The following is an alternative method:

```
char *allocCString(Hjava_lang_String *s);
```

This function allocates the C string from the local heap by using `malloc()`. You are responsible for freeing the resulting pointer when you are finished with it.

When all the rows have been created, the method tries to print the result. Originally, I printed the results from within Java, but I wanted to show you an example of C calling Java. The call was moved into the native library for this purpose.

Calling Back Into Java

Remember the discussion of method signatures? This is where they are used. Any Java method can be invoked from C:

```
s = (HString *)execute_java_dynamic_method(0, (HObject *)stmt,
            "toString",
            "()Ljava/lang/String;");
```

The function `execute_java_dynamic_method()` accomplishes the invocation. A JHandle to the object is passed, along with the method name and its signature. Without the correct signature, Java can't find the method to execute. The invoked method can return any normal Java value. In this case, a String was returned. Do you recognize the previous call? Its Java equivalent would be the following:

```
String s = stmt.toString();
```

There are actually three functions for calling back into Java:

```
Hobject *execute_java_constructor(ExecEnv *,
                                  char *classname,
                                  ClassClass *cb,
                                  char *signature, ...);

long execute_java_statuc_method(ExecEnv *, ClassClass *db,
                                char *method_name,
                                char *signature, ...);

long execute_java_dynamic_method(ExecEnv *, Hobject *,
                                 char *method_name,
                                 char *signature, ...);
```

You must know whether the method is static or dynamic because calling the wrong function will yield an exception. The ellipses at the end of each parameter list indicate a variable number of additional arguments, and the signature determines how many additional parameters there are.

Structure ClassClass describes all the attributes of a Java class. You can find the `ClassClass` pointer from the JHandle structure. In addition, there is a Java "helper" function to find the ClassClass structure of a Java class:

```
ClassClass *FindClass(struct execenv *, char *name, bool_t resolve);
```

The second native method `Database_sql()` uses `FindClass()` to construct an instance of the SQLStmt class.

Constructing Java Objects from C

`Database_sql()` is passed a String object, but it needs to return an SQLStmt object. The return object must be created. Calling `execute_java_constructor()` will both create and initialize the desired object, but what is the signature of a constructor? The following routine will dump the contents of a class's method table:

```
void dumpMethodTable(ClassClass *cb)
{
    int x;
    struct methodblock *mptr;

    fprintf(stderr, "There are %d methods in class %s\n",
        cb->methods_count, cb->name);
    mptr = cb->methods;
    for ( x = 0; x < cb->methods_count; x++, mptr++ )
    {
        fprintf(stderr, "Method %02d: name: '%s'  signature: '%s'\n",
            x, mptr->fb.name, mptr->fb.signature);
    }
}

void dumpMethods(HObject *han)
{
    dumpMethodTable(han->methods->classdescriptor);
}
```

Dumping SQLStmt's method table yields the following:

```
There are 7 methods in class SQLStmt
Method 0: name: '<init>'    signature: '(Ljava/lang/String;)V'
Method 1: name: 'numRows'   signature: '()I'
Method 2: name: 'numCols'   signature: '()I'
Method 3: name: 'getRow'    signature: '(I)Ljava/lang/String;'
Method 4: name: 'getColumn' signature: '(II)Ljava/lang/String;'
Method 5: name: 'allDone'   signature: '(Ljava/lang/String;)V'
Method 6: name: 'toString'  signature: '()Ljava/lang/String;'
```

The signature of the constructor seems as though it should be `"(Ljava/lang/String;)V"`. This is not actually the case. Using this signature will yield an exception:

```
java.lang.NoSuchMethodError
```

The correct signature leaves off the trailing *V*.

NOTE

The signature of a constructor has NO return type at all. It should always be written as `"(...)"`, not as `"(...)V"`.

After the constructor is run, the object is passed into the original query routine before it is returned to the caller.

Creating the Library

The final step is to compile the library. You must have Microsoft Visual C++ Version 2.*x* or above. The libraries on the CD-ROM were compiled with Visual C++ 4.0. To compile the database library, issue the following command:

```
cl Database.c DatabaseImpl.c -FeDatabase.dll -MD -LD odbc32.lib javai.lib
```

If you don't have ODBC32 installed in your system, a synthetic version can be made. Issue the following command to construct the synthetic version:

```
cl Database.c FakeDatabaseImpl.c -FeDatabase.dll -MD -LD javai.lib
```

Obviously, FakeDatabaseImpl.c makes no ODBC calls, but it does supply a simulated version of the data. Both of the above commands create the file Database.dll. The javai library provides access to the Java runtime DLL of the same name. It should be listed as the last library on the command line.

The Database class still needs to be integrated into the server from Chapter 9, but the following Java application is suitable for testing the library itself. It can be found on the CD-ROM in the file TestDatabase.java.

```
import Database;

/**
 * A simple test application for exercising the Database class.
 */
public class TestDatabase
{
    public static void main(String args[])
    {
        // Create the database class and assign the data source
        Database db = new Database("election.dbf");

        // Make the a SQL statement to execute
        SQLStmt stmt = new SQLStmt("select * from election");

        try
        {
            // Execute the 1st native method
            db.query(stmt);
```

```
            // Execute the 2nd native method
            db.sql("select * from election where State = 'Maryland'");
        }
        catch (DBException de)
        {
            System.out.println(de);
        }
    }
}
```

NOTE

The database in this project has five columns: Candidate, State, Votes, % Precincts Reporting, and Electoral Votes. The database file, election.dbf, is in dBASE IV format. You will need to set up an ODBC data source called election.dbf to access this file.

Now that the database access class is written, it's time to integrate it with the client/server applet from the previous chapter.

Database Server

The project architecture consists of three threads. The main HTTP server thread forms the basis of the application and provides HTTP services. This main thread spawns a separate second thread, called ElectionServer, whose purpose is to perform additional server functions unrelated to HTTP. ElectionServer acts as a manager of the DGTP transmission protocol thread and provides access to the database. The DGTP thread is the third and final thread for the project—it's spawned and used by the election server. The main HTTP thread has no communication with either the election server or its DGTP thread.

The client side mirrors the server. Instead of a HTTP server, the client substitutes a Java-enabled browser. The browser spawns the applet, and the applet spawns and manages the DGTPClient thread. Figure 10.1 illustrates the overall architecture.

This project uses the DGTP protocol from Chapter 9, but the protocol has a major limitation that must be addressed first. Currently, the amount of data being sent to a DGTP client must fit within the block size of the protocol (1024 bytes). This is not acceptable for a database server, so the protocol must be amended to serve arbitrarily large amounts of data.

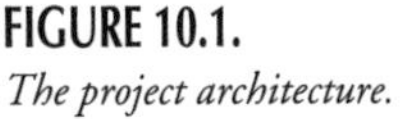

FIGURE 10.1.
The project architecture.

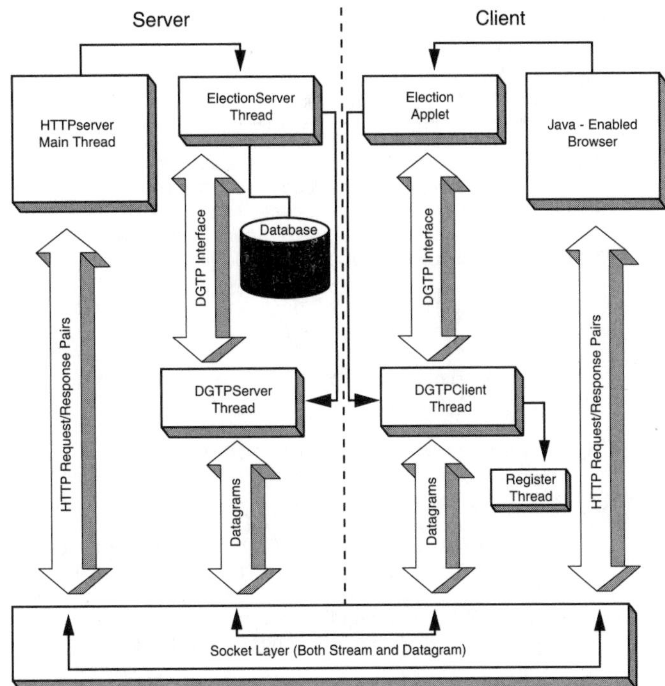

Adding Packet Assembly to DGTP

Serving large data blocks isn't difficult, but it does require some overhead costs. DGTP will use a technique called *chaining* to send the data. Chaining simply means that large data will be sent as a series of smaller sub-blocks; each sub-block is marked to reflect both its position within a chain and the chain itself. In addition, the sub-blocks are marked as first-in-chain, middle-in-chain, or last-in-chain, depending on their chain position. Keep in mind that datagrams are still being used to send the sub-blocks, so it is quite possible for the sub-blocks to arrive at the receiver in a different order than they were sent.

When a chained sub-block is received, it will have to be queued to a packet assembler to reconstruct the original chain. Only when all the sub-blocks are received can the data be forwarded. A *packet assembler* acts as a middle man—assembling packet fragments into a single continuous packet.

Each transmission request is checked for size before it is sent. If the size will not fit into a single packet, the data block is forwarded to a separate send routine for chaining. This new routine will use a new DGTP command for its transmissions:

- `MDATA` *`chain sub-block first-middle-or-last length`*

The new format for DGTP send operations is shown in Listing 10.7.

Listing 10.7. New DGTP send operations.

```
/**
 * Send the block of data to the specified address.
 * @param dest contains the address to send to
 * @param data is the data to send
 * @param srcOffset is where to start sending from
 * @param length is the amount of data to send
 */
public void sendData(ClientAddr dest, byte[] data,
                     int srcOffset, int length)
{
    String hdr = new String("DGTP/" + DGTPver + " ");
    hdr += "DATA " + length + "\r\n\r\n";

    if ( (hdr.length() + length) > PSIZE )
        multiPartSend(dest, data, srcOffset, length);
    else
    {
        byte[] sendbuf = new byte[hdr.length() + length];
        hdr.getBytes(0, hdr.length(), sendbuf, 0);
        System.arraycopy(data, srcOffset, sendbuf, hdr.length(), length);
        DatagramPacket sendPacket = new DatagramPacket(
            sendbuf, sendbuf.length, dest.address, dest.port);
        try
        {
            socket.send(sendPacket);
        }
        catch (IOException ioe)
        {
            System.out.println("IOException: Unable to send. " + ioe);
        }
    }
}

/**
 * Send the a large block of data to the specified address.
 * Large means bigger than the largest packet size (PSIZE).
 * @param dest contains the address to send to
 * @param data is the data to send
 * @param srcOffset is where to start sending from
 * @param length is the amount of data to send
 */
public void multiPartSend(ClientAddr dest, byte[] data,
                          int srcOffset, int length)
{
    int multiNum = chainNum++;
    int blockNum = 0;
    int sentSoFar = 0;

    while ( sentSoFar < length )
    {
        String chain;
        String hdr = new String("DGTP/" + DGTPver + " ");
        hdr += "MDATA " + multiNum + " " + blockNum;
```

```
        // max = current header + sizeof(" xic ") +
        //       sizeof("1024 ") + sizeof("\r\n\r\n");
        int maxHdrSize = hdr.length() + 5 + MAX_PSIZE_STRING + 4;

        // Determine the biggest block we can send
        int blockLength = PSIZE - maxHdrSize;
        if ( blockLength <= 0 )
        {
            System.out.println("Error: PSIZE is too small");
            System.out.println("Header is " + maxHdrSize + " bytes long");
            return;
        }

        // If block is more than we need, make it fit
        if ( (blockLength + sentSoFar) >= length )
        {
            blockLength = length - sentSoFar;
            chain = " lic ";       // last-in-chain
        }
        else if ( blockNum == 0 )
        {
            chain = " fic ";        // first-in-chain
        }
        else
        {
            chain = " mic ";        // middle-in-chain
        }

        // finish wrting the header
        hdr += chain + blockLength + "\r\n\r\n";

        byte[] sendbuf = new byte[hdr.length() + blockLength];
        hdr.getBytes(0, hdr.length(), sendbuf, 0);
        System.arraycopy(data, srcOffset + sentSoFar,
                         sendbuf, hdr.length(), blockLength);
        DatagramPacket sendPacket = new DatagramPacket(
            sendbuf, sendbuf.length, dest.address, dest.port);
        try
        {
            socket.send(sendPacket);
        }
        catch (IOException ioe)
        {
            System.out.println("IOException: Unable to send. " + ioe);
            return;
        }

        // Update counters
        blockNum++;
        sentSoFar += blockLength;
    }
  }
}
```

The DGTPClient class also has to be changed to work with the new transmission scheme. Listing 10.8 shows only the changed methods.

Listing 10.8. Changes to DGTPClient in support of chaining.

```
public DGTPClient(LiveDataNotify handler)
{
        ...
        buildThread = new ClientPacketAssembler(this);
        ...
 }

public void run()
{
    DatagramPacket packet = null;
    try
    {
        regThread.start();
        buildThread.start();
    }
         ...
}

public void parsePacketData(DatagramPacket packet)
    throws IOException, ProtocolException
{
    ...
    else if ( cmd.equals("MDATA") )
    {
        handleNewMultiData(cmds, is);
    }
    ...
}

public void handleNewMultiData(StringTokenizer cmds, DataInputStream is)
    throws ProtocolException
{
    int packetNum = Integer.valueOf(cmds.nextToken()).intValue();
    int subBlockNum = Integer.valueOf(cmds.nextToken()).intValue();
    boolean last = false;
    if ( cmds.nextToken().equals("lic") )
        last = true;
    int length = Integer.valueOf(cmds.nextToken()).intValue();
    byte[] data = new byte[length];
    try
    {
        is.readFully(data);
        buildThread.newSubBlock(packetNum, subBlockNum, last, data);
    }
    catch (EOFException eof)
    {
        throw new ProtocolException(
            "Server packet too short: " + eof);
    }
```

```
        catch (IOException ioe)
        {
            throw new ProtocolException(
                "Error while reading server data: " + ioe);
        }
    }
```

The actual tracking and assembly of chains is done in the ClientPacketAssembly thread. The DGTPClient merely assembles the sub-block and its information, then passes the data into the assembly thread, shown in Listing 10.9.

Listing 10.9. The ClientPacketAssembler class.

```
import java.lang.*;
import java.util.*;
import java.net.*;
import java.io.*;
import DGTPClient;

/**
 * Packet assembler tracks and assembles multi part data blocks.
 */
public class ClientPacketAssembler extends Thread
{
    private static final int TIMEOUT = 30000;    // in milliseconds
    private static final int SLEEP_TIME = 5000;  // in milliseconds
    DGTPClient ct = null;
    Hashtable partials = null;

    public ClientPacketAssembler(DGTPClient cthread)
    {
        ct = cthread;
        partials = new Hashtable();
    }

    public void run()
    {
        while (true)
        {
            try
            {
               Thread.currentThread().sleep(SLEEP_TIME);
            }
            catch (InterruptedException ie)
            {
                System.out.println(
                    "InterruptedException: in packet assembler thread: " + ie);
            }
            checkTimers();
        }
    }

    /**
     * For each partial packet being tracked, decrement the timer
```

continues

Listing 10.9. continued

```
     * and kill the packet if it has expired.
     */
    public synchronized void checkTimers()
    {
         for (Enumeration e = partials.elements(); e.hasMoreElements();)
         {
             PartialPacket pp = (PartialPacket)e.nextElement();
             if ( pp.timer > 0 )
             {
                 pp.timer -= SLEEP_TIME;
                 if ( pp.timer <= 0 )
                 {
                   partials.remove( new Integer(pp.packetNum) );
                   ct.notifyCompleteBlock(null, true);
                 }
             }
         }
    }

    /**
     * Add a new sub block.
     * @param packetNum contains the pnum being assembled
     * @param subBlockNum contains the bnum within this pnum
     * @param last is true if this is the last in a series
     * @param data contains the data for this sub block.
     */
    public synchronized void newSubBlock(int packetNum, int subBlockNum,
                                boolean last, byte data[])
    {
        PartialPacket pp;

        pp = (PartialPacket)partials.get(new Integer(packetNum));
        if ( pp == null )
        {
            pp = new PartialPacket(packetNum);
            partials.put(new Integer(packetNum), pp);
        }

        pp.addSubBlock(subBlockNum, last, data);

        if ( pp.complete() )
        {
            try
            {
                ct.notifyCompleteBlock(pp.getData(), false);
                partials.remove(new Integer(packetNum));
            }
            catch (IOException ioe)
            {
                System.out.println("Error getting data: " + ioe);
            }
        }
        else
          pp.timer = TIMEOUT;
    }
}
```

This class is structured to handle multiple chains simultaneously. A hash table is used to store each chain's assembly. The key to the hash table is the packet number, but it can't be passed directly to the hash table because `int` is a base type, not a class object. The `int` must first be placed in an Integer class wrapper.

The ClientPacketAssembler class is a thread so that it can detect timeouts. The `run()` method checks for timeouts on each packet under assembly. Every time a sub-block is received, the sub-block's chain timer is reset. If the timer expires before a new sub-block arrives, the chain is killed. This protects the client if one of a chain's sub-blocks is lost. When a chain is killed, the DGTPClient is notified through the same function used to signal complete chains:

```
ct.notifyCompleteBlock(null, true);
```

The second parameter to the above function is a boolean error flag. If it is true, the first parameter is undefined. This flag is also added to the `recvNewData()` method within the LiveDataNotify interface:

```
public interface LiveDataNotify
{
    public String getDestHost();
    public int getDestPort();
    public void recvNewData(byte[] newDataBlock, boolean error);
    public void connectRefused();
}
```

A new command has been added to the client to facilitate recovery from lost chains. In each application, you must decide what action to take if it loses a chain, but one option is to send a `REFRESH` request to the server.

When a new sub-block arrives, the assembler checks to see whether a chain has been started. If no previous instance of the chain exists, a PartialPacket class, shown in Listing 10.10, is created to track the new chain. The current sub-block is then added to the chain.

Listing 10.10. The PartialPacket tracking class.

```
/**
 * A private class for assembling packets
 */
class PartialPacket
{
    public int timer;
    public int packetNum;

    private int totalBlocks;
    private int totalSize;
    private Hashtable blocks;
    private BitSet recvd;

    public PartialPacket(int pnum)
    {
```

continues

Listing 10.10. continued

```
        packetNum = pnum;
        timer = 0;
        totalBlocks = -1;
        totalSize = 0;
        blocks = new Hashtable();
        recvd = new BitSet();
    }

    /**
     * Handle a new sub block
     * @param subBlockNum is the strand being added
     * @param last is true if this is the last block
     * @param data contains the data for this strand
     */
    public void addSubBlock(int subBlockNum, boolean last, byte data[])
    {
        // Ignore duplicate packets, shouldn't occur
        if ( recvd.get(subBlockNum) )
            return;

        // if last block, we can set the number of blocks
        // for this packet
        if ( last )
            totalBlocks = subBlockNum + 1;

        totalSize += data.length;
        recvd.set(subBlockNum);
        blocks.put(new Integer(subBlockNum), data);
    }

    /**
     * Function to test whether a packet is completely
     * assembled.
     */
    public boolean complete()
    {
        if ( totalBlocks != -1 )
        {
            for ( int x = 0; x < totalBlocks; x++ )
            {
                if ( recvd.get(x) == false )
                    return false;
            }
            return true;
        }
        return false;
    }

    /**
     * Assembles the strands into one big byte array.
     * @exception IOException if packet is not complete.
     */
    public byte[] getData()
        throws IOException
    {
        byte ret[];
```

```
        if ( complete() )
        {
            ret = new byte[ totalSize ];
            int bytesSoFar = 0;
            for ( int x = 0; x < totalBlocks; x++ )
            {
                byte data[] = (byte[])blocks.remove(new Integer(x));
                if ( data == null )
                    throw new IOException("Internal packet assembler error");
                if ( data.length + bytesSoFar > totalSize )
                    throw new IOException("Internal packet assembler error");

                System.arraycopy(data, 0, ret, bytesSoFar, data.length);
                bytesSoFar += data.length;
            }
        }
        else
        {
            throw new IOException("getData() of incomplete packet");
        }
        return ret;
    }
}
```

PartialPacket uses a hash table of its own to track each piece of a chain. The sub-block number is the key, and the data block is the value. A BitSet class is used to track each piece in relation to the whole. BitSets take up very little storage and operate like an array of booleans. When a sub-block comes in, its bit is set before it's added to the hash table. Once the last-in-chain sub-block appears, the object knows how many blocks are in the chain. The method `complete()` is called to test whether the chain has all its members. When all sub-blocks have been received, the chain is assembled by using method `getData()`.

Only the DGTPServer can initiate MDATA blocks. The client is still limited to sending data that can travel within a single DGTP packet.

The Election Server

The NumUsersServer class from Chapter 9 will be used as the basis for the ElectionServer class. If you recall, NumUsersServer sent text commands to applets that connected to it. There was a single command:

- `CLIENTS num_of_connections`

The ElectionServer adds two new commands:

- `RESULTS #rows #cols database_rows`
- `QUERY_RSP qnum #rows #cols database_rows`

In addition, the ElectionServer will now have to handle incoming data blocks. The election client uses the `QUERY` command:

- `QUERY qnum query_string`

Listing 10.11 shows the ElectionServer class.

Listing 10.11. The ElectionServer class.

```
import java.lang.Thread;
import java.net.DatagramPacket;
import java.util.*;
import DGTPServer;
import LiveDataServer;
import ClientAddr;

public class ElectionServer extends Thread
    implements LiveDataServer
{
    private static final int ONE_SECOND = 1000;
    private DGTPServer servThread = null;
    private Database election = null;
    private SQLStmt results = null;

    public ElectionServer(int hostPort)
    {
        servThread = new DGTPServer(this, hostPort);
        election = new Database("election.dbf");
        try
        {
            results = election.sql("select * from election");
        }
        catch (DBException de)
        {
            System.out.println("ERROR: " + de);
            System.out.println("Server exiting due to lack of data");
        }
    }

    /**
     * Run method for this thread.
     * Issue a new query every 30 seconds.
     */
    public void run()
    {
        boolean toggle = false;

        if ( results != null )
        {
            servThread.start();
            while(true)
            {
                sleep(30);
                try
                {
                    SQLStmt nn;
```

```
                if (toggle)
                {
                    nn = election.sql("select * from election");
                    toggle = false;
                }
                else
                {
                    nn = election.sql("select * from election " +
                                      "where State = 'Maryland'");
                    toggle = true;
                }
                synchronized (results)
                {
                    results = nn;
                }
                servThread.sendToUsers(
                    formatResults("RESULTS", results));
            }
            catch (DBException de)
            {
                System.out.println("Error: " + de);
            }
        }
    }
}

public boolean ValidateRegistrant(ClientAddr user)
{
    return true;
}

/**
 * A private routine to concatenate the number of rows & cols
 * to a response string and then add the SQLStmt data.
 * If the query was invalid, send a NULL response.
 *
 * @param sql contains the data to return
 * @param resultType contains the initial String
 */
private String formatResults(String resultType, SQLStmt sql)
{
    String ret = new String(resultType + " ");
    try
    {
        synchronized(sql)
        {
            ret += sql.numRows() + " " + sql.numCols() + " " + sql;
        }
    }
    catch (DBException de)
    {
        ret += "0 0";
    }
    return ret;
}

/**
```

continues

Listing 10.11. continued

```
     * A new connection was accepted, send the latest data
     * @param user contains the address to send to
     */
    public void NewRegistrant(ClientAddr user)
    {
         // broadcast the new user
         servThread.sendToUsers("CLIENTS " + servThread.Clients.size());

         // send the latest data to only the new user
         servThread.sendData(user, formatResults("RESULTS", results));
    }

    public void refreshRequest(ClientAddr user)
    {
        servThread.sendData(user, formatResults("RESULTS", results));
    }

    /**
     * A connection was dropped.
     * @param user contains the address that was dropped
     */
    public void DropRegistrant(ClientAddr user)
    {
        // broadcast the new number of users
        servThread.sendToUsers("CLIENTS " + servThread.Clients.size());
    }

    /**
     * Recv data block routine
     * @param newDataBlock contains the data
     * @param who is the original recv packet
     */
    public void recvNewData(byte[] newDataBlock,
        DatagramPacket who)
    {
        ClientAddr user = null;
        SQLStmt stmt = null;

        String query = new String(newDataBlock, 0);
        StringTokenizer cmds = new StringTokenizer(query, " \t");
        if (cmds.nextToken().equals("QUERY"))
        {
            String qnum = cmds.nextToken();
            String sql = cmds.nextToken("\r\n");
            System.out.println("Processing: " + sql);
            try
            {
                // Try the query
                stmt = election.sql(sql);
            }
            catch (DBException de)
            {
                System.out.println("Error: " + sql + "\n" + de);
            }
```

```
            user = new ClientAddr(who.getAddress(), who.getPort());

            // Send the response (will be NULL rsp if DBException)
            servThread.sendData(user,
                formatResults("QUERY_RSP " + qnum, stmt));
        }
    }

    /**
     * A simple sleep routine
     * @param a the number of SECONDS to sleep
     */
    private void sleep(int a)
    {
        try
        {
            Thread.currentThread().sleep(a * ONE_SECOND);
        }
        catch (InterruptedException e)
        {
        }
    }
}
```

The run method for this thread will query the database every 30 seconds. Since this is still a demonstration applet, a simple toggle was added to cause the data to change with each read.

The `formatResults()` method accepts a String and an SQLStmt class and creates a single return string consisting of the request type String, followed by the number of rows and columns in the data. This is followed by the data itself. This routine is the only method in the class that reads an SQLStmt object. Because the thread receives connection requests asynchronously, access to SQLStmt objects must be protected:

```
synchronized(sql)
{
    ret += sql.numRows() + " " + sql.numCols() + " " + sql;
}
```

When the thread queries the database, it will update the class variable: `results`. The update must also be synchronized to protect the update from corrupting a transmission.

```
synchronized (results)
{
    results = nn;
}
```

The entire method could have been protected, but good technique keeps protected ranges to the absolute minimum possible. Protecting entire methods will tie up the object for the time that the method executes. It isn't necessary to protect the database access, because the result is stored in temporary variable `nn`. The only critical piece of code is the assignment itself.

In Chapter 9, the `recvNewData()` method performed no actions, but now clients can send queries to the server for evaluation. The method first checks to make sure the request is a valid `QUERY` command. If it is, the query string is extracted from the data along with the query number. The query is sent to the database, and a response is formulated for the caller. If the query fails, a normal response is sent, with the number of rows and columns set to zero.

Election Client

The SimpleClientApplet class will serve as the basis for the Election class. The server needed to implement checking only for the `QUERY` command, but as the client, the applet will have to parse and display both normal `RESULTS` and specific `QUERY_RSP` packets. In addition, logic is added to display the additional database responses. The display showing the number of users is maintained, with the new database fields being displayed under the active connections string. Listing 10.12 shows the Election applet source code.

Listing 10.12. The Election applet class.

```
import java.applet.*;
import java.awt.*;
import java.net.*;
import java.io.*;
import java.util.*;
import DGTPClient;

public class Election extends Applet
    implements LiveDataNotify
{
    private static final int SPACING = 70;
    private boolean init = false;
    DGTPClient ct = null;
    int destPort;
    String destHost = null;
    String users = null;
    String results[][];
    int nRows = 0, nCols = 0;

    /**
     * Standard initialization method for an applet
     */
    public void init()
    {
        if ( init == false )
        {
            init = true;
            resize(500,500);
            String strPort = getParameter("PORT");
            if ( strPort == null )
            {
                System.out.println("ERROR: PORT parameter is missing");
                strPort = "4545";
            }
```

```
            destPort = Integer.valueOf(strPort).intValue();
            destHost = getDocumentBase().getHost();
        }
    }

    /**
     * Standard paint routine for an applet.
     * @param g contains the Graphics class to use for painting
     */
    public void paint(Graphics g)
    {
        g.drawString("Active connections: " + getUsers(), 0, 100);

        // Paint the headings
        g.drawString("Candidate",         SPACING * 0, 120);
        g.drawString("State",             SPACING * 1, 120);
        g.drawString("Votes",             SPACING * 2, 120);
        g.drawString("% Reporting",       SPACING * 3, 120);
        g.drawString("Electorial Votes", SPACING * 4, 120);

        // Display the contents of the database
        for ( int x = 0; x < nRows; x++ )
        {
            for ( int y = 0; y < nCols; y++ )
                g.drawString(results[x][y], SPACING * y, 140 + (20 * x));
        }
    }

    /**
     * Return the name of the server
     */
    public String getDestHost()
    {
        return destHost;
    }

    /**
     * Return the server port number
     */
    public int getDestPort()
    {
        return destPort;
    }

    /**
     * Recv a new block of data.  Parse it for display.
     * @param newDataBlock contains the data to parse
     */
    public synchronized void recvNewData(byte[] newDataBlock)
    {
         String cmd = new String(newDataBlock, 0);
         StringTokenizer cmds = new StringTokenizer(cmd, " \t");
         String current = cmds.nextToken();

         // Number of users update
         if (current.equals("CLIENTS"))
             users = cmds.nextToken();
```

continues

Listing 10.12. continued

```
        // Entire new database image
        else if (current.equals("RESULTS"))
        {
            nRows = Integer.valueOf(cmds.nextToken()).intValue();
            nCols = Integer.valueOf(cmds.nextToken()).intValue();
            results = new String[nRows][nCols];
            for ( int x = 0; x < nRows; x++ )
            {
                for ( int y = 0; y < nCols; y++ )
                {
                    results[x][y] = cmds.nextToken("¦\r\n");
                }
            }
        }

        // QUERY response is unimplemented because
        // this applet currently sends no QUERY commands
        else if (current.equals("QUERY_RSP"))
        {
        }

        // Cause the applet to receive a paint request
        repaint();
    }

    /**
     * Return either the users string if it has been
     * filled in or return the unknown string.
     */
    public synchronized String getUsers()
    {
        if (users != null)
            return users;
        return "Unknown at this time";
    }

    /**
     * Standard applet start method.  Launch the
     * DGTP client thread.
     */
    public void start()
    {
        ct = new DGTPClient(this);
        ct.start();
    }

    /**
     * Standard applet stop method.  Kill the
     * DGTPClient thread.
     */
    public void stop()
    {
        ct.terminate();
    }

    /**
```

```
     * Notification if a server connection was refused
     * by the host.  Needed to satisfy the interface, but
     * otherwise unimplemented.
     */
    public void connectRefused()
    {
    }
}
```

The paint routine uses a `SPACING` constant to position all the data, relying on the sample table having at most four rows. Chapter 11, "Building a Live Data Applet," will dress up the applet display and expand the table to a full 100 rows! The data is stored in a two-dimensional String array within the applet. The `recvNewData()` method parses the data block into this array. Because the data is formatted into columns separated by a pipe character, a simple StringTokenizer object can completely extract the individual columns. Notice that the parsing criteria is altered after the number of rows and columns is extracted. The method `nextToken()` can accept an argument, which, if present, will become the separating characters for successive tokens. In this case, the parser changed from looking for tokens separated by spaces to looking for tokens separated by pipe characters. The routine relies on the server placing at least a single space into an otherwise null column. If this isn't done, the StringTokenizer will completely skip the column and a later `nextToken()` call will fail.

Because the applet behaves in an essentially synchronous fashion, only the asynchronous method `recvNewData()` needs to be protected. This ensures that the applet will not paint while its data is being refreshed. Figure 10.2 shows the display of the Election applet.

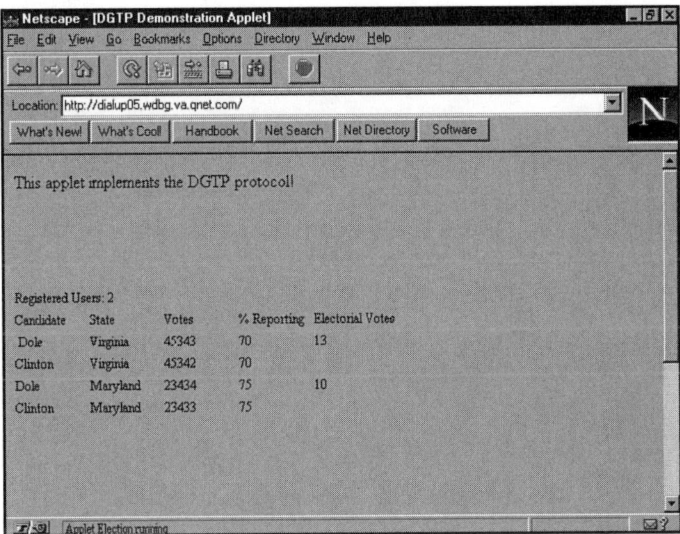

FIGURE 10.2.
Output of the Election applet.

Summary

This chapter covers a lot of ground—you learn how to create native methods in C and how to create and manipulate Java internal objects. You should now be familiar with method signatures, as well as the majority of standard Java helper functions. Both Java calling C and C calling into Java have been covered, and using a static initializer has been introduced for loading native libraries.

In addition to native methods, the data communications concept of chaining has been introduced. The DGTP protocol is now relatively mature and can form the basis for a wide array of client/server applications.

Chapter 11 will complete this section on managing live data, which has developed the internals of a sophisticated client/server applet, and address the one area not yet covered, the applet's user interface.

11

Building a Live Data Applet

This chapter concludes Part IV with an application that brings together most of the JDK features you have seen throughout this book. The application is an Election Night applet that shows election returns as they arrive. It can do this because the applet gets datagrams from a back-end Web server that broadcasts returns as they are entered into a server database. This client-server application is Internet-ready! You can run the server on the host and have multiple clients connect to your site to see the live returns.

This application brings in many of the JDK's major components, such as AWT, threads and synchronization, streams, exception handling, native methods, and sockets. Because of the project's size, many less critical but useful components are also applied—such as the Hashtable class, static methods, and string parsing. Some new concepts are also introduced; for example, the model-view paradigm is covered briefly before you get into the heart of the chapter project.

Observers and the Model-View Paradigm

One problem that programmers often face is showing different views of data that may change over time. A classic example of this is a spreadsheet with multiple graphs (this sounds familiar!). If the spreadsheet were tied to a relational database, traditional programmers would represent the graph by making SQL calls to the same set of tables the spreadsheet uses. However, if the spreadsheet changes (and, therefore, its underlying table structure), the graph programs would need to be modified, also. In other words, the spreadsheet structure is closely tied to both the spreadsheet program and the graphs that use its data.

The problem can get even worse if the graphs must update themselves as the spreadsheet data changes. How do the graphs monitor the data? Should the graphs keep querying the data to see whether it has changed? This would be inefficient from a performance standpoint since such data will probably not change much from second to second, although it can change dramatically over longer periods of time. Furthermore, with multiple graphs and a spreadsheet constantly accessing the data, the database host's performance will be strained.

The *model-view paradigm* offers a solution to these problems with two fundamental tenets: Separate the underlying data model from the programs that view (use) this data, and let the underlying data model inform the views that something has changed, which prevents the view from having to constantly query the data. To illustrate the first tenet being applied, take a look again at the spreadsheet applet developed in Part II. The data was maintained in the CellContainer class, whose only function was the proper upkeep of the spreadsheet data. The CellContainer class provided a "model" for the spreadsheet data. There were three "views" on the data—the two graphs and the spreadsheet itself. The latter was represented by the SpreadsheetContainer class, which simply uses the CellContainer model. For example, the SpreadsheetContainer didn't have any responsibility for verifying a formula or evaluating its results—that was the job of the model. In a sense, the SpreadsheetContainer was little more than a "dumb" view of the model.

The second tenet of the model-view paradigm is how to let a view know when a model has changed. For this situation, the Observable class and Observer interface in the java.util package offer an effective solution. The Observable class represents the model. To create an Observable model, you need to build a subclass of Observable. Observer objects can then attach to your model; when the model changes, you notify the observers.

In the applet portion of the chapter project, a class called ElectionTable maintains a local cache of election results on a state-by-state and grand-total basis; it is a direct subclass of Observable. When its data is modified, it notifies the Observer objects of the changes:

```
setChanged();
notifyObservers();
```

The first method, `setChanged()`, tells the Observable class that the model has been modified. When a notify method is next called (immediately afterward, in this case), the Observable class checks to see whether the data has changed and, if so, broadcasts a notification to the observers. Table 11.1 lists a summary of the Observable class's methods.

Table 11.1. The Observable class's methods.

Method	*Description*
`addObserver`	Add an Observer object to the list of observers.
`deleteObserver`	Remove an Observer from the observer list.
`deleteObservers`	Clear the observer list.
`notifyObservers`	Notify all the Observers that the data has changed. One version of this method has an optional parameter to send data about what was modified.
`setChanged`	Signals internally that a change has occurred.
`hasChanged`	Returns whether the data has changed.
`countObservers`	Returns a count of all the Observers.

The Observer interface has only one method, `update()`. It takes as its parameters the Observable object and an object that can be used to convey more information about what has changed. The Observer object hooks to the Observable object through the `addObserver()` method. In this chapter's project, the two observers simply repaint when they get an `update()` message.

Chapter Project

This chapter project demonstrates an applet and corresponding Java server used to show you election night returns as they come in. When you select the Election home page, the applet connects to the server and is added to a list of registrants to be notified whenever election data changes. The server uses its local database to check for any incoming election returns. When they occur, the server broadcasts the results to the client applets. The applets, in turn, update themselves to show the latest totals.

To add a little fun to the project, the system was designed for the likely 1996 presidential election between the incumbent and his challenger. (Note that it wouldn't be hard to change the project if a third-party candidate throws a monkey wrench into this mix, since the project is mostly driven by the database. However, a few assumptions about there being two candidates were made.) Figure 11.1 shows the Election applet before the returns start rolling in, Figure 11.2 illustrates what the applet might look like later in the evening, and Figure 11.3 shows the applet as the election reaches its possible conclusion. This last figure demonstrates the applet with its graphical view turned on.

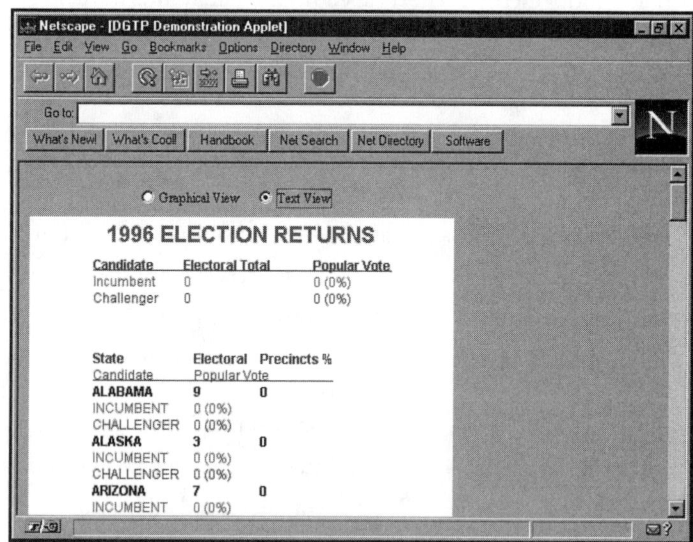

FIGURE 11.1.
The Election applet before the election returns start rolling in.

You are given a database consisting of filled-in states and corresponding electoral votes. However, the totals are left blank. If you want, you can rig the election in favor of the candidate of your choice!

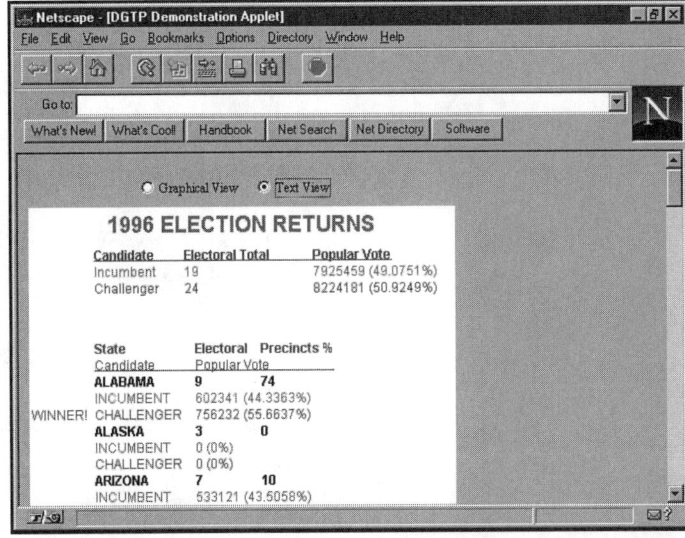

FIGURE 11.2.
The Election applet as the evening progresses. It's a close one!

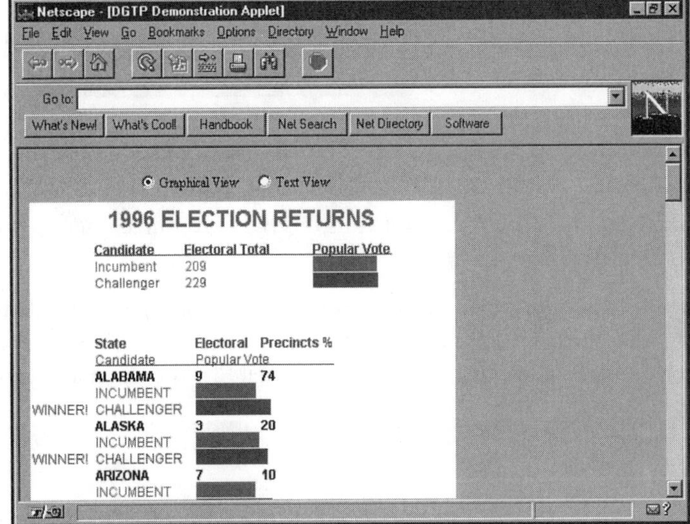

FIGURE 11.3.
The applet as the election reaches its climax—who is going to win?

General Architecture of the Project

The general architecture of this project is based on the project architecture from Chapter 10, "Native Methods and Java." For the sake of clarity, a visual overview of the architecture is repeated in Figure 11.4. Refer to Chapter 10 for a description of the general architecture and detailed server and database implementation, but a couple of additional points about the structure of the project are covered here. Furthermore, a full description of the client applet will follow in the section "Applet Client."

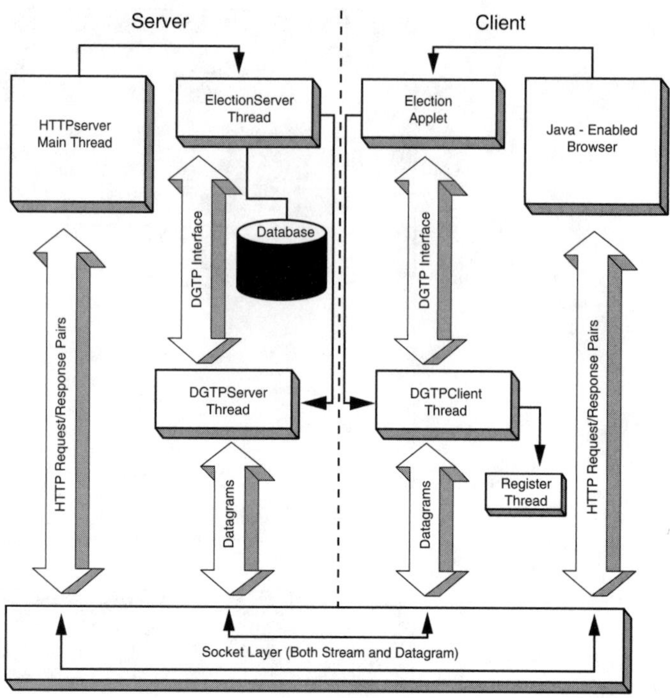

FIGURE 11.4.
The project architecture.

The hierarchy of the server environment is as follows: The server classes should be placed in the parent directory (which could be in a variety of places); the database (ELECT.DBF) can also be in this directory, but if your ODBC data source is set up properly, the database can be located elsewhere.

Underneath the parent is a directory called *htdocs*. The only file it must have is index.html, which is the HTML for the applet at hand. Located underneath htdocs is a *classes* subdirectory. This will contain classes and any additional files the client applet will need.

To start the server, go to the parent directory and type:

```
java BasicWebServer
```

An additional `debug 1` parameter will display debug information about the server.

Changes to the Server

As in the previous chapter, the ElectionServer class is used to send data to multiple client applets. It does this at the behest of the BasicWebServer class because it implements the LiveDataServer interface. The main part of this Thread class is its `run()` method, which constantly looks for new data and broadcasts its results to the client applets. This code was slightly modified from Chapter 10 for a fuller implementation of the election night project. Only the `run()` method was modified, as illustrated in Listing 11.1.

Listing 11.1. Changes to the run() method of the ElectionServer Class.

```
/**
     * Run method for this thread.
     * Recheck the database every 30 seconds
     * and send changed data
     * Resend all data every couple minutes.
     */
    public void run()
    {
     int timestamp = 0;
     int iterationsBeforeFull = 60;  // Fifteen minutes
     int iteration = 0;
        if ( results != null )
        {
            servThread.start();
            while(true)
            {
               sleep(30);
                try
                {
                    SQLStmt nn;
                    // After so many iterations, resend all data...
                    if (iteration >= iterationsBeforeFull) {
                       nn = election.sql("select * from election order by
➥state,candidate");
                       synchronized (results)
                       {
                           results = nn;
                       }
                       servThread.sendToUsers(
                           formatResults("RESULTS", results));
                       iteration = 0;
                    } // end full if
                    else {
                     // Otherwise just check timestamps...
                     String partialSQL =
                      "select * from election where updated > '" +
                        timestampToChar(timestamp) +
                        "' order by state,candidate";
                     nn = election.sql(partialSQL);
                     // Make sure a valid number of rows is returned...
                     if ((nn.numRows() > 0) && ((nn.numRows()%2) == 0) ) {
                        // Send data and update timestamp...
                        servThread.sendToUsers(
                           formatResults("RESULTS", nn));
                        ++timestamp;
                     }
                     ++iteration;
                    }
                }
                catch (DBException de)
                {
                    System.out.println("Error: " + de);
                }
            }
        }
    }
```

NOTE

Note that the database used here does not have a "triggering" capability as many relational databases do. With triggers, the database would update the server, much like the model-view paradigm discussed earlier. This is much better than having the server query the database all the time.

There were mainly two changes to the method. The first was the introduction of partial updates. After broadcasting all the election data (in the `NewRegistrant()` method, which is not listed here), the server loops and waits for partial updates. The server uses the timestamp mechanism discussed in the next section, "Database," to see whether data has changed. Every 30 seconds, the server queries the database to see whether any data has been added with a timestamp older than the current timestamp. If not, the server sleeps again and then retries. If new data is found, the changes are broadcast to the client applets. The timestamp is then incremented and the process repeats itself.

The other change in the server's `run()` method is indicated by the *iteration* variable. Every 15 minutes, the server rebroadcasts *all* of the data to the clients. This might seem unnecessary, but remember that the datagram protocol used to transmit data is unreliable, and packets could be lost. Given this, it's possible that the clients might not have received some earlier updates. However, you could increase the rebroadcast time to a higher value, such as 30 minutes, an hour, or more. The right figure for this will depend on a variety of factors, including the size and sensitivity of your data.

Database

The database used in this chapter is generally the same dBASE IV table described in the previous chapter. An UPDATED field was added so that changes can be timestamped, thus allowing the server to download only the state information that has changed.

A couple of other things should be mentioned about the database. First of all, a blank version of the database can be found in the file NEWELECT.DBF located on the CD-ROM. It has all the states, candidates, and electoral votes. Data that changes over time, such as the popular vote, is initialized to zero. Since the runtime server uses ELECT.DBF, you can simply replace NEWELECT.DBF to generate a clean database after the ELECT.DBF data is modified for testing.

Another peculiarity of the table is that the ELECTORAL field initially has negative numbers. The absolute value of the negative numbers symbolizes the number of electoral votes a state carries. If the number is positive, it indicates that the corresponding candidate has won the state. A normalized database would have been a better solution here (separate tables for state information and declared winners), but it didn't seem appropriate to focus on this aspect of the project.

Yet another curiosity is the UPDATED field. Since the native method's ODBC driver implements only character data types, all the fields in the database need to be of a character type. Unfortunately, this makes timestamping a little tricky, so timestamps in this project have the following format: `000XXX`. That is, all timestamps need to be prefixed by zeroes to produce a timestamp six characters long. So the first stamp would be 000001, the hundredth would be 000100, and so on. If your server updates aren't working properly, be careful how you enter the timestamps in the database.

After sending data down the first time, the server retrieves partial updates based on a timestamp. Although internally it is a number, it's in the format just described in the database. Any database rows with a timestamp higher than the last timestamp are made part of any new partial update broadcasts. Once the database timestamp is surpassed by the external timestamp, the corresponding row is no longer sent down as part of a partial update. The server will always print out the current timestamp it is working on. Suppose it is 000003, and you want to update the data. You can do this by changing *both* entries of the candidates in a state and setting the timestamp to 000004. The data will then be sent down in the next partial update broadcast and should show up in your applet.

Applet Client

The Election applet continually gives you updated election results as they arrive to the server. The applet consists of basically two parts: back-end threads to manage the arrival of datagrams with the latest election results from the server and a front-end that displays the results in either a graphical or text-based format. The network-processing classes were mostly developed in the previous two chapters; the display classes are new for this chapter.

Class Organization

Table 11.2 lists the classes used in this chapter's Election applet. Since many of these classes were created in the previous section, the new classes are specified by having their names in boldface type; the classes that were modified have their names italicized.

Table 11.2. The Election applet classes and interfaces.

Class/Interface	*Description*
Candidate	An accessor class that keeps vote totals for a specific candidate.
ClientPacketAssembler	Tracks and assembles blocks of data packets.
ClientRegistration	For registering as a new client.
ClientUnregistration	For removing client registration with server.
DGTPClient	To receive dynamic data updates from server.

continues

Table 11.2. continued

Class/Interface	*Description*
Election	The class for the Election applet that implements the LiveDataNotify interface to manage dynamic data from the server and creates components for visual display.
ElectionTable	Keeps local copy of election results from the server. Uses synchronization so that incoming DGTP data does not collide with reads from visual components.
ElectionUpdater	Periodically causes update of Election's visual components.
LiveDataNotify	Interface that defines methods for handling dynamic delivery of data from the server.
PartialPacket	Private class used by ClientPacketAssembler for assembling packets.
StateBreakdownCanvas	ElectionTable observer that displays results of individual states in text or graphics format.
StateEntry	Simple accessor class that keeps all election data related to a specific state.
SummaryCanvas	ElectionTable observer that displays national election totals.

How It Works

Figure 11.5 illustrates the workflow of the Election applet. The DGTPClient object receives datagrams from the server indicating the latest election results. This data may be a partial update of just the states that have changed, or it may be a broadcast of the full election results. In either case, the Election object receives the new data since it implements the LiveDataNotify interface.

The Election object parses the data and passes it to the ElectionTable object. The ElectionTable class has only one instance since it has a private constructor; objects that use the data must get a reference to the table object from a public ElectionTable method. The Election object is the only object that updates the table and does so when it's notified by the DGTPClient with new data. When you get the first full batch of election data, with all the states identified, the ElectionTable object creates a private table of the individual state and summary totals. This table is updated by any calls that follow.

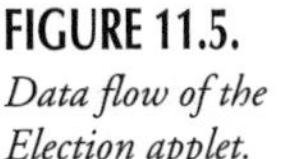

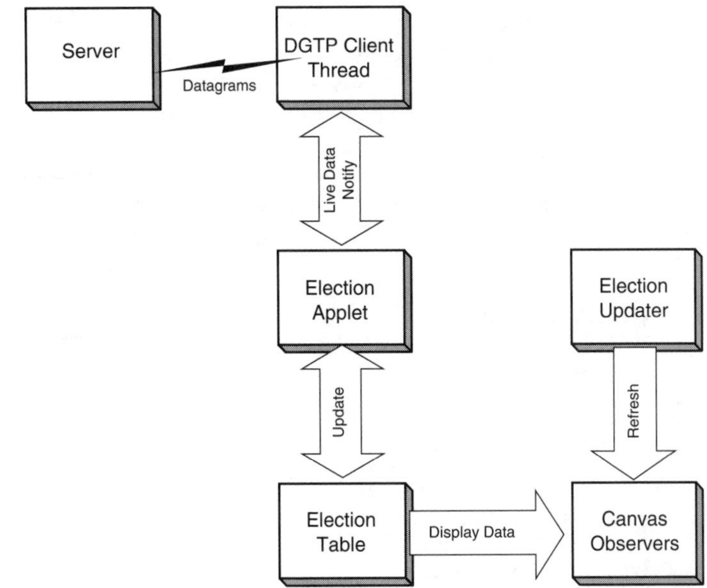

FIGURE 11.5.
Data flow of the Election applet.

ElectionTable is an instance of the Observable class. It notifies its two Observers, the StateBreakdownCanvas and SummaryCanvas, whenever its data change. These two Canvas objects implement the Observer interface and are mainly responsible for displaying the election information. The ElectionUpdater thread runs in the background, periodically forcing refreshes of the Canvas objects.

Since the underlying classes that implement the network interfaces haven't changed since the previous chapter, the discussion that follows will focus on the classes involved in the visual interface.

The Election Class

The Election class runs the Election applet. It implements the LiveDataNotify interface so that it can be notified whenever the DGTPClient gets new election data packets. The Election class also creates the two components that display the election results—the StateBreakdownCanvas and SummaryCanvas classes. Listing 11.2 shows the Election class's code.

Several important things happen at initialization. In the `init()` method, the first step is to get an applet parameter that specifies the port the server is listening on, then initializes the display. It creates a panel at the top of the screen so that you can toggle between a text-based or graphical display. The Election class then creates the components that display the election results and starts a simple thread, ElectionThread, that periodically causes the applet to repaint. This is needed because paint messages could be lost if election returns come in rapid-fire fashion. The last step in the `init()` method is to resize the applet so that it's large enough to show all of the state returns.

The other major thing that happens at initialization occurs when the `start()` method is first called. The Election class creates an instance of the DGTPClient class, specifying itself as the LiveDataNotify parameter—this ensures that the Election applet is notified of all incoming datagrams.

The DGTPClient calls the Election class's `recvNewData()` method when data has arrived. The Election class then parses this data into a large two-dimensional String array, which is then passed to the ElectionTable class that provides the data's final storage location.

Listing 11.2. The Election class.

```
// This class starts the Election applet. It implements
// the LiveDataNotify interface that sends the latest
// results to it.  It creates objects to display the
// returns as they arrive.
public class Election extends Applet
    implements LiveDataNotify
{
    private static final int SPACING = 70;
    private boolean init = false;
    DGTPClient ct = null;
    int destPort;
    String destHost = null;
    String numUsers = "Unknown at this time";
    String users = null;
    String results[][];
    int nRows = 0, nCols = 0;
    // Place canvas drawing objects...
    SummaryCanvas sc;
    StateBreakdownCanvas states;
    Checkbox graphView,textView;
    Panel p;

    public void init()
    {
        if ( init == false )
        {
            // Initialize network connections...
            init = true;
            String strPort = getParameter("PORT");
            if ( strPort == null )
            {
                System.out.println("ERROR: PORT parameter is missing");
                strPort = "4545";
            }
            destPort = Integer.valueOf(strPort).intValue();
            destHost = getDocumentBase().getHost();
            // Initialize AWT components...
          // Do basic setup...
          setLayout(new BorderLayout());
          // Add panel to set views...
          p = new Panel();
          CheckboxGroup cg = new CheckboxGroup();
          graphView = new Checkbox("Graphical View",cg,false);
          textView = new Checkbox("Text View",cg,true);
```

```
        p.add(graphView);
        p.add(textView);
        add("North",p);

        // Add summary information at top of applet
        sc = new SummaryCanvas(this);
        // Show state breakdowns...
        states = new StateBreakdownCanvas(this);
        // Create update thread...
        Thread t = new ElectionUpdater(this);
        t.start();
        // Resize to fit all the states...
        Dimension d = size();
        FontMetrics fm = Toolkit.getDefaultToolkit().getFontMetrics(getFont());
        int height = sc.getHeight() + states.getHeight()
          + (2 * fm.getHeight());
        resize(d.width,height);
        show();
      }
  }

// Update message sent when repainting is needed...
// Prevent paint from getting cleared out...
public void update(Graphics g) {
   paint(g);
}


// If table is ready, paint all the canvases...
public synchronized void paint(Graphics g) {
    if (!(ElectionTable.getElectionTable().ready()) )
      return;
    Dimension d = size();
    int height = g.getFontMetrics(getFont()).getHeight();
    int y = 2 * height;
    y = sc.paint(g,0,y,d.width);
    y += states.paint(g,0,y,d.width,d.height - y);
    g.drawString("Registered Users: " + getUsers(),
         10,d.height - height);
}

// Toggle radio buttons...
public boolean action(Event ev,Object o) {
   if (ev.target instanceof Checkbox) {
      if (ev.target.equals(graphView)) {
            states.setMode(StateBreakdownCanvas.GRAPHICS);
            sc.setMode(SummaryCanvas.GRAPHICS);
      }
      else {
            states.setMode(StateBreakdownCanvas.TEXT);
            sc.setMode(SummaryCanvas.TEXT);
      }
      repaint();
   }
   return true;
}
```

continues

Listing 11.2. continued

```
    public String getDestHost()
    {
        return destHost;
    }

    public int getDestPort()
    {
        return destPort;
    }

    public synchronized void recvNewData(byte[] newDataBlock, boolean error)
    {
         if ( error )
         {
             ct.send("REFRESH");
             return;
         }
         String cmd = new String(newDataBlock, 0);
         StringTokenizer cmds = new StringTokenizer(cmd, " \t");
         String current = cmds.nextToken();
         if (current.equals("CLIENTS"))
             users = cmds.nextToken();
         else if (current.equals("RESULTS"))
         {
             nRows = Integer.valueOf(cmds.nextToken()).intValue();
             nCols = Integer.valueOf(cmds.nextToken()).intValue();
             results = new String[nRows][nCols];
             for ( int x = 0; x < nRows; x++ )
             {
                 for ( int y = 0; y < nCols; y++ )
                 {
                     results[x][y] = cmds.nextToken("¦\r\n");
                 }
             }
             // Update the election table with the new data...
             ElectionTable.getElectionTable().tableUpdate(nRows,results);
         }
         // QUERY response is unimplemented because
         // this applet currently sends no QUERY commands
         else if (current.equals("QUERY_RSP"))
         {
         }
    }

    public synchronized String getUsers()
    {
        if (users != null)
            return users;
        return numUsers;
    }

    public void start()
    {
        ct = new DGTPClient(this);
        ct.start();
```

```
    }

    public void stop()
    {
        System.out.println("Election.stop()");
        ct.terminate();
    }

    public void connectRefused()
    {
    }
}
```

The ElectionTable Class

The ElectionTable class, shown in Listing 11.3, creates a private table of the individual state and summary totals. Since ElectionTable is responsible for keeping the local cache of the election data, it isn't allowed to be instantiated by an external class. The table has only one instance because it has a private constructor; objects that use the data must get a reference to the table object from a public ElectionTable method called `getElectionTable()`.

An internal array, called `states`, maintains each state's election information. It is composed of StateEntry objects that contain electoral information about the state, as well as the state totals of the two candidates. The `states` array is not created in the constructor; rather, it's created when data is first received in the `tableUpdate()` method, the only entry point into the table for updating data. When the `states` array is null, it is set up in the `initializeTable()` method. All subsequent updates (called through the `partialUpdate()` method) are applied to the `states` array created at initialization. These write methods are synchronized to prevent any collisions by other threads reading data.

After each update, ElectionTable compiles the state totals to get the summary figures by using the `updateTotals()` method. Since ElectionTable is an instance of the Observable class, it notifies its observers of the changes at the end of the `tableUpdate()` method.

The observers use the `getStates()` method to walk through the results of the individual states. This method has an interesting solution to the synchronization problem, such as when an update occurs while an observer is reading the state information. The `getStates()` method makes a shallow copy of the `states` array; it's "shallow" because it copies only the array references and not the actual state elements. If an update thread modifies the original States table, it doesn't affect the copy the reader has because the update makes new StateEntry objects for each update. Therefore, the reader won't be adversely affected by any updates.

Listing 11.3. The ElectionTable class.

```
import java.lang.*;
import java.util.Observable;

// This class keeps a local cache of the election results
// The table can only be created once so constructor is private...
// A producer thread keeps the table updated
public class ElectionTable extends Observable {
 // The table is static and so can be created only once
  private static ElectionTable table = new ElectionTable();

  // Data objects...
  Candidate Incumbent;
  Candidate Challenger;
  int totalPopular;
  static StateEntry states[];

  // Create the table information...
  private ElectionTable() {
      // Set up the candidates...
      Incumbent = new Candidate("Incumbent");
      Challenger = new Candidate("Challenger");
      // Not ready yet...
      states = null;
  }

  // Get reference to election table...
  public static synchronized ElectionTable getElectionTable() {
      return table;
  }

  // See if table is ready...
  public static synchronized boolean ready() {
      return ((states != null) ? (true) : (false));
  }

  // Update the states table with new values...
  public void tableUpdate(int rows,String results[][]) {
      if (states == null)
            initializeTable(rows,results);
      else
            partialUpdate(rows,results);
      // Update totals...
      updateTotals();
      // Notify observers of changes...
      setChanged();
      notifyObservers();
  }

  // Initialize the table with the first batch of data...
  // Code ASSUMES that the results are ordered by
  // state and then candidate
  private static synchronized void initializeTable(int rows,String results[][]) {
      int i,j;
      StateEntry newState;
      // Create the state array...
      states = new StateEntry[rows/2];
```

```
      // Go through each row
      for (i = j = 0; i < rows; i+=2,++j) {
         newState = createStateEntry(i,results);
         // Now add to state array...
         states[j] = newState;
      } // end for
   }

   // Update just parts of the table...
   private void partialUpdate(int rows,String results[][]) {
      int i,j;
      StateEntry newState;
      // Kick out if rows is not a multiple of 2
      if ((rows % 2) != 0) {
         System.out.println("Data not formatted right. Rejected.");
         return;
      }
      // Go through each row
      for (i = j = 0; i < rows; i+=2,++j) {
         // Create new state table...
         newState = createStateEntry(i,results);
         // Now update state array...
         stateUpdate(newState);
      } // end for
   }

   // Take index into results table and get a StateEntry
   // object from it...
 private static StateEntry createStateEntry(int index,String results[][]) {
      Candidate newChallenger;
      Candidate newIncumbent;
      String stateName;
      double precincts = 0.0;
      int electoral = 0;
      int candElectoral = 0;
      int IncumbentVotes = 0;
      int ChallengerVotes = 0;
      int i = index;
      String s;
         // First row is Challenger. Get his and state info...
         s = results[i][1];
         stateName = s.trim();
         // Get precinct, electoral,votes...
         try {
            s = results[i][2];
            ChallengerVotes = Integer.valueOf(
               s.trim()).intValue();
            s = results[i][3];
            precincts = Double.valueOf(s.trim()).doubleValue();
            s = results[i][4];
            electoral = Math.abs(Integer.valueOf(s.trim()).intValue());
            candElectoral = Integer.valueOf(s.trim()).intValue();
            if (candElectoral < 0)
                     candElectoral = 0;
         }
         catch (NumberFormatException e) {
            System.out.println("Format error: " + e.getMessage());
```

continues

Listing 11.3. continued

```
        }
        s = results[i][0];
        newChallenger = new Candidate(s.trim(),
              candElectoral, ChallengerVotes);
        // Now get Incumbent info...
        ++i;
        try {
           s = results[i][2];
           IncumbentVotes = Integer.valueOf(s.trim()).intValue();
           s = results[i][4];
           candElectoral = Integer.valueOf(s.trim()).intValue();
           if (candElectoral < 0)
                    candElectoral = 0;
        }
        catch (NumberFormatException e) {
           System.out.println("Format error: " + e.getMessage());
        }
        s = results[i][0];
        newIncumbent = new Candidate(s.trim(),
              candElectoral,IncumbentVotes);
        // Return state entry field...
        return new StateEntry(stateName,precincts,
           electoral,(IncumbentVotes + ChallengerVotes),
           newIncumbent, newChallenger);
}

// Get table of state listings.  This is a copy of the
// state entry TABLE, but not the individual listings.  This
// solves synchronization problems.  The user of the table
// will get the references to the states but does not actually
// have references to the actual keys used by the ElectionTable
// class.
public synchronized StateEntry[] getStates() {
    if (states == null)
          return states;
    StateEntry tempStates[] = new StateEntry[states.length];
    for (int i = 0; i < states.length; ++i)
             tempStates[i] = states[i];
    return tempStates;
}

// Get candidate total information...
public synchronized Candidate getIncumbent() {
 return Incumbent;
}
public synchronized Candidate getChallenger() {
 return Challenger;
}

// Update the totals for each Candidate...
public synchronized void updateTotals() {
    int ChallengerPopular = 0;
    int ChallengerElectoral = 0;
    int IncumbentPopular = 0;
    int IncumbentElectoral = 0;
    totalPopular = 0;
```

```
      // Calculate the totals...
      for (int i = 0; i < states.length; ++i) {
         ChallengerPopular += states[i].getChallenger().getPopular();
         ChallengerElectoral += states[i].getChallenger().getElectoral();
         IncumbentPopular += states[i].getIncumbent().getPopular();
         IncumbentElectoral += states[i].getIncumbent().getElectoral();
         totalPopular += states[i].getTotalVotes();
      } // end for
      // Update the Candidates...
      Incumbent = new Candidate("Incumbent",IncumbentElectoral,IncumbentPopular);
      Challenger = new Candidate("Challenger",ChallengerElectoral,
➥ChallengerPopular);
   }

   // Take a state field and find spot in state
   // table to update...
   public synchronized void stateUpdate(StateEntry newState) {
      String name = newState.getName();
      for (int i = 0; i < states.length; ++i) {
         // Replace state that matches current entry...
         if (name.equals(states[i].getName())) {
               states[i] = newState;
               return;
         }
      } // end for
System.out.println("STATE UPDATE ERROR!");
   }

   // Get total popular vote...
   public synchronized int getTotalPopular() {
    return totalPopular;
   }

   // Get info for a specific state...
   private synchronized StateEntry getState(String name) {
      for (int i = 0; i < states.length; ++i) {
         // Replace state that matches current entry...
         if (name.equals(states[i].getName())) {
               return states[i];
         }
      } // end for
System.out.println("STATE GET ERROR!");
      return null;
   }
}
```

The Candidate Class

Listing 11.4 displays the Candidate class, which contains the name and vote totals of a specific candidate. Although it's a simple accessor class, it effectively functions as a row in a virtual table of candidates.

Listing 11.4. The Candidate class.

```
// This is a simple accessor class to keep information
// about candidates...
public class Candidate {
   String Name;  // Name of candidate
   int totalElectoral;  // Electoral votes so far...
   int votePopular;  // Popular vote...
   // Create object with states long name and abbreviation
   public Candidate(String Name) {
      this.Name = Name;
      totalElectoral = 0;
      votePopular = 0;
   }
   // Candidate with new totals...
   public Candidate(String Name,
    int totalElectoral,int votePopular) {
      this.Name = Name;
      this.totalElectoral = totalElectoral;
      this.votePopular = votePopular;
   }
   // Access the variables...
   public String getName() {
      return Name;
   }
   public int getElectoral() {
      return totalElectoral;
   }
   public int getPopular() {
      return votePopular;
   }
}
```

The StateEntry Class

Listing 11.5 displays the StateEntry class, which contains general electoral votes of the state, the percent of precincts counted so far, and the total number of votes cast. It also holds Candidate objects for the two candidates. The StateEntry class, coupled with the Candidate class, provides for normalized data, something that was missing in the back-end database.

Listing 11.5. The StateEntry class.

```
// This is a simple accessor class to keep information
// about candidates and corresponding state totals...
public class StateEntry {
   String Name;  // Name of state
   int electoral; // Number of electoral votes
   int totalVotes; // Total number of votes in state
   double precincts; // % of precincts counted
   Candidate Incumbent;  // The two candidates
   Candidate Challenger;
   // Create object with states long name and abbreviation
   public StateEntry(String Name) {
```

```
        this.Name = Name;
        precincts = 0;
        electoral = 0;
        totalVotes = 0;
        Incumbent = new Candidate("Incumbent");
        Challenger = new Candidate("Challenger");
     }
     // Candidates with new totals...
     public StateEntry(String Name,double precincts,
      int electoral,int totalVotes,
      Candidate Incumbent, Candidate Challenger) {
        this.Name = Name;
        this.totalVotes = totalVotes;
        this.precincts = precincts;
        this.electoral = electoral;
        this.Incumbent = Incumbent;
        this.Challenger = Challenger;
     }
     // Access the variables...
     public String getName() {
        return Name;
     }
     public int getElectoral() {
        return electoral;
     }
     public int getTotalVotes() {
        return totalVotes;
     }
     public double getPrecincts() {
        return precincts;
     }

     // Get candidate-state information...
     public Candidate getIncumbent() {
      return Incumbent;
     }
     public Candidate getChallenger() {
      return Challenger;
     }
}
```

The StateBreakdownCanvas Class

The StateBreakdownCanvas class displays the election results on a state-by-state basis, as shown in Listing 11.6. The class can show the data graphically or in a primarily text-based format, indicated by its mode. If the canvas is in graphical mode, it shows the popular vote as a bar graph representing the percentages of each candidate in the state.

When the StateBreakdownCanvas is initialized, it sets up a variety of variables used when painting the canvas. Its last step is to declare itself an observer of the ElectionTable by calling its `addObserver()` method. When the table changes, the canvas's `update()` method is called, which results in the canvas being repainted to yield the new results.

The paint() method uses many of the techniques discussed elsewhere in this book. The most interesting thing about it, however, is that the canvas occurs over a large area, bigger than most screens. However, most browsers—such as Netscape Navigator—support large applets. If you scroll down the applet, you will see the other state totals. Figure 11.6 shows what the StateBreakdownCanvas looks like when the Election applet, while set in graphical mode, is scrolled down toward the middle of the state listings.

Listing 11.6. The StateBreakdownCanvas class.

```
import java.awt.*;
import java.lang.*;
import java.applet.Applet;
import java.util.Observable;
import java.util.Observer;

// This canvas shows the breakdown of each state
// by candidate. An Observer of the election table
// is added and is called when election
// data has changed which forces update
public class StateBreakdownCanvas extends Canvas implements Observer {
   Applet a; // The applet
   Font fonts[];  // Font to display...
   int fontHeight; // Quick reference of font height...
   int totalWidth;  // Width coordinates...
   int colStart[];
   Rectangle lastPaint; // Keep track of last paint...
   // Various display strings...
   String titleBanner = "1996 ELECTION RETURNS";
   String winner = "WINNER!";
   String headers[] = { "State", "Electoral",
      "Precincts %",
      "Candidate", "Popular Vote" };
   // Graphics or text mode.
   public static final int TEXT = 0;
   public static final int GRAPHICS = 1;
   int mode = TEXT;

   // Calculate some dimension information...
   public StateBreakdownCanvas(Applet app) {
      // Create display fonts...
      fonts = new Font[2];
      fonts[0] = new Font("Helvetica",Font.BOLD,12);
      fonts[1] = new Font("Helvetica",Font.PLAIN,12);
      // Get font height info...
      FontMetrics fm;
      fm = Toolkit.getDefaultToolkit().getFontMetrics(fonts[0]);
      fontHeight = fm.getHeight();
      // Initialize column width displays...
      colStart = new int[5];
      colStart[0] = fm.stringWidth("  " + winner + "!! ");
      colStart[1] = colStart[0] +
         (int)(1.25 *(double)fm.stringWidth("New Jersey!!!"));
      colStart[2] = colStart[1] +
         (int)(1.25 *(double)fm.stringWidth(headers[1]));
      colStart[3] = colStart[0];
```

```
      colStart[4] = colStart[1];
      totalWidth = colStart[2] + fm.stringWidth(headers[2]);
      // Make Canvas an observer of the ElectionTable...
      a = app;
      ElectionTable.getElectionTable().addObserver(this);
   }

   // Get target height...
   public int getHeight() {
      return 3 * 53 * fontHeight;
   }

   // Set the mode to paint in...
   public void setMode(int mode) {
      this.mode = mode;
   }

   // Called when Table changes....
   public void update(Observable o, Object arg) {
    if (lastPaint != null)
       a.repaint(lastPaint.x,lastPaint.y,
         lastPaint.width,lastPaint.height);
   }

   // Paint the summary totals...
   public int paint(Graphics g,int xOrg,int yOrg,
    int width, int totalHeight) {
      // Set the background color to white...
      int y = yOrg + fontHeight;
      g.setColor(Color.white);
      g.fillRect(xOrg,yOrg,width,totalHeight);
      lastPaint = new Rectangle(xOrg,yOrg,width,totalHeight);

      // Paint the header...
      g.setFont(fonts[0]);
      g.setColor(Color.blue);
      for (int i = 0; i < 5; ++i) {
         g.drawString(headers[i],colStart[i],y);
         if (i == 2) {
            g.setFont(fonts[1]);
            y += fontHeight;
         }
      }

      // Draw line across bottom...
      g.drawLine(colStart[0],y,totalWidth,y);
      y += fontHeight;

      // Now get the listing of states...
      int length;
      double graphicsWidth = (double)(totalWidth - colStart[1]);
      double percent;
      String s;
      StateEntry[] stateData =ElectionTable.getElectionTable().getStates();
      // Walk through each state...
      for (int i = 0; i < stateData.length; ++i) {
         // Print the state information...
```

continues

Listing 11.6. continued

```
        g.setColor(Color.black);
        g.setFont(fonts[0]);
        g.drawString(stateData[i].getName(),colStart[0],y);
        g.drawString(Integer.toString(stateData[i].getElectoral()),
           colStart[1],y);
        g.drawString(Double.toString(stateData[i].getPrecincts()),
           colStart[2],y);
        // Print the candidates...
        // Incumbent...
        g.setColor(Color.red);
        g.setFont(fonts[1]);
        y += fontHeight;
        Candidate c = stateData[i].getIncumbent();
        // See if he won the state...
        if (c.getElectoral() > 0)
           g.drawString(winner,2,y);
        g.drawString(c.getName(),colStart[0],y);
        // Get election percentage...
        if (stateData[i].getTotalVotes() > 0)
           percent = ((double)c.getPopular()) /
              ((double)stateData[i].getTotalVotes());
        else
           percent = 0.0;
        // Draw text or graphics based on mode...
        if (mode != GRAPHICS) {
           s = Integer.toString(c.getPopular()) +
              " (" + ((float)(percent * 100.00) ) + "%)";
           g.drawString(s,colStart[1],y);
        } // end if
        else {
          if (stateData[i].getTotalVotes() > 0) {
           length = (int)(percent * graphicsWidth);
           g.fillRect(colStart[1],y - fontHeight + 2,
              length,fontHeight - 1);
          } // end if
        } // end else
        // then Challenger...
        g.setColor(Color.blue);
        y += fontHeight;
        c = stateData[i].getChallenger();
        // See if he won the state...
        if (c.getElectoral() > 0)
           g.drawString(winner,2,y);
        g.drawString(c.getName(),colStart[0],y);
        // Get election percentage...
        if (stateData[i].getTotalVotes() > 0)
           percent = ((double)c.getPopular()) /
              ((double)stateData[i].getTotalVotes());
        else
           percent = 0.0;
        // Draw text or graphics based on mode...
        if (mode != GRAPHICS) {
           s = Integer.toString(c.getPopular()) +
              " (" + ((float)(percent * 100.00) ) + "%)";
           g.drawString(s,colStart[1],y);
        } // end if
```

```
        else {
          if (stateData[i].getTotalVotes() > 0) {
           length = (int)(percent * graphicsWidth);
           g.fillRect(colStart[1],y - fontHeight + 2,
              length,fontHeight - 1);
          } // end if
        } // end else
        y += fontHeight;
     } // end for

     return totalHeight;
  }
}
```

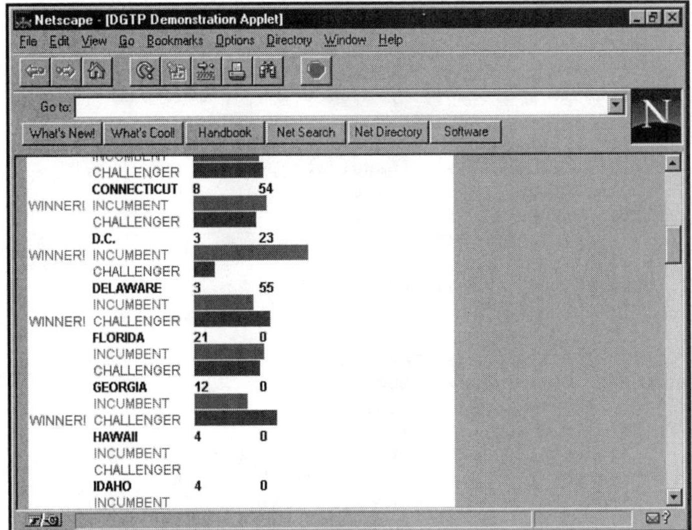

FIGURE 11.6.
The Election applet set in graphical mode.

The SummaryCanvas Class

The SummaryCanvas class, whose code is given in Listing 11.7, displays the election results on a national basis. It, too, can show the data graphically or in a primarily text-based format, depending on its mode. If the canvas is in graphical mode, then it shows the popular vote as a bar graph representing the percentages of each candidate in the state.

When the SummaryCanvas is initialized, it sets up variables used when painting the canvas. The canvas also declares itself an observer of the ElectionTable by calling its `addObserver()` method. When the table changes, then the canvas's `update()` method is called. This repaints the canvas, yielding the new results.

Listing 11.7. The SummaryCanvas class.

```
import java.awt.*;
import java.lang.*;
import java.util.Observable;
import java.util.Observer;
import java.applet.Applet;

// This canvas shows the top banner and the
// election totals...
// The Observer is called when election
// data has changed and, if so, forces update
public class SummaryCanvas extends Canvas implements Observer {
   Applet a; // The applet
   int totalWidth;  // Width coordinates...
   int colStart[];
   Font fonts[];  // Font to display...
   int fontHeights[]; // Quick reference of font heights...
   int topMargin; // Where to start painting...
   int totalHeight; // How much to paint...
   Rectangle lastPaint; // Keep track of last paint...
   // Various display strings....
   String titleBanner = "1996 ELECTION RETURNS";
   String headers[] = { "Candidate",
      "Electoral Total", "Popular Vote" };
   String winner = "WINNER!";
   // Graphics or text mode.
   public static final int TEXT = 0;
   public static final int GRAPHICS = 1;
   int mode = TEXT;

   // Calculate some dimension information...
   public SummaryCanvas(Applet app) {
      // Create display fonts...
      fonts = new Font[3];
      fonts[0] = new Font("Helvetica",Font.BOLD,20);
      fonts[1] = new Font("Helvetica",Font.BOLD,12);
      fonts[2] = new Font("Helvetica",Font.PLAIN,12);
      // Initialize column width array...
      colStart = new int[3];
      // Get the font and use to calculate some margins...
      fontHeights = new int[3];
      FontMetrics fm;
      for (int i = 0; i < 3; ++i) {
         fm = Toolkit.getDefaultToolkit().getFontMetrics(fonts[i]);
         fontHeights[i] = fm.getHeight();
      } // end for
      topMargin = fontHeights[0];
      fm = Toolkit.getDefaultToolkit().getFontMetrics(fonts[1]);
      colStart[0] = fm.stringWidth(" " + winner + "!! ");
      colStart[1] = colStart[0] +
         (int)(1.5 *(double)fm.stringWidth(headers[0]));
      colStart[2] = colStart[1] +
         (int)(1.5 *(double)fm.stringWidth(headers[1]));
      totalWidth = colStart[2] + fm.stringWidth(headers[2]);
      totalHeight = 8 * fontHeights[1];
      // Make Canvas an observer of the ElectionTable...
      a = app;
```

```
   ElectionTable.getElectionTable().addObserver(this);
}

// Get target height...
public int getHeight() {
   return totalHeight;
}

// Set the mode to paint in...
public void setMode(int mode) {
   this.mode = mode;
}

// Called when Table changes....
public void update(Observable o, Object arg) {
 if (lastPaint != null)
    a.repaint(lastPaint.x,lastPaint.y,
      lastPaint.width,lastPaint.height);
}

// Paint the summary totals...
public int paint(Graphics g,int xOrg,int yOrg,int width) {
   // Set the background color to white...
   int y = yOrg + topMargin;
   g.setColor(Color.white);
   g.fillRect(xOrg,yOrg,width,totalHeight);
   lastPaint = new Rectangle(xOrg,yOrg,width,totalHeight);
   // Paint the title banner...
   g.setFont(fonts[0]);
   FontMetrics fm = g.getFontMetrics();
   g.setColor(Color.red);
   int x = (width - fm.stringWidth(titleBanner))/2;
   g.drawString(titleBanner,x,y);
   y += fontHeights[0];

   // *********
   // Paint the header...
   // *********
   g.setFont(fonts[1]);
   fm = g.getFontMetrics();
   g.setColor(Color.blue);
   for (int i = 0; i < 3; ++i) {
      g.drawString(headers[i],colStart[i],y);
   }
   // Draw line across bottom...
   g.drawLine(colStart[0],y,totalWidth,y);
   y += fontHeights[1];

   // Display the candidate totals...
   String s;
   g.setFont(fonts[2]);
   g.setColor(Color.red);
   double graphicsWidth =
     (double)(totalWidth - colStart[2] + fm.stringWidth(winner) );
   ElectionTable t = ElectionTable.getElectionTable();
   int totalPopular = t.getTotalPopular();
   // *********
```

continues

Listing 11.7. continued

```
// Show Incumbent...
// *********
g.setColor(Color.red);
int electoral,length;
Candidate c = t.getIncumbent();
electoral = c.getElectoral();
if (electoral >= 270)
   g.drawString(winner,2,y);
g.drawString(c.getName(),colStart[0],y);
g.drawString(Integer.toString(electoral),
      colStart[1],y);
double percent;
// Get popular vote percentage...
if (totalPopular > 0)
      percent = ((double)c.getPopular()) /
         ((double)totalPopular);
else
      percent = 0.0;
// Paint Text or Graphics?
if (mode != GRAPHICS) {
   s = Integer.toString(c.getPopular()) +
        " (" + ((float)(percent * 100.00) ) + "%)";
   g.drawString(s,colStart[2],y);
}
else {
     if (totalPopular > 0) {
      length = (int)(percent * graphicsWidth);
      g.fillRect(colStart[2],y - fontHeights[2] + 2,
         length,fontHeights[2] - 1);
     } // end if
}
y += fontHeights[2];
// *********
// Show Challenger...
// *********
g.setColor(Color.blue);
c = t.getChallenger();
electoral = c.getElectoral();
if (electoral >= 270)
   g.drawString(winner,2,y);
g.drawString(c.getName(),colStart[0],y);
g.drawString(Integer.toString(electoral),
      colStart[1],y);
// Get popular vote percentage...
if (totalPopular > 0)
      percent = ((double)c.getPopular()) /
         ((double)totalPopular);
else
      percent = 0.0;
// Paint Text or Graphics?
if (mode != GRAPHICS) {
   s = Integer.toString(c.getPopular()) +
        " (" + ((float)(percent * 100.00) ) + "%)";
   g.drawString(s,colStart[2],y);
}
else {
```

```
            if (totalPopular > 0) {
             length = (int)(percent * graphicsWidth);
             g.fillRect(colStart[2],y - fontHeights[2] + 2,
                length,fontHeights[2] - 1);
            } // end if
        }
        return yOrg + totalHeight;
    }
}
```

Summary

This part of the book has brought together many of Java's most powerful elements. Sockets and streams are used to manage network connections, features of AWT are used to display the election results, and multithreading and synchronization constructs are used to run the applet and server application efficiently. The result is a large project that concludes the project-development portion of this book. Part V, "Advanced Applet Development," will focus on smaller, standalone projects, giving you more exposure to the subtleties of Java.

V

Advanced Applet Development

12

Handling Dynamic Content

This chapter introduces the HotJava browser and explains why it is so groundbreaking, then introduces the HotJava source release, used to modify HotJava itself. The HTTP server from previous chapters gets a needed face-lift before being used to serve dynamic content to HotJava. At the end of the chapter, you will actually write and test two HotJava content handlers.

Introducing the HotJava Browser

The developers at Sun had a problem; they had a new language, Java, envisioned as dominating the World Wide Web (WWW), but they didn't have a way to reach the public. People need to see demonstrations before they can fully appreciate a new technology, and they need to work with things before they will adopt them. How could Sun convince people to use their distributed language without a demonstration vehicle? The answer is: They couldn't. A Web browser that could execute Java was needed, so the HotJava browser was developed.

HotJava is completely implemented in the Java language itself! It was started to demonstrate interactive content (Java applets) and to prove that Java was a viable language for advanced applications (the browser).

Dynamic Content

Traditional Web browsers are a monolithic collection of protocol handlers and display routines. Typically, the manufacturer equips them to respond to a certain subset of the huge number of protocols and data formats that make up the Internet. HotJava essentially understands none of the protocols or data formats on the Internet. This distinction is important. HotJava was not conceived to speak any specific protocol; it was developed to speak them all.

HotJava implements a concept called *dynamic content*. When you point HotJava at a URL, the browser searches for the code to converse in whatever protocol is being used. If you entered

```
http://www.javasoft.com/
```

HotJava would load its HTTP protocol handler. If you entered

```
ftp://ftp.some.host/
```

HotJava would load its FTP protocol handler. What if it didn't have an FTP handler? Well, it would ask the host whether it had an FTP handler. If the host had one, HotJava would download it, then use the new handler to fetch the original URL. HotJava upgrades itself on the fly!

Protocol Handlers

HotJava actually does come with a great many protocol handlers already installed—that is, already present on the local computer. When a new protocol is needed, HotJava searches locally first; only then does it resort to asking the remote host.

The distinction is that it makes no difference to HotJava whether the handler is locally available or gotten from halfway around the world. This dynamic behavior extends to display content as well.

Content Handlers

Traditional Web browsers understand a small subset of display formats. Most common are GIF, JPEG, and X11 bitmap. The content type comes encoded in a Multipurpose Internet Mail Extension (MIME) header. You experienced MIME content types when you worked with the HTTP server. Remember how the server sent everything as `Content-type: text/html`? This was a MIME content type. Servers are configured to send each file format with a specific MIME type. Typically, this is done by tying the suffix of a file to a specific content type. Table 12.1 lists some common file extensions and their MIME content types.

When HotJava sees a MIME content type, it tries to load the appropriate handler. Again, if it can't find a local handler, it will ask the remote server for one.

Table 12.1. Common file extensions and their MIME content types.

File Extension	*MIME Content Type*
html	text/html
htm	text/html
txt	text/plain
rtf	text/rtf
ps	text/postscript
doc	text/msword
gif	image/gif
jpg	image/jpeg
mpg	video/mpeg
wav	audio/wav
au	audio/ulaw
tar	file/tar
arc	file/arc
lha	file/lharc
zip	file/zip

Netscape attempts to mimic this behavior with "plug-ins." You can configure Netscape Navigator to run plug-in programs when it encounters certain MIME content types. The one thing that Netscape can't do is use the server to load one on the fly. Even if it could, there are so many different platforms available, who knows if it would load the correct executable for your specific architecture. Java is portable, so you can compile it once and execute it everywhere there's an interpreter present. If you're using the HotJava browser, then you have a running Java interpreter already in action.

Security Model

HotJava has a much more flexible security model than Netscape Navigator. Instead of banning all file access and limiting socket access, HotJava allows the severity of restrictions to be configured.

Network security has four modes:

- **No access**—Applets cannot open any external URLs or socket connections.
- **Applet host**—Applets can open sockets only to the host they were loaded from.
- **Firewall**—Applets can open sockets to the host they were loaded from and to hosts within a configurable list or domain.
- **Unrestricted**—Applets can open sockets to anywhere.

In addition, you can also apply these modes to applet loading:

- **No access**—No Java applets can be loaded.
- **Applet host**—Only applets from the local file system can be loaded.
- **Firewall**—Applets from hosts within a firewall can be loaded.
- **Unrestricted**—Applets can be loaded from any host.

Accessing local file storage is also a configurable option. HotJava uses two environment variables to control file access by applets:

- `HOTJAVA_READ_PATH`
- `HOTJAVA_WRITE_PATH`

Both these variables consist of a semicolon-separated list of directories. Applets can access any files in these directories or their subdirectories.

Firewall Security Model

The *firewall security model* is a powerful option. The corporate world is only now becoming aware of the vast power inherent in HTML. Corporate intranets are sprouting up everywhere; these corporate nets offer full access for machines behind their firewall, but limited or no access to the Internet at large. Allowing a browser to have full access rights within a firewall offers the necessary flexibility that corporations demand. The current Netscape security model is too restrictive for business use. Real-world applications need local storage and flexible connectivity options to be of any use. Browsers will probably adopt this firewall model as business demands for Java grow.

Alpha3 Distribution Differences

Unfortunately, HotJava is mired in the world of Java Alpha3. It can't run applets written for version 1.0, but it still has instructive use. The Java language is quite stable, so you'll find no differences in the language syntax or semantics, but there are some major differences in the class packages and libraries.

To begin with, there is no classes.zip file. All the Java classes are contained in a directory tree that reflects the package name of each class. Actually, if you peered inside the zipped class file from version 1.0, you would find that this same tree has been maintained in the compressed image. Figure 12.1 shows the major packages within the directory hierarchy.

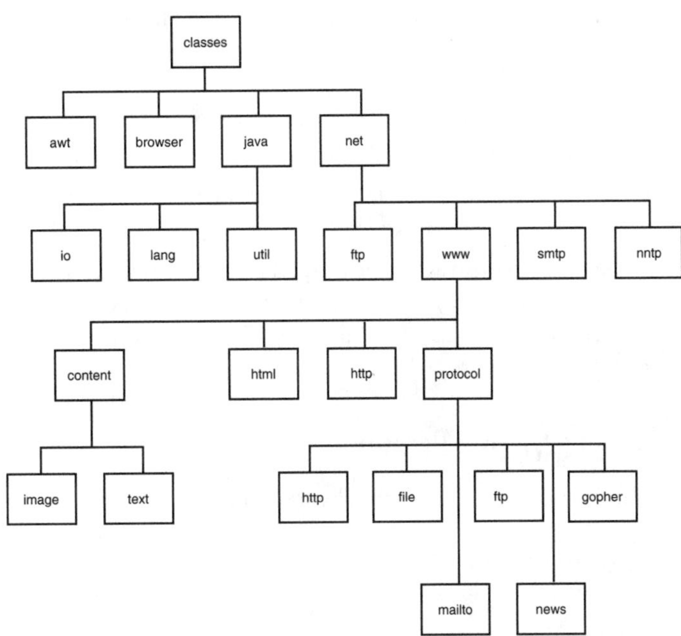

FIGURE 12.1.
Directory structure and major packages.

This layout should look familiar to you, with the exception of the browser package. This package contains classes and interfaces to HotJava's general functionality. In particular, the Applet class is located within the browser package.

The protocol and content handler classes are under the following directories:

```
classes/net/www/protocol
classes/net/www/content
```

When HotJava makes a request to a server for a specific handler, it uses the same path as the local directories. For example, if you encounter MIME type `text/plain` and there's no plain.class within the local text subdirectory, HotJava issues the following request:

```
GET /classes/net/www/content/text/plain.class HTTP/1.0
```

Unfortunately, this request issued to the previous chapter's HTTP server would go unanswered because HotJava is waiting for a socket close notification that will never arrive due to a bug in the JDK. It seems as though `socket.close()` doesn't work under either Windows 95 or Windows NT. You need to change HotJava's source code to use the `Content-length` MIME parameter that the HTTP server dutifully places into the outbound stream.

Altering the HotJava Source

To alter the HotJava source, you must first have a thorough understanding of the inner workings of the HotJava protocol handler; its principle function is to provide the input stream:

```
public InputStream openStream(URL u);
```

The handler for HTTP constructs an instance of the HttpClient class to perform its low-level work; this class extends NetworkClient. Then the socket connection is opened and the request is sent. The input stream is acquired and wrapped in a BufferedInputStream. The HttpClient parses the response header and stores the results.

At this point, the constructor for HttpClient returns. The HTTP protocol handler now processes the response. If the MIME header contains a valid `Content-length:` field, the input stream is further encapsulated in a MeteredStream. The Stream class MeteredStream is the perfect place to make the alterations.

Buffered Streams Primer

The standard input stream hierarchy looks like this:

```
InputStream
    FilterInputStream
        BufferedInputStream
```

The following list shows the public methods of the FilterInputStream class:

FilterInputStream Members
`available()`
`close()`
`mark(int)`
`markSupported()`
`read()`
`read(byte[])`
`read(byte[], int, int)`
`reset()`
`skip(int)`

This class is extended by BufferedInputStream. Buffered streams offer a look-ahead buffer that enables a stream to be read in large chunks, but processed a character at a time. They also provide mark/reset capability. Frequently, applications will need to parse a stream, looking for a specific string. If this string is not found, then the application should reset the stream so other processes can try to parse the same data. Marking a stream tells the BufferedInputStream object to remember the current location within the buffer. If a subsequent reset is called, the object will march backward in its buffer to the previously stored location. New read requests will be satisfied from the old location. The following list shows the public methods of the BufferedInputStream class; all these methods override the equivalent named method in the FilterInputStream class:

Public Methods of BufferedInputStream

```
available()
mark(int)
markSupported()
read()
read(byte[], int, int)
reset()
skip(int)
```

Start with the following InputStream:

```
"BufferedInputStreams are handy!"
```

Next, execute the following code snippet on the stream:

```
byte data[] = new byte[13];
is.read(data);        // read 13 characters [BufferedInput]
mark(200);             // save this position for up to 200 characters
is.read(data, 0, 7);  // read 7 more characters [Streams]
reset();               // go back
byte rest[] = new byte[18];
is.read(rest);        // read 18 more characters [Streams are handy!]
```

A MeteredStream extends FilterInputStream; you can find its source code in the HotJava directory:

```
classsrc\net\www\html\MeteredStream.java
```

Metered Stream and HTTP

HotJava has a progress display, performed by the MeteredStream class, that can show how a transfer is progressing. Whenever the HTTP protocol handler detects a length parameter in the response header, it will encapsulate the current input stream within a MeteredStream:

```
String ct = http.getHeaderField("content-length");
int len = 0;
if (ct != null && (len = Integer.parseInt(ct)) != 0) {
    is = new MeteredStream(is, len, url);
```

Since all subsequent reads will be done through the MeteredStream class, this is the ideal location for the changes.

Making the Changes

Now you simply need to make stream reads return end-of-stream once the length parameter has been read. The following list shows the overriding methods in the MeteredStream class:

MeteredStream Public Methods
`read()`
`read(byte[], int, int)`
`skip(int)`
`close()`

Both read routines must be changed so that there are no further read attempts once the entire length of bytes has been returned:

```
public int read() {
    if ( count >= expected ) return -1;    // add this line
    int c = super.read();
    if (c != -1) {
        justRead(1);
    }
    return c;
}

public int read(byte b[], int off, int len) {
    if ( count >= expected ) return -1;
    if ( count + len > expected ) len = expected - count;    // add both of these
➥lines
    int n = super.read(b, off, len);
    if (n != -1) {
        justRead(n);
    }
    return n;
}
```

In addition, mark and reset operations must be intercepted so the counts can be updated. As you can see from the previous list of public methods, these routines are absent, so add the following two routines:

```
public synchronized void mark(int readlimit) {
        meterMark = count;
        super.mark(readlimit);
    }

    public synchronized void reset() {
        if ( meterMark != -1 )
            count = meterMark;
        super.reset();
    }
```

The class variable `meterMark` also needs to be added to the class:

```
public
class MeteredStream extends FilterInputStream
{
    // Class variables.
       ...

    // Instance variables.
       ...
    int meterMark = -1;     // add this line
       ...
}
```

That's it! Recompile MeteredStream and move the class file into the classes/net/www/html subdirectory.

Compiling Under HotJava

Compiling under HotJava is the same as compiling under the JDK; the only difference is which version of javac you use. I prefer not to alter my path and environment for HotJava. Simply issue the command specifying the full path to HotJava's version of javac:

```
c:\hotjava\bin\javac MeteredStream.java
```

Assuming you made the alterations correctly, this will create a MeteredStream.class file in the current directory. Rename the original MeteredStream.class to MeteredStream.orig, then copy your altered MeteredStream.class into its place. You have just changed the source for HotJava! Now give it a try—run the server from Chapters 9, "Java Socket Programming," 10, "Native Methods and Java," or 11, "Building a Live Data Applet," and point your new HotJava at the server. The files transfer perfectly.

Before addressing content handlers, you need to add some enhancements to the server.

Toward a More Perfect Server

The server used in Part IV, "Managing Live Data," was useful, but it lacked many features of an actual HTTP server. Specifically, there is no configuration file to map file extensions to MIME content strings. In addition, some log information would be helpful.

The first change is to the class name. Up to this point, the main class has been called BasicWebServer. Change this to HTTPServer, then perform a global search and replace to make the change. Now the configuration and logging methods can be added.

Adding a Configuration File

Since the server is an application, it is free to read and even write the disk. The format of the configuration file is very straightforward:

- port = #
- suffix = file_extension Content-type
- log = filename

New methods are added to handle reading the configuration data. Listing 12.1 shows the new routines.

Listing 12.1. New routines for reading configuration files.

```
/**
 * Read the config file.
 */
private void initialize()
{
    String line = null;
    String configFile = "server.cfg";

    // setup defaults
    HTTP_PORT = 80;
    suffix = new Hashtable();

    try
    {
        FileInputStream inFile = new FileInputStream(configFile);
        DataInputStream is = new DataInputStream(inFile);

        while ((line = is.readLine()) != null)
        {
            StringTokenizer icmd = new StringTokenizer(line, " \t=");
            addConfigEntry(icmd);
        }
    }
    catch (FileNotFoundException fnf)
    {
        suffix.put("html", "text/html");
        suffix.put("htm", "text/html");
        suffix.put("class", "text/plain");
        suffix.put("gif", "image/gif");
    }
    catch (IOException ioe)
    {
        System.out.println("Error reading config file: " + ioe);
    }
}

/**
 * Add a config entry.
 * @param icmd contains the tokenized line.
 */
```

```
private void addConfigEntry(StringTokenizer icmd)
{
    if ( icmd.hasMoreTokens() )
    {
        String param = null;
        String command = icmd.nextToken();
        if ( icmd.hasMoreTokens() )
        {
            param = icmd.nextToken();
            if ( command.equalsIgnoreCase("PORT") )
            {
                HTTP_PORT = Integer.valueOf(param).intValue();
                if (debug)
                    System.out.println("Monitoring port " + HTTP_PORT);
            }
            else if ( command.equalsIgnoreCase("SUFFIX") )
            {
                if ( icmd.hasMoreTokens() )
                {
                    String param2 = icmd.nextToken();
                    suffix.put(param, param2);
                    if (debug)
                    {
                        System.out.print(
                            "Adding suffix: '" + param + "'");
                        System.out.println("  '" + param2 + "'");
                    }
                }
            }
            else if ( command.equalsIgnoreCase("LOG") )
            {
                openLog(param);
            }
            else
            {
                System.out.print("Error: Unknown cfg entry: ");
                System.out.println(command);
            }
        }
    }
}

/**
 * Open a log file
 * @param logfile contains the filename to open
 */
public void openLog(String logfile)
{
    try
    {
        logFile = new PrintStream( new FileOutputStream(logfile) );
        logging = true;
    }
    catch (IOException ioe)
    {
        System.out.println("Error opening log file: " + ioe);
    }
}
```

The StringTokenizer is instructed to parse equal sign characters out of the stream. This allows the configuration file to omit the equal sign and still function as expected. Only one config entry per line is allowed because `readLine()` is used to retrieve the entries.

File extension to MIME type mapping is contained in a hash table called `suffix`. The file extension is used as the key. If a configuration file contains multiple entries for an extension, only the last one will be stored. Hash table `put` operations overwrite duplicate entries.

Adding Standard Logging

There are many third-party tools available to analyze server log files, provided they are in a "common log format":

```
hostname identd authuser [date] "request" status length
```

The first entry, `hostname`, is the name of the host this connection was received from. If the name cannot be established, this field will display the numeric IP address of the caller. The next two fields contain information for "login" and authorized user names. The HTTP server does not support remote identification dialogs, so these fields will appear as a single dash (`-`). The date field has this format:

```
DD/MMM/YYY:HH:MM:SS GGGG
```

All these fields are evident except GGGG, which represents the number of time zones away from GMT.

The request field is the first line from the request header. `status` is the HTTP response code that was sent, typically 200, and `length` is the total number of file bytes sent in the response. Here is a sample log entry:

```
some.name.com - - [25/Mar/1996:08:48:23 -0400] "GET / HTTP/1.0" 200 342
```

The 200 indicates that a response containing 342 bytes was sent.

Building Log Information

HTTP requests are already stored in the HTTPrequest class, so it's reasonable to also store the log information in this class. If the server is ever made to work concurrently, the log information will have to travel with each request, so just add it there now:

```
/**
 * This class maintains all of the information from a HTTP request
 */
public class HTTPrequest
{
        ...
```

```
    public StringBuffer log;

    /**
     * Create an instance of this class
     */
    public HTTPrequest()
    {
        ...
        log = null;
    }
        ...
}
```

A StringBuffer is used because the string will grow and be altered. Java String objects are immutable—they can never be altered after they are created. If you use the plus operator to grow a String, you are actually creating a new String:

```
String first = new String("This is the first string.");
first += "  This is the second string";
```

The `first` variable now contains a completely different string, constructed from the first string and the addition of the second string. The original contents of the variable are lost.

The log string will need some tweaking to bring it in line with the common log format. That is why a StringBuffer class is used.

After a request is parsed, a new routine is added to HTTPrequest to format the initial portions of the log entry:

```
/**
 * Log a complete request.
 */
public void logRequest()
{
    Date current = new Date();

    log = new StringBuffer("");
    if ( clientSocket == null )
        log.append("-");
    else
        log.append(clientSocket.getInetAddress().getHostName());
    log.append(" - - ");
    log.append(formatDate(current));
    log.append(" \"" + firstLine + "\" ");
}
```

The Date Class

The Date class is part of the java.util package. It provides full support for both date and time. Six different constructors for the class, shown in the following list, offer a great deal of flexibility in how a date is specified.

Date Class Constructors

```
Date()
Date(long totalSecs)
Date(int yr, int mth, int day)
Date(int yr, int mth, int day, int hrs, int min)
Date(int yr, int mth, int day, int hrs, int min, int sec)
Date(String s)
```

The first constructor, the most commonly used, constructs a Date class reflecting the current date and time. The other constructors are used mainly to construct Date objects that are either forward or backward in time. This could be done for comparison purposes:

```
Date c = new Date();
Date p = new Date( c.getYear() - 1, c.getMonth(), c.getDate() );
Date n = new Date( c.getYear() + 1, c.getMonth(), c.getDate() );
if ( p.before( c ) )
    System.out.println("Date " + p + " is before Date " + c);
if ( n.after( c ) )
    System.out.println("Date " + n + " is after Date " + c);
```

The Date class provides three useful comparison functions:

- `boolean before(Date d)`
- `boolean after(Date d)`
- `boolean equals(Date d)`

Several public methods get and manipulate Date class variables. Table 12.2 lists the remaining public methods of the Date class.

Table 12.2. Public methods of the Date class.

Method	*Synopsis*
`int getYear()`	Year since 1900
`void setYear(int y)`	Year since 1900
`int getMonth()`	Month (0–11)
`void setMonth(int m)`	Month (0–11)
`int getDate()`	Day of month (1–31)
`void setDate(int d)`	Day of month (1–31)
`int getDay()`	Day of week (0–6)[0=Sunday]
`int getHours()`	(0–23)
`void setHours(int h)`	(0–23)
`int getMinutes()`	(0–59)

Method	Synopsis
`void setMinutes(int m)`	(0–59)
`int getSeconds()`	(0–59)
`void setSeconds(int s)`	(0–59)
`long getTime()`	Milliseconds since 1970
`void setTime(long totalSecs)`	Milliseconds since 1970
`int hashCode()`	Return the object's hash code
`String toString()`	Uses UNIX ctime conventions
`String toLocaleString()`	Uses locale conventions
`String toGMTString()`	Uses Internet GMT conventions
`int getTimezoneOffset()`	Minutes from GMT

Creating Common Log Date Format

None of the `toString()` variants in the Date class match common log format. The following routines use a Date class to create the correct common log date format:

```
/**
 * Return the passed date as a common log format String.
 * @param d contains the date to convert
 */
public String formatDate(Date d)
{
    return "[" + formatFor2(d.getDate()) + "/" + getMonthName(d) +
                "/" + (d.getYear() + 1900) +
                ":" + formatFor2(d.getHours()) +
                ":" + formatFor2(d.getMinutes()) +
                ":" + formatFor2(d.getSeconds()) +
                " " + getTimezone(d) + "]";
}

/**
 * return a String of the passed int.  The String will
 * be formatted to take up at least two places.
 */
public String formatFor2(int n)
{
    String ret;

    if ( n < 10 )
        ret = new String("0" + n);
    else
        ret = new String("" + n);
    return ret;
}

/**
```

```
     * Return the timezone formatted for common log format.
     * @param d contains the date to convert
     */
    public String getTimezone(Date d)
    {
        String ret;

        int tz = d.getTimezoneOffset();
        int lf = tz % 60;                   // check for remainders
        tz /= 60;                           // change to hours

        // The polarity of getTimezoneOffset is backwards.
        // Positive values mean you are behind GMT.
        // Negative values mean GMT is behind you.

        if ( tz > 0 )
            ret = "-";
        else if ( tz < 0 )
            ret = "+";
        else
            ret = "";
        ret += formatFor2(tz) + formatFor2(lf);
        return ret;
    }

    /**
     * Return a String representing the month name in
     * common log format.
     * @param d contains the date to convert
     */
    public String getMonthName(Date d)
    {
        switch ( d.getMonth() )
        {
        case 0: return "Jan";
        case 1: return "Feb";
        case 2: return "Mar";
        case 3: return "Apr";
        case 4: return "May";
        case 5: return "Jun";
        case 6: return "Jul";
        case 7: return "Aug";
        case 8: return "Sep";
        case 9: return "Oct";
        case 10: return "Nov";
        case 11: return "Dec";
        }
        return "-";
    }
}
```

Integers will print in their current precision. Common log format calls for two-digit numbers. The method `formatFor2()` will add a zero at the beginning if the passed integer is less than 10.

Notice the polarity switch of `getTimezoneOffset()`. Common log format as well as most other time-zone representations use hours away from GMT (locale - GMT).

> **NOTE**
>
> The `getTimezoneOffset()` method returns the number of minutes GMT is away from your locale (GMT - locale). Normal convention is to use the number of minutes your locale is away from GMT (locale - GMT). Be careful when displaying time-zone information.

Now the HTTPrequest contains the request and the initial parts of the log string. The remaining two pieces of log information, `status` and `length`, are filled in by the send routines.

Altering the Send Routines

A nice feature of many servers is that they send a standard HTML file for error states. For instance, file error404.html is returned when a request is not found, which enables you to configure what is sent for various error conditions. Previously, the status of a transmission was always `200 OK`. Now, negative responses also need to use the services of `sendFile()`. Status and the description string need to be passed in by the caller. This has another advantage because log information is written in the `sendFile()` routine, which means that negative responses are also recorded.

```
/**
 * Send a negative (404 NOT FOUND) response
 * @param request the HTTP request to respond to.
 */
private void sendNegativeResponse(HTTPrequest request)
{
    try
    {
        String fileToGet = "error404.html";
        FileInputStream inFile = new FileInputStream(fileToGet);
        if (debug & level < 4)
        {
            System.out.print("DEBUG: Sending -rsp ");
            System.out.print(fileToGet + " " + inFile.available());
            System.out.println(" Bytes");
        }
        sendFile(request, inFile, 404, "Not Found", fileToGet);
        inFile.close();
    }
    catch (FileNotFoundException fnf)
    {
        System.out.println("Error: No error404.html file for -rsp");
    }
    catch (ProtocolException pe)
    {
    }
```

```
        catch (IOException ioe)
        {
            System.out.println("Unknown file length: " + ioe);
        }
    }

    /**
     * Send the passed file
     * @param request the HTTP request instance
     * @param inFile the opened input file stream to send
     */
    private void sendFile(HTTPrequest request,
                          FileInputStream inFile,
                          int status, String describe,
                          String fileToGet)
    {
        DataOutputStream outbound = null;
        String type = null;

        try
        {
            // Acquire an output stream
            outbound = new DataOutputStream(
                request.clientSocket.getOutputStream());

            // Send the response header
            int period = fileToGet.lastIndexOf('.');
            if ( period != -1 && period != fileToGet.length() )
                type = (String)suffix.get(fileToGet.substring(period + 1));
            if (type == null)
                type = "text/plain";

            if (debug & level < 4)
            {
                System.out.println("DEBUG: Type " + type);
            }
            outbound.writeBytes("HTTP/1.0 " + status + " " + describe + "\r\n");
            outbound.writeBytes("Content-type: " + type + "\r\n");
            outbound.writeBytes("Content-Length: " + inFile.available() + "\r\n");
            outbound.writeBytes("\r\n");

            request.log.append(status + " " + inFile.available());
            System.out.println(request.log.toString());
            if ( logging )
                logFile.print(request.log.toString() + "\r\n");

            // Added to allow Netscape to process header properly
            // This is needed because the close is not recognized
            sleep(5000);

            // If not a HEAD request, send the file body.
            // HEAD requests only solicit a header response.
            if (!request.method.equals("HEAD"))
            {
                byte dataBody[] = new byte[1024];
                int cnt;
                while ((cnt = inFile.read(dataBody)) != -1)
                    outbound.write(dataBody, 0, cnt);
```

```
        }

        // Cleanup
        outbound.flush();
        outbound.close();
        request.inbound.close();
    }
    catch (IOException ioe)
    {
        System.out.println("IOException while sending file: " + ioe);
    }
}
```

Notice how the MIME content type is derived from the file's extension. Using a hash table for this information allows a rapid lookup. If the extension is not found, or if the file has no extension, the file is sent as type `text/plain`.

Creating New Content Types

Now that the server can send various MIME content types, it's time to investigate how to use HotJava content handlers. This exercise is small in scope, but large in know-how.

HotJava comes equipped with four content handlers, in addition to its standard HTML handler:

- `text/plain`
- `image/gif`
- `image/x_xbitmap`
- `image/x_xpixmap`

This exercise adds two new types, `text/fee` and `text/foo`. Since these types aren't within the local system, HotJava will try to load them from the server:

```
GET /classes/net/www/content/text/fee.class HTTP/1.0
GET /classes/net/www/content/text/foo.class HTTP/1.0
```

Writing Content Handlers

A HotJava content handler consists of a single class that extends the ContentHandler class. Its class name must be the same as the MIME sub-type that it handles. In addition, it must have the same path it would have if it were local to HotJava.

The code below implements the `text/fee` content handler:

```
package net.www.content.text;

import net.www.html.ContentHandler;
import net.www.html.URL;
import java.io.InputStream;
```

```
/**
 * A content handler for text/fee objects
 */
public class fee extends ContentHandler
{
    /**
     * Read in an ASCII text file and append an
     * ID string to the end.
     * @param is holds the input stream for the content
     * @param u holds the URL for the object
     */
    public Object getContent(InputStream is, URL u)
    {
        StringBuffer sb = new StringBuffer();
        int c;

        while ((c = is.read()) >= 0)
        {
            sb.appendChar((char)c);
        }
        sb.append("\n\n\nThis is a fee ASCII text file.\n");
        sb.append("Rendered by the fee content handler!\n");
        is.close();
        return sb.toString();      // return a string object
    }
}
```

This handler expects an ASCII text file to be its input. It will continue reading until the end of the stream. When the stream is finished, this handler adds an identification string to the end of the text.

All content handlers return some type of object to the browser. The browser uses `instanceof` calls to figure out how to display the object. Obviously, HotJava can handle string data. More complex types, such as images, would return an instance of the Observable class. Inspecting the GIF content handler shows that it returns a GIFImage, which descends from DIBitmap, which itself descends from class Observable.

Compile the code by invoking HotJava's version of javac:

```
c:\hotjava\bin\javac fee.java
```

Now add the new content type to the server config file: server.cfg.

```
suffix= fee text/fee
```

Finally, run the server and then HotJava. Remember to use the server's new name: HTTPServer. Point the browser at the server test file: test.fee.

```
http://your_host/test.fee
```

You should see the display shown in Figure 12.2.

FIGURE 12.2.
Rendition of test.fee using the fee content handler.

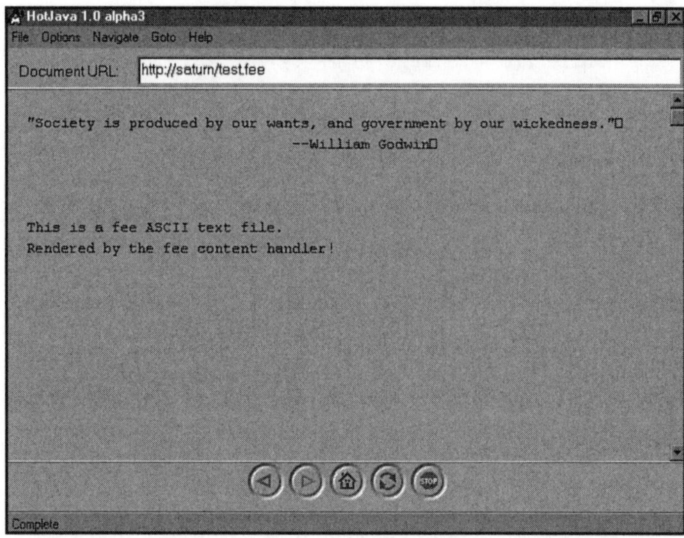

HotJava downloaded the new handler, installed it, and used it to render the new type! You can check this by looking at the output of the server:

```
merlin - - [25/Mar/1996:16:07:56 -0400] "GET /test.fee HTTP/1.0" 200 120
merlin - - [25/Mar/1996:16:08:09 -0400]
          "GET /classes/net/www/content/text/fee.class HTTP/1.0" 200 834
```

Did you notice the strange boxes at the end of each text line in the HotJava display? Those are carriage returns. HotJava doesn't know how to display these, so it uses a box.

Copy the fee.java file to foo.java. Edit the new foo handler so that it removes carriage returns whenever it sees them.

```
package net.www.content.text;

import net.www.html.ContentHandler;
import net.www.html.URL;
import java.io.InputStream;

/**
 * A content handler for text/foo objects
 */
public class foo extends ContentHandler
{
    /**
     * Read in an ASCII text file and append an
     * ID string to the end.
     * @param is holds the input stream for the content
     * @param u holds the URL for the object
     */
    public Object getContent(InputStream is, URL u)
    {
        StringBuffer sb = new StringBuffer();
```

```
        int c;

        while ((c = is.read()) >= 0)
        {
            if ( c == '\r' ) continue;    // remove carriage returns
            sb.appendChar((char)c);
        }
        sb.append("\n\n\nThis is a foo ASCII text file.\n");
        sb.append("Rendered by the foo content handler!\n");
        is.close();
        return sb.toString();      // return a string object
    }
}
```

First, compile the new foo handler:

```
c:\hotjava\bin\javac foo.java
```

Add the new "foo" suffix to the server configuration file:

```
suffix= foo text/foo
```

Next, restart the server and HotJava. Point the browser to the following statement:

```
http://your_host/test.foo
```

The boxes have disappeared! You should see the display shown in Figure 12.3.

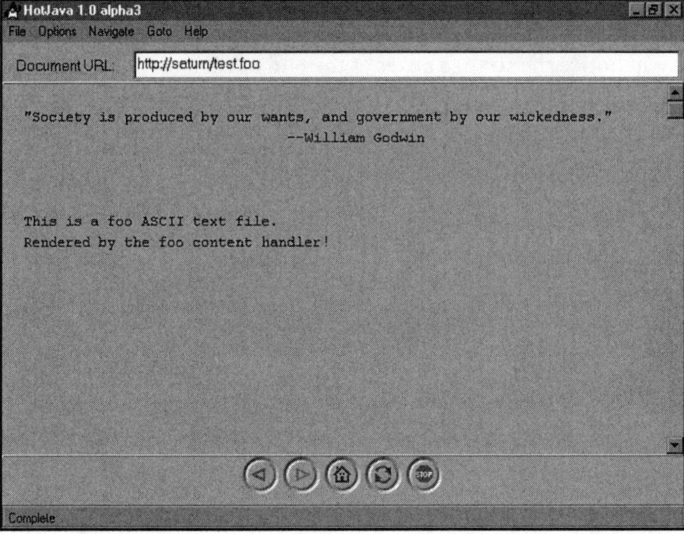

FIGURE 12.3.
Rendition of test.foo using the foo content handler.

The server log shows the following:

```
merlin - - [25/Mar/1996:16:10:17 -0400] "GET /test.foo HTTP/1.0" 200 120
merlin - - [25/Mar/1996:16:10:24 -0400]
         "GET /classes/net/www/content/text/foo.class HTTP/1.0" 200 845
```

Again, the handler was dynamically loaded by HotJava.

Summary

This chapter covers the dynamic Web browser HotJava. After some initial background, the HotJava class hierarchy is reviewed and the HotJava concept of dynamic content handlers is introduced. To demonstrate dynamic content, HotJava's source is patched to enable it to operate with the HTTP server from previous chapters.

The server itself receives a face-lift that brings it more in line with a standard HTTP server. In light of the changes, its name is changed to HTTPServer. You add a configuration file and logging.

You learn about the MIME content types as well as how servers use file extensions to decide what content type to send for a specific file.

The Date class is reviewed, and the common log format is introduced. Finally, you learn the basics of writing a HotJava content handler.

13

Animation and Image Filters

This chapter teaches you the more advanced concepts involved in Java images. It explores Java's image models and how to use images for animation. You learn about both static and dynamic image filters, including how to write your own.

This chapter leads off by exploring animation techniques, and then moves into the fundamental model behind Java images. Image filters are introduced, and two advanced filters are explained, including a special-effects filter. This chapter ends by using the effects filter to create a slide show suitable for corporate presentations.

Simple Animation Using Images

You can use images to produce animation. Listing 13.1 contains the code for an applet called SimpleRoll. The four images used were produced with a third-party paint application. Each yin-yang image has been rotated 90, 180, 270, or 360 degrees. If these images are displayed in rapid succession, the symbol appears to roll. Animation creates the illusion of movement by displaying images in rapid succession.

Listing 13.1. A simple animation applet.

```
import java.applet.*;
import java.awt.*;
import java.awt.image.*;
import java.io.*;
import SpinFilter;

public class SimpleRoll extends Applet
    implements Runnable
{
    private boolean init = false;
    Image myImage = null;
    Image allImages[] = null;
    Thread animation = null;
    MediaTracker tracker = null;
    int roll_x = 0;                    // where to draw
    boolean complete = false;
    int current = 0;

    /**
     * Standard initialization method for an applet
     */
    public void init()
    {
        if ( init == false )
        {
            init = true;
            tracker = new MediaTracker(this);
            allImages = new Image[4];
            allImages[0] = getImage(getCodeBase(), "images/yin0.gif");
            allImages[1] = getImage(getCodeBase(), "images/yin1.gif");
```

```
        allImages[2] = getImage(getCodeBase(), "images/yin2.gif");
        allImages[3] = getImage(getCodeBase(), "images/yin3.gif");
        for ( int x = 0; x < 4; x++ )
            tracker.addImage(allImages[x], x);
    }
}

/**
 * Standard paint routine for an applet.
 * @param g contains the Graphics class to use for painting
 */
public void paint(Graphics g)
{
    if ( complete )
    {
        g.drawImage(allImages[current], roll_x, 40, this);
    }
    else
    {
        g.drawString("Images not yet loaded", 0, 20);
    }
}

public void start()
{
    if ( animation == null )
    {
        animation = new Thread(this);
        animation.start();
    }
}

public void stop()
{
    if ( animation != null )
    {
        animation.stop();
        animation = null;
    }
}

public void run()
{
    while ( !checkRoll() ) sleep(250);
    complete = true;
    while (true)
    {
        roll(0, this.size().width-42);        // roll left to right
        roll(this.size().width-42, 0);        // roll right to left
    }
}

boolean checkRoll()
{
    boolean finished = true;
    for ( int i = 0; i < 4; i++ )
```

continues

Listing 13.1. continued

```
        {
            if ( (tracker.statusID(i, true) & MediaTracker.COMPLETE) == 0 )
                finished = false;
        }
        return finished;
    }

    void roll(int begin, int end)
    {
        if ( begin < end )
        {
            for ( int x = begin; x <= end; x += 21 )
            {
                roll_x = x;
                repaint();
                current--;
                if ( current == -1 ) current = 3;
                sleep(150);
            }
        }
        else
        {
            for ( int x = begin; x >= end; x -= 21 )
            {
                roll_x = x;
                repaint();
                current++;
                if ( current == 4 ) current = 0;
                sleep(150);
            }
        }
    }

    /**
     * A simple sleep routine
     * @param a the number of milliseconds to sleep
     */
    private void sleep(int a)
    {
        try
        {
            Thread.currentThread().sleep(a);
        }
        catch (InterruptedException e)
        {
        }
    }
}
```

The first thing the `run()` method does is start loading the four images; this is done by using a MediaTracker object. It would have been more efficient to assign the same ID to all four, but I wanted to show you how to track individual images as well. When all the images have loaded, the animation can start. The `run()` thread updates the `roll_x` variable and image number every 150 milliseconds, and then issues a repaint request.

The `paint()` method simply draws the current image to the requested location.

> **NOTE**
>
> This applet will work even if the images are not preloaded with MediaTracker; however, failing to preload causes incomplete images to display. The object's position updates even though there are no images to paint. It's much more professional to wait until all the images are complete before beginning an animation.

To really appreciate the power behind Java images, you need to understand the consumer/producer model in detail. Powerful graphics applications use the advantages of this model to perform their visual wizardry. In particular, you can write effective image filters only if you understand the underlying model.

Image Producers

The ImageProducer interface has the following methods:

- `public void addConsumer(ImageConsumer ic);`
- `public boolean isConsumer(ImageConsumer ic);`
- `public void removeConsumer(ImageConsumer ic);`
- `public void startProduction(ImageConsumer ic);`
- `public void requestTopDownLeftRightResend(ImageConsumer ic);`

Notice that all the methods require an ImageConsumer object. There are no backdoors; an ImageProducer can output only through an associated ImageConsumer. A given producer can have multiple objects as client consumers, though this is not usually the case. Typically, as soon as a consumer registers itself with a producer [`addConsumer()`], the image data is immediately delivered through the consumer's interface.

Image Consumers

The ImageProducer interface is clean and straightforward, but the ImageConsumer is quite a bit more complex. It has the following methods:

- `public void setDimensions(int width, int height);`
- `public void setProperties(Hashtable props);`
- `public void setColorModel(ColorModel model);`
- `public void setHints(int hintflags);`

- `public void setPixels(int x, int y, int w, int h, ColorModel model, byte pixels[], int off, int scansize);`
- `public void setPixels(int x, int y, int w, int h, ColorModel model, int pixels[], int off, int scansize);`
- `public void imageComplete(int status);`

Figure 13.1 shows the normal progression of calls to the ImageConsumer interface. Several methods are optional: `setProperties()`, `setHints()`, and `setColorModel()`. The core methods are first `setDimensions()`, followed by one or more calls to `setPixels()`. Finally, when there are no more `setPixels()` calls, `imageComplete()` is invoked.

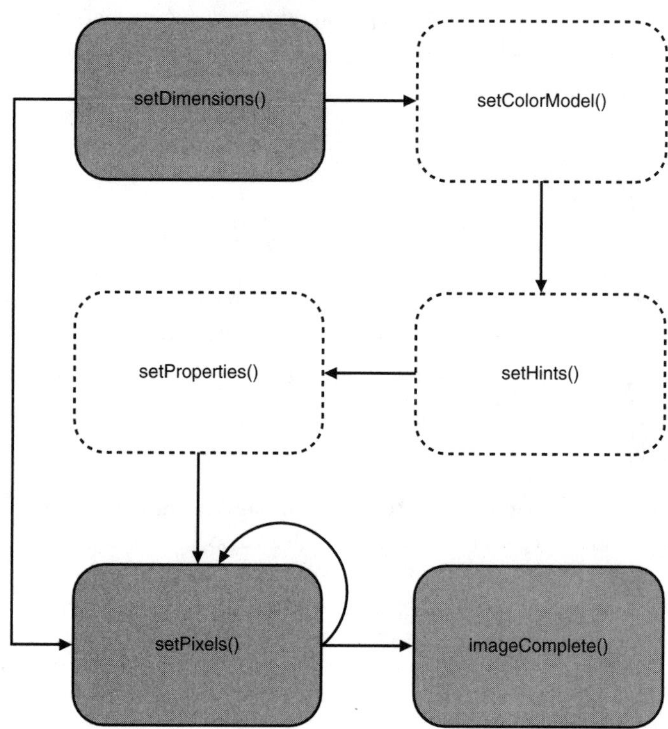

FIGURE 13.1.
Normal flow of calls to an ImageConsumer.

Each image has fixed rectangular dimensions, which are passed in `setDimensions()`. The consumer needs to save this data for future reference. The `setProperties()` method has no discernible use right now, and most consumers don't do anything with it. The hint flags, however, are a different story. *Hints* are supposed to give clues about the format of the producer's data. Table 13.1 lists the values for hint flags.

Table 13.1. Hint flag values for `setHints()`.

Name	*Meaning*
`RANDOMPIXELORDER=1`	No assumptions should be made about the delivery of pixels.
`TOPDOWNLEFTRIGHT=2`	Pixel delivery will paint in top to bottom, left to right.
`COMPLETESCANLINES=4`	Pixels will be delivered in multiples of complete rows.
`SINGLEPASS=8`	Pixels will be delivered in a single pass. No pixel will appear in more than one `setPixel()` call.
`SINGLEFRAME=16`	The image consists of a single static frame.

When all the pixel information has been transmitted, the producer will call `imageComplete()`. The status parameter will have one of three values: `IMAGEERROR=1`, `SINGLEFRAMEDONE=2`, or `STATICFRAMEDONE=3`.

`SINGLEFRAMEDONE` indicates that additional frames will follow; for example, a video camera would use this technique. Special-effect filters could also use `SINGLEFRAMEDONE`. `STATICFRAMEDONE` is used to indicate that no more pixels will be transmitted for the image. The consumer should remove itself from the producer after receiving `STATICFRAMEDONE`.

The two `setPixels()` calls provide the image data. Keep in mind that the image size was set by `setDimensions()`. The array within `setPixels()` calls does not necessarily contain all the pixels within an image. In fact, it usually contains only a rectangular subset of the total image. Figure 13.2 shows a rectangle of `setPixels()` within an entire image.

The row size of the array is the `scansize`. The width and height parameters indicate the usable pixels within the array, and the offset contains the starting index. It is up to the consumer to map the passed array onto the entire image. The sub-image's location within the total image is contained in the `x` and `y` parameters.

The ColorModel contains all needed color information for the image. The call to `setColorModel()` is purely informational because each `setPixels()` call passes a specific ColorModel parameter. No assumptions should be made about the ColorModel from `setColorModel()` calls.

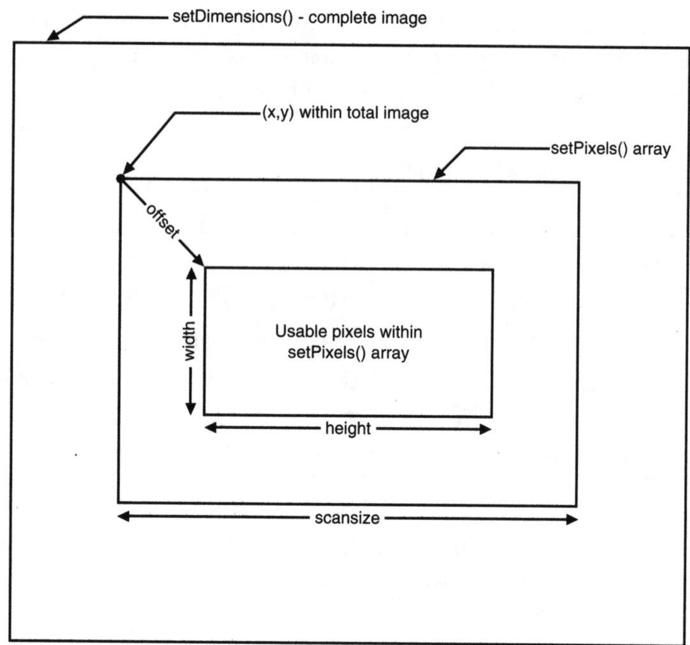

FIGURE 13.2.
The relationship of `setPixels()` *calls to an entire image.*

Filtering an Image

Image filters sit between an ImageProducer and an ImageConsumer and must implement both these interfaces. Java supplies two separate classes for using filters: FilteredImageSource and ImageFilter.

FilteredImageSource

The FilteredImageSource class implements the ImageProducer interface, which allows the class to masquerade as a real producer. When a consumer attaches to the FilteredImageSource, it's stored in an instance of the current filter. The filter class object is then given to the actual ImageProducer. When the image is rendered through the filter's interface, the data is altered before being forwarded to the actual ImageConsumer. Figure 13.3 illustrates the filtering operation.

The following is the constructor for FilteredImageSource:

```
FilteredImageSource(ImageProducer orig, ImageFilter imgf);
```

The producer and filter are stored until a consumer attaches itself to the FilterImageSource. The following lines set up the filter chain:

```
// Create the filter
ImageFilter filter = new SomeFilter();
// Use the filter to get a producer
```

```
ImageProducer p = new FilteredImageSource(myImage.getSource(), filter);
// Use the producer to create the image
Image img = createImage(p);
```

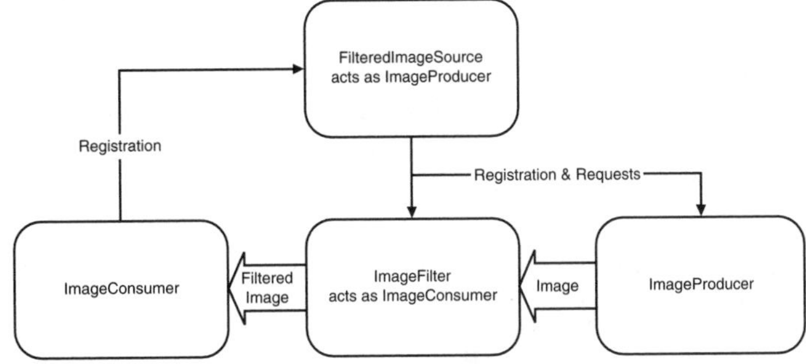

FIGURE 13.3.
Image filtering classes.

Writing a Filter

Filters always extend the ImageFilter class, which implements all the methods for an ImageConsumer. In fact, the ImageFilter class is itself a pass-through filter. It passes the data without alteration but otherwise acts as a normal image filter. The FilteredImageSource class works only with ImageFilter and its subclasses. Using ImageFilter as a base frees you from having to implement a method you have no use for, such as `setProperties()`. ImageFilter also implements one additional method:

- `public void resendTopDownLeftRight(ImageProducer ip);`

When a FilteredImageSource gets a request to resend through its ImageProducer interface, it will call the ImageFilter instead of the actual producer. ImageFilter's default resend function will call the producer and request a repaint. There are times when the filter does not want to have the image regenerated, so it can override this call and simply do nothing. One example of this type of filter is described in the section "Dynamic Image Filter: FXFilter." A special-effects filter may simply remove or obscure certain parts of an underlying image. To perform the effect, the filter merely needs to know the image dimensions, not the specific pixels it will be overwriting. `SetPixel()` calls are safely ignored, but the producer must be prevented from repainting. If your filter does not implement `setPixels()` calls, a subsequent resend request will destroy the filter's changes by writing directly to the consumer.

NOTE

If `setPixels()` is not overridden in your filter, you will probably want to override `resendTopDownLeftRight()`to prevent the image from being regenerated after your filter has altered the image.

Static Image Filter: Rotation

The SimpleRoll applet works by loading four distinct images; remember that an external paint application was used to rotate each image. Unfortunately, the paint program cannot maintain the transparency of the original image. You can see this if you change the background color of the applet. The bounding rectangle of the image shows up in gray. Instead of loading the four images, a Java rotation filter can be substituted to allow any image to be rolled. Not only would this minimize the download time, but it would also maintain the image's transparency information. A transparent foreground image also allows a background image to be added.

Pixel Rotation

To perform image rotation, you need to use some math. You can perform the rotation of points with the following formulas:

```
new_x = x * cos(angle) - y * sin(angle)
new_y = y * cos(angle) + x * sin(angle)
```

Rotation is around the z-axis. Positive angles cause counterclockwise rotation, and negative angles cause clockwise rotation. These formulas are defined for Cartesian coordinates. The Java screen is actually inverted, so the positive y-axis runs down the screen, not up. To compensate for this, invert the sign of the sine coefficients:

```
new_x = x * cos(angle) + y * sin(angle)
new_y = y * cos(angle) - x * sin(angle)
```

In addition, the sine and cosine functions compute the angle in radians. The following formula converts degrees to radians:

```
radians = degrees * PI/180;
```

This works because there are `2*PI` radians in a circle. That's all the math you'll need; now you can set up the ImageConsumer routines.

Handling `setDimensions()`

The `setDimensions()` call tells you the total size of the image. Record the size and allocate an array to hold all the pixels. Because this filter will rotate the image, the size may change. In an extreme case, the size could grow much larger than the original image because images are rectangular. If you rotate a rectangle 45 degrees, a new rectangle must be computed that contains all the pixels from the rotated image, as shown in Figure 13.4.

To calculate the new bounding rectangle, each vertex of the original image must be rotated. After rotation, the new coordinate is checked for minimum and maximum x and y values. When all four points are rotated, then you'll know what the new bounding rectangle is. Record this information as rotation space, and inform the consumer of the size after rotation.

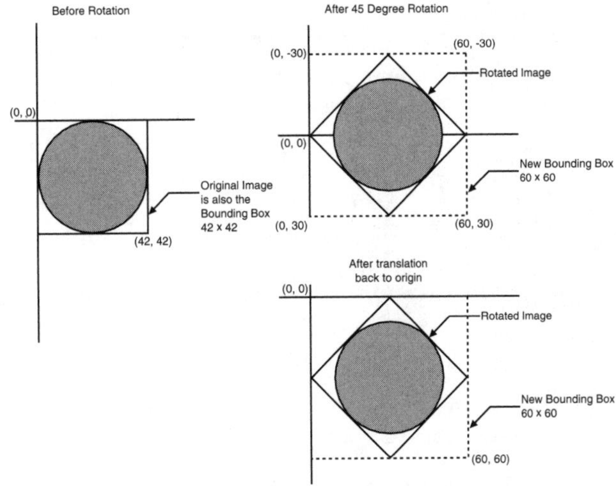

FIGURE 13.4.
New bounding rectangle after rotation.

Handling `setPixels()`

The `setPixels()` calls are very straightforward. Simply translate the pixel color into an RGB value and store it in the original image array allocated in `setDimensions()`.

Handling `imageComplete()`

The `imageComplete()` method performs all the work. After the image is final, populate a new rotation space array and return it to the consumer through the consumer's `setPixels()` routine. Finally, invoke the consumer's `imageComplete()` method. Listing 13.2 contains the entire filter.

Listing 13.2. The SpinFilter class.

```
import java.awt.*;
import java.awt.image.*;

public class SpinFilter extends ImageFilter
{
    private double angle;
    private double cos, sin;
    private Rectangle rotatedSpace;
    private Rectangle originalSpace;
    private ColorModel defaultRGBModel;
    private int inPixels[], outPixels[];

    SpinFilter(double angle)
    {
        this.angle = angle * (Math.PI / 180);
        cos = Math.cos(this.angle);
```

continues

Listing 13.2. continued

```
        sin = Math.sin(this.angle);
        defaultRGBModel = ColorModel.getRGBdefault();
    }

    private void transform(int x, int y, double out[])
    {
        out[0] = (x * cos) + (y * sin);
        out[1] = (y * cos) - (x * sin);
    }

    private void transformBack(int x, int y, double out[])
    {
        out[0] = (x * cos) - (y * sin);
        out[1] = (y * cos) + (x * sin);
    }

    public void transformSpace(Rectangle rect)
    {
        double out[] = new double[2];

        double minx = Double.MAX_VALUE;
        double miny = Double.MAX_VALUE;
        double maxx = Double.MIN_VALUE;
        double maxy = Double.MIN_VALUE;
        int w = rect.width;
        int h = rect.height;
        int x = rect.x;
        int y = rect.y;

        for ( int i = 0; i < 4; i++ )
        {
            switch (i)
            {
            case 0: transform(x + 0, y + 0, out); break;
            case 1: transform(x + w, y + 0, out); break;
            case 2: transform(x + 0, y + h, out); break;
            case 3: transform(x + w, y + h, out); break;
            }
            minx = Math.min(minx, out[0]);
            miny = Math.min(miny, out[1]);
            maxx = Math.max(maxx, out[0]);
            maxy = Math.max(maxy, out[1]);
        }
        rect.x = (int) Math.floor(minx);
        rect.y = (int) Math.floor(miny);
        rect.width = (int) Math.ceil(maxx) - rect.x;
        rect.height = (int) Math.ceil(maxy) - rect.y;
    }

    /**
     * Tell the consumer the new dimensions based on our
     * rotation of coordinate space.
     * @see ImageConsumer#setDimensions
     */
    public void setDimensions(int width, int height)
```

```
{
    originalSpace = new Rectangle(0, 0, width, height);
    rotatedSpace = new Rectangle(0, 0, width, height);
    transformSpace(rotatedSpace);
    inPixels = new int[originalSpace.width * originalSpace.height];
    consumer.setDimensions(rotatedSpace.width, rotatedSpace.height);
}

/**
 * Tell the consumer that we use the defaultRGBModel color model
 * NOTE: This overrides whatever color model is used underneath us.
 * @param model contains the color model of the image or filter
 *              beneath us (preceding us)
 * @see ImageConsumer#setColorModel
 */
public void setColorModel(ColorModel model)
{
    consumer.setColorModel(defaultRGBModel);
}

/**
 * Set the pixels in our image array from the passed
 * array of bytes.  Xlate the pixels into our default
 * color model (RGB).
 * @see ImageConsumer#setPixels
 */
public void setPixels(int x, int y, int w, int h,
                ColorModel model, byte pixels[],
                int off, int scansize)
{
    int index = y * originalSpace.width + x;
    int srcindex = off;
    int srcinc = scansize - w;
    int indexinc = originalSpace.width - w;
    for ( int dy = 0; dy < h; dy++ )
    {
        for ( int dx = 0; dx < w; dx++ )
        {
            inPixels[index++] = model.getRGB(pixels[srcindex++] & 0xff);
        }
        srcindex += srcinc;
        index += indexinc;
    }
}

/**
 * Set the pixels in our image array from the passed
 * array of integers.  Xlate the pixels into our default
 * color model (RGB).
 * @see ImageConsumer#setPixels
 */
public void setPixels(int x, int y, int w, int h,
                ColorModel model, int pixels[],
                int off, int scansize)
{
    int index = y * originalSpace.width + x;
```

continues

Listing 13.2. continued

```
        int srcindex = off;
        int srcinc = scansize - w;
        int indexinc = originalSpace.width - w;
        for ( int dy = 0; dy < h; dy++ )
        {
            for ( int dx = 0; dx < w; dx++ )
            {
                inPixels[index++] = model.getRGB(pixels[srcindex++]);
            }
            srcindex += srcinc;
            index += indexinc;
        }
    }

    /**
     * Notification that the image is complete and there will
     * be no further setPixel calls.
     * @see ImageConsumer#imageComplete
     */
    public void imageComplete(int status)
    {
        if (status == IMAGEERROR || status == IMAGEABORTED)
        {
            consumer.imageComplete(status);
            return;
        }
        double point[] = new double[2];
        int srcwidth = originalSpace.width;
        int srcheight = originalSpace.height;
        int outwidth = rotatedSpace.width;
        int outheight = rotatedSpace.height;
        int outx, outy, srcx, srcy;

        outPixels = new int[outwidth * outheight];
        outx = rotatedSpace.x;
        outy = rotatedSpace.y;
        double end[] = new double[2];
        int index = 0;
        for ( int y = 0; y < outheight; y++ )
        {
            for ( int x = 0; x < outwidth; x++)
            {
                // find the originalSpace point
                transformBack(outx + x, outy + y, point);
                srcx = (int)Math.round(point[0]);
                srcy = (int)Math.round(point[1]);

                // if this point is within the original image
                // retrieve its pixel value and store in output
                // else write a zero into the space. (0 alpha = transparent)
                if ( srcx < 0 || srcx >= srcwidth ||
                     srcy < 0 || srcy >= srcheight )
                {
                    outPixels[index++] = 0;
                }
```

```
                else
                {
                    outPixels[index++] = inPixels[(srcy * srcwidth) + srcx];
                }
            }
        }
        // write the entire new image to the consumer
        consumer.setPixels(0, 0, outwidth, outheight, defaultRGBModel,
                           outPixels, 0, outwidth);

        // tell consumer we are done
        consumer.imageComplete(status);
    }
}
```

The rotation is complex. First, as Figure 13.4 shows, the rotated object is not completely within the screen's boundary. All the rotated pixels must be translated back in relation to the origin. You can do this easily by assuming that the coordinates of rotated space are really 0,0—the trick is how the array is populated. An iteration is made along each row in rotated space. For each pixel in the row, the rotation is inverted. This yields the position of this pixel within the original space. If the pixel lies within the original image, grab its color and store it in rotated space; if it isn't, store a transparent color.

SimpleRoll Revisited

Now redo the SimpleRoll applet to incorporate the SpinFilter and background image. Instead of loading the four distinct images, apply the filter to perform the rotation:

```
/**
 * Check for the initial image load.  Once complete,
 * rotate the image for (90, 180, 270 & 360 degrees)
 * When all rotations are complete, return true
 * @returns true when all animation images are loaded
 */
boolean checkRoll()
{
    finished = false;
    // if we have not rotated the images yet
    if ( complete == false )
    {
       if ( first.checkID(0, true) )
       {
            for ( int x = 0; x < 4; x++ )
            {
                // Generate the angle in radians
                double amount = x * 90;

                // Create the filter
                ImageFilter filter = new SpinFilter(amount);

                // Use the filter to get a producer
```

```
                ImageProducer p = new FilteredImageSource(
                                      myImage.getSource(),
                                      filter);

                // Use the producer to create the image
                allImages[x] = createImage(p);
                tracker.addImage(allImages[x], 0);
            }
            complete = true;
        }
    }
    // else wait for all images to generate
    else
    {
        finished = tracker.checkID(0, true);
    }
    return finished;
}
```

Instead of waiting for the four individual images to load, the routine now waits for the four rotated images to generate. In addition, a background image is loaded.

Try running the new applet, which is in the file SpinRoll.java on the CD-ROM that comes with this book. What happened when you ran it? All that flashing is a common animation problem. Don't despair; you can eliminate it with double buffering.

Double Buffering

Double buffering is the single best way to eliminate image update flashing. Essentially, you update an offscreen image. When the drawing is complete, the offscreen image is drawn to the actual display. It's called double buffering because the offscreen image is a secondary buffer that mirrors the actual screen.

To create the offscreen buffer, use `createImage()` with only the width and height as arguments. After creating the offscreen buffer, you can acquire a graphics context and use the image in the same manner as `paint()`. Add the following lines to the `init()` method of the applet:

```
Image offScreenImage = createImage(this.size().width,
                                   this.size().height);
Graphics offScreen = offScreenImage.getGraphics();
```

When the image is completely drawn, use the following line to copy it to the real screen:

```
g.drawImage(offScreenImage, 0, 0, this);
```

In addition, the `update()` method of the component needs to be overridden in the applet. Component's version of `update()` clears the screen before calling `paint()`. The screen clear is the chief cause of flashing. Your version of `update()` should just call `paint()` without clearing the screen.

```
public void update(Graphics g)
{
    paint(g);
}
```

These changes have been incorporated in SpinRoll2, also on the CD-ROM in the file SpinRoll2.java. The new version will animate smoothly.

Dynamic Image Filter: FXFilter

SpinFilter is static; the FXFilter is dynamic. A *static filter* alters an image and sends `STATICIMAGEDONE` when the alteration is done, but a *dynamic filter* makes the effect take place over multiple frames, much like an animation. The FXFilter has four effects: *wipe left*, *wipe right*, *wipe from center out*, and *dissolve*. Each effect operates by erasing the image in stages. The filter will call `imageComplete()` many times, but instead of passing `STATICIMAGEDONE`, it specifies `SINGLEFRAMEDONE`.

Because each effect is simply a matter of writing a block of a particular color, there is no need to refer to the pixels in the original image. Therefore, you don't need to use the `setPixels()` method, so the filter functions very quickly.

Each of the wipes operates by moving a column of erased pixels over the length of the image. The width of the column is calculated to yield the number of configured iterations. The dissolve works by erasing a rectangular block at random places throughout the image. Of all the effects, dissolve is the slowest to execute because it has to calculate each random location.

In `setHints()`, the consumer is told that the filter will send random pixels. This causes the consumer to call `resendTopDownLeftRight()` when the image is complete. The filter needs to intercept the call to avoid having the just-erased image repainted by the producer in pristine form.

The filter has two constructors. If you don't specify a color, the image dissolves into transparency, allowing you to phase one image into a second image. You can also specify an optional color, which causes the image to gradually change into the passed color. You can dissolve an image into the background by passing the background color in the filter constructor. The number of iterations and paints is completely configurable. There is no hard-and-fast formula for performing these effects, so feel free to alter the values to get the result you want. Listing 13.3 contains the source for the filter.

Listing 13.3. The special-effects filter.

```
import java.awt.*;
import java.awt.image.*;
import java.util.*;

public class FXFilter extends ImageFilter
{
    private int outwidth, outheight;
    private ColorModel defaultRGBModel;
    private int dissolveColor;
```

continues

Listing 13.3. continued

```
    private int iterations = 50;
    private int paintsPer = 2;
    private static final int SCALER = 25;
    private static final int MINIMUM_BLOCK = 7;
    private int dissolve_w, dissolve_h;
    private boolean sizeSet = false;
    private Thread runThread;

    public static final int DISSOLVE = 0;
    public static final int WIPE_LR =  1;
    public static final int WIPE_RL =  2;
    public static final int WIPE_C =   3;
    private int type = DISSOLVE;

    /**
     * Dissolve to transparent constructor
     */
    FXFilter()
    {
        defaultRGBModel = ColorModel.getRGBdefault();
        dissolveColor = 0;
    }

    /**
     * Dissolve to the passed color constructor
     * @param dcolor contains the color to dissolve to
     */
    FXFilter(Color dcolor)
    {
        this();
        dissolveColor = dcolor.getRGB();
    }

    /**
     * Set the type of effect to perform.
     */
    public void setType(int t)
    {
        switch (t)
        {
        case DISSOLVE: type = t; break;
        case WIPE_LR:  type = t; break;
        case WIPE_RL:  type = t; break;
        case WIPE_C:   type = t; break;
        }
    }

    /**
     * Set the size of the dissolve blocks (pixels removed).
     */
    public void setDissolveSize(int w, int h)
    {
        if ( w < MINIMUM_BLOCK ) w = MINIMUM_BLOCK;
        if ( h < MINIMUM_BLOCK ) w = MINIMUM_BLOCK;
        dissolve_w = w;
        dissolve_h = h;
```

```
    sizeSet = true;
}

/**
 * Set the dissolve parameters. (Optional, will default to 200 & 2)
 * @param num contains the number of times to loop.
 * @param paintsPerNum contains the number of blocks to remove per paint
 */
public void setIterations(int num, int paintsPerNum)
{
    iterations = num;
    paintsPer = paintsPerNum;
}

/**
 * @see ImageConsumer#setDimensions
 */
public void setDimensions(int width, int height)
{
    outwidth = width;
    outheight = height;
    consumer.setDimensions(width, height);
}

/**
 * Don't tell consumer we send complete frames.
 * Tell them we send random blocks.
 * @see ImageConsumer#setHints
 */
public void setHints(int hints)
{
    consumer.setHints(ImageConsumer.RANDOMPIXELORDER);
}

/**
 * Override this method to keep the producer
 * from refreshing our dissolved image
 */
public void resendTopDownLeftRight(ImageProducer ip)
{
}

/**
 * Notification that the image is complete and there will
 * be no further setPixel calls.
 * @see ImageConsumer#imageComplete
 */
public void imageComplete(int status)
{
    if (status == IMAGEERROR || status == IMAGEABORTED)
    {
        consumer.imageComplete(status);
        return;
    }
    if ( status == SINGLEFRAMEDONE )
```

continues

Listing 13.3. continued

```
        {
            runThread = new RunFilter(this);
            runThread.start();
        }
        else
            filter();
    }

    public void filter()
    {
        switch ( type )
        {
        case DISSOLVE: dissolve();   break;
        case WIPE_LR:  wipeLR();     break;
        case WIPE_RL:  wipeRL();     break;
        case WIPE_C:   wipeC();      break;
        default:       dissolve();   break;
        }
        consumer.imageComplete(STATICIMAGEDONE);
    }

    /**
     * Wipe the image from left to right
     */
    public void wipeLR()
    {
        int xw = outwidth / iterations;
        if ( xw <= 0 ) xw = 1;
        int total = xw * outheight;
        int dissolvePixels[] = new int[total];
        for ( int x = 0; x < total; x++ )
            dissolvePixels[x] = dissolveColor;

        for ( int t = 0; t < (outwidth - xw); t += xw )
        {
            consumer.setPixels(t, 0, xw, outheight,
                               defaultRGBModel, dissolvePixels,
                               0, xw);
            // tell consumer we are done with this frame
            consumer.imageComplete(ImageConsumer.SINGLEFRAMEDONE);
        }
    }

    /**
     * Wipe the image from right to left
     */
    public void wipeRL()
    {
        int xw = outwidth / iterations;
        if ( xw <= 0 ) xw = 1;
        int total = xw * outheight;
        int dissolvePixels[] = new int[total];
        for ( int x = 0; x < total; x++ )
            dissolvePixels[x] = dissolveColor;
```

```
    for ( int t = outwidth - xw - 1; t >= 0; t -= xw )
    {
        consumer.setPixels(t, 0, xw, outheight,
                           defaultRGBModel, dissolvePixels,
                           0, xw);
        // tell consumer you are done with this frame
        consumer.imageComplete(ImageConsumer.SINGLEFRAMEDONE);
    }
}

/**
 * Wipe the image from the center out
 */
public void wipeC()
{
    int times = outwidth / 2;
    int xw = times / iterations;
    if ( xw <= 0 ) xw = 1;
    int total = xw * outheight;
    int dissolvePixels[] = new int[total];
    for ( int x = 0; x < total; x++ )
        dissolvePixels[x] = dissolveColor;

    int x1 = outwidth /2;
    int x2 = outwidth /2;
    while ( x2 < (outwidth - xw) )
    {
        consumer.setPixels(x1, 0, xw, outheight,
                           defaultRGBModel, dissolvePixels,
                           0, xw);
        consumer.setPixels(x2, 0, xw, outheight,
                           defaultRGBModel, dissolvePixels,
                           0, xw);

        // tell consumer we are done with this frame
        consumer.imageComplete(ImageConsumer.SINGLEFRAMEDONE);
        x1 -= xw;
        x2 += xw;
    }
}

/**
 * Dissolve the image
 */
public void dissolve()
{
    // Is the image too small to dissolve?
    if ( outwidth < MINIMUM_BLOCK && outheight < MINIMUM_BLOCK )
    {
        return;
    }
    consumer.imageComplete(ImageConsumer.SINGLEFRAMEDONE);

    if ( !sizeSet )
    {
        // Calculate the dissolve block size
```

continues

Listing 13.3. continued

```
            dissolve_w = (outwidth * SCALER) / (iterations * paintsPer);
            dissolve_h = (outheight * SCALER) / (iterations * paintsPer);

            // Minimum block size
            if ( dissolve_w < MINIMUM_BLOCK ) dissolve_w = MINIMUM_BLOCK;
            if ( dissolve_h < MINIMUM_BLOCK ) dissolve_h = MINIMUM_BLOCK;
        }

        // Initialize the dissolve pixel array
        int total = dissolve_w * dissolve_h;
        int[] dissolvePixels = new int[total];
        for ( int i = 0; i < total; i++ )
            dissolvePixels[i] = dissolveColor;

        int pos;
        double apos;
        for ( int t = 0; t < iterations; t++ )
        {
            for ( int px = 0; px < paintsPer; px++ )
            {
                // remove some pixels
                apos = Math.random() * outwidth;
                int xpos = (int)Math.floor(apos);
                apos = Math.random() * outheight;
                int ypos = (int)Math.floor(apos);
                if ( xpos - dissolve_w >= outwidth )
                    xpos = outwidth - dissolve_w - 1;
                if ( ypos - dissolve_h >= outheight )
                    ypos = outheight - dissolve_h - 1;
                consumer.setPixels(xpos, ypos, dissolve_w, dissolve_h,
                                   defaultRGBModel, dissolvePixels,
                                   0, dissolve_w);
            }
            // tell consumer we are done with this frame
            consumer.imageComplete(ImageConsumer.SINGLEFRAMEDONE);
        }
    }
}

class RunFilter extends Thread
{
    FXFilter fx = null;

    RunFilter(FXFilter f)
    {
        fx = f;
    }

    public void run()
    {
        fx.filter();
    }
}
```

You need RunFilter for image producers created from a memory image source. GIF and JPEG images both spawn a thread for their producers. Because the filter needs to loop within the `imageComplete()` method, you need a separate thread for the production. Memory images do not spawn a separate thread for their producers, so the filter has to spawn its own.

The only way to differentiate the producers is to key on their status. GIF and JPEG image producers send `STATICIMAGEDONE`, and memory images send `SINGLEFRAMEDONE`.

NOTE

If you spawn an additional thread for GIF and JPEG images, you won't be able to display the image at all. Producers that are already a separate thread need to be operated within their existing threads.

The variables `SCALER` and `MINIMUM_BLOCK` apply only to dissolves. Because a dissolve paints into random locations, there will be many overlapping squares. If the blocks are sized to exactly cover the image over the configured number of iterations, the image won't come close to dissolving. The `SCALER` parameter specifies what multiple of an image the blocks should be constructed to cover. Increasing the value yields larger dissolve blocks and guarantees a complete dissolve. A value that's too large will erase the image too quickly and ruin the effect, but a value that's too small will not dissolve enough of the image. A middle value will completely dissolve the image, but a dissolve is most effective when most of the image is erased in the beginning stages of the effect.

Corporate Presentation Applet

Many companies need presentation tools, so by using programs such as PowerPoint, you can create a slide-show–type presentation. In the remainder of this chapter, you'll create the equivalent for the Internet.

Instead of just painting images, use the FXFilter to create visually pleasing transitions between the slides. The applet is called PresentImage. It reads in a series of images labeled with an *s* and the image number (for example, s0.gif, s1.gif, and so on). The images form the input for the slide show.

How the PresentImage Applet Works

Listing 13.4 shows the complete PresentImage applet. The `paint()` method has been broken into separate routines. First, `paint()` clears the offscreen image, then one of the update routines is executed according to the class variable `inFX`.

Listing 13.4. The PresentImage applet.

```
import java.applet.*;
import java.awt.*;
import java.awt.image.*;
import java.io.*;
import SpinFilter;
import FXFilter;

public class PresentImage extends Applet
    implements Runnable
{
    private int max_images;
    private int pause_time;
    private boolean init = false;  // true after init is called
    Image allImages[] = null;      // holds the rotated versions
    Thread animation = null;
    MediaTracker tracker = null;   // to track rotations of initial image
    boolean applyFX = false;       // true to switch the backgrounds
    boolean inFX = false;          // true when performing FX
    boolean FXstarted = false;     // true after imageUpdate called for FX
    Image offScreenImage = null;   // the double buffer
    Graphics offScreen = null;     // The graphics for double buffer
    int currentID = 0;             // Image number to retrieve
    Image currentImage = null;     // Image to draw
    Image newImage = null;         // Image to transition to
    Image FXoldImg, FXnewImg;      // the FX background images
    Image text1, text2;
    long waitTime;
    int textID = 0;
    int MAX_MSG = 5;

    /**
     * Standard initialization method for an applet
     */
    public void init()
    {
        if ( init == false )
        {
            init = true;
            tracker = new MediaTracker(this);
            max_images = getIntegerParameter("IMAGES", 6);
            pause_time = getIntegerParameter("PAUSE", 10);
            allImages = new Image[max_images];
            for ( int x = 0; x < max_images; x++ )
            {
                allImages[x] = getImage(getCodeBase(),
                                        "images/s" + x + ".gif");
                tracker.addImage(allImages[x], x);
            }
            offScreenImage = createImage(this.size().width,
                                         this.size().height);
            offScreen = offScreenImage.getGraphics();
            text1 = createImage(384, 291);
            text2 = createImage(384, 291);
            currentImage = nextText();
        }
    }
```

```
public int getIntegerParameter(String p, int def)
{
    int retval = def;

    String str = getParameter(p);
    if ( str == null )
        System.out.println("ERROR: " + p + " parameter is missing");
    else
        retval = Integer.valueOf(str).intValue();
    return retval;
}

/**
 * Standard paint routine for an applet.
 * @param g contains the Graphics class to use for painting
 */
public void paint(Graphics g)
{
    offScreen.setColor(getBackground());
    offScreen.fillRect(0, 0, this.size().width, this.size().height);
    if ( inFX )
        updateFX();
    else
        updateScreen();
    g.drawImage(offScreenImage, 0, 0, this);
}

public void updateScreen()
{
    if ( currentImage != null )
        offScreen.drawImage(currentImage, 0, 0, this);
    if ( applyFX )
    {
       applyFX = false;
       FXfromto(currentImage, newImage);
    }
}

/**
 * Override component's version to keep from clearing
 * the screen.
 */
public void update(Graphics g)
{
    paint(g);
}

/**
 * Do the FX.  Draw the new image if the FX image
 * is complete and ready to display
 */
public void updateFX()
{
    if ( FXstarted)
        offScreen.drawImage(FXnewImg, 0, 0, this);
```

continues

Listing 13.4. continued

```
        offScreen.drawImage(FXoldImg, 0, 0, this);
    }

    /**
     * Dissolve from one image into another
     * @param oldImg is the top image to dissolve
     * @param new Img is the background image to dissolve into
     */

    int filterType = FXFilter.WIPE_C;
    public void FXfromto(Image oldImg, Image newImg)
    {
        ImageProducer p;
        FXFilter filter = new FXFilter();
        filter.setType(filterType);
        switch ( filterType )
        {
        case FXFilter.WIPE_LR: filterType = FXFilter.WIPE_RL;  break;
        case FXFilter.WIPE_RL: filterType = FXFilter.WIPE_C;   break;
        case FXFilter.WIPE_C:  filterType = FXFilter.DISSOLVE; break;
        case FXFilter.DISSOLVE: filterType = FXFilter.WIPE_LR; break;
        }

        // Use the filter to get a producer
        p = new FilteredImageSource(oldImg.getSource(), filter);

        // Use the producer to create the image
        FXoldImg = createImage(p);
        FXnewImg = newImg;
        inFX = true;
        FXstarted = false;
        offScreen.drawImage(FXoldImg, 0, 0, this);  // start the FX
    }

    /**
     * Monitor the FX
     */
    public boolean imageUpdate(Image whichOne, int flags,
                               int x, int y, int w, int h)
    {
        if ( whichOne != FXoldImg ) return false;
        if ( (flags & (FRAMEBITS ¦ ALLBITS) ) != 0 )
        {
            FXstarted = true;
            repaint();
        }
        if ( (flags & ALLBITS) != 0 )
        {
            currentImage = FXnewImg;
            inFX = false;
            repaint();
        }
        return inFX;
    }

    /**
```

```
     * Standard start method for an applet.
     * Spawn the animation thread.
     */
    public void start()
    {
        if ( animation == null )
        {
            currentID = 0;
            animation = new Thread(this);
            animation.start();
        }
    }

    /**
     * Standard stop method for an applet.
     * Stop the animation thread.
     */
    public void stop()
    {
        if ( animation != null )
        {
            animation.stop();
            animation = null;
        }
    }

    public Image nextText()
    {
        Image img;

        if ( (textID & 0x01) != 0 )
            img = text1;
        else
            img = text2;
        Graphics g = img.getGraphics();

        switch ( textID )
        {
        case 0:
            g.setColor(getBackground());
            g.fillRect(0, 0, 384, 291);
            g.setColor(Color.blue);
            g.drawString("About to begin...", 152, 130);
            break;
        case 1:
            g.setColor(Color.blue);
            g.fillRect(0, 0, 384, 291);
            g.setColor(Color.white);
            g.drawString("A presentation by...", 152, 130);
            break;
        case 2:
            g.setColor(Color.black);
            g.fillRect(0, 0, 384, 291);
            g.setColor(Color.white);
            g.drawString("Steve Ingram", 152, 130);
            break;
```

continues

Listing 13.4. continued

```
        case 3:
            g.setColor(Color.blue);
            g.fillRect(0, 0, 384, 291);
            g.setColor(Color.white);
            g.drawString("From the book...", 152, 130);
            break;
        case 4:
            g.setColor(Color.black);
            g.fillRect(0, 0, 384, 291);
            g.setColor(Color.white);
            g.drawString("Developing Professional Java Applets", 100, 130);
            break;
        case 5:
            g.setColor(Color.yellow);
            g.fillRect(0, 0, 384, 291);
            g.setColor(Color.black);
            g.drawString("Publishing in June!", 140, 130);
            break;
        case -1:
            g.setColor(Color.black);
            g.fillRect(0, 0, 384, 291);
            g.setColor(Color.white);
            g.drawString("Thanks for watching!", 140, 130);
            break;
        default:
            img = null;
            break;
        }
        textID++;
        return img;
    }

    /**
     * This applet's run method.
     */
    public void run()
    {
        for ( int x = 0; x < max_images; x++ )
            allImages[x].flush();
        // Wait for the first image to load
        while ( !checkLoad() || textID <= MAX_MSG )
        {
            newImage = nextText();
            if ( newImage != null )
            {
                setTimer(6);
                applyFX = true;
                repaint();
                waitTimer();
            }
            else
                sleep(1000);
        }
        while (true)
```

```
    {
        setTimer();
        newImage = allImages[currentID];
        applyFX = true;
        repaint();
        currentID++;
        if ( currentID == max_images )
        {
            waitTimer();
            textID = -1;
            newImage = nextText();
            applyFX = true;
            repaint();
            setTimer();
            waitTimer();
            return;
        }
        while ( !checkLoad() )
            sleep(250);
        waitTimer();
    }
}

public void waitTimer()
{
    long newTime = System.currentTimeMillis();

    if ( newTime < waitTime )
        sleep((int)(waitTime - newTime));
    while ( inFX ) sleep(1000);
}

public void setTimer()
{
    waitTime = System.currentTimeMillis() + (pause_time * 1000);
}

public void setTimer(int t)
{
    waitTime = System.currentTimeMillis() + (t * 1000);
}

/**
 * @returns true new image is loaded
 */
boolean checkLoad()
{
    return tracker.checkID(currentID, true);
}

/**
 * A simple sleep routine
 * @param a the number of milliseconds to sleep
 */
private void sleep(int a)
```

continues

Listing 13.4. continued

```
    {
        try
        {
            Thread.currentThread().sleep(a);
        }
        catch (InterruptedException e)
        {
        }
    }
}
```

When `inFX` is `false`, `updateScreen()` is executed to paint the current image. If `applyFX` is `true`, then it's time to switch images.

Method `Fxfromto()` prepares the image transition. First a filter is created, and the filter type is set. Each transition uses a different effect of the filter. The current image is used as the producer for the filter:

```
// Use the filter to get a producer
p = new FilteredImageSource(oldImg.getSource(), filter);
```

The new producer is then used to create an image that is stored in the variable `FXoldImg`. This will become the new foreground image during the transition:

```
FXoldImg = createImage(p);
```

Because `updateScreen()` does not reference this new image, a separate routine needs to perform the paint. Setting flag `inFX` causes `updateFX()`, instead of `updateScreen()`, to be called.

Normally, `updateFX()` would first paint the new image followed by the filtered old image. Unfortunately, the filtered image takes some time before it will begin painting. The new image can be drawn only after the filtered image is available. Flag `FXstarted` is used to signal when the filtered image is ready. The flag is set within an `imageUpdate()` method. If you recall, `imageUpdate()` is within the ImageObserver interface. When the filtered image is prepared, ImageObserver's update routine is invoked with `FRAMEBITS` set. Until `FXstarted` is `true`, `updateFX()` will not paint the new image.

All the update routines draw to the offscreen image created in the `init()` method. The last act of the `paint()` routine is to draw the offscreen image onto the actual screen.

The basic architecture of the applet is to read in a series of images from the images directory. Applet parameters control the number of images read, as well as the minimum amount of time each image takes to appear. The reason this time is a minimum is because a new image will not be displayed until it has fully loaded. Large images will take much longer to load than the minimum time. Timing is managed by `setTimer()` and `waitTimer()`.

Before the first image displays, a series of credits appears, which are text strings painted as images. Besides providing a nice introduction, they also offer a visual distraction while the first image is loaded.

Currently, photorealistic images need too much bandwidth for effective presentation over the Internet, but this will probably be a short-term problem. This applet is very good for small text slides, but large images take too long to load. Corporate intranets don't have bandwidth limitations, so PresentImage is ideal for elaborate LAN-based productions.

Summary

This chapter covers advanced image concepts, such as animation and double buffering, as well as the details behind the Java image model. This chapter also demonstrates writing and using image filters, rotation concepts, and special effects. Finally, a corporate slide show applet is demonstrated to illustrate the principles explained in this chapter.

Images give Java tremendous flexibility. Once you master image concepts, the endless possibilities of the Java graphics system are yours to explore.

14

Advanced Image Processing

This chapter's project, one that views the Mandelbrot set, gives you examples of some of the more advanced concepts you have been introduced to. The Mandelbrot set is the most spectacular example of fractals, which represents one of the hot scientific topics of recent years. With the applets in this chapter, you can view or generate an original Mandelbrot image and zoom in and out of it to produce new portions of the set.

Since the Mandelbrot set can take a while to generate—requiring millions of calculations—it gives you a chance to combine threads and image filters so you can view the set as it's being generated. You might also want to save the Mandelbrot images. The BmpClass, introduced in Part III, that converts a BMP formatted file into a Java image, is enhanced so you can save the Mandelbrot data as a BMP file. You can then view or modify it with any tool that can handle the BMP format. Finally, the chapter concludes by showing how you can auto-document the source of a Java class into a HTML file. This can be viewed by a browser and has links to other classes.

Since you have already been introduced to most aspects of Java, this chapter will jump straight into the project. Topics will be introduced as appropriate.

Chapter Project

There are actually two applets in this chapter. The first applet, MandelApp, is used to generate a full Mandelbrot set. The tools and BMP file produced by this applet are input into the second applet, called MandelZoomApp. This applet displays a Mandelbrot set, then allows you to zoom (magnify) portions of the set so you can inspect its fractal qualities. You can also return to previous images and zoom into another area.

If you want to use the file-saving capabilities of this program, you need to run it from something that does not prevent file saving, such as the appletviewer program. You can run the program in a browser like Netscape, though; it will be able to do everything except save the images as files.

Class Organization

Table 14.1 lists the classes used in this chapter's applets. Most of the classes are new, so their names are set in boldface type. Existing classes that were modified have their names italicized.

Table 14.1. Mandelbrot project classes and interfaces.

Class/Interface	*Description*
BmpImage	For BMP-Image conversion.
CalculatorFilter	ImageFilter that produces updates of images as they are generated.

Class/Interface	*Description*
CalculatorFilterNotify	Interface that defines ways an ImageFilter can receive data updates.
CalculatorImage	Used to tie a calculation object, an image, and a CalculatorFilter together.
CalculatorProducer	Interface that defines a mechanism for establishing how an ImageFilter can update a calculation class.
MandelApp	An Applet that produces a full Mandelbrot image and lets you save it to a file.
MandelEntry	Accessor class for keeping information about a Mandelbrot image.
Mandelbrot	A Thread that produces Mandelbrot data for the specified parameters. It implements CalculatorProducer to get started by a filter. It uses CalculatorFilterNotify to update a filter with new data.
MandelZoomApp	An Applet that displays the full Mandelbrot set and allows you to zoom in and out of the set.

How It Works

Because the Mandelbrot set can take quite a while to generate, it was designed by combining a calculation thread with an image filter so you can see the results as they are generated. However, understanding how the classes interrelate is a little tricky. Figure 14.1 shows the workflow involved in producing a Mandelbrot image. Understanding this flow is the key to understanding this project.

FIGURE 14.1.
Workflow of producing a Mandelbrot image.

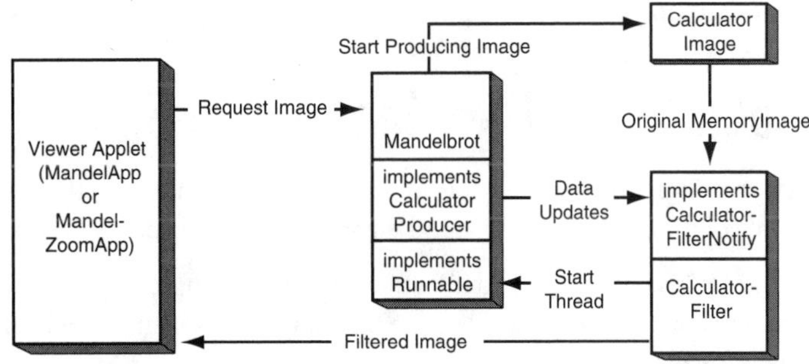

The process begins when an applet displaying Mandelbrot sets constructs a Mandelbrot object. (In this project, the two Applet classes are MandelApp and MandelZoomApp.) The

Mandelbrot object, in turn, creates an instance of the CalculatorImage class. The Mandelbrot set passes itself as a part of the CalculatorImage constructor. It is referenced as a CalculatorProducer object, an interface that the Mandelbrot class implements. This interface implementation will be used to communicate with the image filter.

In the next step, the applet requests a Mandelbrot image. This is initiated by calling the `getImage()` method of the Mandelbrot object, which in turn leads to a call to a like-named method of the CalculatorImage object. At this point, the CalculatorImage object first creates a color palette by using an instance of the ImageColorModel class, then creates a MemoryImageSource object. This object, which implements ImageProducer, produces an image initialized to all zeros (black); it's combined with an instance of the CalculatorFilter class to produce a FilteredImageSource.

When the MemoryImageSource object produces its empty image, it is passed to the CalculatorFilter, which takes the opportunity to produce the calculated image. It does this by kicking off the thread of the image to be calculated. The CalculatorFilter doesn't know that it is the Mandelbrot set that's calculated—it just knows that some calculation needs to occur in the CalculatorProducer object in which it has a reference.

Once the Mandelbrot thread is started, it begins the long calculations to produce a Mandelbrot set. Whenever it finishes a section of the set, it notifies the filter with new data through the CalculatorFilterNotify interface. The filter, in turn, lets the viewing applet know that it has new data to display by updating the corresponding ImageConsumer, which causes the applet's `imageUpdate()` method to be called. This causes a repaint, and the new image data to be displayed. This process repeats until the full image is created.

As you have probably observed, this is a complicated process. Although the mechanics of image processing were introduced in Part III, it doesn't hurt to have another example. The Calculator classes here are meant to provide a generic approach toward manipulating images that need long calculations. You can replace the Mandelbrot class with some other calculation thread that implements CalculatorProducer, and everything should work. A good exercise would be to replace Mandelbrot with another fractal calculation or some other scientific imaging calculation (I found that replacing Mandelbrot with a Julia fractal class calculation was very easy).

Fractals and the Mandelbrot Set

Before going into the internals of the classes that make up this project, it's worth spending a couple of moments to understand what's behind the images produced by the Mandelbrot class.

In the 1970s, Benoit Mandelbrot at IBM was using computers to study curves generated by iterations of complex formulas. He found that these curves had unusual characteristics, one of which is called *self-similarity*. The curves have a series of patterns that repeat themselves when inspected more closely.

One of the characteristics of the curves Mandelbrot studied was that they could be described as having a certain dimensional quality that Mandelbrot termed "fractal." One of the fractals that

Mandelbrot was investigating is called a *Julia set*. By mapping the set in a certain way, Mandelbrot came across a set that turned out to include all the Julia sets—a kind of a master set that was deemed the *Mandelbrot set*. This set has several spectacular features, all of them beautiful. The most striking of these is its self-similarity and a extraordinary sensitivity to initial conditions. As you explore the Mandelbrot set, you will be amazed by both its seeming chaos and exquisite order.

Figure 14.2 shows the famous Mandelbrot set, produced by this chapter's MandelApp applet. The figures in this chapter show the kind of images that appear when you zoom into various places in this set. The Mandelbrot set is based on a seemingly simple iterated function, shown in Formula 14.1.

FIGURE 14.2.
The full Mandelbrot set image.

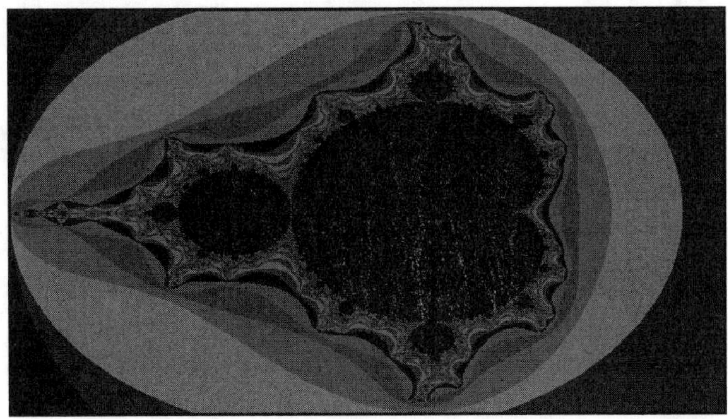

Formula 14.1. Formula for calculating the Mandelbrot set.

$$z_{n+1}=z_n^2 + c$$

In Formula 14.1, `z` and `c` are complex numbers. The Mandelbrot set is concerned with what happens when `z0` is zero and `c` is set over a range of values. The real part of `c` is set to the x-axis, and the complex portion corresponds to the y-axis. A color is mapped to each point based on how quickly the corresponding value of `c` causes the iteration to reach infinity. The process of "zooming" in and out of the Mandelbrot set is equivalent to defining what ranges of `c` are going to be explored. It is amazing that something so simple can yield patterns so sophisticated!

NOTE

If you are more interested in chaos and fractals, there are a lot of places to turn. *Chaos* by James Gleick (Penguin, 1987) is a layman's introduction to the ideas and discoveries that gave rise to chaos theory and the study of fractals. Mandelbrot's *The Fractal Geometry of Nature* (W.H. Freeman, 1983) lays out his ideas on fractals and nature.

For a rigorous mathematical treatment of fractals, see the beautiful book *Fractals Everywhere* (Academic Press, 1988), written by one of the foremost figures in fractals, Michael Barnsley. Among other things, Barnsley is a major innovator on how to use fractal geometrics to achieve high rates of data compression.

For a no-nonsense approach to writing programs that display fractals, see *Fractal Programming in C* by Roger T. Stevens (M&T Books, 1989). The algorithms for the Mandelbrot set were developed from this book. The C programs in this book map very easily to Java—except for the underlying graphics tools, which were developed for MS-DOS. However, the image calculation classes created in this chapter aim to fill this gap. With Stevens's book and these classes, you should be able to move his C code right over to Java and begin exploring the amazing world of fractals!

Using the Applets

There are two applets in this chapter. The first applet, MandelApp, generates the full Mandelbrot set. This will take a little while, depending on your computer; for example, on a 486DX2-50 PC, it takes a couple of minutes. When the image is complete, indicated by a message on the browser's status bar, you can save the image to a BMP formatted file by clicking anywhere on the applet's display area. The file will be called mandel.bmp. Remember to run this applet from a program, such as appletviewer, that lets applets write to disk.

The other applet, MandelAppZoom, is more full-featured. It begins by loading the Mandelbrot bitmap specified by an HTML applet parameter tag. The default `mandel1` corresponds to a BMP file and a data file that specifies x-y parameter values—included on this book's CD-ROM.

Once the image is up, you can pick regions to zoom in on by clicking on a point in the image, then dragging the mouse to the endpoint of the region you want to display. Enter `z` or `Z` on the keyboard, and the applet creates the image representing the new region of the Mandelbrot set. The key to this applet is patience! The calculations can take a little while to set up and run. The applet tries to help your patience by updating the status bar to indicate what is going on. Furthermore, the image filter displays each column of the set as the calculations advance.

You might select a region that doesn't appear to have anything interesting to show when you zoom in on it. You can stop a calculation in the middle by entering `a` or `A` on the keyboard. The applet will take a moment to wrap up, but then you can proceed. When you are having problems finding an interesting region to look at, try increasing the size of the highlighted area. This will yield a bigger area that is generated, giving you a better feel for what should be inspected. You get the best results by working with medium-sized highlighted regions, rather than large or small ones.

Figures 14.3 to 14.6 show what some of the zoomed-in regions of the Mandelbrot set look like. Figure 14.3 is a large area picked above the black "circles" of the full Mandelbrot set; Figure 14.5 explores an area between two of the black areas. The richest displays seem to occur at the boundaries of the black areas. The black color indicates that the particular value takes a long time to reach infinity. Consequently, these are also the regions that take the longest to calculate. You get what you pay for!

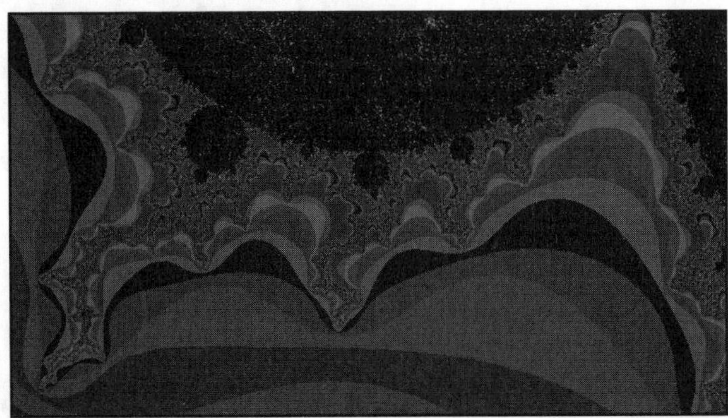

FIGURE 14.3.
Zoom in over black regions of Figure 14.2.

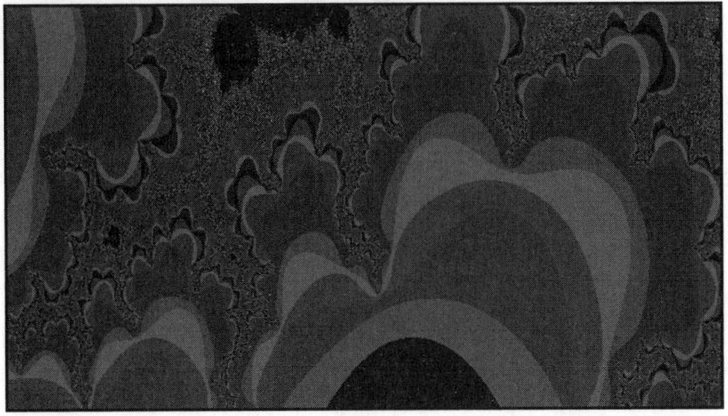

FIGURE 14.4.
Zoom in of Figure 14.3.

The zoom applet maintains a cache of processed images so you can move back and forth among the processed images. Table 14.2 lists the text codes for using the zoom applet.

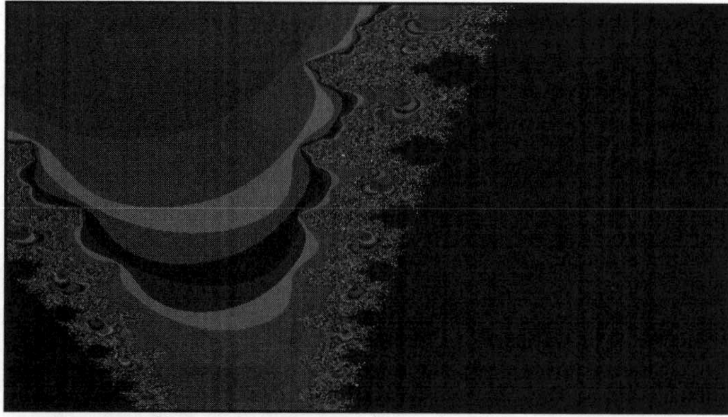

FIGURE 14.5.
Zoom in between black regions of Figure 14.2.

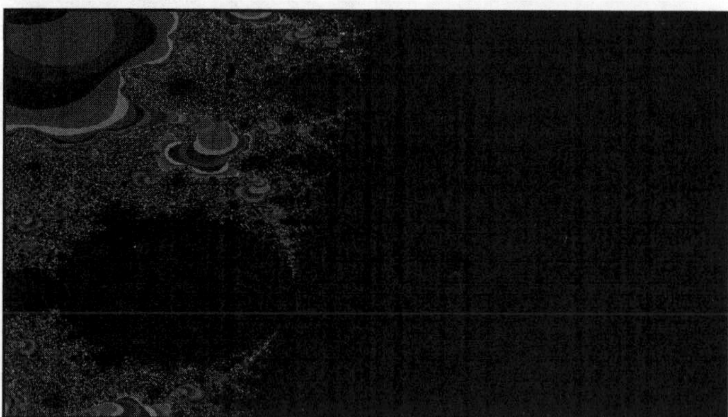

FIGURE 14.6.
Zoom in of Figure 14.5.

Table 14.2. Codes for controlling the Mandelbrot applet.

Characters	*Action*
`A` or `a`	Abort current Mandelbrot calculation.
`B` or `b`	Go to previous image.
`F` or `f`	Go to next image.
`C` or `c`	Remove all but full image from memory.
`N` or `n`	Go to next image.
`P` or `p`	Go to previous image.
`S` or `s`	Save the current image to a BMP file prefixed by `tempMandel`.
`Z` or `z`	Zoom in on currently highlighted region.

The Mandelbrot Class

The Mandelbrot class, shown in Listing 14.1, calculates the Mandelbrot set. It implements the Runnable interface, so it can run as a thread, and also implements the CalculatorProducer interface, so it can update an image filter of progress made in its calculations.

There are two constructors for the Mandelbrot class. The default constructor produces the full Mandelbrot set and takes the dimensions of the image to calculate. The Real and Imagine variables in the constructors and the `run()` method are used to map the x-y axis to the real and imaginary portions of `c` in Formula 14.1. The other constructor is used to zoom in on a user-defined mapping.

A couple of the other variables are worth noting. The variable `maxIterations` represents when to stop calculating a number. If this number, set to `512`, is reached, then the starting value of `c` takes a long time to head toward infinity. The variable `maxSize` is a simpler indicator of how quickly the current value grows. How the current calculation is related to these variables is mapped to a specific color; the higher the number, the slower the growth. If you have a fast computer, you can adjust these variables to get a richer or duller expression of the Mandelbrot set.

Once the thread is started (by the CalculatorFilter object through the `start()` method), the `run()` method calculates the Mandelbrot values and stores a color corresponding to the growth rate of the current complex number into a pixel array. When a column is complete, it uses the CalculateFilterNotify to let the related filter know that new data has been produced. It also checks to see whether you want to abort the calculation. Note how it synchronizes the `stopCalc` boolean object in the `run()` and `stop()` methods.

The calculation can take a while to complete. Still, it takes only a couple of minutes on a 486-based PC. This performance is quite a testament to Java! With other interpreted, portable languages you would probably be tempted to use the reset button because the calculations would take so long. With Java you get fast visual feedback on how the set unfolds.

A good exercise is to save any partially developed Mandelbrot set; you can use the `saveBMP()` method here. You also need some kind of data file to indicate where the calculation was stopped.

Listing 14.1. The Mandelbrot class.

```
import java.awt.image.*;
import java.awt.Image;
import java.lang.*;

// Class for producing a Mandelbrot set image...
public class Mandelbrot implements Runnable, CalculatorProducer {
   int width;  // The dimensions of the image...
   int height;
```

continues

Listing 14.1. continued

```
CalculateFilterNotify filter; // Keeps track of image production...
int pix[]; // Pixels used to construct image...
CalculatorImage img;
// General Mandelbrot parameters...
int numColors = 256;
int maxIterations = 512;
int maxSize = 4;
double RealMax,ImagineMax,RealMin,ImagineMin;  // Define sizes to build...
private Boolean stopCalc = new Boolean(false);  // Stop calculations...

// Create standard Mandelbrot set
public Mandelbrot(int width,int height) {
   this.width = width;
   this.height = height;
   RealMax = 1.20;  // Default starting sizes...
   RealMin = -2.0;
   ImagineMax = 1.20;
   ImagineMin = -1.20;
}

// Create zoom of Mandelbrot set
public Mandelbrot(int width,int height,double RealMax,double RealMin,
 double ImagineMax,double ImagineMin) {
   this.width = width;
   this.height = height;
   this.RealMax = RealMax;  // Default starting sizes...
   this.RealMin = RealMin;
   this.ImagineMax = ImagineMax;
   this.ImagineMin = ImagineMin;
}

// Start producing the Mandelbrot set...
public Image getImage() {
   img = new CalculatorImage(width,height,this);
   return img.getImage();
}

// Start thread to produce data...
public void start(int pix[],CalculateFilterNotify filter) {
   this.pix = pix;
   this.filter = filter;
   new Thread(this).start();
}

// See if user wants to stop before completion...
public void stop() {
   synchronized (stopCalc) {
      stopCalc = Boolean.TRUE;
   }
   System.out.println("GOT STOP!");
}

// Create data here...
public void run() {
   // Establish Mandelbrot parameters...
   double Q[] = new double[height];
```

```
      // Pixdata is for image filter updates...
      int pixdata[] = new int[height];
      double P,diffP,diffQ, x, y, x2, y2;
      int color, row, column,index;

      System.out.println("RealMax = " + RealMax + " RealMin = " + RealMin +
          " ImagineMax = " + ImagineMax + " ImagineMin = " + ImagineMin);
      // Setup calculation parameters...
      diffP = (RealMax - RealMin)/(width);
      diffQ = (ImagineMax - ImagineMin)/(height);
      Q[0] = ImagineMax;
      color = 0;

      // Setup delta parameters...
      for (row = 1; row < height; row++)
         Q[row] = Q[row-1] - diffQ;
      P = RealMin;

      // Start calculating!
      for (column = 0; column < width; column++) {
         for (row = 0; row < height; row++) {
            x = y = x2 = y2 = 0.0;
            color = 1;
            while ((color < maxIterations) &&
               ((x2 + y2) < maxSize)) {
                  x2 = x * x;
                  y2 = y * y;
                  y = (2*x*y) + Q[row];
                  x = x2 - y2 + P;
                  ++color;
            }
            // plot...
            index = (row * width) + column;
            pix[index] = (int)(color % numColors);
            pixdata[row] = pix[index];
         } // end row
         // Update column after each iteration...
         filter.dataUpdateColumn(column,pixdata);
         P += diffP;
         // See if we were told to stop...
         synchronized (stopCalc) {
            if (stopCalc == Boolean.TRUE) {
               column = width;
               System.out.println("RUN: Got stop calc!");
            }
         }  // end sync
      } // end col

      // Tell filter that we're done producing data...
      System.out.println("FILTER: Data Complete!");
      filter.setComplete();
   }

   // Save the Mandelbrot set as a BMP file...
   public void saveBMP(String filename) {
      img.saveBMP(filename,pix);
   }
}
```

CalculateFilterNotify Interface

The CalculateFilterNotify interface defines the methods needed to update an image filter that works with a calculation thread. As shown in Listing 14.2, the "data" methods are used for conveying a new batch of data to the filter. The `setComplete()` method indicates that the calculations are complete.

Listing 14.2. The CalculateFilterNotify interface.

```
/* Interface for defining methods for updating a
   Calculator Filter... */
public interface CalculateFilterNotify {
   public void dataUpdate();   // Update everything...
   public void dataUpdateRow(int row); // Update one row...
   public void dataUpdateColumn(int col,int pixdata[]);  // Update one column...
   public void setComplete();
}
```

CalculatorProducer Interface

The CalculatorProducer interface, as shown in Listing 14.3, defines the method called when a calculation filter is ready to kick off a thread that produces the data used to generate an image. The CalculateFilterNotify object passed to the `start()` method is called by the producer whenever new data is yielded.

Listing 14.3. The CalculatorProducer interface.

```
// Interface for a large calculation to produce image...
interface CalculatorProducer {
   public void start(int pix[],CalculateFilterNotify cf);
}
```

The CalculatorFilter Class

The CalculatorFilter class in Listing 14.4 is a subclass of ImageFilter. Its purpose is to receive image data produced by some long calculation (like the Mandelbrot set) and update any consumer of the the new data's image. The CalculatorProducer, indicated by variable `cp`, is what produces the data.

Since the ImageFilter class was explained in detail in Part III, issues related to this class are not repeated here. However, a couple of things should be pointed out. When the image is first requested, the filter gets the dimensions the consumer wants by a call of the `setDimensions()`

method. At this point, the CalculatorFilter will allocate a large array holding the color values for each pixel.

When the original ImageProducer is finished creating the original image, the filter's `imageComplete()` method will be called, but the filter needs to override this method. In this case, the CalculatorFilter will start the CalculatorProducer thread, passing it the pixel array to put in its updates. Whenever the CalculatorProducer has new data, it will call one of the four methods specified by the CalculateFilterNotify interface: `dataUpdate()`, `dataUpdateRow()`, `dataUpdateColumn()`, or `setComplete()`. (The `dataUpdateColumn()` method is called by the Mandelbrot calculation since it operates on a column basis.) In each of these cases, the filter updates the appropriate consumer pixels by using the `setPixels()` method, then calls the consumer's `imageComplete()` method to indicate the nature of the change. For the three "data" methods, the updates are only partial, so a SINGLEFRAMEDONE flag is sent. The `setComplete()` method, on the other hand, indicates that everything is complete, so it sets a STATICIMAGEDONE flag.

Listing 14.4. The CalculatorFilter class.

```
import java.awt.image.*;
import java.awt.Image;
import java.awt.Toolkit;
import java.lang.*;

public class CalculatorFilter extends ImageFilter
 implements CalculateFilterNotify {
   private ColorModel defaultRGBModel;
   private int width, height;
   private int pix[];
   private boolean complete = false;
   private CalculatorProducer cp;
   private boolean cpStart = false;

   public CalculatorFilter(ColorModel cm,CalculatorProducer cp) {
      defaultRGBModel = cm;
      this.cp = cp;
   }

   public void setDimensions(int width, int height) {
      this.width = width;
      this.height = height;
      pix = new int[width * height];
      consumer.setDimensions(width,height);
   }

   public void setColorModel(ColorModel model) {
      consumer.setColorModel(defaultRGBModel);
   }

   public void setHints(int hints) {
      consumer.setHints(ImageConsumer.RANDOMPIXELORDER);
   }
```

continues

Listing 14.4. continued

```
    public void resendTopDownLeftRight(ImageProducer p) {
     }


    public void setPixels(int x, int y, int w, int h,
       ColorModel model, int pixels[],int off,int scansize) {
    }

    public void imageComplete(int status) {
      if (!cpStart) {
         cpStart = true;
         dataUpdate();  // Show empty pixels...
         cp.start(pix,this);
      } // end if
      if (complete)
          consumer.imageComplete(ImageConsumer.STATICIMAGEDONE);
    }

    // Called externally to notify that more data has been created
    // Notify consumer so they can repaint...
    public void dataUpdate() {
      consumer.setPixels(0,0,width,height,
                defaultRGBModel,pix,0,width);
      consumer.imageComplete(ImageConsumer.SINGLEFRAMEDONE);
    }

    // External call to update a specific pixel row...
    public void dataUpdateRow(int row) {
      // The key thing here is the second to last parameter (offset)
      // which states where to start getting data from the pix array...
      consumer.setPixels(0,row,width,1,
                defaultRGBModel,pix,(width * row),width);
      consumer.imageComplete(ImageConsumer.SINGLEFRAMEDONE);
    }

    // External call to update a specific pixel column...
    public void dataUpdateColumn(int col,int pixdata[]) {
      // The key thing here is the second to last parameter (offset)
      // which states where to start getting data from the pix array...
      consumer.setPixels(col,0,1,height,
                defaultRGBModel,pixdata,0,1);
      consumer.imageComplete(ImageConsumer.SINGLEFRAMEDONE);
    }

    // Called from external calculating program when data has
    // finished being calculated...
    public void setComplete() {
       complete = true;
       consumer.setPixels(0,0,width,height,
          defaultRGBModel,pix,0,width);
       consumer.imageComplete(ImageConsumer.STATICIMAGEDONE);
    }
}
```

The CalculatorImage Class

The CalculatorImage class, shown in Listing 14.5, is the glue between the CalculatorProducer class that produces the image data and the CalculatorFilter that manages it. When an image is requested with the `getImage()` method, the CalculatorImage creates a color palette through an instance of the ImageColorModel class, then creates a MemoryImageSource object. This ImageProducer object produces an image initialized to all zeros (black). It is combined with an instance of the CalculatorFilter class to produce a FilteredImageSource. When the `createImage()` method of the Toolkit is called, production of the calculated image begins.

The color palette is a randomly generated series of pixel values. Depending on your luck, these colors can be attractive or uninspiring. The `createPalette()` method is a good place to create a custom set of colors for this applet, if you want to have some control over its appearance. You should replace the random colors with hard-coded RGB values, and you might want to download a URL file that specifies a special color mapping.

Listing 14.5. The CalculatorImage class.

```
// This class takes a CalculatorProducer and sets up the
// environment for creating a calculated image.  Ties the
// producer to the CalculatorFilter so incremental updates can
// be made...
public class CalculatorImage {
   int width;  // The dimensions of the image...
   int height;
   CalculatorProducer cp;  // What produces the image data...
   IndexColorModel palette;  // The colors of the image...
   // Create Palette only once per session...
   static IndexColorModel prvPalette = null;
   int numColors = 256;  // Number of colors in palette...

   // Use defines how big of an image they want...
   public CalculatorImage(int width,int height,CalculatorProducer cp) {
      this.width = width;
      this.height = height;
      this.cp = cp;
   }

   // Start producing the Calculator image...
   public synchronized Image getImage() {
      // Hook into the filter...
      createPalette();
      ImageProducer p = new FilteredImageSource(
       new MemoryImageSource(width,height,palette,
            (new int[width * height]),0,width),
            new CalculatorFilter(palette,cp));
      // Return the image...
      return Toolkit.getDefaultToolkit().createImage(p);
   }
```

continues

Listing 14.5. continued

```
    // Create a 256 color palette...
    // Use Default color model...
    void createPalette() {
      // Create palette only once per session...
      if (prvPalette != null) {
          palette = prvPalette;
          return;
      }
      // Create a palette out of random RGB combinations...
      byte blues[], reds[], greens[];
      reds = new byte[numColors];
      blues = new byte[numColors];
      greens = new byte[numColors];
      // First and last entries are black and white...
      blues[0] = reds[0] = greens[0] = (byte)0;
      blues[255] = reds[255] = greens[255] = (byte)255;
      // Fill in other entries...
      for ( int x = 1; x < 254; x++ ){
       reds[x] = (byte)(255 * Math.random());
       blues[x] = (byte)(255 * Math.random());
       greens[x] = (byte)(255 * Math.random());
      }
      // Create Index Color Model...
      palette = new IndexColorModel(8,256,reds,greens,blues);
      prvPalette = palette;
    }

    // Save the image set as a BMP file...
    public void saveBMP(String filename,int pix[]) {
       try {
          BmpImage.saveBitmap(filename,palette,
             pix,width,height);
       }
       catch (IOException ioe) {
          System.out.println("Error saving file!");
       }
    }
}
```

The MandelApp Class

The MandelApp class, shown in Listing 14.6, creates and displays the full Mandelbrot set; the end result is shown in Figure 14.2. An instance of the Mandelbrot class is created in the `init()` method. Whenever the Mandelbrot calculation has produced some new data, it calls the ImageObserver-based method, `imageUpdate()`. This will probably result in the applet being repainted to show the new data. If the image is complete, an internal flag is set. After this, if you click the mouse, the image will be saved to a BMP formatted file called mandel.bmp.

Listing 14.6. The MandelApp class.

```
import java.awt.*;
import java.lang.*;
import java.applet.Applet;

// This applet displays the Mandlebrot set through
// use of the Mandelbrot class...
public class MandelApp extends Applet  {
   Image im;   // Image that displays Mandelbrot set...
   Mandelbrot m; // Creates the Mandelbrot image...
   int NUMCOLS = 640;   // Dimensions image display...
   int NUMROWS = 350;
   boolean complete = false;

   // Set up the Mandelbrot set...
   public void init() {
      m = new Mandelbrot(NUMCOLS,NUMROWS);
      im = m.getImage();
   }

   // Will get updates as set is being created.
   // Repaint when they occur...
   public boolean imageUpdate(Image im,int flags,
      int x, int y, int w, int h) {
      if ((flags & FRAMEBITS) != 0) {
         showStatus("Calculating...");
         repaint();
         return true;
      }
      if ((flags & ALLBITS) != 0) {
         showStatus("Image Complete!");
         repaint();
         complete = true;
         return false;
      }
      return true;
   }

   // Paint on update...
   public void update(Graphics g) {
      paint(g);
   }
   public synchronized void paint(Graphics g) {
       g.drawImage(im,0,0,this);
   }

   // Save Bitmap on mouse down when image complete...
   public boolean mouseDown(Event evt,int x, int y) {
        if (complete) {
            showStatus("Save Bitmap...");
            m.saveBMP("mandel.bmp");
            showStatus("Bitmap saved!");
            return true;
         } // end if
         return false;
        }
}
```

The MandelZoomApp Class

Listing 14.7 shows the MandelZoomApp class, which represents this chapter's main applet; its function was described earlier, in the section "Using the Applets." See this section and Table 14.1 for how to use the applet.

The most interesting features in the code are the routines for marking the region to be highlighted. Each pixel on the displayed Mandelbrot image maps an x-y value to a real-imaginary value of the `c` value of the Mandelbrot formula shown in Formula 14.1. Whenever you move the cursor, the current real-imaginary values are shown in the browser's status bar. When you highlight an area to zoom in on, you are really picking a range of `c` values to be explored. All the double variables are used for tracking this range of values. These values are read in at initialization by the `loadParameters()` method to match the bitmap that's displayed. You can specify other Mandelbrot BMP files and corresponding data files by changing the `filename` parameter of the applet's `<APPLET>` tag.

The `Zoom()` method takes the currently highlighted range and brings up a new Mandelbrot image that corresponds to this range. It uses the same calculation-image filtering techniques that the MandelApp class does.

Listing 14.7. The MandelZoomApp class.

```
// This applet displays the Mandelbrot set bitmap specified
// in the APPLET tag parameters.  You can then zoom and in
// and out of the bitmap by dragging a region to paint.
// And then clicking on the appropriate option...
// Z or z - Zoom
// S or s - Save.
public class MandelZoomApp extends Applet  {
   Image img;
   boolean zoomOn = false;
   double XLeft,XRight,YTop,YBottom,XDelta,YDelta;
   double currentX,currentY;
   double startX,startY,endX,endY;  // Zooming coordinates...
   Rectangle markingRectangle;  // Zooming rectangle...
   Mandelbrot m; // Creates the Mandelbrot image...
   int NUMCOLS = 640;   // Dimensions image display...
   int NUMROWS = 350;
   boolean complete = false;
   // Array for keeping track of Mandelbrot entries...
   MandelEntry me[];
   int lastIndex;  // Top of array...
   int currentIndex;

   // Set up the Mandelbrot set specified in the parameters...
   public void init() {
      img = null;
      m = null;
      // Get parameter of bitmap to display...
      String filename;
      if ((filename = getParameter("filename")) == null)
```

```
            filename = "mandel1";
        // Load the bitmap...
        loadBitmap(filename);
        // Initialize Mandelbrot array...
        me = new MandelEntry[40];
        me[0] = new MandelEntry(null,img,XLeft,XRight,YTop,YBottom);
        lastIndex = 0;
        currentIndex = 0;
    }


    // ZOOM onto Mandelbrot set if all is good...
    void Zoom() {
        // No Zooming if off or no rectangle...
        if ((!zoomOn) || (markingRectangle == null)) {
            showMsg("Nothing marked or Zooming disable...");
            return;
        } // end if

        // See if Mandelbrot table is full...
        if ((lastIndex + 1) >= me.length) {
            showMsg("Mandelbrot table full. Clear with C before zooming");
            return;
        }
        showMsg("ZOOM: SX=" + startX + " SY=" + startY + " EX=" + endX + " EY=" +
endY);
        // Load new Mandelbrot...
        complete = false;
        zoomOn = false;
        markingRectangle = null; // Reset marking rectangle...
        m = new Mandelbrot(NUMCOLS,NUMROWS,endX,startX,
            endY,startY);
        img = m.getImage();
        // Store in Mandelbrot table...
        XLeft = startX;
        XRight = endX;
        YTop = startY;
        YBottom = endY;
        XDelta = Math.abs(XRight - XLeft);
        YDelta = Math.abs(YBottom - YTop);
        ++lastIndex;
        me[lastIndex] = new MandelEntry(m,img,startX,endX,startY,endY);
        currentIndex = lastIndex;
        showMsg("Calculating...");
        repaint();
    }

    // Paint on update...
    public void update(Graphics g) {
        paint(g);
    }
    public synchronized void paint(Graphics g) {
        if (img == null)
            return;
        // Show image...
        g.drawImage(img,0,0,this);
```

continues

Listing 14.7. continued

```
      // Show marking rectangle if exists...
      if (markingRectangle != null) {
         g.drawRect(markingRectangle.x,markingRectangle.y,
            markingRectangle.width,markingRectangle.height);
      } // end if
   }

   // Will get updates as set is being created.
   // Repaint when they occur...
   public boolean imageUpdate(Image im,int flags,
      int x, int y, int w, int h) {
      if ((flags & FRAMEBITS) != 0) {
         repaint();
         return true;
      }
      if ((flags & ALLBITS) != 0) {
         showMsg("Image Complete!");
         repaint();
         complete = true;
         zoomOn = true;
         return false;
      }
      return true;
   }

   // Load a bitmap and accompanying data file...
   void loadBitmap(String filename) {
      // Zoom is false unless both succeed...
      zoomOn = false;
      markingRectangle = null; // Reset marking rectangle...
      // Load the bitmap...
      try  {
         showMsg("Load image...");
         ImageProducer producer = BmpImage.getImageProducer(
            getDocumentBase(), filename + ".bmp");
         img = createImage(producer);
         showMsg("Image loaded...");
      }
      catch (AWTException e){
         img = null;
         showMsg("Cannot open file " + filename);
         return;
      }

      // Load the zoom parameters.
      // Turn Zoom on if all works...
      try {
         loadParameters(filename);
         zoomOn = true;
         complete = true;
      }
      catch (IOException e){
         showMsg("Cannot load parameter data. " + e.getMessage());
      }
   }
```

```
// Load the parameters.  Throw IO Exception...
public void loadParameters(String filename) throws IOException {
 // Create URL for data...
 URL u;
 try {
   u = new URL(getDocumentBase(),filename + ".dat");
 }
 catch (MalformedURLException e) {
   showMsg("Bad Data URL");
   throw new IOException("Bad URL");
 }
 // Now load the data by opening up a stream
 // to the URL...
 DataInputStream dis = new DataInputStream(
   new BufferedInputStream(u.openStream() ) );
  // Read only the first line...
  String param = dis.readLine();
  // Tokenize out the boundary values....
  StringTokenizer s = new StringTokenizer(param,",");
  try {
    XLeft = Double.valueOf(s.nextToken()).doubleValue();
    XRight = Double.valueOf(s.nextToken()).doubleValue();
    YTop = Double.valueOf(s.nextToken()).doubleValue();
    YBottom = Double.valueOf(s.nextToken()).doubleValue();
    XDelta = Math.abs(XRight - XLeft);
    YDelta = Math.abs(YBottom - YTop);
  }
  catch (NumberFormatException e) {
   throw new IOException("Improperly formatted data...");
  }
  catch (NoSuchElementException e) {
   throw new IOException("Improperly formatted data...");
  }
}


// Track mouse to show fractal values and to
// mark area to zoom
public boolean handleEvent(Event evt) {
  switch(evt.id) {
      case Event.KEY_PRESS: {
         // Z or z means Zoom
         if ((evt.key == 'z') || (evt.key == 'Z'))
               Zoom();
         // S or s means Save
         if ((evt.key == 's') || (evt.key == 'S'))
               saveFile();
         // A or a means Abort Zoom calculation...
         if ((evt.key == 'a') || (evt.key == 'A')) {
            if (m != null) {
               showMsg("Aborting calculation...");
               m.stop();
            } // end if
         }
         // P or p means previous image...
```

continues

Listing 14.7. continued

```
            if ((evt.key == 'p') || (evt.key == 'P'))
                  previousImage();
            // B or b means previous image...
            if ((evt.key == 'B') || (evt.key == 'b'))
                  previousImage();
            // N or n means next image...
            if ((evt.key == 'N') || (evt.key == 'n'))
                  nextImage();
            // F or f means next image...
            if ((evt.key == 'F') || (evt.key == 'f'))
                  nextImage();
            // C or c means clear images
            if ((evt.key == 'C') || (evt.key == 'c'))
                  clearImage();
            return true;
         }
         // Mouse clicks. Start marking...
         case Event.MOUSE_DOWN: {
            startMarking(evt.x,evt.y);
            return false;
         }
         case Event.MOUSE_DRAG: {
            dragMarking(evt.x,evt.y);
            return false;
         }
         case Event.MOUSE_UP: {
            stopMarking(evt.x,evt.y);
            return false;
         }
         case Event.MOUSE_MOVE: {
            showPosition(evt.x,evt.y);
            return false;
         }
         default:
            return false;
      }
}

   // Save the image as a file...
   void saveFile() {
      // Don't save if we are loading...
      if (!complete)
         return;
      // Get Mandelbrot reference, if exists...
      Mandelbrot mb = me[currentIndex].getMandelbrot();
      if (mb == null) {
         showStatus("Cannot save. Not generated in this session");
         return;
      } // end if

      // Generate the filename...
      String filename = "tempMandel" + (currentIndex + 1) + ".bmp";
      // Security test...
      try {
         System.getSecurityManager().checkWrite(filename);
      }
```

```
   catch (SecurityException e) {
      showStatus("Write not permitted!");
      return;
   }
   // Save the image...
   showStatus("Saving image as " + filename + "...");
   mb.saveBMP(filename);
   showStatus("Image saved as " + filename);
}


// Routines for moving through Mandelbrot table...
// Load previous image...
void previousImage() {
   // Nothing if we are loading...
   if (!complete)
      return;
   // Do nothing if at top index...
   if (currentIndex == 0) {
      showMsg("At Top index");
      return;
   }
   // Go to previous image...
   reloadImage(currentIndex - 1);
}

// Load next image...
void nextImage() {
   // Nothing if we are loading...
   if (!complete)
      return;
   // Do nothing if at last index...
   if (currentIndex == lastIndex) {
      showMsg("At Last index");
      return;
   }
   // Go to next image...
   reloadImage(currentIndex + 1);
}

// Reload index from Mandelbrot array...
void reloadImage(int index) {
   showMsg("Reloading image...");
   currentIndex = index;
   complete = true;
   zoomOn = true;
   markingRectangle = null; // Reset marking rectangle...
   // Get data from Mandelbrot table...
   img = me[currentIndex].getImage();
   XLeft = me[currentIndex].getXLeft();
   XRight = me[currentIndex].getXRight();
   YTop = me[currentIndex].getYTop();
   YBottom = me[currentIndex].getYBottom();
   XDelta = Math.abs(XRight - XLeft);
```

continues

Listing 14.7. continued

```
      YDelta = Math.abs(YBottom - YTop);
      repaint();
   }

   // Remove everything but first image from stack...
   void clearImage() {
      for (int i = 1; i <= lastIndex; ++i)
         me[i] = null;
      // Go back to first image...
      lastIndex = 0;
      reloadImage(0);
   }

   // ************************************
   // Routines for mouse tracking...
   // ************************************
   boolean TrackingOn = false;
   int leftX,topY;

   // Start marking a zoom rectangle, erase existing one...
   void startMarking(int x,int y) {
      // Get current positions... Clear marking if invalid...
      if (!showPosition(x,y)) {
         TrackingOn = false;
         markingRectangle = null;
         repaint();
         return;
      } // end if
      // Else, start marking...
      TrackingOn = true;
      startX = currentX;
      startY = currentY;
      endX = currentX;
      endY = currentY;
      leftX = x;
      topY = y;
      // Set marking rectangle and repaint...
      markingRectangle = new Rectangle(x,y,1,1);
      repaint();
   }


   // Expand square of dragging unless invalid...
   void dragMarking(int x,int y) {
      // Get current positions... Clear marking if invalid...
      boolean good = showPosition(x,y);
      // See if other marking conditions hold.
      // Such as going in a bad direction...
      if (good) {
         if ((!TrackingOn) || (x < leftX) || (y < topY))
            good = false;
      }
      // Clear out if marking is bad...
      if (!good) {
         TrackingOn = false;
         markingRectangle = null;
```

```
         repaint();
         return;
      } // end if
      // Set new marking rectangle and repaint...
      endX = currentX;
      endY = currentY;
      markingRectangle = new Rectangle(leftX,topY,
            x - leftX,y - topY);
      repaint(leftX,topY,markingRectangle.width + 1,
         markingRectangle.height + 1);
   }

   // Stop marking...
   void stopMarking(int x,int y) {
      showPosition(x,y);
      TrackingOn = false;
      // Kill if too small...
      if (markingRectangle != null) {
         if ((markingRectangle.width < 3) ¦¦
          (markingRectangle.height < 3)) {
            markingRectangle = null;
         } // end if
      }
      repaint();
   }

   // Show current position to status if an image has
   // been prepared...
   // Returns true if good position, else bad...
   boolean showPosition(int x,int y) {
      // Return if not ready to zoom...
      if ((img == null) ¦¦ (!zoomOn))
         return false;
      // See if we are in the display area...
      int width = img.getWidth(this);
      int height = img.getHeight(this);
      if ((x > width) ¦¦ y > height) {
         showStatus("");
         return false;
      } // end if
      currentX = XLeft + (XDelta * (((double)x)/((double)width)));
      currentY = YTop + (YDelta * (((double)y)/((double)height)));
      showStatus(currentX + " : " + currentY);
      return true;
   }


   // Print a message to standard out and the status bar...
   public void showMsg(String s) {
      System.out.println(s);
      showStatus(s);
   }
}
```

A cache is maintained so that you can move back and forth between images. The cache is an array of MandelEntry accessor objects; the MandelEntry class is shown in Listing 14.8. The cache is set to store up to 40 images. If you fill up the cache, press `C` or `c` to clear the cache of everything but the full Mandelbrot set image. As an exercise, you might want to make the caching mechanism more sophisticated so that it can bring in existing files, delete individual images, and so forth.

Note that there is a little trick in the `saveFile()` method. It uses the SecurityManager to see whether file writes are allowed. This is a way of checking the browser's security before a write is attempted. If file writing is prohibited, a SecurityException is thrown. How this works will differ from browser to browser.

Listing 14.8. The MandelEntry class.

```
// Store Mandelbrot images and corresponding coordinates...
class MandelEntry {
   Mandelbrot m;
   Image img;
   double XLeft,XRight,YTop,YBottom;
   // Constructor: Store data...
   public MandelEntry(Mandelbrot m,Image img,double XLeft,
      double XRight,double YTop,double YBottom) {
         this.m = m;
         this.img = img;
         this.XLeft = XLeft;
         this.XRight = XRight;
         this.YTop = YTop;
         this.YBottom = YBottom;
   }
   // Accessor methods...
   public Mandelbrot getMandelbrot() {
      return m;
   }
   public Image getImage() {
      return img;
   }
   public double getXLeft() {
      return XLeft;
   }
   public double getXRight() {
      return XRight;
   }
   public double getYTop() {
      return YTop;
   }
   public double getYBottom() {
      return YBottom;
   }
}
```

The BmpImage Class

The BmpImage class, introduced in Part III of this book, reads images stored in the BMP format and converts them into a form Java can use. In this chapter, more functions were added to the class so that it could write the BMP back out to a file (shown in Listing 14.9). It's basically the opposite of the reading process discussed in Part III.

Listing 14.9. Adding BMP saving to the BmpImage class.

```
import java.lang.String;
import java.io.*;
import java.net.*;
import java.awt.*;
import java.awt.image.*;

/**
 * This is a class that reads and writes a
 * BMP formatted file
*/
public class BmpImage
{
// ... EXISTING CODE GOES HERE!!!
/**
     * Write out a bitmap...
     * Current only supporting 8 bits per pixel...
     * @String filename - The file to save it as...
     * @IndexColorModel ICM - Palette to use
     * @int pix[] - Pixels to save
     * @int width - Width of data
* @int height - Height of data
     */
    public static void saveBitmap(String filename,
     IndexColorModel ICM, int pix[],
     int width, int height) throws IOException {
         // Create output stream...
         BmpImage b = new BmpImage(filename);
         DataOutputStream os = new DataOutputStream(
            new BufferedOutputStream(
             new FileOutputStream(filename) ) );
         b.writeFileHeader(os,ICM,width,height);
         b.write8bitWindowsHeader(os,ICM,width,height);
         b.write8bitColorIndex(os,ICM);
         b.write8bitData(os,pix,width,height);
         os.close();
    }

    /**
     * Write out the file header
     * @DataOutputStream os - The output stream to write
     * @IndexColorModel ICM - Palette to use
     * @int width - Width of data
* @int height - Height of data
    */
```

continues

Listing 14.9. continued

```
    public void writeFileHeader(DataOutputStream os,
     IndexColorModel ICM,
     int width, int height) throws IOException {
      byte b[] = new byte[4];
      // Write out magic code...
      b[0] = 'B';
      b[1] = 'M';
      os.write(b,0,2);

      // Calculate size and offset..
      int paletteSize = (ICM.getMapSize() * 4);
      int offset = 54 + paletteSize;
      int fileSize = offset + (width * height);

      // Write out size & offset...
      pushVal(os,fileSize,4);
      pushVal(os,0,4);
      pushVal(os,offset,4);
    }

    /**
     * Write the bitmap header out to Windows...
     * @DataOutputStream os - The output stream to write
     * @IndexColorModel ICM - Palette to use
     * @int width - Width of data
     * @int height - Height of data
    */
    public void write8bitWindowsHeader(DataOutputStream os,
     IndexColorModel ICM,
     int width, int height) throws IOException {
      pushVal(os,40,4);  // Bytes in header
      pushVal(os,width,4);  // Size in pixels...
      pushVal(os,height,4);
      pushVal(os,1,2);    // # Color Planes
      pushVal(os,8,2);  // Bits per pixel...
      pushVal(os,0,4);  // NO Compression...
      pushVal(os,width * height,4);  // Size of image...
      // LATER PUT IN REAL DATA pixels/meter
      pushVal(os,3790,4);  // TBD: Horizontal Res pixels/meter
      pushVal(os,3790,4);  // TBD: Vertical Res pixels/meter
pushVal(os,ICM.getMapSize(),4);  // Indexes in bitmap...
      pushVal(os,ICM.getMapSize(),4);  // Indexes in bitmap...
    }

    /**
     * Write the bitmap header out to Windows...
     * @DataOutputStream os - The output stream to write
     * @IndexColorModel ICM - Palette to use
    */
    public void write8bitColorIndex(DataOutputStream os,
      IndexColorModel ICM) throws IOException {
         // Create RGB array...
         int paletteSize = ICM.getMapSize();
         byte blues[] = new byte[paletteSize];
         byte greens[] = new byte[paletteSize];
         byte reds[] = new byte[paletteSize];
         byte b[] = new byte[4];
```

```
        // Copy RGB arrays...
        ICM.getBlues(blues);
        ICM.getGreens(reds);
        ICM.getReds(reds);
// Write out palette...
        for (int i = 0; i < paletteSize; ++i) {
           b[0] = (byte)blues[i];
           b[1] = (byte)greens[i];
           b[2] = (byte)reds[i];
           b[3] = (byte)0;
           os.write(b,0,4);
        } // end for
    }

    /**
     * Write out data of bitmap...
     * @DataOutputStream os - The output stream to write
     * @IndexColorModel ICM - Palette to use
     * @int pix[] - Pixels to save
     * @int width - Width of data
     * @int height - Height of data
     */
    public void write8bitData(DataOutputStream os,
     int pix[],int width, int height) throws IOException {
     // Bytes b...
byte b[] = new byte[width];
     for (int i = 0; i < 4; ++i)
         b[i] = 0;
     // Calculate padding
     int padding = 0;
     int overage = width % 4;
     if (overage != 0)
      padding = 4 - overage;
     // Write out starting from bottom of height
     int index,x,y;
     for (y = (height - 1); y >= 0; —y) {
         // Write out each row, send to big buffer...
         index = (y * width);
         for (x = 0; x < width; ++x,++index)
               b[x] = (byte)pix[index];
         // Write out a big block...
         os.write(b,0,width);
         // Send out padding...
         if (padding != 0) {
            for (int i = 0; i < 4; ++i)
                  b[i] = 0;
            os.write(b,0,padding);
}
         System.out.print("."); System.out.flush();
     } // end y for
     System.out.println("Write done!");
    }


    /**
     * Write out integer to little endian stream...
     * @DataOutputStream os - The output stream to write
```

continues

Listing 14.9. continued

```
     * @int data - Data to convert
     * @int len - Length of array to convert
     */
    private void pushVal(DataOutputStream os,
     int data,int len) throws IOException {
      byte b[] = new byte[len];
      for (int i = 0; i < len; ++i) {
         b[i] = (byte)(data >> (i * 8));
      }
      os.write(b,0,len);
    }
```

Automatic Documentation with `javadoc`

The last thing covered in this chapter is how to auto-document your code. The tool `javadoc`, provided with the JDK, can take a properly formatted file and convert it into an HTML file, complete with links to the classes it references (assuming those classes are also run through `javadoc`). The BmpImage.java is such a file; its HTML output from `javadoc` is shown in Figure 14.7 and is included on this book's CD-ROM.

Comments that should appear in the HTML are marked by appearing between `/**` and `*/`, as shown at the beginning of the source code in Listing 14.9. The `javadoc` tool figures out a lot of things on its own, such the superclass, what external classes are used, and the individual parts of a method or variable declaration. You can specify additional information for each method by preceding certain keywords with an `@`. These keywords include `param`, `returns`, and `exception` for documenting parameters, return values, and exceptions thrown, respectively. For example, here is the declaration for `getImageProducer()`:

```
/**
     * A method to retreive an ImageProducer given just a BMP URL.
     * @param context contains the base URL (from getCodeBase() or such)
     * @returns an ImageProducer
     * @exception AWTException on stream or bitmap data errors
*/
```

Look at the HTML to see what this looks like.

You will need to place the HTML output in the right directory for everything to work properly. You can also document an entire package by passing the package name to `javadoc`.

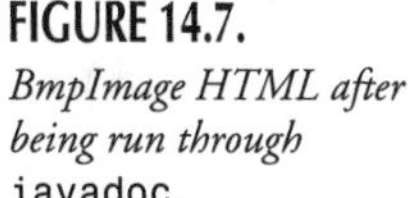

FIGURE 14.7.
BmpImage HTML after being run through `javadoc`.

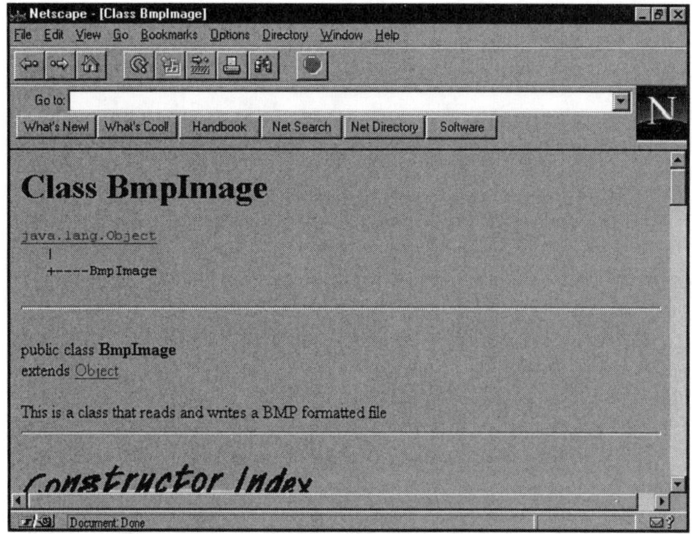

Summary

The major work of this book began in Part II with a series of discussions on how to use the AWT package. The spreadsheet applet was used to show how to incrementally build an applet using AWT. Since AWT is the basis for constructing the user interface of your Java applets, you need to know the package well. While constructing the spreadsheet, you also learned the subtleties of the java.io package and how to create exception handlers. By the end of Part II, you had seen most of the basics of Java applet programming.

Part III took everything a step further. You discovered the underlying classes behind applets and images and saw how threads can be used to enhance your application. Part III concluded with showing you how AWT, the applet classes, images, and threads could be brought together to create a Catalog applet, whose key element was a background image loader running as a thread. Although this applet was not a final product, it could—combined with the client/server mechanisms of Part IV—be the basis for producing a serious catalog application for use on the World Wide Web.

In Part IV, you incorporated the lessons of the previous chapters to create the most complex application of the book. You saw how to use the Java network classes to create a client-server application, and how to use native methods to take full advantage of a particular platform's features. The client applet demonstrated how Java could be used to represent data as it changes in real time. The election applet in Part IV was just the beginning of what you can create with Java client-server technology.

Part V allowed you to focus on some of the more advanced features of Java. You saw how HotJava, although still in its infancy, has features that indicate the future of browsers and Java programming. You also saw how to use Java's image classes to create advanced animation and image-processing applets. With a knowledge of these advanced imaging techniques, you can now use Java to produce images more sophisticated than just a banner moving across the screen.

You have been given the tools to write great Java applets for the Internet, the intranet, or anywhere else Java calls. Go for it!

VI

Appendixes

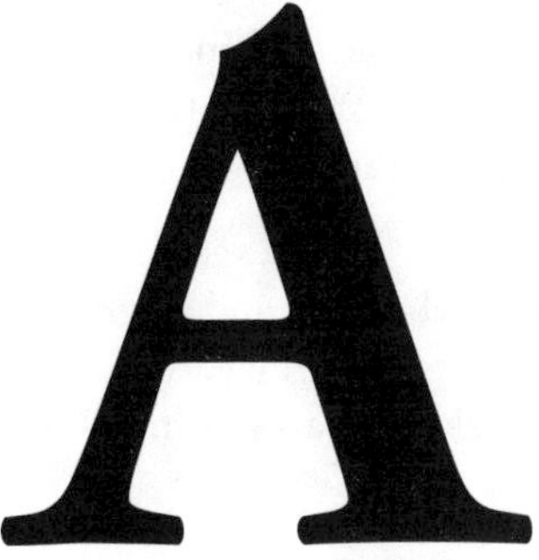

Inside the Java Virtual Machine

Looking at a virtual machine from the outside in is probably the best way to understand its workings. Incremental learning results when you move from the known to the unknown, so this section starts with the item you are most familiar with: the class file.

The Class File

The class file is similar to standard language object modules. When a C language file is compiled, the output is an object module. Multiple object modules are linked together to form an executable program. In Java, the class file replaces the object module and the Java virtual machine replaces the executable program.

You'll find all the information needed to execute a class contained within the class file, as well as extra information that aids debugging and source file tracking. Remember that Java has no "header" include files, so the class file format also has to fully convey class layout and members. Parsing a class file yields a wealth of class information, not just its runtime architecture.

Layout

The overall layout uses an outer structure and a series of substructures that contain an ever-increasing amount of detail. The outer layer is described by the following structure:

```
ClassFile
{
    u4 magic;
    u2 minor_version;
    u2 major_version;
    u2 constant_pool_count;
    cp_info constant_pool[constant_pool_count - 1];
    u2 access_flags;
    u2 this_class;
    u2 super_class;
    u2 interfaces_count;
    u2 interfaces[interfaces_count];
    u2 fields_count;
    field_info fields[fields_count];
    u2 methods_count;
    method_info methods[methods_count];
    u2 attributes_count;
    attribute_info attributes[attribute_count];
}
```

In addition to the generic class information (this_class, super_class, version, and so forth), there are three major substructures: constant_pool, fields, and methods. Attributes are considered minor substructures because they recur throughout the class file at various levels. Fields and methods contain their own attributes. Some individual attributes also contain their own private attribute arrays.

The u2 and u4 types represent unsigned 2-byte and 4-byte quantities.

This simple class will be used throughout this appendix as the basis for class file exploration.

```
public class test
{
    public static int st_one;

    public test()
    {
        st_one = 100;
    }

    public test(int v)
    {
        st_one = v;
    }

    public native boolean getData(int data[] );

    public int do_countdown()
    {
        int x = st_one;

        System.out.println("Performing countdown:");
        while ( x— != 0 )
            System.out.println(x);
        return st_one;
    }

    public int do_countdown(int x)
    {
        int save = x;

        System.out.println("Performing countdown:");
        while ( x— != 0 )
            System.out.println(x);
        return save;
    }
}
```

This class doesn't actually do very much, but it does provide a basis for class file exploration. Once compiled, the outer layer of the resulting class file is as follows:

```
file name: test.class
      magic: cafebabe
    version: 45.3
  constants: Valid indexes: 1 - 39
     access: PUBLIC
 this class: Class: test
super class: Class: java/lang/Object
 interfaces: none
     fields: [1] st_one
    methods: [4] <init> <init> do_countdown do_countdown
 attributes: SourceFile(test.java)
```

> **NOTE**
>
> The above output was generated with a Java tool I wrote called ClassView. The full source code is available on this book's CD-ROM. ClassView parses and outputs the various features and levels of a given class file. It also provides a good basis for other class file parsers, such as disassemblers.

The magic number of a class is 0xcafebabe. This number must appear in a class file, or the file is assumed to be invalid. The current major version is 45; the current minor version is 3.

Access Flags

Access flags are used throughout the class file to convey the access characteristics of various items. The flag itself is a collection of 11 individual bits. Table A.1 lays out the masks.

Table A.1. Access flag bit values.

Flag Value	*Indication*
`ACC_PUBLIC = 0x0001`	Global visibility
`ACC_PRIVATE = 0x0002`	Local class visibility
`ACC_PROTECTED = 0x0004`	Subclass visibility
`ACC_STATIC = 0x0008`	One occurrence in system (not per class)
`ACC_FINAL = 0x0010`	No changes allowed
`ACC_SYNCHRONIZED = 0x0020`	Access with a monitor
`ACC_VOLATILE = 0x0040`	No local caching
`ACC_TRANSIENT = 0x0080`	Not a persistent value
`ACC_NATIVE = 0x0100`	Native method implementation
`ACC_INTERFACE = 0x0200`	Class is an interface
`ACC_ABSTRACT = 0x0400`	Class or method is abstract

Access flags are present for a class and its fields and methods. Only a subset of values appears in any given item. Some bits apply only to fields (VOLATILE and TRANSIENT); others apply only to methods (SYNCHRONIZED and NATIVE).

Attributes

Attributes, like access flags, appear throughout a class file. They have the following form:

```
GenericAttribute_info
{
    u2 attribute_name;
    u4 attribute_length;
    u1 info[attribute_length];
}
```

A generic structure exists to enable loaders to skip over attributes they don't understand. The actual attribute has a unique structure that can be read if the loader understands the format. As an example, the following structure specifies the format of a source file attribute:

```
SourceFile_attribute
{
    u2 attribute_name;
    u4 attribute_length;
    u2 sourcefile_index;
}
```

The name of an attribute is an index into the constant pool. You'll learn about constant pools momentarily. If a loader did not understand the source file attribute structure, it could skip the data by reading the number of bytes specified in the length parameter. For the source file attribute, the length is 2.

Constant Pool

The constant pool forms the basis for all numbers and strings within a class file. Nowhere else do you ever find strings or numbers in a class file. Any time there is a need to reference a string or number, an index into the constant pool is substituted. Consequently, the constant pool is the dominant feature of a class. The pool is even used directly within the virtual machine itself.

There are twelve different types of constants:

- `CONSTANT_Utf8` = 1
- `CONSTANT_Unicode` = 2
- `CONSTANT_Integer` = 3
- `CONSTANT_Float` = 4
- `CONSTANT_Long` = 5
- `CONSTANT_Double` = 6
- `CONSTANT_Class` = 7
- `CONSTANT_String` = 8
- `CONSTANT_Fieldref` = 9

- CONSTANT_Methodref = 10
- CONSTANT_InterfaceMethodref = 11
- CONSTANT_NameAndType = 12

Each constant structure leads off with a tag identifying the structure type. Following the type is data specific to each individual structure. The layout of each constant structure follows:

```
CONSTANT_Utf8_info
{
    u1 tag;
    u2 length;
    u1 bytes[length];
}

CONSTANT_Unicode_info
{
    u1 tag;
    u2 length;
    u2 words[length];
}

CONSTANT_Integer_info
{
    u1 tag;
    u4 bytes;
}

CONSTANT_Float_info
{
    u1 tag;
    u4 bytes;
}

CONSTANT_Long_info
{
    u1 tag;
    u4 high_bytes;
    u4 low_bytes;
}

CONSTANT_Double_info
{
    u1 tag;
    u4 high_bytes;
    u4 low_bytes;
}

CONSTANT_Class_info
{
    u1 tag;
    u2 name_index;
}

CONSTANT_String_info
{
    u1 tag;
```

```
    u2 string_index;
}

CONSTANT_Fieldref_info
{
    u1 tag;
    u2 class_index;
    u2 name_and_type_index;
}

CONSTANT_Methodref_info
{
    u1 tag;
    u2 class_index;
    u2 name_and_type_index;
}

CONSTANT_InterfaceMethodref_info
{
    u1 tag;
    u2 class_index;
    u2 name_and_type_index;
}

CONSTANT_NameAndType_info
{
    u1 tag;
    u2 name_index;
    u2 signature_index;
}
```

The `CONSTANT_Utf8` contains standard ASCII text strings. These are not null-terminated because they use an explicit length parameter. Notice that most of the constants reference other constants for information. Methods, for instance, specify a class and type by providing indexes to other constant pool members. Constant pool cross-references eliminate repetition of data.

The constant pool for the test class appears as follows:

```
String #28 -> Performing countdown:
Class: java/lang/System
Class: java/lang/Object
Class: test
Class: java/io/PrintStream
Field: java/lang/System.out Ljava/io/PrintStream;
Field: test.st_one I
Method: java/io/PrintStream.println(I)V
Method: java/lang/Object.<init>()V
Method: java/io/PrintStream.println(Ljava/lang/String;)V
NameAndType: println (I)V
NameAndType: println (Ljava/lang/String;)V
NameAndType: out Ljava/io/PrintStream;
NameAndType: <init> ()V
NameAndType: st_one I
Utf8: [7] println
Utf8: [4] (I)V
Utf8: [3] ()I
Utf8: [13] ConstantValue
```

```
Utf8: [4] (I)I
Utf8: [19] java/io/PrintStream
Utf8: [10] Exceptions
Utf8: [15] LineNumberTable
Utf8: [1] I
Utf8: [10] SourceFile
Utf8: [14] LocalVariables
Utf8: [4] Code
Utf8: [21] Performing countdown:
Utf8: [3] out
Utf8: [21] (Ljava/lang/String;)V
Utf8: [16] java/lang/Object
Utf8: [6] <init>
Utf8: [21] Ljava/io/PrintStream;
Utf8: [16] java/lang/System
Utf8: [12] do_countdown
Utf8: [5] ([I)Z
Utf8: [6] st_one
Utf8: [7] getData
Utf8: [9] test.java
Utf8: [3] ()V
Utf8: [4] test
```

NOTE

The ClassView tool substitutes pool indexes with actual pool data whenever possible.

Fields

Field structures contain the individual data members of a class. Any class item that is not a method is placed into the fields section. The field structure looks like the following:

```
field_info
{
    u2 access_flags;
    u2 name_index;
    u2 signature_index;
    u2 attribute_count;
    attribute_info attributes[attribute_count];
}
```

The test class contains the following field:

```
st_one I
  PUBLIC STATIC
  No attributes
```

Methods

The method section contains all of the executable content of a class. In addition to the method name and signature, the structure contains a set of attributes. One of these attributes has the actual byte codes that the virtual machine will execute. The method structure follows:

```
method_info
{
    u2 access_flags;
    u2 name_index;
    u2 signature_index;
    u2 attributes_count;
    attribute_info attributes[attribute_count];
}
```

The test class produces the following method section:

```
<init>()V
  PUBLIC
  Code(stack=1 locals=1 code=10 exceptions=none)
<init>(I)V
  PUBLIC
  Code(stack=1 locals=2 code=9 exceptions=none)
getData([I)Z
  PUBLIC NATIVE
  No attributes
do_countdown()I
  PUBLIC
  Code(stack=2 locals=2 code=33 exceptions=none)
do_countdown(I)I
  PUBLIC
  Code(stack=2 locals=3 code=29 exceptions=none)
```

Each method has a name and signature. You learned about signatures in Chapter 10, "Native Methods and Java." Each non-native method contains a code attribute that has the following format:

```
Code_attribute
{
    u2 attribute_name;
    u4 attribute_length;
    u2 max_stack;
    u2 max_locals;
    u4 code_length;
    u1 code[code_length];
    u2 exception_table_length;
    ExceptionItem exceptions[exception_table_length];
    u2 attributes_count;
    attribute_info attributes[attribute_count];
}
```

Code attributes contain a private list of other attributes. Typically, these are debugging lists, such as line number information. Now that you've hit the code attribute, it's time to jump into the virtual machine.

The Virtual Machine

The Java virtual machine interprets Java byte codes that are contained in code attributes. The virtual machine is stack based. Most computer architectures perform their operations on a mixture of memory locations and registers. The Java virtual machine performs its operations exclusively on a stack. This is done primarily to support portability. No assumptions could be made about the size or number of registers in a given CPU. Intel microprocessors are especially limited in their register composition.

Registers

The virtual machine does contain some registers, but these are used for tracking the current state of the machine:

- `pc` register points to the next bytecode to execute
- `vars` register points to the local variables for a method
- `optop` register points to the operand stack
- `frame` register points to the execution environment

All these registers are 32 bits wide and point into separate storage blocks. The blocks, however, can be allocated all at once because the code attribute specifies the size of the operand stack, the number of local variables, and the length of the bytecodes.

Operand Stack

Most Java byte codes work on the operand stack. For instance, to add two integers together, each integer is pushed onto the operand stack. The addition operator removes the top two integers, adds them, and places the result in its place back on the stack:

```
..., 4, 5 -> ..., 9
```

> **NOTE**
>
> The operand stack notation is used throughout the remainder of this appendix. The stack reads from left to right, with the stack top on the extreme right. Ellipses indicate indeterminate data buried on the stack. The arrow indicates an operation; the data to the right of the arrow represents the stack after the operation is performed.

Each stack location is 32 bits wide. Long and doubles are 64 bits wide, so they take up two stack locations.

Primitive Types

The virtual machine provides support for nine primitive types:

- `byte`—single byte signed 2's complement
- `short`—2-byte signed 2's complement

- `int`—4-byte signed 2's complement
- `long`—8-byte signed 2's complement
- `float`—4-byte IEEE 754 single precision
- `double`—8-byte IEEE 754 double precision
- `char`—2-byte unsigned Unicode character
- `object`—4-byte reference to a Java object
- `returnAddress`—4-byte reference

The virtual machine specification does not mandate the internal format of object references. In Sun's implementation, object references point to a Java handle consisting of two pointers. One points to the method table for the class and the other points to the object's instance data.

Local Variables

Each code attribute specifies the size of the local variables. A local variable is 32 bits wide, so long and double primitives take up two variable slots. Unlike C, all method arguments appear as local variables. The operand stack is reserved exclusively for operations.

The Verifier

When a class is loaded, it is passed through a bytecode verifier before it is executed. The verifier checks the internal consistency of the class and the validity of the code. Java uses a late binding scheme that puts the code at risk. In traditional languages, the object linker binds all of the method calls and variable accesses to specific addresses. In Java, the virtual machine doesn't perform this service until the last possible moment. As a result, it is possible for a called class to have changed since the original class was compiled. Method names or their arguments may have been altered, or the access levels may have been changed. One of the verifier's jobs is to make sure that all external object references are correct and allowed.

No assumptions can be made about the origin of bytecodes. A hostile compiler could be used to create executable bytecodes that conform to the class file format, but specify illegal codes.

The verifier uses a conservative four-pass verification algorithm to check bytecodes.

Pass 1

This pass reads in the class file and ensures that it is valid. The magic number must be present and all the class data must be present with no truncation or extra data after the end of the class. Any recognized attributes must have the correct length and the constant pool must not have any unrecognized entries.

Pass 2

The second pass involves validating class features other than the bytecodes. All methods and fields must have a valid name and signature and every class must have a super class. Signatures are not actually checked, but they must appear valid. The next pass is more specific.

Pass 3

This is the most complex pass because the bytecodes are validated. The bytecodes are analyzed to make sure that they have the correct type and number of arguments. In addition, a data-flow analysis is performed to determine each path through the method. Each path must arrive at a given point with the same stack size and types. Each path must call methods with the proper arguments, and fields must be modified with values of the appropriate type. Class accesses are not checked in this pass. Only the return type of external functions is verified.

Forcing all paths to arrive with the same stack and registers can lead the verifier to fail some otherwise legitimate bytecodes. This is a small price to pay for this high level of security.

Pass 4

This pass loads externally referenced classes and checks that the method name and signatures match. It also validates that the current class has access rights to the external class. After complete validation, each instruction is replaced with a `_quick` alternative. These `_quick` bytecodes indicate that the class has been verified and need not be checked again.

Exception Handling

The `pc` register points to the next bytecode to execute. Whenever an exception is thrown, the method's exception table is searched for a handler. Each exception table entry has this format:

```
ExceptionItem
{
    u2 start_pc;
    u2 end_pc;
    u2 handler_pc;
    u2 catch_type;
}
```

If the `pc` register is within the proper range and the thrown exception is the proper type, the entry's handler code block is executed. If no handler is found, the exception propagates up to the calling method. The procedure repeats itself until either a valid handler is found or the program exits.

Bytecodes

The bytecodes can be divided into 11 major categories:

- Pushing constants onto the stack
- Moving local variable contents to and from the stack
- Managing arrays
- Generic stack instructions (dup, swap, pop & nop)
- Arithmetic and logical instructions
- Conversion instructions
- Control transfer and function return
- Manipulating object fields
- Method invocation
- Miscellaneous operations
- Monitors

Each bytecode has a unique tag and is followed by a fixed number of additional arguments. Notice that there is no way to work directly with class fields or local variables. They must be moved to the operand stack before any operations can be performed on the contents.

Generally, there are multiple formats for each individual operation. The addition operation provides a good example. There are actually four forms of addition: `iadd`, `ladd`, `fadd`, and `dadd`. Each type assumes the top two stack items are of the correct format: integers, longs, floats, or doubles.

Pushing Constants Onto the Stack

Java uses the following instructions for moving object data and local variables to the operand stack:

Push One-Byte Signed Integer

```
bipush=16 byte1       Stack: ... -> ..., byte1
```

Push Two-Byte Signed Integer

```
sipush=17 byte1 byte2    Stack: ... -> ..., word1
```

Push Item From the Constant Pool (8-bit index)

```
ldc1=18 indexbyte1     Stack: ... -> ..., item
```

Push Item from the Constant Pool (16-bit index)

```
ldc2=19 indexbyte1 indexbyte2   Stack: ... -> ..., item
```

Push Long or Double from Constant Pool (16-bit index)

```
ldc2w=20 indexbyte1 indexbyte2   Stack: ... -> ..., word1, word2
```

Push Null Object

```
aconst_null=1    Stack: ... -> ..., null
```

Push Integer Constant -1

```
iconst_m1=2   Stack: ... -> ..., -1
```

Push Integer Constants

```
iconst_0=3    Stack: ... -> ..., 0
iconst_1=4    Stack: ... -> ..., 1
iconst_2=5    Stack: ... -> ..., 2
iconst_3=6    Stack: ... -> ..., 3
iconst_4=7    Stack: ... -> ..., 4
iconst_5=8    Stack: ... -> ..., 5
```

Push Long Constant

```
lconst_0=9    Stack: ... -> ..., 0, 0
lconst_1=10   Stack: ... -> ..., 0, 1
```

Push Float Constants

```
fconst_0=11   Stack: ... -> ..., 0
fconst_1=12   Stack: ... -> ..., 1
fconst_2=13   Stack: ... -> ..., 2
```

Push Double Constants

```
dconst_0=14   Stack: ... -> ..., 0, 0
dconst_1=15   Stack: ... -> ..., 0, 1
```

Accessing Local Variables

The most commonly referenced local variables are at the first four offsets from the `vars` register. Because of this, Java provides single byte instructions to access these variables for both reading and writing. A two-byte instruction is needed to reference variables greater than 4 deep. The variable at location zero is the class pointer itself (the `this` pointer).

Load Integer from Local Variable

```
iload=21 vindex   Stack: ... -> ..., contents of varaible at vars[vindex]
iload_o=26        Stack: ... -> ..., contents of variable at vars[0]
iload_1=27        Stack: ... -> ..., contents of variable at vars[1]
iload_2=28        Stack: ... -> ..., contents of variable at vars[2]
iload_3=29        Stack: ... -> ..., contents of variable at vars[3]
```

Load Long Integer from Local Variable

```
lload=22 vindex   Stack: .. -> ..., word1, word2  from vars[vindex] & vars[vindex+1]
lload_0=30        Stack: .. -> ..., word1, word2  from vars[0] & vars[1]
```

```
lload_1=31        Stack: .. -> ..., word1, word2  from vars[1] & vars[2]
lload_2=32        Stack: .. -> ..., word1, word2  from vars[2] & vars[3]
lload_3=33        Stack: .. -> ..., word1, word2  from vars[3] & vars[4]
```

Load Float from Local Variable

```
fload=23 vindex   Stack: ... -> ..., contents from vars[vindex]
fload_0=34        Stack: ... -> ..., contents from vars[0]
fload_1=35        Stack: ... -> ..., contents from vars[1]
fload_2=36        Stack: ... -> ..., contents from vars[2]
fload_3=37        Stack: ... -> ..., contents from vars[3]
```

Load Double from Local Variable

```
dload=24 vindex   Stack: ... -> ..., word1, word2  from vars[vindex] &
vars[vindex+1]
dload_0=38        Stack: ... -> ..., word1, word2  from vars[0] & vars[1]
dload_1=39        Stack: ... -> ..., word1, word2  from vars[1] & vars[2]
dload_2=40        Stack: ... -> ..., word1, word2  from vars[2] & vars[3]
dload_3=41        Stack: ... -> ..., word1, word2  from vars[3] & vars[4]
```

Load Object from Local Variable

```
aload=25 vindex   Stack: ... -> ..., object  from vars[vindex]
aload_0=42        Stack: ... -> ..., object  from vars[0]
aload_1=43        Stack: ... -> ..., object  from vars[1]
aload_2=44        Stack: ... -> ..., object  from vars[2]
aload_3=45        Stack: ... -> ..., object  from vars[3]
```

Store Integer into Local Variable

```
istore=54 vindex Stack: ..., INT -> ...  into vars[vindex]
istore_0=59      Stack: ..., INT -> ...  into vars[0]
istore_1=60      Stack: ..., INT -> ...  into vars[1]
istore_2=61      Stack: ..., INT -> ...  into vars[2]
istore_3=62      Stack: ..., INT -> ...  into vars[3]
```

Store Long Integer into Local Variable

```
lstore=55 vindex Stack: ..., word1, word2 -> ...  into vars[vindex] &
vars[vindex+1]
lstore_0=63      Stack: ..., word1, word2 -> ...  into vars[0] & vars[1]
lstore_1=64      Stack: ..., word1, word2 -> ...  into vars[1] & vars[2]
lstore_2=65      Stack: ..., word1, word2 -> ...  into vars[2] & vars[3]
lstore_3=66      Stack: ..., word1, word2 -> ...  into vars[3] & vars[4]
```

Store Float into Local Variable

```
fstore=56 vindex Stack: ..., FLOAT -> ...  into vars[vindex]
fstore_0=67      Stack: ..., FLOAT -> ...  into vars[0]
fstore_1=68      Stack: ..., FLOAT -> ...  into vars[1]
fstore_2=69      Stack: ..., FLOAT -> ...  into vars[2]
fstore_3=70      Stack: ..., FLOAT -> ...  into vars[3]
```

Store Double into Local Variable

```
dstore=57 vindex Stack: ..., word1, word2 -> ...  into vars[vindex] &
vars[vindex+1]
dstore_0=71      Stack: ..., word1, word2 -> ...  into vars[0] & vars[1]
```

```
dstore_1=72      Stack: ..., word1, word2 -> ...  into vars[1] & vars[2]
dstore_2=73      Stack: ..., word1, word2 -> ...  into vars[2] & vars[3]
dstore_3=74      Stack: ..., word1, word2 -> ...  into vars[3] & vars[4]
```

Store Object into Local Variable

```
istore=58 vindex Stack: ..., OBJ -> ...  into vars[vindex]
istore_0=75      Stack: ..., OBJ -> ...  into vars[0]
istore_1=76      Stack: ..., OBJ -> ...  into vars[1]
istore_2=77      Stack: ..., OBJ -> ...  into vars[2]
istore_3=78      Stack: ..., OBJ -> ...  into vars[3]
```

Increment Local Variable

This applies only to integers.

```
iinc=132 vindex constant   Stack: ... -> ...  vars[vindex] += constant
```

Managing Arrays

Arrays are treated as objects, but as you learned in Chapter 10, they don't use a method table pointer. Because of this uniqueness, arrays have special bytecodes to create and access them.

Allocate a New Array

```
newarray=188 type Stack: ..., size -> ..., OBJ
```

Allocate a New Array of Objects

```
anewarray=189 classindex1 classindex2 Stack: ..., size -> ..., OBJ
```

Allocate a New Multi-Dimensional Array

```
newarray=197 indexbyte1 indexbyte1 indexbyte2  Stack: ..., size1, size2, etc ->
..., OBJ
```

Get the Array Length

```
arraylength=190 Stack: ..., OBJ -> ..., length
```

Load Primitives from the Array

```
iaload=46 Stack: ..., OBJ, index -> ..., INT
laload=47 Stack: ..., OBJ, index -> ..., LONG1, LONG2
faload=48 Stack: ..., OBJ, index -> ..., FLOAT
daload=49 Stack: ..., OBJ, index -> ..., DOUBLE1, DOUBLE2
aaload=50 Stack: ..., OBJ, index -> ..., OBJ
baload=51 Stack: ..., OBJ, index -> ..., BYTE
caload=52 Stack: ..., OBJ, index -> ..., CHAR
saload=53 Stack: ..., OBJ, index -> ..., SHORT
```

Store Primitives into the Array

```
iastore-79 Stack: ..., OBJ, index, INT -> ...
lastore=80 Stack: ..., OBJ, index, LONG1, LONG2 -> ...
```

```
fastore=81 Stack: ..., OBJ, index, FLOAT -> ...
dastore=82 Stack: ..., OBJ, index, DOUBLE1, DOUBLE2 -> ...
aastore=83 Stack: ..., OBJ, index, OBJ -> ...
bastore=84 Stack: ..., OBJ, index, BYTE -> ...
castore=85 Stack: ..., OBJ, index, CHAR -> ...
sastore=86 Stack: ..., OBJ, index, SHORT -> ...
```

Generic Stack Instructions

These are basic operations that alter the stack:

Do Nothing

```
nop=0   Stack: ... -> ...
```

Pop Stack Values

```
pop=87  Stack: ..., VAL -> ...
pop2=88  Stack: ..., VAL1, VAL2 -> ...
```

Duplicate Stack Values and Possibly Insert Below Stack Top

```
dup=89      Stack: ..., V -> ..., V, V
dup2=92     Stack: ..., V1, V2 -> ..., V1, V2, V1, V2
dup_x1=90   Stack: ..., V1, V2 -> ..., V2, V1, V2
dup2_x1=93 Stack: ..., V1, V2, V3 -> ..., V2, V3, V1, V2, V3
dup_x2=91   Stack: ..., V1, V2, V3 -> ..., V3, V1, V2, V3
dup2_x2=94 Stack: ..., V1, V2, V3, V4 -> ..., V3, V4, V1, V2, V3, V4
```

Swap Two-Stack Items

```
swap=95    Stack: ..., V1, V2 -> ..., V2, V1
```

Arithmetic and Logical Instructions

All the arithmetic operations operate on four possible types: integer, long, float, or double. Logical instructions operate only on integer and long types.

Addition

```
iadd=96  Stack: ..., INT1, INT2 -> ..., INT1+INT2
ladd=97  Stack: ..., L1_1, L1_2, L2_1, L2_2 -> ..., L1+L2 (high), L1+L2 (low)
fadd=98  Stack: ..., FLOAT1, FLOAT2 -> ..., FLOAT1+FLOAT2
dadd=99  Stack: ..., D1_1, D1_2, D2_1, D2_2 -> ..., D1+D2 (high), D1+D2 (low)
```

Subtraction

```
isub=100 Stack: ..., INT1, INT2 -> ..., INT1-INT2
lsub=101 Stack: ..., L1_1, L1_2, L2_1, L2_2 -> ..., L1-L2 (high), L1-L2 (low)
fsub=102 Stack: ..., FLOAT1, FLOAT2 -> ..., FLOAT1-FLOAT2
dsub=103 Stack: ..., D1_1, D1_2, D2_1, D2_2 -> ..., D1-D2 (high), D1-D2 (low)
```

Multiplication

```
imul=104  Stack: ..., INT1, INT2 -> ..., INT1*INT2
lmul=105  Stack: ..., L1_1, L1_2, L2_1, L2_2 -> ..., L1*L2 (high), L1*L2 (low)
```

```
fmul=106  Stack: ..., FLOAT1, FLOAT2 -> ..., FLOAT1*FLOAT2
dmul=107  Stack: ..., D1_1, D1_2, D2_1, D2_2 -> ..., D1*D2 (high), D1*D2 (low)
```

Division

```
idiv=108  Stack: ..., INT1, INT2 -> ..., INT1/INT2
ldiv=109  Stack: ..., L1_1, L1_2, L2_1, L2_2 -> ..., L1/L2 (high), L1/L2 (low)
fdiv=110  Stack: ..., FLOAT1, FLOAT2 -> ..., FLOAT1/FLOAT2
ddiv=111  Stack: ..., D1_1, D1_2, D2_1, D2_2 -> ..., D1/D2 (high), D1/D2 (low)
```

Remainder

```
irem=112  Stack: ..., INT1, INT2 -> ..., INT1%INT2
lrem=113  Stack: ..., L1_1, L1_2, L2_1, L2_2 -> ..., L1%L2 (high), L1%L2 (low)
frem=114  Stack: ..., FLOAT1, FLOAT2 -> ..., FLOAT1%FLOAT2
drem=115  Stack: ..., D1_1, D1_2, D2_1, D2_2 -> ..., D1%D2 (high), D1%D2 (low)
```

Negation

```
ineg=116  Stack: ..., INT -> ..., -INT
lneg=117  Stack: ..., LONG1, LONG2 -> ..., -LONG1, -LONG2
fneg=118  Stack: ..., FLOAT -> ..., -FLOAT
dneg=119  Stack: ..., DOUBLE1, DOUBLE2 -> ..., -DOUBLE1, -DOUBLE2
```

Integer Logical Instructions

>>> denotes an unsigned right shift.

```
ishl=120  Stack: ..., INT1, INT2 -> INT1<<(INT2 & 0x1f)
ishr=122  Stack: ..., INT1, INT2 -> INT1>>(INT2 & 0x1f)
iushr=124 Stack: ..., INT1, INT2 -> INT1>>>(INT2 & 0x1f)
```

Long Integer Logical Instructions

>>> denotes an unsigned right shift.

```
lshl=121  Stack: ..., L1, L2, INT -> L1<<(INT & 0x3f), L2<<(INT & 0x3f)
lshr=123  Stack: ..., L1, L2, INT -> INT1>>(INT & 0x3f), L2>>(INT & 0x03)
lushr=125 Stack: ..., L1, L2, INT -> INT1>>>(INT & 0x3f), L2>>>(INT & 0x3f)
```

Integer Boolean Operations

```
iand=126  Stack: ..., INT1, INT2 -> ..., INT1&INT2
ior=128   Stack: ..., INT1, INT2 -> ..., INT1|INT2
ixor=130  Stack: ..., INT1, INT2 -> ..., INT1^INT2
```

Long Integer Boolean Operations

```
land=127  Stack: ..., L1_1, L1_2, L2_1, L2_2 -> ..., L1_1&L2_1, L1_2&L2_2
lor=129   Stack: ..., L1_1, L1_2, L2_1, L2_2 -> ..., L1_1|L2_1, L1_2|L2_2
lxor=131  Stack: ..., L1_1, L1_2, L2_1, L2_2 -> ..., L1_1^L2_1. L1_2^L2_2
```

Conversion Instructions

Because most of the previous bytecodes expect the stack to contain a homogenous set of operands, Java uses conversion functions. In code, you can add a float and an integer, but Java will first convert the integer to a float type before performing the addition.

Integer Conversions

```
i2l=133        Stack: .., INT -> ..., LONG1, LONG2
i2f=134        Stack: .., INT -> ..., FLOAT
i2d=135        Stack: .., INT -> ..., DOUBLE1, DOUBLE2
int2byte=145   Stack: .., INT -> ..., BYTE
int2char=146   Stack: .., INT -> ..., CHAR
int2short=147  Stack: .., INT -> ..., SHORT
```

Long Integer Conversions

```
l2i=136        Stack: .., LONG1, LONG2 -> ..., INT
l2f=137        Stack: .., LONG1, LONG2 -> ..., FLOAT
l2d=138        Stack: .., LONG1, LONG2 -> ..., DOUBLE1, DOUBLE2
```

Float Conversions

```
f2i=139        Stack: .., FLOAT -> ..., INT
f2l=140        Stack: .., FLOAT -> ..., LONG1, LONG2
f2d=141        Stack: .., FLOAT -> ..., DOUBLE1, DOUBLE2
```

Double Conversions

```
d2i=142        Stack: .., DOUBLE1, DOUBLE2 -> ..., INT
d2l=143        Stack: .., DOUBLE1, DOUBLE2 -> ..., LONG1, LONG2
d2f=144        Stack: .., DOUBLE1, DOUBLE2 -> ..., FLOAT
```

Control Transfer and Function Return

All branch indexes are signed 16-bit offsets from the current pc register.

Comparisons with Zero

```
ifeq=153 branch1 branch2   Stack: ..., INT -> ...
ifne=154 branch1 branch2   Stack: ..., INT -> ...
iflt=155 branch1 branch2   Stack: ..., INT -> ...
ifge=156 branch1 branch2   Stack: ..., INT -> ...
ifgt=157 branch1 branch2   Stack: ..., INT -> ...
ifle=158 branch1 branch2   Stack: ..., INT -> ...
```

Comparison with Null

```
ifnull=198 branch1 branch2    Stack: ..., OBJ -> ...
ifnonnull=199 branch1 branch2 Stack: ..., OBJ -> ...
```

Compare Two Integers

```
if_icmpeq=159 branch1 branch2  Stack: ..., INT1, INT2 -> ...
if_icmpne=160 branch1 branch2  Stack: ..., INT1, INT2 -> ...
if_icmplt=161 branch1 branch2  Stack: ..., INT1, INT2 -> ...
if_icmpge=162 branch1 branch2  Stack: ..., INT1, INT2 -> ...
if_icmpgt=163 branch1 branch2  Stack: ..., INT1, INT2 -> ...
if_icmple=164 branch1 branch2  Stack: ..., INT1, INT2 -> ...
```

Compare Two Long Integers

```
lcmp=148  Stack: ..., L1_1, L1_2, L2_1, L2_2 -> ..., INT (One of [-1, 0, 1])
```

Compare Two Floats

l->-1 on NaN, g->1 on NaN.

```
fcmpl=149  Stack: ..., FLOAT1, FLOAT2 -> ..., INT (One of [-1, 0, 1])
fcmpg=150  Stack: ..., FLOAT1, FLOAT2 -> ..., INT (One of [-1, 0, 1])
```

Compare Two Doubles

l->-1 on NaN, g->1 on NaN.

```
dcmpl=151  Stack: ..., D1_1, D1_2, D2_1, D2_2 -> ..., INT (One of [-1, 0, 1])
dcmpg=152  Stack: ..., D1_1, D1_2, D2_1, D2_2 -> ..., INT (One of [-1, 0, 1])
```

Compare Two Objects

```
if_acmpeq=165 branch1 branch2  Stack: ..., OBJ1, OBJ2 -> ...
if_acmpne=166 branch1 branch2  Stack: ..., OBJ1, OBJ2 -> ...
```

Unconditional Branching

16-bit and 32-bit branching

```
goto=167 branch1 branch2                    Stack: ... -> ...
goto_w=200 branch1 branch2 branch3 branch4  Stack: ... -> ...
```

Jump Subroutine

16-bit and 32-bit jumps

```
jsr=168 branch1 branch2                     Stack: ... -> ..., returnAddress
jsr_w=201 branch1 branch2 branch3 branch4   Stack: ... -> ..., returnAddress
```

Return from Subroutine

The return address is retrieved from a local variable, not the stack.

```
ret=169 vindex   Stack: ... -> ...   (returnAddress <- vars[vindex])
ret_w=209 vindex1 vindex2   Stack: ... -> ...   (returnAddress <- vars[vindex])
```

Returning Primitives

The current stack frame is destroyed. The top primitive is pushed onto the caller's operand stack.

```
ireturn=172  Stack: ..., INT -> [destroyed]
lreturn=173  Stack: ..., LONG1, LONG2 -> [destroyed]
freturn=174  Stack: ..., FLOAT -> [destroyed]
dreturn=175  Stack: ..., DOUBLE1, DOUBLE2 -> [destroyed]
areturn=176  Stack: ..., OBJ -> [destroyed]
return=177  Stack: ... -> [destroyed]
```

Calling the Breakpoint Handler

```
breakpoint=202  Stack: ..., -> ...
```

Manipulating Object Fields

Construct a 16-bit index into the constant pool to retrieve the class and field name, then resolve these names to determine the field offset and width. Use the object reference on the stack as the target. The value will be 32 or 64 bits, depending on the field information in the constant pool.

```
Getstatic=178  index1 index2   Stack: ..., -> ..., VAL
Putstatic=179  index1 index2   Stack: ..., VAL -> ...
Getfield=180   index1 index2   Stack: ..., OBJ -> ..., VAL
Putfield=181   index1 index2   Stack: ..., OBJ, VAL -> ...
```

Method Invocation

There are four types of method invocation:

- `invokevirtual=182`—Normal method dispatch in Java. Use the index bytes to create a 16-bit index into the constant table of the current class. Extract the method name and signature. Search the method table of the stack object to determine the method address. Use the method signature to remove the method arguments from the operand stack and transfer them to the new method's local variables.
- `invokenonvirtual=183`—Used when a method is called with the super keyword. Use the index bytes to create a 16-bit index into the constant pool of the current class. Extract the method name and signature. Search the named class's method table to determine the method address. Extract the object and arguments and place them in the new method's local variables.
- `invokestatic=184`—Used to call static methods. Create a 16-bit index into the current class's constant pool. Extract the method and search the named class's method table for the address. Transfer the arguments as before. There is no object to pass.
- `invokeinterface=185`—Invoke an interface function. Again, a 16-bit index is created to find the method name and signature. This time, however, the number of arguments is determined from the bytecodes, not the signature.

```
virtual index1 index2              Stack: ..., OBJ, [arg1, [arg2, ...]] ->
...
nonvirtual index1 index2           Stack: ..., OBJ, [arg1, [arg2, ...]] ->
...
static index1 index2               Stack: ..., [arg1, [arg2, ...]] -> ...
interface index1 index2 nargs resv Stack: ..., OBJ, [arg1, [arg2, ...]] ->
...
```

Miscellaneous Operations

These instructions don't fall under any other heading; they deal with generic object operations, such as creation and casting.

Throw Exception

```
athrow=191   Stack: ..., OBJ -> [undefined]
```

Create a New Object

```
new=187 index1 index2  Stack: ... -> ..., OBJ
```

Check a Cast Operation

```
checkcast=192 index1 index2  Stack: ..., OBJ -> ..., OBJ
```

Instanceof

```
instanceof=193 index1 index2  Stack: ..., OBJ -> ... INT (1 or 0)
```

Monitors

Monitor instructions are used for synchronization.

Enter a Monitored Region of Code

```
monitorenter=194  Stack: ..., OBJ -> ...
```

Exit a Monitored Region of Code

```
monitorexit=195  Stack: ..., OBJ -> ...
```

Test Class Bytecodes

Sun supplies a tool, `javap`, that enables you to disassemble and view the bytecodes of a class. If the -c option is passed to `javap`, a listing of bytecodes is produced. These are the test class's bytecodes:

```
Compiled from test.java
public class test extends java.lang.Object {
    public static int st_one;
    public test();
    public test(int);
    public native boolean getData(int []);
    public int do_countdown();
    public int do_countdown(int);

Method test()
   0 aload_0
   1 invokenonvirtual #9 <Method java.lang.Object.<init>()V>
   4 bipush 100
   6 putstatic #7 <Field test.st_one I>
   9 return

Method test(int)
   0 aload_0
   1 invokenonvirtual #9 <Method java.lang.Object.<init>()V>
   4 iload_1
   5 putstatic #7 <Field test.st_one I>
   8 return

Method int do_countdown()
   0 getstatic #7 <Field test.st_one I>
   3 istore_1
```

```
   4 getstatic #6 <Field java.lang.System.out Ljava/io/PrintStream;>
   7 ldc #1 <String "Performing countdown:">
   9 invokevirtual #10 <Method java.io.PrintStream.println(Ljava/lang/String;)V>
  12 goto 22
  15 getstatic #6 <Field java.lang.System.out Ljava/io/PrintStream;>
  18 iload_1
  19 invokevirtual #8 <Method java.io.PrintStream.println(I)V>
  22 iload_1
  23 iinc 1 -1
  26 ifne 15
  29 getstatic #7 <Field test.st_one I>
  32 ireturn

Method int do_countdown(int)
   0 iload_1
   1 istore_2
   2 getstatic #6 <Field java.lang.System.out Ljava/io/PrintStream;>
   5 ldc #1 <String "Performing countdown:">
   7 invokevirtual #10 <Method java.io.PrintStream.println(Ljava/lang/String;)V>
  10 goto 20
  13 getstatic #6 <Field java.lang.System.out Ljava/io/PrintStream;>
  16 iload_1
  17 invokevirtual #8 <Method java.io.PrintStream.println(I)V>
  20 iload_1
  21 iinc 1 -1
  24 ifne 13
  27 iload_2
  28 ireturn
}
```

The left-hand column displays the offset of the instruction. `Javap` automatically converts jump displacements to actual offsets. In addition, it looks up constant pool references in order to output the corresponding strings.

Garbage Collection

Java uses a multitiered security mechanism. The bytecode verifier provides the lowest layer of security. Above the verifier, the security manager is the next sentry. In addition to these two explicit checks, there are a number of language features that provide security as well. Chief among these is the garbage collector.

Failing to free memory blocks or file handles is a common bug in most modern programs. The problem quickly escalates until the system crashes in some unforeseen manner. Java, like Smalltalk before it, uses implicit garbage collection to solve the problem. The virtual machine spec does not mandate a particular type of garbage collection; it requires only that some type be used.

In Sun's runtime, a mark and sweep algorithm is used. This enables the garbage collector to run incrementally in the background.

B

Language Grammar

This appendix provides a commented Java grammar. A *grammar* is a series of rules that have the following form:

```
nonterminal = meta-expression ;
```

Any quoted symbols (such as "0") indicate a literal symbol or keyword. The comments should help you understand the more formal grammar.

Meta-expressions use the following additional notation:

- `(some expression)` for grouping
- `postfix?` for 0 or 1 occurrences required
- `postfix+` for 1 or more occurrences required
- `postfix*` for 0 or more occurrences required
- `:¦` for alteration (either-or)

The grammar is not exactly BNF (Backus-Naur Form), but it gets the job done. I prefer a more formal notation, but it's Sun's prerogative to choose the grammar specification format.

NOTE

The following terminal symbols are undefined: DocComment, Identifier, Number, String, and Character. "Undefined" specifically means that the terminal symbols are referenced in a right-hand rule, but never defined as a left-hand quantity.

```
CompilationUnit =
  PackageStatement? ImportStatement* TypeDeclaration*
;
```

A compilation unit is the outermost definition in this grammar. An application or applet can be made up of multiple compilation units. The stars after the last two names indicate zero or more occurrences, and the question mark indicates zero or one occurrence.

```
PackageStatement =
  'package' PackageName ';'
;

ImportStatement =
  'import' PackageName '.' '*' ';'
¦ 'import' ( ClassName ¦ InterfaceName ) ';'
;

TypeDeclaration =
  ClassDeclaration
¦ InterfaceDeclaration
¦ ';'
;
```

This rule forces all fields and methods to appear within a class. In C, this rule also contains variable and function definition options:

```
ClassDeclaration =
  Modifier* 'class' Identifier
  ('extends' ClassName)?
  ('implements' InterfaceName (',' InterfaceName)*)?
  '{' FieldDeclaration* '}'
;
```

This rule looks a little confusing because of its optional notation. A class declaration may have one or more modifiers before the keyword `class`. The extends clause and interface clause are optional. If the interface clause is present, there may be multiple comma-separated interface names. The class must be followed by braces, but there do not have to be any fields defined within them.

```
InterfaceDeclaration =
  Modifier* 'interface' Identifier
  ('extends' InterfaceName (',' InterfaceName)*)?
  '{' FieldDeclaration* '}'
;
```

Interface declarations are similar to classes. The main difference between them is that interface declarations can extend one or more existing interfaces.

```
FieldDeclaration =
  DocComment? MethodDeclaration
¦ DocComment? ConstructorDeclaration
¦ DocComment? VarableDeclaration
¦ StaticInitializer
¦ ';'
;
```

DocComment is an undefined terminal. It takes the form of a multiline comment beginning with `/**` and ending with the standard `*/`.

```
MethodDeclaration =
  Modifier* Type Identifier '(' ParameterList? ')' ( '[' ']' )*
  ( '{' Statement* '}' ¦ ';' )
;
```

Grammars enable syntactic constructs that cause the compiler to issue semantic errors. Notice that the body of a method is optional. Syntactically, this is correct. Semantically, however, this is correct only if a native or abstract modifier is present.

```
ConstructorDeclaration =
  Modifier* Identifier '(' ParameterList? ')'
  '{' Statement* '}'
;

VariableDeclaration =
  Modifier* Type VariableDeclarator (',' VariableDeclarator)* ';'
;

VariableDeclarator =
  Identifier ('[' ']')* ('=' VariableInitializer)?
;
```

A variable declarator may specify an array: `int name[]`. It also is legal for a Type to specify an array: `int[] name`. Either form is correct.

```
VariableInitializer =
  Expression
| '{' (VariableInitializer ( ',' VariableInitializer )* ','? )? '}'
;
```

The second rule is for array initializations:

```
int x[] = { 1, 2, 3, 5, 9 };
```

The preceding statement creates an array of integers with a length of 5.

```
StaticInitializer =
  'static' '{' Statement* '}'
;
```

You used a static initializer in Chapter 10, "Native Methods and Java," to load a native library:

```
ParameterList =
  Parameter (',' Parameter)*
;

Parameter =
  Type Identifier ('[' ']')*
;

Statement =
  VariableDeclaration
| Expression ';'
| '{' Statement* '}'
| 'if' '(' Expression ')' Statement ('else' Statement)?
| 'while' '(' Expression ')' Statement
| 'do' Statement 'while' '(' Expression ')' ';'
| 'for' '(' (VariableDeclaration | Expression ';' | ';')
            Expression? ';' Expression?')' Statement
| 'try' Statement ('catch' '(' Parameter ')' Statement)*
   ('finally' Statement)?
| 'switch' '(' Expression ')' '{' Statement* '}'
| 'synchronized' '(' Expression ')' Statement
| 'return' Expression? ';'
| 'throw' Expression ';'
| 'case' Expression ':'
| 'default' ':'
| Identifier ':' Statement
| 'break' Identifier? ';'
| 'continue' Identifer? ';'
| ';'
;
```

Unlike C, break and continue have an optional identifier. This enables branching to a label. `For` loops may declare a new variable just as in C++. Notice that each loop expression is optional.

Several control statements (`if`, `while`, and `for`) specify an expression in parentheses. Semantically, the expression must evaluate to a boolean type or an error is issued.

```
Expression =
  Expression '+' Expression
| Expression '-' Expression
| Expression '*' Expression
| Expression '/' Expression
```

```
| Expression '%' Expression
| Expression '^' Expression
| Expression '&' Expression
| Expression '|' Expression
| Expression '&&' Expression
| Expression '||' Expression
| Expression '<<' Expression
| Expression '>>' Expression
| Expression '>>>' Expression
| Expression '=' Expression
| Expression '+=' Expression
| Expression '-=' Expression
| Expression '*=' Expression
| Expression '/=' Expression
| Expression '%=' Expression
| Expression '^=' Expression
| Expression '&=' Expression
| Expression '|=' Expression
| Expression '<<=' Expression
| Expression '>>=' Expression
| Expression '>>>=' Expression
| Expression '<' Expression
| Expression '>' Expression
| Expression '<=' Expression
| Expression '>=' Expression
| Expression '==' Expression
| Expression '!=' Expression
| Expression '.' Expression
| Expression ',' Expression
| Expression 'indtanceof' ( ClassName | InterfaceName )
| Expression '?' Expression ':' Expression
| ''++'' Expression
| ''—''Expression
| '++' Expression
| '—'Expression
| Expression '++'
| Expression '—'
| '-' Expression
| '!' Expression
| '~' Expression
| '('Expression ')'
| '(' Type ')' Expression
| Expression '(' ArgList? ')'
| 'new' ClassName '(' ArgList? ')'
| 'new' TypeSpecifier ( '[' Expression ']' )+ ('[' ']')*
| 'new' '(' Expression ')'
| 'true'
| 'false'
| 'null'
| 'super'
| 'this'
| Identifier
| Number
| String
| Character
;
```

Comparison expressions always evaluate to a boolean expression.

Declaring new arrays can be confusing. The syntax states that there must be a `new` keyword followed by a type and one or more defined dimensions: `new int[2][3]`. A trailing undefined dimension is also allowed: `new int[2][3][]`. The following is not legal because there must be one or more defined dimensions: `new int[]`.

```
ArgList =
  Expression (',' Expression )*
;

Type =
  TypeSpecifier ('[' ']')*
;
```

Here is the second method for declaring an array: `int[] name`.

```
TypeSpecifier =
   'boolean'
 ¦ 'byte'
 ¦ 'char'
 ¦ 'short'
 ¦ 'int'
 ¦ 'float'
 ¦ 'long'
 ¦ 'double'
 ¦ ClassName
 ¦ InterfaceName
;

Modifier =
   'public'
 ¦ 'private'
 ¦ 'protected'
 ¦ 'static'
 ¦ 'final'
 ¦ 'native'
 ¦ 'synchronized'
 ¦ 'abstract'
 ¦ 'threadsafe'
 ¦ 'transient'
;

PackageName =
  Identifier
¦ PackageName '.' Identifier
;

ClassName =
  Identifier
¦ PackageName '.' Identifier
;

InterfcaeName =
  Identifer
¦ PackageName '.' Identifier
;
```

I

Index

A

B

D

E

I

M

N

Q

R

T

Add to Your Sams.net Library Today with the Best Books for Internet Technologies

ISBN	Quantity	Description of Item	Unit Cost	Total Cost
1-57521-039-8		Presenting Java	$25.00	
1-57521-030-4		Teach Yourself Java in 21 Days	$39.99	
1-57521-049-5		Java Unleashed	$49.99	
1-57521-007-X		Netscape 2 Unleashed	$49.99	
1-57521-041-X		The Internet Unleashed, 1996	$49.99	
1-57521-040-1		The World Wide Web Unleashed, 1996	$49.99	
0-672-30745-6		HTML and CGI Unleashed	$49.99	
1-57521-051-7		Web Publishing Unleashed	$49.99	
1-57521-018-5		Web Site Administrator's Survival Guide	$49.99	
1-57521-009-6		Teach Yourself CGI Programming with Perl in a Week	$39.99	
1-57521-068-1		Teach Yourself Netscape 2 Web Publishing in a Week	$35.00	
0-672-30718-9		Navigating the Internet, Third Edition	$25.00	
1-57521-064-9		Teach Yourself Web Publishing with HTML 3.0 in a Week, Second Edition	$29.99	
1-57521-014-2		Teach Yourself Web Publishing with HTML in 14 Days, Premiere Edition	$39.99	
1-57521-072-X		Web Site Construction Kit for Windows 95	$49.99	
		Shipping and Handling: See information below.		
		TOTAL		

Shipping and Handling: $4.00 for the first book, and $1.75 for each additional book. If you need to have it NOW, we can ship product to you in 24 hours for an additional charge of approximately $18.00, and you will receive your item overnight or in two days. Overseas shipping and handling adds $2.00. Prices subject to change. Call between 9:00 a.m. and 5:00 p.m. EST for availability and pricing information on latest editions.

201 W. 103rd Street, Indianapolis, Indiana 46290

1-800-428-5331 — Orders 1-800-835-3202 — FAX 1-800-858-7674 — Customer Service

Book ISBN 1-57521-083-5

Web Site Administrator's Survival Guide

— *Jerry Ablan, et al*

The *Web Site Administrator's Survival Guide* is a detailed, step-by-step book that guides the Web administrator through the process of selecting Web server software and hardware, installing and configuring a server, and administering the server on an ongoing basis. Includes a CD-ROM with servers and administrator tools. The book provides complete step-by-step guidelines for installing and configuring a Web server.

Price: $49.99 USA/$70.95 CDN *User Level: Intermediate-Advanced*
ISBN: 1-57521-018-5 *700 pages*

Web Publishing Unleashed

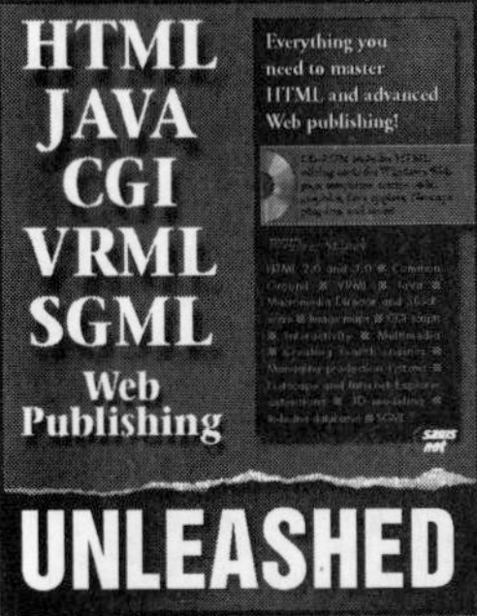

— *Stanek, et al*

Includes sections on how to organize and plan your information, design pages, and become familiar with hypertext and hypermedia. Choose from a range of applications and technologies, including Java, SGML, VRML, and the newest HTML and Netscape extensions. The CD-ROM contains software, templates, and examples to help you become a successful Web publisher.

Price: $49.99 USA/$70.95 CDN *User Level: Casual-Expert*
ISBN: 1-57521-051-7 *1,000 pages*

Web Site Construction Kit for Windows 95

— *Christopher Brown and Scott Zimmerman*

The *Web Site Construction Kit for Windows 95* provides readers with everything you need to set up, develop, and maintain a Web site with Windows 95. It teaches the ins and outs of planning, installing, configuring, and administering a Windows 95–based Web site for an organization, and it includes detailed instructions on how to use the software on the CD-ROM to develop the Web site's content: HTML pages, CGI scripts, image maps, etc.

Price: $49.99 USA/$70.95 CDN *User Level: Casual-Accomplished*
ISBN: 1-57521-072-X *500 pages*

Java Unleashed

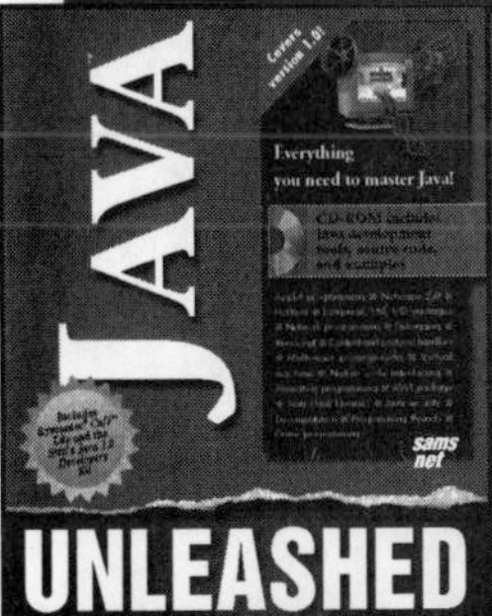

— *Various*

Java Unleashed is the ultimate guide to the year's hottest new Internet technologies, the Java language, and the HotJava browser from Sun Microsystems. *Java Unleashed* is a complete programmer's reference and a guide to the hundreds of exciting ways Java is being used to add interactivity to the World Wide Web. It describes how to use Java to add interactivity to Web presentations, and shows how Java and HotJava are being used across the Internet. Includes helpful and informative CD-ROM.

Price:$49.99 USA/$70.95 CDN *User Level: Casual-Expert*
ISBN: 1-57521-049-5 *1,000 pages*

Creating Web Applets with Java

— David Gulbransen and Kendrick Rawlings

Creating Web Applets with Java is the easiest way to learn how to integrate existing Java applets into your Web pages. This book is designed for the non-programmer who wants to use or customize preprogrammed Java applets with a minimal amount of trouble. It teaches the easiest way to incorporate the power of Java in a Web page, and covers the basics of Java applet programming. Find out how to use and customize preprogammed Java applets. Includes a CD-ROM that is full of useful applets.

$39.99 USA/$56.95 CDN User Level: Casual-Accomplished
ISBN: 1-57521-070-3 350 pages

Teach Yourself CGI Programming with Perl in a Week

— Eric Herrmann

This book is a step-by-step tutorial of how to create, use, and maintain Common Gateway Interfaces (CGI). It describes effective ways of using CGI as an integral part of Web development. Adds interactivity and flexibility to the information that can be provided through your Web site. Includes Perl 4.0 and 5.0, CGI libraries, and other applications to create databases, dynamic interactivity, and other enticing page effects.

Price: $39.99 USA/$56.95 CDN User Level: Intermediate-Advanced
ISBN: 1-57521-009-6 500 pages

Teach Yourself Java in 21 Days

— Laura Lemay and Charles Perkins

The complete tutorial guide to the most exciting technology to hit the Internet in years—Java! A detailed guide to developing applications with the hot new Java language from Sun Microsystems, *Teach Yourself Java in 21 Days* shows readers how to program using Java and develop applications (applets) using the Java language. With coverage of Java implementation in Netscape Navigator and HotJava, along with the Java Developer's Kit, including the compiler and debugger for Java, *Teach Yourself Java in 21 Days* is a must-have!

Price: $39.99 USA/$56.95 CDN User Level: Intermediate-Advanced
ISBN: 1-57521-030-4 600 pages

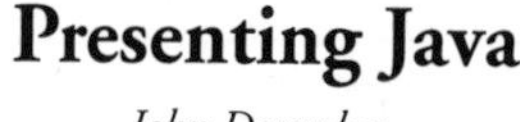

Presenting Java

— John December

Presenting Java gives you a first look at how Java is transforming static Web pages into living, interactive applications. Java opens up a world of possibilities previously unavailable on the Web. You'll find out how Java is being used to create animations, computer simulations, interactive games, teaching tools, spreadsheets, and a variety of other applications. Whether you're a new user, a project planner, or developer, *Presenting Java* provides an efficient, quick introduction to the basic concepts and technical details that make Java the hottest new Web technology of the year!

Price: $25.00 USA/$35.95 CDN User Level: All Levels
ISBN: 1-57521-039-8 207 pages

Netscape 2 Unleashed

— Dick Oliver, et al

This book provides a complete, detailed, and fully fleshed-out overview of the Netscape products. Through case studies and examples of how individuals, businesses, and institutions are using the Netscape products for Web development, *Netscape 2 Unleashed* gives a full description of the evolution of Netscape from its inception to today, and its cutting-edge developments with Netscape Gold, LiveWire, Netscape Navigator 2.0, Java and JavaScript, Macromedia, VRML, Plug-ins, Adobe Acrobat, HTML 3.0 and beyond, security, and Intranet systems.

Price: $49.99 USA/$70.95 CDN *User Level: All Levels*
ISBN: 1-57521-007-X *Pages: 800 pages*

The Internet Unleashed 1996

— Barron, Ellsworth, Savetz, et al

The Internet Unleashed 1996 is the complete reference to get new users up and running on the Internet while providing the consummate reference manual for the experienced user. *The Internet Unleashed 1996* provides the reader with an encyclopedia of information on how to take advantage of all the Net has to offer for business, education, research, and government. The companion CD-ROM contains over 100 tools and applications. The only book that includes the experience of over 40 of the world's top Internet experts, this new edition is updated with expanded coverage of Web publishing, Internet business, Internet multimedia and virtual reality, Internet security, Java, and more!

Price: $49.99 USA/$70.95 CDN *User Level: All Levels*
ISBN: 1-57521-041-X *1,456 pages*

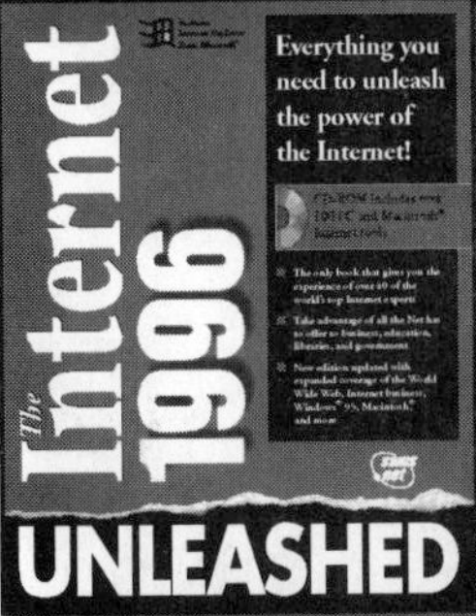

The World Wide Web Unleashed 1996

— December and Randall

The World Wide Web Unleashed 1996 is designed to be the only book a reader will need to experience the wonders and resources of the Web. The companion CD-ROM contains over 100 tools and applications to make the most of your time on the Internet. Shows readers how to explore the Web's amazing world of electronic art museums, online magazines, virtual malls, and video music libraries, while giving readers complete coverage of Web page design, creation, and maintenance, plus coverage of new Web technologies such as Java, VRML, CGI, and multimedia!

Price: $49.99 USA/$70.95 CDN *User Level: All Levels*
ISBN: 1-57521-040-1 *1,440 pages*

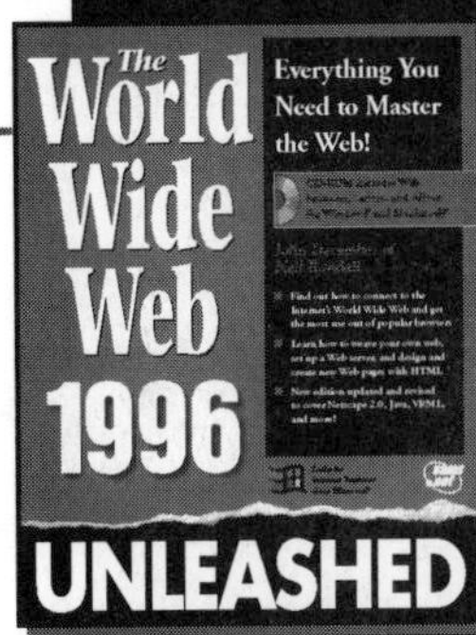

Teach Yourself Web Publishing with HTML in 14 Days, Premier Edition

— Laura Lemay

This book teaches everything about publishing on the Web. In addition to its exhaustive coverage of HTML, it also gives readers hands-on practice with more complicated subjects such as CGI, tables, forms, multimedia programming, testing, maintenance, and much more. The CD-ROM is Mac- and PC-compatible and includes a variety of applications that help readers create Web pages using graphics and templates.

Price: $39.99 USA/$56.95 CDN *User Level: All Levels*
ISBN: 1-57521-014-2 *804 pages*

Teach Yourself Web Publishing with HTML 3.0 in a Week, Second Edition

— Laura Lemay

Ideal for those people who are interested in the Internet and the World Wide Web—the Internet's hottest topic! This updated and revised edition teaches readers how to use HTML (Hypertext Markup Language) version 3.0 to create Web pages that can be viewed by nearly 30 million users. Explores the process of creating and maintaining Web presentations, including setting up tools and converters for verifying and testing pages. The new edition highlights the new features of HTML, such as tables and Netscape and Microsoft Explorer extensions. Provides the latest information on working with images, sound files, and video, and teaches advanced HTML techniques and tricks in a clear, step-by-step manner with many practical examples of HTML pages.

Price: $29.99 USA/$42.95 CDN User Level: Beginner-Intermediate
ISBN: 1-57521-064-9 518 pages

Web Page Construction Kit (Software)

Create your own exciting World Wide Web pages with the software and expert guidance in this kit! Includes HTML Assistant Pro Lite, the acclaimed point-and-click Web page editor. Simply highlight text in HTML Assistant Pro Lite, and click the appropriate button to add headlines, graphics, special formatting, links, etc. No programming skills needed! Using your favorite Web browser, you can test your work quickly and easily without leaving the editor. A unique catalog feature allows you to keep track of interesting Web sites and easily add their HTML links to your pages. Assistant's user-defined toolkit also allows you to add new HTML formatting styles as they are defined. Includes the #1 best-selling Internet book, *Teach Yourself Web Publishing with HTML 3.0 in a Week, Second Edition,* and a library of professionally designed Web page templates, graphics, buttons, bullets, lines, and icons to rev up your new pages!

PC Computing magazine says, "If you're looking for the easiest route to Web publishing, HTML Assistant is your best choice."

Price: $39.95 US/$55.95 CAN User Level: Beginner-Intermediate
ISBN: 1-57521-000-2 518 pages

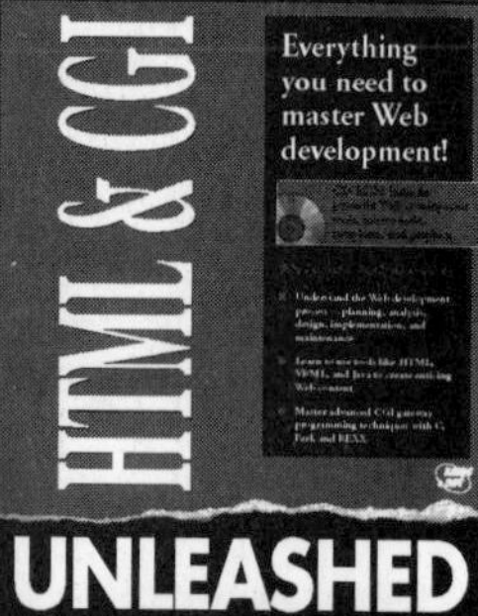

HTML & CGI Unleashed

— John December and Marc Ginsburg

Targeted to professional developers who have a basic understanding of programming and need a detailed guide. Provides a complete, detailed reference to developing Web information systems. Covers the full range of languages—HTML, CGI, Perl, C, editing and conversion programs, and more—and how to create commercial-grade Web applications. Perfect for the developer who will be designing, creating, and maintaining a Web presence for a company or large institution.

Price: $49.99 USA/$70.95 CDN User Level: Intermediate-Advanced
ISBN: 0-672-30745-6 830 pages

Teach Yourself JavaScript in a Week

— Arman Danesh

Teach Yourself JavaScript in a Week is the easiest way to learn how to create interactive Web pages with JavaScript, Netscape's Java-like scripting language. It is intended for non-programmers, and will be equally of value to users on the Macintosh, Windows, and UNIX platforms. Teaches how to design and create attention-grabbing Web pages with JavaScript, and shows how to add interactivity to Web pages.

Price: $39.99 USA/$56.95 CDN User Level: Intermediate-Advanced
ISBN: 1-57521-073-8 450 pages

A VIACOM SERVIC-E

The Information SuperLibrary™

CHECK OUT THE BOOKS IN THIS LIBRARY.

You'll find thousands of shareware files and over 1600 computer books designed for both technowizards and technophobes. You can browse through 700 sample chapters, get the latest news on the Net, and find just about anything using our massive search directories.

All Macmillan Computer Publishing books are available at your local bookstore.

We're open 24-hours a day, 365 days a year.

You don't need a card.

We don't charge fines.

And you can be as **LOUD** as you want.

The Information SuperLibrary

http://www.mcp.com/mcp/ ftp.mcp.com

Get Café at a Special Price

Symantec® Café™ contains the latest Java Developer's Kit and many exciting new features and tools:

- Debug your Java applets with Symantec's new integrated Visual Java Debugger
- View the class relationships and their methods with the Hierarchy Editor
- Navigate your classes and edit your class methods with the Class Editor

Go to our Web page and check out the latest version of Café:

`http://www.symantec.com/lit/dev/javaindex.html`

Stay on top of Java development and order Symantec Café today!

SYMANTEC.

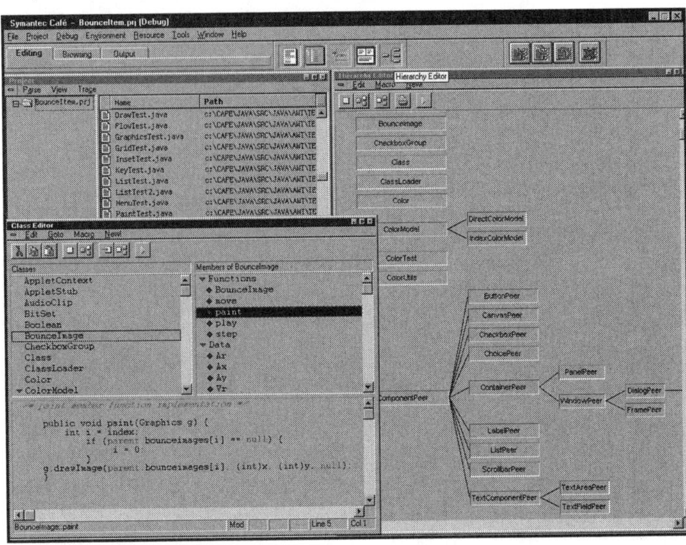

Symantec Café includes a Hierarchy Editor that displays the relationships of both the Java source classes and your custom classes. You can zoom in on any class and see its data and methods.

Yes! I want the most advanced Java development tool for Windows NT and Windows 95.
Please rush me Symantec Café at this special discount offer! Offer expires 6/30/96.
Available in U.S. only

(Please print neatly)

Name: ______________________________

Company: ______________________________

Title: ______________________________

Address: ______________________________

____

City: ______________________________

State/Province: ______________________________

Country (if not USA): ______________________________

Phone: ______________________________

E-mail: ______________________________

You can receive updates on new developments regarding Symantec Café approximately once per month via e-mail. Do you wish to be added to our information bulletin list?

☐ Yes ☐ No

Purchase Café **$129.00**
Product Code: FULL CAFÉ

Number of Units Requested: **$** ________

Applicable Sales Tax: **$** ________

Shipping **$** ________
$8.00 for each product shipped in U.S.

PAYMENT TOTAL: **$** ________

Payment Method: ☐ Check ☐ Money Order ☐ Visa
(Please do not send cash) ☐ American Express ☐ MasterCard

Name on card: ______________________________

Expiration date: ______________________________

Signature (required): ______________________________

Mail to: Café Purchase
P.O. Box 10849
Eugene, OR 97440-9711
Call 1-800-240-2275 24Hrs/7days a week
or Fax your order to 800-800-1438
Product Code FULL CAFÉ

State Sales/Use Tax

In the following states, add sales/use tax: CO–3%; GA, LA, NY–4%; VA–4.5%; KS–4.9%; AZ, IA, IN, MA, MD, OH, SC, WI–5%; CT, FL, ME, MI, NC, NJ, PA, TN–6%; CA, IL, TX–6.25%; MN, WA–6.5%; DC–5.75%.

Please add local tax for: AZ, CA, FL, GA, MO, NY, OH, SC, TN, TX, WA, WI.

Order Information:

- Please allow 2-4 weeks for processing your order.
- Please attach the order form with your payment.
- No P.O. Boxes and no C.O.D.s accepted.
- Order form good in the U.S. only.
- If you are tax-exempt, please include exemption certificate or letter with tax-exempt number.
- Resellers not eligible.
- Offer not valid with any other promotion.
- One copy per product, per order.
- Special offer expires 6/30/96.

What's on the CD-ROM

The companion CD-ROM contains the Java™ Developer's Kit from Sun Microsystems. Other shareware programs mentioned in the book and dozens of useful third-party tools and utilities are also included.

Windows 3.1 or NT Installation Instructions

1. Insert the CD-ROM disc into your CD-ROM drive.
2. From File Manager or Program Manager, choose Run from the File menu.
3. Type `<drive>:\CDSETUP` and press Enter, where `<drive>` corresponds to the drive letter of your CD-ROM. For example, if your CD-ROM is drive D:, type **`D:\CDSETUP`** and press Enter.

Follow the onscreen instructions in the installation program. Files will be installed to a default directory, unless you choose a different directory during installation.

CDSETUP creates a Windows program manager group called "Developing Java Applets." This group contains icons for exploring the CD-ROM.

Windows 95 Installation Instructions

If Windows 95 is installed on your computer and you have the AutoPlay feature enabled, the Guide to the CD-ROM program starts automatically whenever you insert the disc into your CD-ROM drive.

Macintosh Installation Instructions

1. Insert the CD-ROM disc into your CD-ROM drive.
2. When an icon for the CD appears on your desktop, open the disc by double-clicking on its icon.
3. Double-click on the icon named Guide to the CD-ROM, and follow the directions that appear.

Technical Support from Macmillan

We can't help you with Windows or Macintosh problems or software from third parties, but we can assist you if a problem arises with the CD-ROM itself.

E-mail Support: Send e-mail to `support@mcp.com`.

CompuServe: `GO SAMS` to reach the Macmillan Computer Publishing forum. Leave us a message, addressed to `SYSOP`. If you want the message to be private, address it to `*SYSOP`.

Telephone: (317) 581-3833

Fax: (317) 581-4773

Mail: Macmillan Computer Publishing
Attention: Support Department
201 West 103rd Street
Indianapolis, IN 46290-1093

Here's how to reach us on the Internet:

World Wide Web *(The Macmillan Information SuperLibrary)*
`http://www.mcp.com/samsnet`